# FROM THE AGE
# THAT IS PAST

## HARVARD CLUB OF NEW YORK CITY
### *A HISTORY*

ORMONDE de KAY '45

Produced by Marek & Charles

Printed in the United States of America

ISBN: 0-9643088-0-0
10 9 8 7 6 5 4 3 2 1

First Edition

*"By these festival-rites, from the Age that is past,*
*To the Age that is waiting before"*

# TABLE OF CONTENTS

# INTRODUCTION

To read this history of our glorious Club is to enter its doors a century ago, to feel at home and to meet your fellow members, long departed. It is to live through the history of our city and university, during boom and bust, war and peace. It is to meet giants in their time: Lowell and Eliot, Choate and the Roosevelts. It is to understand our Club more deeply and appreciate it more profoundly.

This work has been nearly six years in the making. Indeed, as you will read herein, it has been attempted unsuccessfully several times before. As a result, we owe a deep debt of gratitude to the creator of this work, Ormonde de Kay '45, a former president of the *Harvard Advocate* and contributing editor of *Harvard Magazine*, and the author of numerous books and magazine articles, whose labor of love over the years of work far exceeded his contractual compensation. Further, George Kramer '50 L'53, who saw the project from inception to completion, has rendered yet another great service to the Club, in addition to his years of careful and caring service as Secretary. Finally, Crocker Luther B'62, a former House Committee Chairman, also devoted many hours of effort and thought to this project.

What they have produced far transcends a typical institutional history. It is a portrait of the Club and its members as an organic, evolving whole. This history traces our decisions, entertainments, sports and attitudes over thirteen decades. It also illuminates the physical configuration of the Club by explaining expansions undertaken and foregone. After reading this book, you will look at the clubhouse with new eyes, as if seeing it for the first time in color after years of black and white.

So read on, friend, and discover your unknown brothers and sisters and their stories. Now, about that big blue elephant. . . .

Charles T. Lee '72
Secretary of the Club

## ACKNOWLEDGMENTS AND SOURCES

Work on this book began on September 1, 1988, when, having been recruited by Club Secretary George P. Kramer '50 L'53, I signed on to research and write it. I reported initially to Communications Committee Chairman Walter S. Isaacson '74, but as the year allotted to the book's creation stretched to five and a half years, George Kramer patiently watched over and directed its slow growth, so assiduously that I consider the end product almost as much his as mine.

Former House Committee Chairman Crocker Luther B'62 also read emerging chapters and proffered helpful suggestions over the years. For me, the crucial reading, however, occurred in 1991, when biographer, historian and retired banker Sheridan A. Logan '23 read the first 400 pages of what ultimately became a 1,257-page typescript. The enthusiastic response of a cultivated gentleman who had belonged to the Club through the greater part of its existence (since 1925), serving as its treasurer during the Great Depression and World War II (1936–45), reassured me that I was on the right track—or at least *a* right track. (Another early reader was James Parton '34, a co-founder of *American Heritage*.)

At the outset I was informed that the University Archives in Cambridge (Harley P. Holden, curator) held much material on the Club. Do they not just! The vast collection includes letters, newspaper clippings, magazine articles, lists of members, invitations, playbills, programs, menus, wine lists, printed and typed texts of speeches and occasional verse, songbooks, circular letters, questionnaires and important publications like the McKinsey Report—a rich hoard. For charting developments within the Club, however, I relied chiefly on records in the Club's own archives, in particular, of course, the minutes of meetings of, first, the Club, and, soon thereafter, the Board of Managers, with the addition in recent years of the minutes of the Executive Committee, January 1873 through December 1993 (121 years, forty-one volumes, seven and a half feet of shelf space, millions upon millions of words). These sources are supplemented by Board of Managers annual reports since the 1880s and copies of the *Bulletin* since January 1931. Changes over almost a century in the bylaws and rules, in the officers, managers and committees and in the membership are recorded in thirty-five Club books spanning the years 1894–1980.

Most of these materials have been stored for the last five years in the eighth-floor office of Mary Saunders, curator since 1986 of the Club's art collection and archives. Mrs. Saunders's important collaboration on the book began at the outset, with her conducting research at, inter alia, the Avery Library (Columbia), the Museum of the City of New York, the New-York Historical Society, the New York Society Library and, of course, the New York Public Library. She came up with all but a handful of the illustrations herein. I am indebted to her, too, for catching a number of errors.

For several decades after its founding the Club's activities were deemed to be of public interest, and its dinners and other doings were regularly reported in the press. As well as the *New York Times* on microfilm, 1865–1994, other useful sources on the Club include the *Harvard Graduates' Magazine* and *Harvard Alumni Bulletin* (in bound volumes in the Club library) and *Harvard Magazine*. Anent New York City and men's clubs between the Civil War and World War II, I consulted local histories and club histories (of the Union, University, Knickerbocker and Metropolitan Clubs, and the Century Association centenary volume, 1947), together with street directories, telephone books and other contemporary reference works, notably successive editions of *King's Handbook of New York City*. Elliot Willensky and Norval White's *AIA Guide to New York City* (1988) contains much relevant historical and architectural data.

But the historian of a university club can hardly ignore the concurrent history of the institution that gave it birth and has since continuously served as its sole reason for being, especially if that institution happens to be the country's oldest and, arguably, the world's foremost fount of learning. For pertinent developments in Cambridge and Boston, 1865–1935, I depended largely on *Three Centuries of Harvard* (1936) by Samuel Eliot Morison '08, for those of 1935–36 on *The Tercentenary of Harvard College* (1937) and for those of subsequent years on various books in the Club's Harvardiana collection, the most useful for my purposes being

## ACKNOWLEDGMENTS AND SOURCES

*Harvard: Through Change and Through Storm* (1969) by E. J. Kahn, Jr. '37. Records of Crimson teams and athletes during the Club's first century, together with information on events such as the construction, with funds supplied exclusively by Club members, of the University or Newell boathouse, are to be found in two volumes put out by the Harvard Varsity Club: *The H Book of Harvard Athletics, 1852–1922* (1923) and *The Second H Book of Harvard Athletics, 1923–1963* (1964).

Several stories in this book are taken from other books. The failure of the country's most promising young artist to produce an acceptable presidential portrait is recounted in Charles Hill Morgan's *George Bellows: Painter of America* (1965); a famous humorist's disgusted resignation in *Robert Benchley: A Biography* (1955) by Nathaniel Benchley '38; and the tragic end of activist-idealist member Travis Howard Whitney L'03 in Thomas Kessner's *Fiorello H. La Guardia and the Making of Modern New York* (1991). More passages are based on information supplied by members and former members. Sherry Logan clued me in on that quasi-legendary interviewer of applicants Gilman ("Colly") Collamore; Daniel W. Jones, Jr. '42 on the origins of the television series *Victory at Sea*; Donald E. Cummings '47 on the tortuous route Eleanor Roosevelt once took within the clubhouse in order to spare the sensibilities of male members; and Gavin P. Murphy L'54 on how he and certain other Harvardians came to represent the United States in the 1968 Olympic Games in a sport none of them had ever played before.

Additional information about some of the tens of thousands of individuals who have contributed to the history of the Club since 1865 was culled from standard sources such as *Who's Who, Who Was Who, Webster's Biographical Dictionary* and the *Dictionary of American Biography*, but the most vital and revealing personal data came, predictably, from autobiographical entries in the class reports, those crimson-bound, glassed-in volumes that constitute, in my opinion, the Club library's greatest glory.

Many people in addition to those cited earlier contributed in one way or another to this book. Dorothy F. Kimball R'47, a friend since undergraduate days, reintroduced me to the Club, which had changed considerably (though not in appearance) since I had been a member (1948–65).

Evelyn McQuade furnished me with Irene Van Fossen's notes toward a Club history and Adrienne Fischier with a key to the Harvardiana collection, while Carol Ann Danko saw to it that the Club records were brought together, first, in a case outside the old Radcliffe Club office, and later in Mary Saunders's office. After Evelyn McQuade's retirement Carol Danko and Adrienne Fischier continued to provide intelligent and helpful counsel, while Assistant Librarian Lauren Garay cheerfully checked innumerable facts, dates, spellings, years of graduation, advanced degrees and other such details.

From General Manager Robert J. Arnold down, the Club staff was unfailingly cooperative. I want to extend special thanks to Director of Facilities Robert E. Burch, Executive Housekeeper Eithne Doniguian, Program Coordinator David K. Goldstein and Controller William B. Reader. Niall McGovern, the longtime "proprietor" of the cigar stand, was a dependable source of amusing talk and anecdotes.

Among former officers and committee chairmen I consulted, the following were particularly helpful: Robert R. Barker '36, Harold E. Buttrick '52 GSD'59, D. Broward Craig '50 L'53, E. Thayer Drake '44 L'49, Albert H. Gordon '23 B'25, Peter S. Heller '48 L'52, E. Kennedy Langstaff '44 B'49, Roswell B. Perkins '47 L'49, Volney F. Righter '26 B'28, Richard Rodwin '52 L'55, Walter N. Rothschild, Jr. '42, Edward L. Saxe '37 B'39, William Stackpole '49 and Frank Streeter '40. The warm support of Secretary Charles T. Lee '72 was much appreciated. Robert C. Seaver '50, my subcommittee chairman when I interviewed would-be freshmen in the 1970s and 1980s, taught me to appreciate the vitally important work of the Schools Committee. Cyrus W. Brown II '60 filled me in on the Club's computer system. Painters William F. Draper '35 and Everett Raymond Kinstler provided information about certain portraits, and writers E. J. Kahn, Jr. '37 and Cleveland Amory '39 creative suggestions and encouragement. Editor John G. Stewart '40 got me to write three historical pieces for the *Bulletin*, one of which *Harvard Magazine* editor John T. Bethell '54 summarized in "The College Pump." And *Harvard Magazine*'s associate managing editor, Jean Martin '70, supplied important data on the 1957–60 fund drive, A Program for Harvard College.

## ACKNOWLEDGMENTS AND SOURCES

Former Communications Committee Chairman James O'Shea Wade '62, a book editor, gave generously of his time and expertise. It was he who recommended the production team that brought this book into being.

Finally, I am grateful to a certain few members who somehow possess the ability to cheer me up on dark days, among them J. Sinclair ("Sinc") Armstrong '38 L'41, indefatigable joke-teller Frederick A. Parker, Jr. '51 and *Bulletin* editor Jack Stewart. But the person to whom this book owes most is my wife, Barbara, without whose steadfast and unstinting support over five and a half years I could not possibly have brought it to completion.

Ormonde de Kay '45

# PRESIDENTS OF THE CLUB

SAMUEL OSGOOD
'32, DV'35, HON'55, 1866

No Portrait
Known

FREDERICK A. LANE
'49, 1867

JOHN O. STONE
'33, M'36, 1868

HENRY W. BELLOWS
'32, DV'37, HON'54, 1869

JAMES C. CARTER
'50, L'53, HON'85,
1870 – 1872

WILLIAM G. CHOATE
'52, L'54, 1872 – 1874

JOSEPH H. CHOATE
'52, L'54, HON'88,
1874 – 1878

JOHN O. SARGENT
'30, 1878 – 1881

FRANCIS M. WELD
'60, M'64, 1881 – 1883

CHARLES C. BEAMAN
'61, 1883 – 1885

EDMUND WETMORE
'60, HON'13, 1885 – 1888

FRANCIS O. FRENCH
'57, L'59, 1888 – 1890

EDWARD KING
'53, 1890 – 1895

JAMES C. CARTER
'50, L'53, HON'85,
1895 – 1899

EDMUND WETMORE
'60, HON'13, 1899 – 1901

CHARLES S. FAIRCHILD
'63, L'65, HON'88,
1901 – 1905

AUSTEN G. FOX
'69, L'71, 1905 – 1906

JOSEPH H. CHOATE
'52, L'54, HON'88
1906 – 1908

AUSTEN G. FOX
'69, L'71, 1908 – 1909

JAMES J. HIGGINSON
'57, 1909 – 1911

# PRESIDENTS OF THE CLUB

PETER B. OLNEY
'64, L'66, 1911 – 1913

AMORY G. HODGES
'74, 1913 – 1916

FRANCIS R. APPLETON
'75, 1916 – 1919

ROBERT P. PERKINS
'84, HON'21, 1919 – 1922

JAMES BYRNE
'77, L'82, HON'27,
1922 – 1924

THOMAS W. SLOCUM
'90, 1924 – 1927

HOWARD ELLIOTT
'81, 1927 – 1928

THOMAS W. LAMONT
'92, 1928 – 1932

LANGDON P. MARVIN
'98, L'01, 1932 – 1936

FRANCIS M. WELD
'97, 1936 – 1938

FREDERICK ROY MARTIN
'93, 1938 – 1941

EUGENE H. POOL
'95, 1941 – 1943

SAMUEL A. WELLDON
'04, L'08, 1943 – 1946

GEORGE WHITNEY
'07, 1946 – 1949

ARTHUR W. PAGE
'05, 1949 – 1951

DEVEREUX C. JOSEPHS
'15, HON'57, 1951 – 1953

EDWARD STREETER
'14, 1953 – 1955

GEORGE A. BROWNELL
'19, G'20, L'22,
1955 – 1957

CORNELIUS C. FELTON
'16, 1957 – 1959

PHILIP B. KUNHARDT
'23, B'25, 1959 – 1961

# PRESIDENTS OF THE CLUB

FREDERICK A. O.
SCHWARZ
'24, L'27, 1961 – 1963

H. IRVING PRATT
'26, B'29, HON'60,
1963 – 1966

ROY E. LARSEN
'21, HON'53,
1966 – 1968

MORGAN D. WHEELOCK
'31, 1968 – 1971

ALBERT H. GORDON
'23, B'25, 1971 – 1975

ROSWELL B. PERKINS
'47, L'49, 1975 – 1977

WALTER N.
ROTHSCHILD, JR.
'42, 1977 – 1979

FREDERICK R.
MOSELEY, JR.
'36, 1979 – 1981

ROBERT R. BARKER
'36, 1981 – 1984

RICHARD W. KIMBALL
'50, 1984 – 1986

D. BROWARD CRAIG
'50, L'53, 1986 – 1988

EDWARD L. SAXE
'37, B'39, 1988 – 1990

J. DINSMORE ADAMS, JR.
'66, 1990 – 1993

DONALD L. SHAPIRO
'57, B'61, 1993 –

FAIR HARVARD! *thy sons to thy Jubilee throng,*
*And with blessings surrender thee o'er,*
*By these festival-rites, from the Age that is past,*
*To the Age that is waiting before.*
*O Relic and Type of our ancestors' worth,*
*That hast long kept their memory warm!*
*First flower of their wilderness! Star of their night,*
*Calm rising through change and through storm!*

# 1

# THE CLUB
# IS LAUNCHED
# (1865–1866)

As 1865 began, Harvard College—which since the Revolution had put forth branches: schools of medicine, divinity and law, as well as the Lawrence Scientific School—was marking its 229th year and its third under President Thomas Hill '43 AM'45 STD'60, a Unitarian minister. Physically, it consisted of thirteen buildings in the Harvard Yard: Massachusetts, Harvard and University Halls; Hollis, Stoughton, Holworthy and Holden Chapel; Appleton Chapel, Boylston Hall and Grays Hall; Wadsworth House, the President's House, and, where Widener Library now stands, Gothic-towered Gore Hall. On the site of present-day Lehman Hall stood Dane Hall, housing the law school. The divinity school and the Lawrence Scientific School were nearby, in Cambridge, and the medical school in Boston.

It was a provincial institution: most of its students hailed from eastern New England, with a few from the Middle Atlantic states and a scattering from the Middle West. Until the outbreak of the Civil War in 1861 it had harbored a modest contingent from the South, but no longer. Hundreds of its undergraduates, graduate students and graduates were away under arms, the majority, of course, with the Federal forces, among them President Lincoln's son Robert Todd Lincoln '64, on the staff of General Grant in Virginia. But most Harvard alumni were civilians living in or near Boston and Cambridge, or within a day's journey of them.

Harvard College, 1865

Typically, these Yankees continued, in wartime, to converge on Cambridge in late June and early July for Commencement, and to attend class dinners, but although the Harvard Alumni Association had been in existence since 1840, they showed little interest in banding together in local brotherhoods. Ten years before, to be sure, a young mathematics instructor at the College by the name of Charles William Eliot '53 had, with a classmate, organized a graduates' club occupying rented rooms on Tremont Street, but by October 1857 attendance had fallen off so badly that the enterprise had been abandoned. The Harvard Club of Boston would not be founded until 1908.

If, however, as seems likely, proximity to Harvard Yard had conduced to apathy, distance apparently lent enchantment, for even as the first Boston club was failing, alumni a thousand miles to the west had formed the Harvard Club of Chicago. But that sodality, too, would come unstuck and have to be reorganized. The first Harvard club destined to survive had been set up in Philadelphia in March 1864, and was now, nine months later, flourishing.

Farther south, as that winter wore on, rebel resistance crumbled. On April 3 the Confederate government fled Richmond, and on the ninth General Lee surrendered to Grant at Appomattox, in effect ending the war. But on the fourteenth, Good Friday, a Southern sympathizer shot and killed Lincoln. After a state funeral, the president's embalmed corpse started north by rail on a circuitous journey home to Illinois; on the twenty-fourth it arrived in America's biggest city and was taken to City Hall, where it stayed on view, as 100,000 New Yorkers filed past it, until the following noon.

Early that afternoon Lincoln's coffined body, atop a hearse surmounted by towering black plumes and drawn by sixteen gray horses, moved slowly up Broadway between ranks of hushed citizens. Having passed Astor Place, the funeral car entered Union Square, center of the city's most fashionable district, where the city rendered homage to the martyred president with appropriate ceremony. The historian and public official George Bancroft delivered the principal oration, and to conclude the program the Reverend Samuel Osgood read two poems composed for the occasion by William Cullen Bryant.

Both Bancroft and Osgood, chosen to speak for New York at the most solemn event the city would ever witness, were, as it happened, Harvard men. Bancroft, born in Worcester in 1800 during the presidency of John Adams AB 1755, had graduated from the College in 1817 (at sixteen!), then received a doctorate from Göttingen before returning to Cambridge to teach. Later, when not working on his monumental *History of the United States*, he had served as secretary of the Navy (1845–46), incidentally founding the Naval Academy, and minister to Great Britain (1846–49), on quitting which post he had settled in New York, the only American city he found sufficiently cosmopolitan. Bostonian Osgood, an 1832 graduate, had taken two graduate degrees at the Divinity School, after which his growing renown as a preacher had brought him a call to a Unitarian church on Waverly Place.

In coming to the metropolis—both, by coincidence, in 1849—these men had been, in terms of their old school, pioneers, for as the famous lawyer Joseph H. Choate '52 L'54 of Salem would recall long afterward, anent his own arrival in 1855, "there was no relation at all existing between New York and Harvard College. Harvard was looked upon, as perhaps it was, as a provincial, heretical concern, hardly worthy of recognition by the great dignitaries of the metropolis of New York. Nobody ever then thought, in New York State, of sending their boys to Harvard, and very few people ever thought of coming to settle in New York after graduating from Harvard College."

During the decade since, however, more graduates of the "provincial, heretical concern" had come to the big city, for no place else in the country offered such opportunities to young men with brains and ambition. New York was America's leading center of manufacturing and commerce, and the prime source of the capital that financed enterprises like the railroads, still opening up the Wild West. Not only businessmen and

James Harrison Fay

bankers, but lawyers, doctors, preachers, architects, publishers and journalists, among others, could earn more there in both cash and kudos than they could anywhere else.

And now that the war was over the influx of Harvard graduates into the city was bound to increase.

With the coming of peace came the enactment of long-deferred reforms. Thus in Boston, on April 28, 1865, a new law severed the last ties between the governments of Massachusetts and Harvard, leaving the election of the latter's thirty Overseers to holders of the

A.B., A.M. and honorary degrees voting in Cambridge on Commencement Day. And in May some Bostonian graduates met to discuss erecting a permanent memorial to their comrades who had died fighting for the Union. (Of the 1,311 Harvard men who had served in the Federal forces 138 had lost their lives, and of the 257 who had borne arms for the Confederacy 64 had perished.)

In New York, meanwhile, five young graduates, all as yet unmarried, conceived a plan to meet regularly with other Harvard men for good fellowship based on shared memories of their alma mater. The youngest, twenty-two-year-old Philadelphian Albert C. Haseltine '63, had already had some experience in this line: after serving briefly with Pennsylvania volunteers, he had helped organize the Philadelphia Harvard Club and had become its first secretary. He and classmate James Truesdell Kilbreth '63 L'65 of Cincinnati would have known Bostonian Arthur Amory '62 in Cambridge, but it was presumably in New York that these three had met their older confederates, lawyer James Harrison Fay '59 of Boston and Worcester-born Thomas Kinnicutt '56 L'60. (Kinnicutt, a former lawyer and insurance man turned tobacco merchant, lent the quintet a modicum of gravitas, being all of thirty years old.)

Founders plaque

One evening in late October these five men and a handful of others assembled in an upstairs room in the Mercantile Library Building on Astor Place. As Fay would remember, "It was not a particularly enthusiastic or hopeful gathering. The social atmosphere of New York City at that period was not especially favorable to the propagation of Harvard enterprises. There was no general interest demanding an outlet in that direction." Even so, the five subsequently drafted a proposal in the form of an invitation and the next week mailed out copies to every Harvard graduate known to reside in the metropolis:

New York City, October 31st, 1865

A meeting of a few of the ALUMNI OF HARVARD COLLEGE, resident in New York, was held October 26th, to consider the feasibility of instituting a society, to bring together, more intimately, the members of their College in this city. The peculiar spirit and influence of Cambridge education and associations would seem a sufficient bond of sympathy on which to base such a society, even among persons widely diverse in age and pursuits.

A committee was appointed to submit a plan of organization at an adjourned meeting, to be held *FRIDAY, NOV. 3rd,* at the rooms of the "AMERICAN GEOG. & STATISTICAL SOCIETY," Clinton Hall, at which your attendance is invited.

Arthur Amory, Jas. H. Fay, Thos. Kinnicutt, J. T. Kilbreth, A. C. Haseltine. Committee.

On the appointed evening the Harvard Club of New York City (or, by the usual spelling, New-York City) came into precarious existence. Its founders may by then have asked George Bancroft, the most distinguished Harvard man in town, to lead them; if so, he had declined, no doubt explaining that he already headed the Century Association and was busy framing President Andrew Johnson's first annual message to Congress. However, Bancroft's fellow-eulogist of Lincoln, Reverend Samuel Osgood, had agreed to take office as president in January. Assisting him would be three vice-presidents, all transplanted Bostonians: George B. Blake, Jr. '59 L'61, Frederick A. Lane '49 and John O. Stone '33 MD'36. Albert Haseltine was to be secretary—again—and his classmate Charles Emerson '63 treasurer, while Arthur Amory and A. W. Green '63 would constitute an executive committee and Thomas Kinnicutt serve on the admissions committee.

On February 22, 1866, the anniversary of the birth of George Washington LLD (hon.) 1776, the new Club held a gala reception and supper at the city's premier restaurant, Delmonico's, at Fifth Avenue and 14th Street. Conceived, produced and paid for by Vice-President Lane, a prosperous businessman and lawyer, it would be remembered ever afterward as the Lane dinner. Anticipating it, the *Evening Post* reminded its readers that on July 3, 1775, General Washington had taken command of his army in Cambridge, adding that "Old Cambridge has ever since kept up close affinity with the principles of Washington; and it is well that the first conspicuous meeting of her graduates in New York should be on Washington's birthday."

Before then, volunteer head-counters had located a total of 145 Harvard men living in New York and Brooklyn. Lane invited all 145 and saw to it that some were approached personally: Thus William G. Choate '52 L'54, older brother and classmate of Joseph, would decades later remember calling on a classmate of George Bancroft's, clergyman Stephen Tyng '17 STD'51, in Tyng's parsonage. "He seemed interested in the College," Choate would recall, "and expressed himself as delighted to come to the dinner. I bade him goodbye and got to the door when he called me back. 'Look here,' said he, 'will they smoke?' 'Well,' I said, 'I suppose after dinner some of them will smoke.' 'Well, then,' said he, 'I can't come, I can't come'; and he didn't come."

Fortunately, enough Harvardians did come—smokers and nonsmokers, members and nonmembers—to make the evening a success. What made it more than that was the presence of a top-level delegation from Cambridge headed by President Hill and former President Jared Sparks '15 Dv '18 LLD'43, the historian. Other guests (and speakers) included College librarian John Sibley '25, the Rev. Edward Everett Hale '39, George Bancroft, the Rev. Henry W. Bellows '32 STD'54, "Hero of Fort Fisher" Albert G. Lawrence '56 L'58 (Fort Fisher, North Carolina, defending the Confederates' last seaport, Wilmington, had been captured in January 1865), and, representing Yale, the brilliant advocate and future secretary of state William M. Evarts. Their speeches must have pleased their host, for as Joseph Choate would recall, "Lane's idea was to have the Harvard men in New York cooperate with the College for its benefit, and the whole burden of what was said at the dinner was the importance to the College of the Harvard men in New York cooperating to do what they could for the benefit of the College. . . .The great representation of the College at the dinner showed how important the matter seemed to those in authority at Cambridge." Confirming this last point were some lines that Oliver Wendell Holmes '29 MD'36 had composed for the dinner:

> She to whose faithful breast each child is dear
>    Hears the far murmur of your voices meeting,
> Ah! sweetest music to her loving ear!
>    And sends a mother's greeting.
>
> When first enrobed her radiant form she dressed
>    Truth was the pearl that on her forehead glistened,
> Freedom her message to the virgin West,
>    And the whole world listened.
>
> Whate'er she gave you—learning, science, art—
>    Shed from the mystic tree whose leaves are letters,
> One gift excelled them all, a manly heart,
>    Freed from all earthly fetters.
>
> Guard well the pearl of Harvard, all too white
>    For the coarse hordes to clutch that buy and barter,
> Conquer with Freedom in her life-long fight,
>    Or fall her noble martyr.

"A large and generous spirit prevailed," the *Evening Post* reported the next day. "The Harvard enthusiasm did not degenerate into exclusive pride or self-admiration. Fine music from a choice band, with old College songs from the Glee Club of Harvard men, gave zest to the proceedings at intervals, and the whole company at the close joined in 'Auld Lang Syne' with clasped hands and right good will. The general feeling was that this must not be the last social meeting of the Sons of Harvard in New York City."

Jonathan Fisher, View of Harvard College, 1790

# 2

# THE FIRST
# DECADE
# (1866–1876)

After this heartening send-off, the Club settled into a routine from which it would depart only rarely over the next twenty years. An initiation fee of ten dollars was fixed upon, annual dues set at the same amount, and meetings of the Club scheduled eight times a year, on the evening of the third Saturday of each month from October through May. At first,

835 Broadway today

these monthly meetings were held at 835 Broadway, a five-story building, still standing, at the southwest corner of Broadway and East 13th Street, in rented rooms upstairs from Clark's Restaurant; when not in use by the Club, these rooms were often rented out—presumably by Nathan Clark, proprietor of the restaurant and owner of the building—to other organizations, for most of the clubs and societies proliferating in the city at that time wanted quarters in the "club district," on or just off the six-block stretch of Broadway between Astor Place and Union

Square. (Among the few New York clubs with clubhouses were the Union Club, founded 1836, at Fifth Avenue and 21st Street, the Century Association, founded 1847, at 42 East 15th Street, and the Union League Club, founded 1863, at 26 East 17th Street.)

Before the start, in October 1866, of its first full season, the Club published a broadsheet listing its officers and members. (The Harvard arms, at the top, look today oddly "blind," for although the shield, partly encircled by the motto *CHRISTO ET ECCLESIAE*, displays the familiar open books, their pages are, as was then customary, blank.) The ninety-eight members listed, two-thirds of all the Harvard men known to live in the metropolis, included, in addition to George Bancroft, Samuel Osgood, Frederick A. Lane, the Choate brothers and several future presidents of the Club, at least three other men of note: Willard Parker '26 MD'30, a distinguished surgeon, H. H. Richardson '59, the great architect-to-be and future designer of Sever Hall and Austin Hall in Cambridge (who, though born and raised in New Orleans, had spent most of the recent war years in Paris at the Ecole des Beaux-Arts) and Charles D. Gambrill '54, Richardson's future partner.

At the Club's first annual meeting for the election of officers, on the evening of Saturday, January 10, 1867, President Osgood noted, as the *Evening Post* would report, "satisfactory evidence that the enterprise had been successful, alike from the good number of members, their social feeling and thriving finances." He resigned his post, congratulating his fellow members "on the good management shown in their business affairs and the uniformly gentlemanly demeanor that had marked their conduct." And he urged them to choose as his successor a younger man who did not belong to the clergy. Accordingly, the Club elected its dinner host of the previous February, Frederick A. Lane. Dr. Parker became a vice-president, with Joseph H. Choate and Henry D. Sedgwick '43. Charles Emerson remained treasurer and James H. Fay an admissions committeeman, while A. W. Green took over as secretary from Albert Haseltine, who joined the executive committee.

Before adjourning, the members present voted to dine together again on Washington's birthday, and to make that day, or a day as close to it as circumstances would allow, their "annual festival."

Billed as the Club's first annual dinner, that next banquet was booked, not into Delmonico's but into the Maison Dorée, at 123 East 13th Street. Evening dress was required. Scheduled for 6:30 P.M., the stag dinner cost six dollars; this was a hefty sum, but the repast, as described in a bill of fare that sported another *Veritas*-less seal and contained tiny errors doubtless undetected by diners better versed in ancient Greek and Latin than modern French, was incontestably Lucullan:

HUITRES.

POTAGES.

Tortue.                                          À la Royale.

POISSON.

Basse rayée à la Maintenon.              Corbeille d'Eperlans.

Croquettes de Pommes de terre.

ENTREES.

Bouchées à la Montglas.

Filets de Boeuf à la Maison Dorée.          Chapons à la Maréchale.

Filets de Chevreuil à la Cumberland.

Harricots verts.                                Tomates au Gratin.

Asperges en branches.

PUNCH A LA ROMAINE

ROTI.

Selles de Mouton à la Gelée de Groseille.

Cailles bordées.                                Salade Celeri.

ENTREMETS ET DESSERT.

Plum Pudding à l'Anglaise,                  Croute à l'ananas,

Milles-Feuille,                                Chalets Suisse,

Charlotte à la Maison Dorée,

Croquembouche,     Mousses au peches,     Bavarois au Café,

Gelée à l'Orientale                          Bombe au Champagne,

Biscuits Glacés,                            Compotes de Fruits,

Patisserie assortie.

At some point that evening the banqueters rose and sang in unison, to the tune of "Fair Harvard," some words printed in their menus. These verses told of how a "Wanderer roaming in desolate ways" comes upon a "brother or chum of his happier days" and is forthwith restored to a pristine state of innocence. Then the scene shifts to the here and now, to New York City in 1867:

> So, Brothers, as we, in this city of trade,
>   From our Mother's halls drifted away,
> Forgetting the pledges we fervently made
>   When she blessed us and warned, the last day,
> Meet together tonight, perchance soiled by the stain
>   Which greed and ambition impart,
> O, what to us now seems the gold of our gain
>   To the gold we have lost from our heart?

In this dilemma, the final stanza advised, we should cut down on (without abandoning altogether) the pursuit of pelf, and instead embrace once more the values and virtues of our youthful college years, wherefor

> The chaplets of fame and the prizes of barter
>   Henceforth shall less dear to us be
> Than a Brother's true love, and, O Alma Mater!
>   Than a smile of approval from thee!

These lines were the work of a new member, originally from Revere, Massachusetts, named Horatio Alger, Jr. '52 Dv'60. At five feet two inches he was the shortest man in his class—and in the Club. Another Unitarian minister, Alger had recently begun serving as chaplain of the Newsboys' Lodging House in Manhattan and had simultaneously discovered his true calling as a writer of inspirational books for boys. While the antimaterialistic sentiments of his "Ode" seem quite appropriate for a clergyman, they do sound a little odd, in retrospect, coming from an author who would become, starting that very year with his *Ragged Dick* series, one of the biggest money-makers in the annals of American letters, whose name would soon be a byword for rising in the world from rags to riches.

In March 1867 the Club issued its first directory, listing just ninety-five members; then, in May, President Johnson named George Bancroft minister to Prussia. Would the Club have to lose him? Apparently not, for throughout Bancroft's seven years in Berlin, years that would witness the consolidation of many German states into a single empire and that empire's crushing military defeat of France, he would remain on the Club's roster, becoming its first nonresident member—or one of its first—in fact if not yet in name.

In January 1868 the Club called on physician John O. Stone to be its leader during the coming year, but next month the annual Washington's birthday dinner was, for some reason, omitted. On a Saturday evening late the following October, however, when members of the Club reassembled after the long summer recess, they had much to talk about concerning developments in Cambridge. The previous July, a Harvard varsity baseball team had taken on a Yale nine for the first time, and beaten it, 25–17. At Commencement, Charles W. Eliot had been elected an Overseer. And in September, President Hill had resigned, citing ill health. The Corporation had offered the presidency to Charles Francis Adams '25, home from London after prolonged service as American minister there, but he had declined it. The Reverend Andrew P. Peabody '26 G'32 STD'52, preacher to the College and professor of Christian morals, was temporarily in charge, but who the next president of Harvard would be was anyone's guess.

Who the next president of the United States would be was, by contrast, rather obvious, but even so, when, in November, General Grant outpolled his Democratic opponent, Governor Horatio Seymour of New York, the Club members, Republicans almost to a man, rejoiced.

In January 1869 they, too, elected a chief executive, still another Unitarian divine. Although he was to play a somewhat equivocal role, a decade thence, in a memorable confrontation between the Club and the University, Henry Whitney Bellows was, by any measure, a highly distinguished citizen. Born in Boston in 1813 and raised in New Hampshire, he had been summoned to the metropolis to preach the gospel according to William Ellery Channing '98 AM'02 STD'20 in 1839; he had since helped to found the Century Association, the Union League Club and Antioch College and published three thick volumes of sermons, but his chief claim to fame, and to his country's gratitude, was to have organized and administered, during the Civil War, the Sanitary Commission, which had cared for countless thousands of sick and wounded men, saving the lives of many.

The Club's annual dinner on February 24—its second, not counting the Lane dinner, but billed as its third—was again held at Delmonico's. William Cullen Bryant, a onetime Williams College undergraduate, spoke about poetry, observing that America's foremost living poets were "nurselings of Harvard" and speculating that "the fount of Castaly or of Hippocrene, or of the Pierian Spring, or some other of those fountains, a draught from which is said to impart poetic inspirations, must flow into the Charles River." (One Harvard nurseling, James Russell Lowell '38 L'40, had sent his regrets, explaining that he was detained in Cambridge celebrating his fiftieth birthday.) But the rest of the evening was far from poetic, consisting of prosaic speeches by no fewer than five clergymen.

Eight days later President Grant took office, and eight days after that word came from Cambridge that the Corporation had picked thirty-four-year-old Charles W. Eliot to be president of Harvard. Wanting an older, more conservative man, the Overseers twice balked at confirming him, but on May 19 they finally relented. At Commencement, the last class was graduated whose members could, in accordance with a medieval custom carried over from Cambridge University by the College's founders, earn a master's degree simply by "keeping out of jail for five years and paying five dollars." And in August, Harvard men sweltering in New York could read in the papers about the first international intercollegiate rowing contest ever held, on the Thames above London, between Harvard and Oxford. In the main race, of four-oared boats, Oxford outrowed Harvard by three lengths, and a few days later both crews were treated to a "grand fête" at which Charles Dickens spoke.

Charles W. Eliot's installation as president of Harvard on October 19 was front-page news, the *New York Times* noting that "There has probably been no change in the administration of the College, from the day of its foundation down to the present time, which has excited such general, serious and various comment." Reading his inaugural address, one could see that, while not a radical, he was certainly a reformer. "The endless controversies," Eliot began, "whether language, philosophy, mathematics or science supplies the best mental training, whether general education should be chiefly literary or chiefly scientific, have no political lesson for us today. This University recognizes no real antagonism between literature and science, and consents to no such narrow alternatives as mathematics or classics, science or metaphysics. We would have them all, and at their best." Regarding the purpose of higher education, he declared that "A university is not closely concerned with the applications of knowledge, until its general education branches into professional. Poetry and philosophy and science do

Charles W. Eliot

indeed conspire to promote the material welfare of mankind; but science no more than poetry finds its best warrant in its utility. Truth and right are above utility in all realms of thought and action." As to "the prevailing discussion touching the education and fit employment of women," Eliot declared that the Corporation would "not receive women as students into the College proper, nor into any school whose discipline requires residence in the school. The difficulties involved in a common residence of hundreds of young men and women of immature character and marriageable age are very grave. The necessary police regulations are exceedingly burdensome." Besides, the president added, "The world knows next to nothing about the natural mental capacities of the female sex. Only after generations of civil freedom and social equality will it be possible to obtain the data necessary for an adequate discussion of women's natural tendencies, tastes and capabilities."

Eliot also spoke about what was already being called the elective system: "The young man of nineteen or twenty ought to know what he likes best and is most fit for. If his previous training had been sufficiently wide, he will know by that time whether he is most apt at language or philosophy or natural science or mathematics. If he feels no loves, he will at least have his hates . . . when the revelation of his own peculiar taste and capacity comes to a young man, let him reverently give it welcome, thank God and take courage. Thereafter he knows his way to happy, enthusiastic work, and, God willing, to usefulness and success."

In scarcely more than a decade President Eliot would, in the words of Joseph H. Choate, transform "the little, provincial, out-of-the-way College of Harvard into a great, national university."

Up to this point the Club had had two ministers, a businessman and a physician as presidents, each for just a year; now it chose a lawyer, a member of a profession from whose ranks a number of the Club's presidents would henceforth be drawn, to serve for at least two years. He was James Coolidge Carter '50 L'53, a native of Lancaster, Massachusetts. Still unmarried at forty-two, Carter would remain so, and through single-minded devotion to his work would rise to the summit of his profession.

As it chanced, the law, lawyers and legal skirmishes would all figure largely in the affairs of the Club during the coming decade. One development that would affect the entire profession was President Eliot's appointment, in January 1870, of Christopher Columbus Langdell '51 L'53 AM (hon.) '54 to the principal professorship of the Law School. A New Hampshire man, Langdell, whom Eliot had come to know and admire during his own undergraduate years, had not completed College, but had worked his way through the Law School, living very modestly; he had then gone to New York and was toiling obscurely in a downtown office when Eliot located him. In all likelihood few lawyer members of the Club were more than dimly aware of his existence, but before long they would be discussing or even heatedly arguing about the radical changes he was introducing, with Eliot's backing, in the teaching of law, for Langdell was determined to scrap the ages-old method of learning by rote in favor of learning by studying actual cases at law, the "case method" that was destined to become standard in American law schools.

By March 1870 the Club had 127 members and convened monthly at Delmonico's, the upstairs room at 835 Broadway having proved less congenial for get-togethers than any restaurant, let alone the best one in town.

Reporting on the Club's fifth annual dinner, in February 1871, the *Times* called it "a very elegant affair," at which "Delmonico's *chef du cuisine* [*sic*] had his ability fully tried." But many diners probably came not so much for the food as to see and hear Eliot, who was rumored to be transforming the college they remembered with affection into something quite different. "After more than two hours had passed in purely gastronomic delights," the *Times* piece continued, President Carter called the banqueters' attention to the presence not only of the president of the University but several Overseers. It was good to have them all here in New York, Carter said, straightfaced, so that they might take in a little of the practical working of life: "how benefactors of the race can successfully water one share of stock into two, and how the principles of political economy, as illustrated in the corners of Wall Street, [are] entirely at variance with those laid down theoretically by Adam Smith." And when he introduced the principal speaker a roar of welcome went up.

President Eliot rose to the ovation. "Our Alma Mater," the *Times* had him replying, "is blushing and trembling with delight at the hearty cheers of his [*sic*] children, and can but faintly return his thanks." Responding to charges that his innovations were sweeping away cherished Harvard traditions, he insisted that every change he had introduced had been planned at least twenty years before. And to prove the wisdom of his course, he cited some telling figures: Whereas twenty years before, he said, there had been only eight students from New York and Brooklyn at Harvard, there were now 39 out of 608, and their numbers were increasing.

At which Eliot's hearers, nearly all of them native New Englanders, applauded heartily.

But if these former Yankees were now proud to call New York their home, they were far from pleased that its government had fallen into the clutches of "Boss" William Marcy Tweed and his henchmen of Tammany Hall. From President Carter down, Club members joined in a crusade to oust the corrupt boss and his "ring," particularly after the *Times* began, on July 8, 1871, to document the latter's swindles. Once, cornered by a reporter who read him a list of such allegations, Tweed growled, defiantly, "What are you going to do about it?" It would fall to Carter's friend Joseph H. Choate to provide an answer.

The occasion was a mass meeting in the Cooper Union on the evening of September 4, 1871. After older and better-known speakers had spelled out the case against the Ring, Choate strode to center stage, in his hand a resolution calling for repeal of the charter that enabled Tweed to do as he pleased without fear of reprisal and for recovery of the millions the Ring had stolen. There was a pause; then he raised his resolution aloft.

"This is what we're going to do about it!" he yelled.

In an instant a thousand people were on their feet, the hall echoing to their shouts. Choate's resolution was adopted. A Committee of Seventy was formed, and Choate was named chairman of its committee on elections. Before September was out, three of Tweed's cronies had fled to France. In November Tweed himself, though under arrest, was reelected to the state senate. But Tammany had suffered frightful losses; the Ring was finished. And although it would require two trials, Tweed would finally be convicted on more than 100 counts of fraud.

Meanwhile, several lawyer members of the Club, among them President Carter and the Choate brothers, had participated prominently in founding, in 1870, an organization destined to become the Club's oldest neighbor on West 44th Street: the Association of the Bar of the City of New York.

In January 1872 William G. Choate became president of the Club, and in the same month the University's governing boards established a Graduate Department of Arts and Sciences. That year, three dormitories—Matthews, Weld and Thayer Halls—went up in the Yard, together with Holyoke House, across Massachusetts Avenue. The Club, too, was growing: Its annual directory listed 147 members.

When, late in 1872, a disastrous fire inflicted severe financial losses on the College, the Club responded at once. President Choate summoned hastily appointed committeemen to Dr. Bellows's study adjoining All Souls' Church (popularly known, for its black-and-white striped front, as the Church of the Holy Zebra), told them of their alma mater's need for cash and sent them out to raise it. Their task was not easy, for while a number of Harvard men in the city were by now comfortably off, few were yet wealthy. As for those men and women, without Harvard connections, who possessed large fortunes and contributed to worthy causes, the majority, firm believers in the doctrine of the Holy Trinity, hesitated to lend their support to that hotbed of Unitarian heresy called Harvard. William Choate would remember being turned down on that very ground:

> I called on an eminent citizen who was known to be very rich and very liberal to charities generally, but a pillar, yes, two or three pillars, of the Presbyterian Church. I stated the case of the College, the great loss of its funds by the failure of the insurance companies . . . in which the funds of the College were invested. . . . This gentleman heard me patiently and then said, "Young man, you might be in better business than collecting money for a Godless college," adding something to the effect that the fire was an obvious visitation from Providence. Of course I got no money from him. Yet personally I felt kindly treated. He evidently had a big heart, yearning for the heathen, both foreign and domestic. He invited me to sit in his pew some Sunday. It seemed to me that he saw an opportunity to pluck a brand from the burning fire. We parted with mutual respect.

In the end, however, enough broadminded affluent New Yorkers joined alumni givers to enable President Choate to send Harvard several thousand dollars.

By March 1873 the Club had 162 members, including former ace batsman Charles F. McKim, Lawrence Scientific School '67, back from the Ecole des Beaux-Arts in Paris. But some months later the concurrent failures of several large banks plunged the nation's economy into depression. During the lean years ahead many of the city's sodalities would go under, but the Harvard Club would continue to grow. This happy consummation owed much to two policies it had adopted at the outset and hewed to ever since, the first being to keep the dues low enough so that young members struggling to get by on inadequate starting salaries could still afford to belong, and the second to defray the costs of refreshments at the annual meetings out of general funds, thereby encouraging even the least pecunious to attend.

In January 1874 Joseph H. Choate took over the presidency of the Club from his older brother, and in February the annual dinner was, the *Times* reported,

> most numerously attended, by every class and kind of alumnus, from the graduate of 1873, with the light down upon his chin, restless in his dress coat and uneasy in his white choker, up to the men of mark who have made their way in the world, and know it. . . . Every course had its appropriate wine, and when the game arrived the famous Delmonico champagne brightened every eye and unbosomed every tongue.

Memorial Hall, 1874

At the end of June those members, the great majority, who did not go to Cambridge for Commencement could read in their daily papers about the dedication of Memorial Hall, honoring the memory of Harvard's sons who had died in the war for the Union, toward the erection of which many of them had contributed. In the coming weeks, moreover, leading magazines would carry photographs and drawings of the imposing structure's majestic interior spaces.

Early in 1875 his clubmates reelected Joseph H. Choate their president, and twelve months later they chose him again, exceptionally, for a third year. That February, a *Times* account of the Club's tenth annual dinner began flatteringly: "There is probably," it declared, "no social club of college alumni in this country which has more real vitality, or a membership numbering so many who are prominent in professional and mercantile life, than the Harvard Club of New York." President Choate had told the diners that "The older I grow, the more I believe that this Harvard Club is worth cherishing. I believe that it contributes to the virtue, the honor and power of our old Alma Mater." Then, citing President Eliot's annual report, he had made a dramatic announcement: "Formerly," he said, "the New Yorkers entered at Cambridge were scanty stragglers, and now they constitute *one-eighth* of the whole number of Freshmen!"

This statement had reportedly evoked "[Great Applause]," whereupon President Eliot shrewdly expanded on the increase in New York's representation within the undergraduate body, attributing it to the fact that Harvard men in the metropolis were preeminent in the learned professions of the ministry, medicine and the law. These remarks, too, appear to have gone down well—and provided the *Times* reporter with his lead; next, the speaker segued nimbly to the question of certifying lawyers. No one should be admitted to the bar, he asserted, without passing a public examination; no law school needed a guarantee that its students would be admitted after a given term of study and no bar examination should be limited to a candidate's knowledge but inquire into his character as well. Lawyers in Eliot's audience perceived that he was defending the rigorous standards set for the Harvard Law School by his protégé, Professor, and now Dean, Langdell, standards which, along with a rise in tuition, had caused a worrying flight of applicants to other, less demanding schools of law.

At the end of the evening, the *Times* report concluded, " 'Auld Lang Syne' was sung in the old familiar fashion, and the president retired, but midnight found the younger alumni singing over the old college songs."

# 3

# CHALLENGING THE UNIVERSITY (1876–1880)

As New York City expanded northward up Manhattan Island many of its residents, including some conspicuous style-setters, moved uptown with it, and the proprietors of Delmonico's, following their clients, reestablished their restaurant at West 26th Street and Fifth Avenue, where that most fashionable of thoroughfares flows together with Broadway. The Club members would no longer meet off Union Square, then, but off

Crews practice at Springfield, Massachusetts (*Frank Leslie's Illustrated Newspaper*, July 7, 1877)

Madison Square. Several of them, at that time, were keenly interested in promoting rowing at Cambridge; to raise funds "in aid of the Harvard University Crew" they rented the Union League Club's theater across the park from Delmonico's, and on the evening of May 8, 1876, presented a single performance of a comic show they had cobbled together:

---

WILLIAM TELL
with a vengeance!
Or, the Pet, the Patriot, and the Pippin.

CHARACTERS:

GESLER (the tyrannical Governor of Altorf, who exercises
    his rule in the City, but misses his *Sway* in the
    Mountains)........................................................................Mr. S. Henry Hooper

SARNEM (a bilious Jailer, with a secret).............................Mr. Henry C. Andrews

WILLIAM TELL (a young Patriot, who has married
    an elderly Lady with a slight Incumbrance)....................Mr. Nathaniel S. Smith
EMMA (the elderly Lady, with a slight Incumbrance)........ Mr. Ernest Szemelenyi

ALBERT (the slight Incumbrance)........................................Mr. William G. Hosea

ERNI (a Patriot, who, though scarcely ready to die
    for his country, objects to Erni's living)..........................Mr. George H. Adams

FURST      ⎫  Patriots pure and.......................................Mr. Francis M. Weld
MELCHTAL  ⎬  more than usually ....................................Mr. James S. Walker
VERNER     ⎭  simple .......................................................Mr. Charles McKim

BEAR................................................................................Mr. James S. McCobb

GENSDARMES [*sic*] ⎰ ......................................................... Mr. William T. Bull
                      ⎱ ......................................................... Mr. Henry W. Poor

ROSETTA (Daughter of Sarnem, who thinks a good
    deal of herself, but more of Albert)..........................Mr. Montgomery D. Parker

Peasantry, ready for unpleasantry, Tag, Rag, and Bobtail in reckless profusion.

---

Unfortunately, no description of *William Tell* survives apart from the playbill, but it seems remarkable that the Club's first organized attempt at humor appeared the same year as did the *Harvard Lampoon*. (The *Advocate* had made its debut in 1866, and the *Crimson*, originally the *Magenta*, in 1873.) As for the cause the cast members had sought to benefit, it flourished: A month later, for the first time, eight-man crews from Harvard and Yale raced, on the Connecticut River at Springfield. Yale won. Over the coming decades, however, Harvard eights would more than make up for this initial defeat, cheered on and financially supported by, among others, dedicated enthusiasts within the Club—who incidentally left the production of further farces to the Hasty Pudding Club.

It was also in the spring of 1876, by the way, that Harvard athletes first competed in an intercollegiate track meet.

That November, it is safe to assume, many members were dismayed when it looked as if the Democratic candidate for president, New York Governor Samuel Tilden, had won the election, and were much relieved when, several weeks later, a special electoral commission on which Republicans outnumbered Democrats awarded the contested votes of four states to the Republican standard bearer, Ohio Governor Rutherford B. Hayes, giving him a majority of one in the Electoral College. Although Tilden had received substantially more popular votes, Hayes was thus elected. The president-elect, a graduate of Kenyon College, had earned an LL.B. from Harvard Law School in 1845, but neither he nor anyone else supposed that that made him a Harvard man: Only in recent times, indeed, has the University itself included Hayes in its roster of Harvard graduates who became American presidents. On the other hand, the Club had always welcomed candidates lacking a Harvard bachelor's degree but possessing a Harvard graduate degree. Already, too, the old, narrow inter-pretation of the concept "Harvard" had begun to give way within the Club to a broader definition: Whereas previous directories had stated that the Club existed "for the advancement of the interests of the College," the 1877 Club book defined its purpose as being "to advance the interest of the University."

That spring, an incident occurred that, as recorded in the minutes by Secretary Francis M. Weld '60 MD'64 AM'71, made for entertaining reading. A certain member—John J. Doe will serve as his name—had been accused of financial hanky-panky; he had asked for an investigation, offering to pay the costs thereof, and at the monthly meeting of May 19 Chairman William G. Choate of the investigating committee reported finding that while Doe "had been careless in the management of funds entrusted to him, he had done nothing to call for any action on the part of the Club or to affect his position as a gentleman." This conclusion having been adopted as the judgment of the Club, Dr. Thomas Kinnicutt, one of the Club's founders, moved that the committee be thanked, and when this was done,

> Dr. Kinnicutt again rose, and struggling with ill-disguised emotion, said that no one would be more pleased and delighted with the result than himself, and that hereafter he should regard [Doe] as a man and a brother.
>
> The secretary controlled his enthusiasm as far as to hold his tongue, but he grasped [Doe's] hand convulsively.
>
> The meeting then resolved itself into a general love-feast, there being nothing else to eat. [Doe] received many congratulations, and afterwards, it is understood, gave a recherché souper à la Madame la duchesse de Pompadour at his elegant apartments on the corner of 23rd Street and Fourth Avenue.

But the story did not end there, for in April 1878, after ignoring repeated requests from Treasurer T. Frank Brownell '65 that he pay the Club expenses of $107 incurred by the investigators, Doe would be expelled.

That renowned wit Joseph W. Choate had been reelected to an unprecedented fourth year as president after an unprecedented third one; clearly his was a hard act to follow, but in January 1878 the Club picked a first-rate successor in charter member John O. Sargent '30 of Gloucester, Massachusetts. Though almost seventy, Sargent, a retired lawyer and journalist with a passion for translating Horace,

Oliver Wendell Holmes

brimmed with energy and self-confidence, attributes on which he would, two years later, have ample occasion to call.

Once elected, the new president wrote the physician-poet Oliver Wendell Holmes in Boston, inviting him to the annual meeting the following month. "I would almost crawl to New York to please you, old friend and constant friend as you are," Holmes replied, but "I do not feel quite up to the winter expedition you so kindly and warmly propose."

Two or three weeks later, however, Sargent received in the post a bulky parcel containing printed copies of a pair of sonnets. "I would not have done this for any other president of the Harvard Club," Holmes told Sargent in a covering note, "but it has been a great pleasure to do my best . . . to help you through the evening."

Late on that February evening, at Delmonico's, President Sargent, having first seen to it that the printed sonnets were distributed among the cigar-smoking, coffee-and-liqueur-sipping company, read aloud a communication from Holmes to the members. "I send you," the poet had written, "a couple of sonnets which I would have read if I could have been with you," adding that "as the construction of a sonnet often renders it somewhat difficult to follow when listened to, I have had a few copies struck off, in case any of the company should care to understand what many of them have heard with more or less dim perception of its significance." Then Dr. Holmes offered

> a few words of explanation. At the first meeting of the Governors of the College under the Charter of 1642, held in 1643, it was "ordered that there should be a College seal in the form of the following," namely a shield with three open books bearing the work *Veritas*. This motto was soon exchanged for *In Christi Gloriam*, and this again shortly superseded by the one so long used, *Christo et Ecclesiae*. The latter change took place, as President [Josiah] Quincy believed, "during the presidency of Increase Mather, when a violent struggle was making to secure the College under the influences of the old established Congregational Church." The date (1700), which I have assigned to this last motto, must be considered as only approximate. [The actual year was 1692.]
>
> The Harvard College of today wants no narrower, no more exclusive motto than Truth—truth, which embraces all that is highest and purest in the precepts of all teachers, human or divine, all that is best in the creeds of all churches, whatever their name. . . .
>
> This is what I meant to express in these two squares of metrical lines wrought in the painful prolixity of the sonnet, a form of verse which suggests a slow minuet of rhythms stepping in measured cadences over a mosaic pavement of rhyme, and which not rarely combines a minimum of thought with a maximum of labor.

Pocketing Holmes's letter, Sargent read out the sonnets:

HARVARD
"CHRISTO ET ECCLESIAE." 1700
TO GOD'S ANOINTED AND HIS CHOSEN FLOCK:
So ran the phrase the black-robed conclave chose
To guard the sacred cloisters that arose
Like David's altar on Moriah's rock.
Unshaken still those ancient arches mock
The ram's-horn summons of the windy foes
Who stand like Joshua's army while it blows
And wait to see them toppling with the shock.
Christ and the Church. *Their* church, whose narrow door
Shut out the many, who if overbold
Like hunted wolves were driven from the fold,
Bruised with the flails those godly zealots bore,
Mindful that Israel's altar stood of old
Where echoed once Araunah's threshing-floor.

1648. "VERITAS." 1878.
TRUTH: So the frontlet's older legend ran,
On the brief record's opening page displayed,
Not yet those clear-eyed scholars were afraid
Lest the fair fruit that wrought the woe of man
By far Euphrates—where our sire began
His search for truth, and, seeking, was betrayed—
Might work new treason in their forest shade,
Doubling the curse that brought life's shortened span.
Nurse of the future, daughter of the past,
That stern phylactery best becomes thee now:
Lift to the morning star thy marble brow!
Cast thy brave truth on every warning blast!
Stretch thy white hand to that forbidden bough,
And let thine earliest symbol be thy last!

Holmes's precaution had been a wise one: Having followed the poet's argument in print, Sargent's hearers had grasped it fully, and they greeted it with tumultuous approval. All at once, restoring Harvard's ancient and secular motto to the three blank books on her shield was a burning issue. Not everyone took up the cause: on March 4 the Club's first president, Samuel Osgood—presumably partial, as a clergyman, to *Christo et Ecclesiae*—asserted in the *Times* "that there is no purpose or wish on the part of the college to change its seal," but two days later the Club's eighth and incumbent president publicly doubted, in the same columns, his predecessor's claim. "That the restoration of the original seal, in its grand simplicity, would be favorably entertained by a considerable portion of the college," Sargent wrote, "we have reason to know."

That very day Dr. Holmes confessed to his old friend, in a letter, that "I had no idea of my sonnets making such a stir. It was rather with the idea that *Veritas* should be recognized as the understood motto of the College, than with that of having it cut upon a new die as the College seal, that I wrote the verses." By then, however, President Sargent had had the sonnets printed and bound in pamphlet form, with an explanatory text, for circulation throughout the Harvard community, including the half dozen Harvard clubs that had come into being alongside Philadelphia's and New York's. As Sargent hoped and expected, Holmes's poetic appeal was to touch a responsive chord in the hearts of alumni, whose agitation in favor of restoring the old motto would at last reach the point where, in 1885, the Corporation would adopt the modified *Veritas* design of 1643 that is still in use.

At the Club's next meeting, in March, the only important business, soon accomplished, was the adoption of a constitution, which read, in toto, as follows:

Article I.
This Club shall be perpetual.
Article II.
This Constitution may be altered or amended by a two-thirds vote of the members present at two successive regular meetings; provided, however, that this article shall not apply to, or authorize any amendment, alteration, or repeal of, Article I.

This marvel of compression, in force, unaltered, to this day, was the handiwork of former President William G. Choate, who, appointed that year to a Southern District of New York judgeship, would be known ever afterward as Judge Choate.

Although aftereffects of the 1873 depression still inhibited building in the city, some novel structures had sprung up there, not least elevated railways. The news from Cambridge likewise reported novelties: young women seeking admittance to the College, lengthening lists of courses undergraduates could choose from, a student body that included young men from remote Western territories not yet states of the Union. Meanwhile, in all branches of the University, New Yorkers made up an ever-increasing portion of the student population.

Knowing this, and aware that within their own ranks were men a match in all ways for the Yankee grandees perpetually presiding over Harvard's affairs, thoughtful older members, President Sargent among them, longed to be heard in their alma mater's governing councils and felt entitled, in fairness, to such a hearing. But certain laws, it seemed, barred them. A committee appointed in the fall of 1878 to look into "the laws that regulate the election of Overseers of Harvard College" submitted a report to the membership on March 15, 1879: It confirmed that the latest and most liberal statute covering the matter, passed in 1865, still limited candidates for Overseer to graduates residing in Massachusetts, but noted, too, that the governing boards of both Williams and Amherst Colleges included men who lived outside the state (or commonwealth). That was encouragement enough: It was moved and, after discussion, voted "that the name of the Rev. Dr. Henry W. Bellows be formally recommended by the Harvard Club of New York City to the alumni of the University as a candidate for Overseer at the next commencement."

In person and by letter, members pressed the case for Dr. Bellows's election with classmates and other alumni. How many New Yorkers actually traveled to Cambridge to vote was not recorded, but visitors from the big city were clearly more numerous than at past Commencements; in any case, the Yankee graduates who outnumbered them unexpectedly demonstrated solidarity with their brothers, helping to elect Dr. Bellows with the biggest vote ever cast, until then, for an Overseer.

Would he, even so, be allowed to take his seat? His partisans feared he might not be, but the College authorities put no obstacle in his path. For several months Dr. Bellows attended every meeting of the board and served on two of its committees. Toward the end of 1879 the official University catalogue listed him among the Overseers. And on January 14, 1880, the Overseers' committee on elections, all lawyers, ruled him eligible for membership.

But two weeks later, the Overseers, by a vote of 13–8, found Dr. Bellows ineligible, as a nonresident of Massachusetts, to serve on the board.

At the Club's annual dinner in February members waxed indignant over this affront to their chosen representative, but President Sargent assured them that the offending statute would be amended in time for the

Commencement elections—as, indeed, it would be, largely through the efforts of Massachusetts legislator Robert M. Morse, Jr. '57, a classmate of Governor John D. Long. The Club would, however, have to field a new candidate, as its quondam man in Cambridge had dropped out of contention, moving the *Times* to comment scathingly that "to the surprise and mortification of those who had promoted Dr. Bellows to be the champion of their rights and expected him to fight it out on that line, the reverend gentleman announced himself a convert to the belief that he had no right to the seat on the board to which he had been elected."

Late in April, the Club nominated President John O. Sargent for one of the five vacant places on the board, but on May 5, to his and his nominators' intense annoyance, the Overseers' nominating committee issued a list of twenty approved candidates that omitted Sargent's name but included the names of two other New Yorkers, James C. Carter and Joseph H. Choate. "It seems to be unfortunate," the *Times* observed, "that a small number of the little clique who cannot reconcile themselves to the changed condition of affairs should refuse to recognize the growing importance of the university outside of the college grounds. The Harvard Club of this city has nominated an eminently fit candidate for Overseer in their President, who is a gentleman with ample leisure to attend to the duties of office, and is second to none in his devotion to his alma mater. . . . Now that the question of the eligibility of nonresidents of Massachusetts has finally been decided, it would seem to be only fair that the modest claim of the 'outsiders' to suggest their own candidate should be received with at least a show of courteous respect."

Apparently stung by this, Henry Cabot Lodge '71 L'74 of the Overseers' nominating committee wrote the newspaper to explain that the Club's request to add Sargent's name had arrived too late, the list having already been printed. But the *Times* was unimpressed: "As the election does not take place till June 30," it pointed out, "there was time enough to print another list, and if the means of the committee were inadequate to pay the cost, it is more than probable that the Harvard Clubs of Portland, Albany, New-York, Philadelphia, Cincinnati, Chicago, St. Louis and San Francisco might have combined to come to the rescue. In this connection, it may be mentioned that Mr. Joseph H. Choate, who was suggested by the Boston committee, has positively declined to be a candidate."

The Club now categorically insisted on nominating Sargent, but the "little clique" was not yet ready to surrender without a struggle its ancient prerogative of deciding whom the electors could vote for. While the Bay State insiders added Sargent's name to the approved list and removed Carter's, they left Choate's in place, ignoring his publicly expressed decision not to run and rather obviously hoping that his candidacy would draw votes away from the Club's candidate. On the evening of June 30, in Cambridge, Sargent, having cast his ballot, attended a dinner celebrating the fiftieth anniversary of his class, and the next morning, July 1, learned that he had been elected. "Good sense," purred the *Times*, "and a manly desire for fair play resulted in Mr. Sargent's election, though he was number four on the list of five Overseers elected. [The fifth, fittingly, was the man who had done most to secure Sargent's right to sit on the board, lawmaker Robert M. Morse, Jr.] Adding to Mr. Sargent's score the votes which were carried off, however, it is evident that the great body of Harvard Alumni are seriously in favor of giving a fair representation in the Board of Overseers to the nonresident graduates. The question may be regarded as settled today, and it is doubtful if the obstruction party will attempt again to defeat the expressed will of the majority."

In January 1881, Sargent having declined a fourth year as president, the Club picked as his successor Francis M. Weld, a wartime campaigner with General Sherman who had since practiced medicine in his native Massachusetts and then New York, serving the Club as both treasurer and secretary. Weld's first act as president was to offer resolutions, "unanimously and heartily approved," recognizing that "the great reform of opening the Board of Overseers... to non-residents of Massachusetts" had been chiefly due to his predecessor's "untiring exertions," and that Sargent's name was "indissolubly connected with the history of this important movement."

Sargent, styling himself "the first recognized representative of all the Alumni," would be reelected in 1886 after his six-year term and serve until his death in 1889. He would be followed onto the Board of Overseers by future members of the Club, numbering, by now, well up in the hundreds.

# 4

# IN CAMBRIDGE, CHANGE;
# IN NEW YORK, GROWTH
# (1880–1887)

Even while supporting their leaders' efforts to restore *Veritas* to the Harvard arms and open up the University's government, many members of the Club, doubtless including some with growing daughters, had been closely watching developments in Cambridge involving another campaign of reform: that fostering higher education for women.

Beginning in June 1874 the College, following the lead of Oxford and Cambridge, had offered examinations to young women seventeen and older, similar but not identical to the regular entrance exams, and in 1876 it had started giving them annually in New York as well as Cambridge. Young women who passed them had been admitted to special courses of "liberal culture" taught by members of the University faculty, courses that, according to one newspaper, "have no direct professional value... but which enlarge both intellect and character." So successful had this experiment proved that in September 1879 twenty-seven young women had been admitted to the Harvard "Annex" at 15 Appian Way; they had opted to take courses not only in music (2), botany (5) and French (6); and not only Latin (9), Greek (6) and Sanskrit (1); but also in physics (3) and mathematics (7).

In May 1880, as the new institution's first school year neared its end, Thomas Wentworth Higginson '41 Dv'47 AM'69, the author, pronounced it a success:

> For all practical purposes a woman's college has been organized at Cambridge, without anyone's calling it such, and without involving the President and Fellows

of the university in any difficulty. The college authorities did the very best thing for it simply by letting it alone. . . . All this has been accomplished so quietly as hardly to have made a ripple on the surface.

But others, viewing the matter from a less elevated perspective, were ready to consider a possibility far from the thoughts of the president and fellows, as was evidenced in a brief item in the *Boston Commonwealth* for December 19:

The Harvard boys have become quite rebellious about their sisters of the "Annex." The opinion of many of them is that it is time for the authorities to officially open the university to women, or to take a decided stand against coeducation at Harvard.

This—in 1880!

However, as individuals, they might view the prospect of their alma mater going coeducational, her alumni, in New York and everywhere else, were likely to be more interested in the fortunes of her varsity teams. For under President Eliot, organized athletics burgeoned at Cambridge. In the still-evolving sport of football, the rugby-based game Harvard players preferred had won out over the soccerlike game Yale and Columbia athletes favored; in 1875 a Harvard eleven had defeated Yale by four goals and four touchdowns, but ever since the prodigious Walter Camp had appeared on the scene as a player in 1878 the Elis had ruled the gridiron, and would continue to do so throughout the 1880s and beyond, under Camp's coaching. (Incidentally, Samuel Eliot Morison '08 maintained in his *Three Centuries of Harvard* that it was the need to conceal one's chagrin over these successive drubbings under a mask of not caring that gave rise to the pose of "Harvard indifference" subsequently affected by generations of would-be "sophisticated" undergraduates.)

On the baseball diamond, by contrast, Harvard nines usually prevailed, their catchers sporting the masks reputedly invented by F. W. Thayer '78. (It was not he but his distant kinsman Ernest L. Thayer '85 who in 1888 would pen, for a San Francisco newspaper, the immortal ballad "Casey at the Bat.") Cricket, lacrosse and lawn tennis, fencing, wrestling and boxing all had their devotees (among the last group, Theodore Roosevelt '80), but the events that drew the biggest crowds were the boat races, in particular the annual Harvard-Yale contest on the Thames River at New London

As for track—in which A. Lawrence Lowell '77 had hung up the first College records for the mile and the half mile—Harvard had lagged behind Princeton and Columbia until Evert J. Wendell '82 arrived in Cambridge: A phenomenal sprinter (he accomplished the 100-yard dash in ten seconds flat, without benefit of the yet-to-be-introduced crouching start), Wendell led Harvard to an overwhelming victory in the intercollegiate meet of 1880, scoring three firsts himself in the process. (Wendell, who would soon become an active member of the Club, was a younger brother of Barrett Wendell '77, the future great Harvard professor of English, who had already joined the Club.)

The Club now entered on a phase of quiet growth, its membership more than doubling between 1880 and 1886, from 210 to 431. This development reflected a considerable increase in enrollments at Cambridge, both at the College (by two-thirds for the decade) and at the graduate schools, in particular those of law and medicine. The reforms imposed on these institutions by President Eliot and his aides—much stiffer entrance standards, improved and expanded curricula, longer residence requirements for a degree—had caused applications to fall off alarmingly during the 1870s, but as the superior quality of the schools' new graduates became apparent, applications had begun to rise again.

The Club would not again confront the University head-on over a particular issue, but as a loyal offshoot it reserved the right to advise its venerable parent on diverse matters, while the University continued to take the Club seriously as the voice of alumni living in the nation's biggest and most important city. President Eliot would faithfully attend the annual dinners. And if the Club was still without a fixed abode, certain incidents suggested that it might not remain homeless much longer, as when, in January 1881, Secretary Nathaniel Smith '69 wrote all of the surviving secretaries of past College classes as far back as 1818 requesting copies of their class reports. The reports, many since rebound, continue to form part of the Club's collection of Harvardiana, second only to that of the Harvard University Archives.

The Club's fifteenth annual dinner, on February 21, 1881, introduced a novel feature: as the *Times* reported, Delmonico's large hall, accommodating about 150 diners, was "entirely without decorations," but "the little balcony over the entrance, usually occupied by musicians, was concealed behind pink drapery, and several ladies occasionally showed small portions of their faces as they peeped through the openings and enjoyed the festive scene below." These highly placed observers were the wives of officers and distinguished guests, and similar galleryfuls of intermittently visible voyeuses were to grace annual dinners for many Februarys to come.

On that occasion, President Eliot candidly acknowledged that Harvard counted on the continuing financial support of "this wealthy community." Another speaker, President H. H. Anderson of the newly reorganized University Club, gave tongue to some interesting observations anent New York in the Gilded Age.

> In this great commercial city, everybody is so intent upon enriching himself, and wealth has counted so heavily in determining social standing, that until recently the fact of a man's having received a finished education did not, for many years, entitle him to any social standing whatever. That was far from what it should have been, and it was only changed when the University Club was established. In its two short years of usefulness this club has demonstrated the necessity of its existence, and has firmly and substantially established itself. It is still, I am sorry to say, the only social organization in this city in which it is impossible for money alone to gain entrance.

How Anderson's hearers reacted to his implied criticism of their own social organization—or whether they did react—was not recorded.

Next spring, the Club again nominated its president for Overseer, but this time the board's nominating committee neither raised objections nor put up rival candidates from New York, so that on Commencement Day the New Yorkers saw their man elected by a comfortable margin. Thus Dr. Francis M. Weld became the second fully accredited Overseer from outside Massachusetts. And the following January the Club elected Charles C. Beaman '61 AM'65 L (Columbia) '63 president in his place.

The annual dinner in February 1883 went off smoothly, with just one minor incident briefly threatening decorum. Among the thirteen at President Beaman's table was General Benjamin Butler, the "Beast"

Butler of the wartime occupation of New Orleans, who, as nominee of the radical Greenback Party, had gotten himself elected governor of Massachusetts; President Eliot, not naming him outright yet making his meaning unmistakable, spoke of the predicament in which the University had found itself on being obliged to honor Butler, as governor, with a doctorate of letters. The next moment, however, Eliot had changed the subject and was praising the Club's plan, recently adopted, to establish scholarships for needy students in the city.

The following spring, on learning that the Harvard Club of Philadelphia was proposing a distinguished older member for Overseer, President Beaman saw to it that the Club "cordially recommended" the candidate "as a suitable person" for the post. Again, cooperation among the various Harvard clubs proved effective, and on the day after Commencement, in Cambridge, the magisterially named Charlemagne Tower '30 L'47 joined his classmate John O. Sargent on the Board of Overseers, its third member from outside Massachusetts. Incidentally, returning alumni could admire a new larger-than-life bronze statue of a seated John Harvard, as imagined by sculptor Daniel Chester French, atop a pedestal on a grassy plot west of Memorial Hall. (Not until 1909 would the statue be installed in its present location in front of University Hall.)

The Club, at its November meeting, approved a change in the bylaws advancing the annual meeting to April and confronted at last the question of acquiring a permanent home: A committee made up of the twenty-four-year-old sprinter Evert Wendell and six older men was charged with checking how the members would feel about the Club's renting "permanent rooms" and the feasibility of its doing so. In December the committeemen, unanimously in favor of the plan, set forth certain proposals in a letter to the members.

The committee proposed to lease a house, somewhere between 17th and 34th Streets and between Fourth and Sixth Avenues, spacious enough to accommodate club activities, with bedrooms upstairs to let out as lodgings, preferably to members. Each year, the Club's seven monthly meetings would be held in the "Club rooms," with suppers supplied by a caterer and wine and cigars provided at cost, but the annual dinner would continue to be held at Delmonico's. "It is proposed," the letter went on, that the Club not seek to rival larger, established clubs in its amenities, but simply "provide rooms open every day where the leading periodicals may be seen, games, such as chess and backgammon, played, and a pleasant rendezvous afforded for such Harvard men as may care to drop in to smoke and chat with their fellows."

Implementing their proposals might, the committeemen warned, entail raising the members' dues, but surely by no more than five dollars a year. And at the end of the circular letter, above the names of Chairman W. A. Purrington '73 and his colleagues, there appeared, in large italics, a question: *Are you or are you not in favor of the proposition to secure permanent accommodations for the Club, provided they can be had without increasing the annual dues to a greater sum than $15?*

In the next few days a torrent of affirmative replies flowed into Chairman Purrington's Wall Street office.

Not long after this some member of the Annual Dinner Committee, perhaps inspired by the College's dropping Latin and Greek as required freshman courses, persuaded his fellows to present the dinner as a Roman banquet. The cover of the menu announced "Coena Anniversaria Undevigesima Circuli Harvardiani, Qui Est in Civitate Novi-Eboraci, in Republica Imperiali," to take place "in Coenatione Delmonicorum"; on the Club seal, at the center, the motto *VERITAS*, once again printed across the three books, stood out boldly, while the normally circumambient *CHRISTO ET ECCLESIAE* was absent—as it would have been, of course, in pagan Rome. Opening his menu, a diner confronted the bill of fare ("billefarius") in ancient and modern forms of bogus Latin purportedly dating from the epochs of, respectively, the Emperor Augustus and the republican (or Republican) ruler Arthurus (who but President Chester A. Arthur?). The only English words on the document were those of "Fair Harvard"—in which the "festival rites" in the third verse was rendered, unaccountably, as "festival rights."

| INDEX CIBORUM | BILLEFARIUS |
|---|---|
| *Temp. Aug.* | *Temp. Arth.* |

OSTREA SUPER CONCHAS.　　　OYSTERIA SUPER SHELLAS

*Temp. Aug.*　　　　　　　　　*Temp. Arth.*

Ostrea que in conchis tuta.

*Ovid. Fast. 6, 174.*

JURA.

Jusculum Berchouxii.　　　　　Biscoctum Cancerorum.

Coenae caput.

*Cic. Tusc. 5, 34.*

PROMULSIS.

Raphani Hortenses.　　　　　　Olivae.

Qualia lassum pervellunt stomachum.

*Hor. Sat. II, 6, 9.*

PISCES.

Perca in modum Massenae　　　Eperlani fricti.

Solana tuberosa petroselino.

Quasi piscis itidem est amator; nequam est nisi recens.

*Plautus, Asin, 1, 3, 26.*

MOVENDUM.

Caro bubulae tener Perigueiuxii.

Fabaciae virides igne lento coctae.

INTERJECTA.

Gallus Indicus nucibus castaneae,　　　Turkeius Chestnuttibus,

modo Lugduni.　　　　　　　　　　ut supra.

*Temp. Aug.*　　　　　　　　　　*Temp. Arth.*

Parvae Pisae Gallicae.

Vituli pancreas in modum Cancellarii.

Amoris Poma cum caseo.　　　　Tomatones Cheesiacae.

*Temp. Aug.*　　　　　　　　　*Temp. Arth.*

INDEX CIBORUM.                    BILLEFARIUS.
*Temp. Aug.*                              *Temp. Arth.*

AQUA LIMONATA GELATA,
In modum regni procuratoris.

CIGARETTI.
*Temp. Arth.*

ASSUM.                                   ROASTUM.
*Temp. Aug.*                              *Temp. Arth.*

Ruficapitis Anates Ferae.

Acetaria Lactucae.

Claudere quae coenas lactuca solebat avorum.

*Martial XIII, 14.*

EDULIA  MELLITA.

Jus mirabellis Gelatum.

Globus uvis siccatis refertus.

Placentaae flore lactis imbutae.

MAGNUM OPUS DULCIARII.

Gelu Neapolitanum.

Fructus et Bellaria.

COFFEA.

TUBULI TABACI.

LIQUORES GENEROSI.

VINA.

Iberium.                                 Rubens.

Merum Fulgens Matronae.
Vina quies sequitur.
*Ovid. Fast. III, 305.*

The "coena" consumed and the banqueters puffing on their "tubuli tabaci" and sipping "liquores generosi," the speechmaking began, and after President Beaman had noted the Club's hope of acquiring a home, President Eliot, with a smile, offered him a suggestion. "We have a motto at Harvard," he said, "with regard to a new house: 'Never build one; get somebody to give you one.'"

On March 13, 1885, the country's newly inaugurated president, Grover Cleveland, appointed a prominent member of the Club, former New York State attorney general Charles S. Fairchild '63 L'65, assistant secretary of the Treasury. The Club's annual meeting, on April 18, departed from precedent not only in taking place three months later than in past years but in being held, not at Delmonico's but in the theater of the University Club, an organization that could, as Treasurer William Montgomery, Jr. '67 had discovered, provide suppers at a considerably lower cost per head. But the meeting was notable, too, in its own terms, for it was then that, in electing a new president, corporation lawyer Edmund Wetmore '60, it gave the Club, at long last, a president born and raised outside New England, in his case Utica, New York, while among the five new vice-presidents one, young Theodore Roosevelt, was, extraordinarily, a native of New York *City*. Finally, the Club adopted an amendment to the bylaws establishing nonresident membership for alumni who lived and worked thirty miles or more from New York's City Hall, these nonresident members to pay annual dues of just five dollars, half those paid by resident members, and enjoy all the privileges of membership except voting and holding office.

Before the meeting adjourned, a committee was appointed to look into the teaching of Latin and Greek at Harvard to determine whether such instruction should be compulsory, as it had always been in the past, or, as President Eliot wanted, left to the discretion of individual students.

Throughout the remainder of 1885, the members of what came to be called the Committee on Elective Studies sporadically pursued their inquiry in Cambridge, and in December they submitted a preliminary report to the Club, promising a final report in January. Before then, however, they learned that President Eliot would very soon produce copious data on how the elective system had actually worked with two recent

College classes, so they put off presenting their views until March, instead distributing to the members copies of two papers on the subject, one by a Harvard professor and the other by one of their number, Samuel Brearley, Jr. '78, who was soon to found the girls' school that would be named for him. Before long the hour for the Club's annual dinner, its twentieth, rolled around, and on February 21, 1886, the *Times* opened its account of A JOLLY GATHERING AT DELMONICO'S with some uncharacteristically breezy exposition:

> Delmonico's was painted red last night. It was an intellectual red, however, [as] The dinner . . . was that of the Harvard Club. . . . There were several things that combined to make it successful. In the first place there was a crimson, gold and black menu, on which figured a number of cheering viands, ranging all the way from "consommé de la varenne" [*sic*] to cognac. Then there was 200 men of Harvard seated at five tables. . . . . There was a band, in which a cornet and a double-barreled piano were conspicuously frequent, and it poured out its soul in selections from "The Mikado," "The Black Hussar," ancient and dilapidated college songs, and the classic symphonies of Mr. David Braham.
>
> Then there was a scarlet-covered book of songs compiled expressly for the dinner by E. J. Wendell of the Class of '82, who was once a sprint runner and did 100 yards in 10 seconds, but who is now a calm dude with a brown bang on his forehead. From this book the merry Harvard lads sang such inspiring songs as "The Bull Dog," "Are You There, Moriarty?" "I'm Off for Baltimore" and "Nelly Was a Lady." With all these elements of joy at hand the Harvard men could not fail to have a good time, and at the close of the evening most of them looked as happy as if their Alma Mater had just beaten Princeton at football, Yale at rowing and the Bostons at baseball.

Before the singing began, Chauncey Depew, Joseph H. Choate's principal rival for the title of America's favorite after-dinner speaker, had spoken words of amiable raillery on behalf of Yale, while President Eliot had assured his hearers that despite the encroachment of new subjects onto the curriculum the old standbys of Latin, Greek and metaphysics were being cultivated in Cambridge "as much as ever and to a much higher degree."

Next month, those members who had been personally checking out Eliot's Harvard submitted their report, and at the annual meeting in April it was

> RESOLVED: That the Harvard Club of New York, having considered the Report of its Committee on the Elective System, approves of said system as at present in operation, and urges the College authorities to press forward in perfecting it, and the method of administering it, with confidence in their zeal and wisdom.

With his governing boards and faculties in a state of near-rebellion and many alumni disaffected over his insistence that undergraduates be free to choose their own courses and map out their own study plans, Eliot was undoubtedly relieved to have the backing of the New Yorkers. His acknowledgment of the committee report and the accompanying resolution, read aloud at the May meeting, sounded a note of sincere gratitude.

How far, meanwhile, had the search for permanent quarters progressed? Not an inch, it appeared, even though the Club had, month after month, been taking in new members, making the need for such a home ever more urgent. In October, however—while Club members followed with interest their fellow member Theodore Roosevelt's campaign for the mayoralty—the matter was referred to the Club's executive committee. On November 2, Republican Roosevelt was roundly defeated at the polls. The next day, as a few members, at least, may have noted, the Club attained its majority. And on November 5, in Cambridge, in the presence of 2,200 alumni, including a goodly number from New York City, there began a four-day celebration marking Harvard's 250th birthday. Although President Cleveland was there (declining an LL.D. on the ground that his skimpy legal education did not qualify him for such an honor); although visitors could watch a parade of professors in academic gowns, boat races, a football game and a jolly procession of undergraduates in costume; although Dr. Holmes read an occasional poem (one of his last) and notable orations were delivered by Phillips Brooks '55 STD'77, James Russell Lowell and the presidents of Yale, Williams and the University of Michigan, the star of the swirling pageant was Charles William Eliot, for whom the occasion seemed, to some, a vindication.

# 5

# THE FIRST CLUBHOUSE (1887–1894)

The decision to seek permanent quarters would bring about great changes in the Club during 1887 and the first half of 1888.

At the January 1887 monthly meeting Secretary Smith read aloud a communication from Nathan Clark, the same man who, twenty-one years before, had supplied the Club with its first hired rooms. The former restaurateur owned a pair of four-story brownstone houses with yards behind them that backed onto each other: 12 West 23rd Street and 11 West 22nd Street. He lived in the first house but rented out rooms in both, operating them as residence hotels or rooming houses. In his letter, he proposed to lease the 22nd Street brownstone to the Club.

The members present approved the plan, 57–13.

Located in a fashionable district, 11 West 22nd Street was the standard twenty-five feet in width, but deeper than most New York brownstones, hence more capacious, with good-sized rooms on the two lower floors and smaller ones, including bedrooms, higher up. It could, without much

The first clubhouse

difficulty, be made over into a satisfactory clubhouse. Clark wanted $6,000 a year in rent, $2,400 more than the highest estimate of the Committee on Permanent Quarters, which may explain why the men who had just voted to take the house put up no objection to a change in

Clement Cleveland

the bylaws raising the annual dues of resident members five years or more out of college or university to $20 and those of all other members to $10.

As word spread throughout the greater Harvard community that New York graduates were converting a house off Madison Square into a clubhouse with overnight accommodations, proposals for membership in the Club increased dramatically. Whereas, at the March meeting, five men were put up for resident membership and nine (including Overseer Robert M. Morse, Jr., of Boston) for non-

resident, a month later candidacies in the two categories had risen to sixteen and thirty-one respectively. President Wetmore urged on the Club the necessity to incorporate without delay, and on the evening of the sixteenth he and sixteen men met first, to sign a certificate of incorporation. The incorporators were, in the order and style in which they signed their names: Edmund Wetmore, Edward King, Edward L. Parris, T. Frank Brownell, G. S. Greene, Jr., J. W. Hawes, A. K. Fiske, Clement Cleveland, Camillus G. Kidder, Wm. Montgomery, Jr., Nathaniel S. Smith, Wm. S. Seamans, Eugene D. Hawkins, W. A. Purrington, Samuel H. Ordway, Nathaniel A. Prentiss and Charles C. Beaman. At that very hour the Board of Managers was adopting a set of nineteen house rules, which began

I    The Club Rooms shall be opened at 8 o'clock A.M., from November 1st to May 1st, and at 7 o'clock A.M., from May 1st to November 1st. The Rooms shall be closed at 1 o'clock A.M. except on the evenings when meetings of the Club shall be held. Members shall not be admitted to the Club Rooms after 1 o'clock A.M.

II    The Restaurant shall be closed from 12:30 o'clock A.M. The Wine Room shall be closed at 1 o'clock A.M.

III   The Card Room shall be closed from 12 o'clock on Saturday nights until 8 o'clock on Monday mornings.

Not exactly words to lift the heart. But these flat assertions and dry injunctions must have been sweet reading to men eager to indulge in the pleasures of club life whenever (within reason) they chose to.

With the Club about to occupy its own house, it needed a house committee, and at the annual meeting on April 29 newly reelected President Wetmore appointed T. Frank Brownell, Charles H. Russell, Jr. '72 and Samuel H. Ordway L'83 to fill this important function. To help the Admissions Committee deal with the expected flood of candidacies it was enlarged to twenty-one members. And before the meeting adjourned for supper and song the men present elected forty-seven new members.

It is unlikely that the Club has ever, at any juncture in its history, welcomed to its ranks a more distinguished group than the thirty-one new nonresident members it casually took in, within a few minutes, that evening. They included Overseer Charlemagne Tower of Philadelphia; Collector of the Port of Boston Leverett Saltonstall '44 L'47; Secretary of War William C. Endicott '47 LLD'82; Boston magnate Martin Brimmer '49; Thomas Jefferson Coolidge '50, a future minister to France; John Quincy Adams '53 of the famous clan; Alexander Agassiz '55 L'85, son of the great naturalist and a world-famous zoologist in his own right; Charles Pickering Bowditch '63, archeologist and Harvard professor; Brooks Adams '70, the future historian; lawyer Charles Bonaparte '71 L'74, a future secretary of the Navy and attorney general; Henry Cabot Lodge, the future senator and author; and Percival Lowell '76, the future astronomer who was to "discover" canals on Mars and to predict, correctly, the existence of the solar system's outermost planet, Pluto.

The Club's first meeting in its new home was supposed to take place on May 21, but as the work of conversion was behind schedule it was postponed. However, on June 1, the members were invited to drop by to inspect the ten "sleeping rooms." Then President Wetmore invited all Harvard men, whether members of the Club or not, to an opening reception on June 9, an event that the *Times* duly covered.

> After 22 years of existence without a home the Harvard Club last night celebrat-
> ed the acquisition of one with appropriate ceremonies. The new clubhouse is at 11
> West Twenty-second Street. . . .When all is complete the first floor will be used
> for the restaurant, and in it also the regular monthly meetings will be held. The
> second floor will contain a singing room, parlor, library, and reading and card
> rooms. The third will have a billiard room and several bedrooms for the accommo-
> dation of members, and the fourth will be wholly occupied by bedrooms. . . . A
> beginning has been made toward the library, and the reading room is well sup-
> plied. It is intended to have in the reading room a full collection of all documents
> relating to Harvard.

On that inaugural evening, sixty-eight new members were inducted
into the Club, including the famous pastor of Boston's Trinity Church,
Phillips Brooks. It was remarked that with Secretary of War Endicott in
the fold a quarter of President Cleveland's eight-man Cabinet were members, Assistant Secretary of the Treasury Charles S. Fairchild having been
appointed secretary two months before on the resignation of Secretary
Daniel Manning.

Besides establishing a library, another top priority of the Club was to
decorate its new home with appropriate materials, and Evert Wendell, as
chairman of the Committee on Literature and Art, spearheaded both
efforts. He doled out a modest appropriation for subscriptions to leading
periodicals, metropolitan dailies and student publications, and for basic
reference works. Periodicals and papers taken by the Club included
*Harper's Monthly, The Century, The Atlantic Monthly, Scribner's* and
*Lippincott's; Harper's Weekly, Puck, Judge, Life* and *The Illustrated
London News* (American edition); *The New York Clipper, The Spirit of
the Times, The Amusement Gazette, Fliegende Blaetter,* and *Le Journal
Amusant.* Daily papers taken were the *New York Herald, Times, Tribune,
World, Evening Post, Daily Graphic, Mail & Express,* and *Commercial
Advertiser.* College (and one University) publications subscribed to were
the *Harvard Advocate, Harvard Lampoon, Harvard Monthly, Harvard
Crimson,* and *Harvard Law Review,* together with the *Yale Daily News*
and *The Princetonian.*

Responding to Wendell's appeals for anything and everything relating
to Harvard, members and other alumni brought or sent in a variety of
objects: group photographs of College classes, teams and social organizations; banners and pennants; "shingles" notifying a student of his election

to a club, society or publication, and notices of upcoming meetings thereof; badges, keys, and pins; and invitations, dance cards, posters, programs, and tickets to Commencement exercises, Hasty Pudding shows and the like.

The oddest gift was two chunks of dried flesh, which, as their Bostonian donor explained in a letter accompanying them, had once belonged to Dr. George Parkman '09 of Beacon Hill, who in 1849 had been murdered and dismembered by his lifelong acquaintance and desperate creditor, Harvard Medical School chemistry professor John W. Webster '11 MD'15, in what former President of the University Edward Everett '11 called "the most disgraceful event in our domestic history." Searches of the premises at 27 West 44th Street conducted in 1989 and 1990 failed, however, to uncover either the pieces of flesh or any clue to their present whereabouts.

The ground floor restaurant seems to have been a success from the start. It was almost certainly operated by Nathan Clark as a private venture; entries in the Club's financial records of the period relating to food and drink are limited to the costs of particular entertainments and never mention the wages of kitchen and restaurant workers, expenditures for comestibles or receipts from the sale of meals. This arrangement would have been to the advantage of both parties: Clark's experience as a restaurateur would have served him well, and as club restaurants were notorious money-losers the Club's managers would probably have been happy to let Clark shoulder the risks.

The all-purpose carte du jour, covering breakfast, lunch and dinner, helps explain why this probably was the case. In its variety, the restaurant's fare could obviously gratify all but the most demanding and idiosyncratic of tastes, at reasonable prices. Beginning with clams in six guises (including on the half shell, fifteen cents; in fritters, forty cents), eleven kinds of soup and ten fish dishes (among them lobster, at forty cents), it went on to list 225 more items of food. The fifty-six main dishes ranged from Welsh rarebit, at thirty cents, to Châteaubriand with truffles at $2.25; sandwiches started at a dime for ham, cheese or tongue and rose to a quarter for chicken; vegetables included most of those served today, with potatoes prepared in fifteen different ways; pies, cakes and pastries amounted to some two dozen, half of them at ten cents; and the thirty other desserts climaxing

Annual dinner, 1887

the bill of fare numbered among them charlotte russe (fifteen cents), ice cream and ices, nine flavors, at twenty cents, and, at a quarter, such confections as plum pudding glacé, biscuit tortoni, Fifth Avenue bombe, café mousse, and sorbet au kirsch.

The wine list was printed, conveniently, on the carte itself. It listed nine champagnes, including Heidsieck "Piper," Mumm's Extra Dry, Roederer, and Veuve Cliquot, all at three dollars a quart; nine Bordeaux wines, from a Château Margaux at $2.50 the quart down to the bargain Harvard Club vin ordinaire at sixty cents; five Burgundies, five Rhine wines and three inexpensive American wines. A pint of New York lager could be had for fifteen cents, but imports like Budweiser beer, Bass's ale, Muir's and Younger's Scotch ale, and Guinness's London porter set a quaffer back a quarter. No cocktails were listed, the vogue for mixed drinks being far in the future, but a diner could down a preprandial tot of sherry, bourbon, Scotch or Holland gin for fifteen cents, and top off his dinner with a ten-cent pony of any of seven liqueurs, among them brandy, curaçao and absinthe.

The Club restaurant was much too small to accommodate the annual dinner, which in February 1888 attracted 222 men to its traditional venue, the members having rejected economy in favor of luxury and glamour. The subject of intercollegiate sports dominated the evening, as the *Times* account noted:

ATHLETES WERE THE LIONS
Harvard Alumni Chant
Their Heroes' Praises

A reverend and distinguished graduate of Harvard stood in the parlors of Delmonico's last evening ceremoniously receiving the greetings of his friends as the Alumni of the university swarmed in to partake of their annual dinner. Clad in the conventional dress suit, erect of carriage, solemn of demeanor, it seemed that little could move him. Suddenly an exultant friend, just brought up in the elevator, rushed up and, grasping him heartily by the hand, exclaimed: "Who is here?"

"Who is here?" The reverend and distinguished gentleman grew enthusiastic, as enthusiastic as a newly-accepted lover describing his affianced—"Who is here? Why, all the best men are here. There is Wendell Baker, the champion sprinter; William Borland, the Captain of '86's crew; Evert Wendell, the champion, the great runner of '82; Seamans, the Captain of the football team of '77; Richards of the famous Loring crew of '68, which never was beaten by Yale; Wendell Goodwin, the famous quarter of a mile runner; Bob Perkins, the Captain of the '84 crew; Arthur Devens, the bow oar of '84 and the champion sculler of his day; Frank Appleton of the '75 crew; Howard Taylor, the tennis champion of '85; Mumford of the crew of '84, and Mumford, the Captain of the crew of '86; Ezra P. Miles of the '85 crew, Wendell Goodwin of the crew of '84, Lucien Littauer, the bow oar of the '79 crew, and one of the football team which fought with All Canada. What more can you want? There hasn't been such a famous gathering since the Harvard Club was founded."

The exuberant friend parted, satisfied, to do homage to the heroes, who, stalwart of form and handsome of face, entertained their knots of admiring friends with becoming condescension.

The reverend and distinguished gentleman had struck the keynote of the dinner. . . .The athletes were the heroes.

Three weeks after this, between March 11 and 14, the great Blizzard of 1888 buried the city in snow, but the Club records did not mention the event. Nor did they note that following the death on March 23 of Chief Justice Morrison R. White many citizens, including many Club members, expected President Cleveland to replace him with a lawyer widely regarded as the foremost member of the New York bar, former Club president James C. Carter, who might well have been named chief justice had his health been less problematical.

In April, the Club nominated yet another former president, Charles C. Beaman, for Overseer, then launched an ultimately successful campaign on his behalf.

The clubhouse had long been staffed by a superintendent, a "clubroom servant" and a doorkeeper, and in April a hall boy was hired. Even so, the Club still remained tied to its landlord in a curious partnership, for Nathan Clark, who had originally engaged the servant, continued to pay the man's wages, with the Club adding an extra ten dollars a month. He also furnished board (at two dollars a week each!) to the doorkeeper and the hall boy, and even supplied the Club with linen at a monthly rental of fifteen dollars.

The managers' first annual report, dated May 1, a year and two weeks after the Club's incorporation, listed receipts during that time of $14,356.20 against expenditures of $14,347.34, with cash and deposits on hand amounting to $4,731.92. It also showed an extraordinary net gain of 153 members, bringing total membership to 531—384 resident and 147 nonresident.

With the coming of spring, the attention of countless Americans had turned, as always, to baseball. Alarmed in recent years by the extensiveness of the Harvard varsity team's schedule (in 1882, twenty-eight games, nineteen of them away) and by the fact that its opponents included professional teams, the University had sought to regulate the sport, and the Overseers had decreed that the nine must thereafter face only amateurs, and only in New England. New York devotees of Harvard baseball deplored these decrees—especially, of course, the second—and on May 12, when the Club elected banker Francis O. French '57 L'59 its president, it petitioned the Overseers to rescind them.

Eventually, University authorities would persist, sensibly, in barring Harvard teams from competing with professionals, but the rule restricting Harvard's intercollegiate athletic encounters to New England would become a dead letter.

Next fall saw the introduction of two practices destined to become familiar and routine. Just before their November meeting the managers, as an experiment, dined together in evening dress; finding the experience agreeable, they would repeat it, and in time the custom would take on the authority of custom. At that same November meeting, moreover, Treasurer Charles H. Russell, Jr., suggested that distinguished University graduates be invited to lecture at the clubhouse, and in December the committee considering the proposal approved it, so long as there were no "tiresome debates, as is customary at the Yale Club." (The reference was actually to the Yale Alumni Association of New York, as the Yale Club of New York would not be founded until 1897.)

At the start of 1889 the Club took a new two-year lease on the premises, to run from May 1, 1889, to May 1, 1891, Nathan Clark having reduced the annual rent by $500. In March, the treasurer won permission to invest Club funds in interest- or dividend-bearing securities. And in June the House Committee informed the members that the regular weeknight table d'hôte dinner would thereafter be served on Saturday evenings as well.

The big development of that year, however, was the installation of electric lights in the Club rooms and restaurant. That summer happened to be unusually hot and humid, so damp, indeed, that some cigarettes in the cigar stand actually mildewed, yet members remarked happily on how much cooler the place was than it would have been with the gaslights still in place.

In October, the managers reluctantly terminated the custom of handing out cigars at monthly meetings, certain members having been observed stuffing their pockets with free stogies, and the House Committee purchased new liveries for two Club servants, that of the highly visible doorman from Brooks Brothers, at $45, and that of the less conspicuous (and smaller) hall boy from Rogers Peet, at $11.50. On instructions, the doorman kept a count of members entering the clubhouse, and at the November meeting it was reported that in the twenty days from October 17 to November 5 inclusive, 546 members had come in.

A dispute with Mr. Clark over payments for improvements to the Club's office was settled when he agreed to pay for the newly laid carpet therein in return for being released from his promise to provide curtains. And on that homely note the 1880s slipped into history.

In March 1890, Nathan Clark told the House Committee he wanted the Club to retain his house for another year, until May 1892, and offered to take another $500 off the rent. And in May the Club elected banker Edward King '53 president and lawyer Austen G. Fox '69 L'71 vice-president, Messrs. Russell and Wendell retaining the posts of treasurer and secretary.

That fall, with the Yale game scheduled to be played at Springfield, Massachusetts, on Saturday, November 22, the Club hired a special train, composed entirely of parlor cars, to transport members from "the Grand Central Depot" to the game and back. And for the benefit of members who could not go—including most office workers, whose work week extended until noon or even later on Saturdays—a man on the sideline of the field, with access to a portable transmitter, telegraphed news of the game to the clubhouse, where the dispatches were immediately posted on a bulletin board.

Loud and frequent was the rejoicing among Harvard partisans on the scene—and, moments later, at 11 West 22nd Street—as, for the first time in eight years, the Crimson eleven defeated the Blue team, 12–6. Within days a few Club members were soliciting contributions toward the purchase of appropriate mementoes of the victory, and on December 13, in the presence of Captain A. J. Cumnock '91 and nine teammates, 200 members, crowded together in the ground floor meeting room and over-flowing into an adjacent room and corridor, heard President King announce that Harvard men in New York had bought a silver cup for each team member who had played in the famous game as well as a larger sil-ver cup to be competed for in future seasons. It would be known as the Cumnock Cup. Former president and Overseer Beaman delivered a graceful presentation speech, whereupon the crowd raised cheer after cheer for the team. "Afterwards," the Secretary's minutes concluded, "Supper was served and the usual round of Song and Story was had."

The Club, now almost 600 strong, needed more room. On January 10, 1891, President King appointed a five-man committee headed by Arthur M. Sherwood '77 "to consider the question of the purchase or lease of a new club-house . . . and the ways and means of raising the necessary funds, the probable cost of land and building, expenses of maintenance, and general plan for the arrangement of a club-house."

On June 1, the expanded committee issued a report, in the form of a circular, of interest today largely for its might-have-beens. Noting that the Club's lease was to run out eleven months thence, the committee pro-claimed itself unanimously agreed that any building the Club was to occupy must be its own, and asserted that the Club's income of about $11,000 would warrant its either building or buying a house for, at most, $75,000. A 25-by-100-foot lot on 27th or 28th Streets, between Madison Avenue and Fourth Avenue (now Park Avenue South), could be pur-chased for $30,000 and a club building erected thereon and furnished for another $45,000. Alternatively, a house of the same dimensions in a more desirable location—on 32nd or 33rd Street between Fifth and Madison Avenues, for example, or on Madison Avenue near 30th Street—could be bought for about $50,000 and refurbished and fur-nished for another $25,000. Under either plan there would be sleeping rooms for nonresident members. The committee unanimously opposed maintaining a restaurant, but favored having a grill room that would be open only in the evening.

What kind of club did the members want? the committee asked. A social club in the full sense, or a center for the collection of Harvard memorabilia and for the dissemination of information about the University? And was desire for a club strong enough among Harvard men in New York to insure that if offered Club income bonds yielding four or five percent they would subscribe for them in the amount required, around $40,000?

In view of the Club's unbroken record of growth and the loyal support of the great majority of its members, the uncertainty implicit in these questions is puzzling, but the committee doubtless needed to feel absolutely sure that the members were behind them. Soon enough, the replies to a questionnaire sent out with the circular established beyond any doubt that the members overwhelmingly wanted a real club with a clubhouse unambiguously its own. In October, Chairman Sherwood reported that the committee was thinking of purchasing a house at 16 East 33rd Street for conversion into a clubhouse. By December 18, however, proponents of erecting a clubhouse, and so ending up with exactly the building required, won out.

By this time, the celebrated architect and former member Charles F. McKim had been asked to draw up a preliminary plan for a clubhouse, and at the end of 1891 an illustrated circular on the subject went out to the members. "As will be seen by the plans submitted," a key sentence read, "the exterior of the proposed building would be of red brick, and the intention would be to preserve as far as possible some of the characteristics of the old colonial buildings at Cambridge." A month later the committee addressed a circular to nearly one thousand Harvard men living in and around New York, urging them to subscribe to a fund for erecting a building to be known as "Harvard House." The committee stressed the intention not to increase the present dues, "a matter of importance to the younger members of the Club." It was expected, the circular continued, to build Harvard House on a lot 25 by 100 feet, but "it is thought possible, if all the graduates subscribe according to their means as liberally as those who have already subscribed, to erect a building on a larger scale, and thus meet any possible wants of graduates in the future." Appended to the circular was a list of subscriptions received from eighty-four subscribers, totaling $22,250.

This appeal proved effective: by May 2, 1892, the committee, even while launching yet another drive with the aim of getting every New York alumnus to subscribe something, however modest, reported that the clubhouse fund now amounted to $31,500, and by the time of the annual meeting twelve days later it had grown to "upwards of $33,000."

The Club House Committee resumed its search for a place to build, but not until October did it report to the members, and then only to state, in a letter, that it was negotiating for a site in an undisclosed location. Early the next year, however, word got out that the site-seekers were considering a lot on the north side of West 44th Street, between Fifth and Sixth Avenues. This development occasioned a certain amount of surprise in some quarters, for although both the Century and the Racquet and Tennis Clubs had erected clubhouses immediately to the south, on West 43rd Street, the 44th Street block was lined on both sides with stables, the only modern buildings in its entire length being the Berkeley School (now the General Society library), the Berkeley Lyceum, at Number 23 and the Brearley School, at Number 17.

The 25-by-100-foot lot under consideration was at Number 13, but the committee had also looked into the possibility of purchasing one or more of two adjacent lots farther west at Numbers 27 and 29. Arrangements were proceeding toward the purchase of the lot at Number 13 when, on February 17, 1893, the subcommittee on site, comprised of President King, Vice-President George Blagden '56 and former President Beaman, received an extraordinary letter; on reading it, King called a meeting of the entire Club House Committee, at which, after affirming that the letter's signer or signers were wholly responsible and wished to conceal his or their identity from everyone except Messrs. King, Blagden and Beaman, he read the communication out loud:

Dear Sirs—

We learn from you that your Committee has received subscriptions for the proposed Harvard House of $34,000, of which $31,000 is now on deposit in the Union Trust Company. We also learn from you that you have been thinking of buying a lot on No. 13 West 44th Street, 25 feet wide, but that you are particularly desirous of buying more land if you can, in order that the new Harvard House may be better adapted and more suitable for its purpose. You tell us that you can arrange to buy a thirty-five foot lot further along 44th Street, about No. 27, for

$57,000 while the 25 foot lot could be bought for $40,000. Of course you could not be justified in buying this 35 foot lot with the money now in hand and with the limitations you have to make a mortgage. We learn from you that your estimate is

| | |
|---|---|
| that the 35 foot lot would cost | $57,000 |
| and that the cost of the house, estimated, would be | $36,000 |
| and that the cost of the furniture, estimated, would be | $7,000 |
| Making total cost | $100,000 |
| This with your subscriptions of | $34,000 |
| your mortgage of | $40,000 |
| would leave you short about | $26,000 |

We have such an interest in the College and in the proposed Harvard House that we hereby guarantee you that you shall receive additional subscriptions to the amount of twenty thousand dollars ($20,000) and we authorize you to go ahead and buy the lot, and contract for the building as if this subscription for $20,000 had actually been made by us, leaving you to get the additional six thousand dollars ($6,000) by other subscriptions, or by additional mortgage. We expect your cooperation in obtaining additional subscriptions, so that all subscriptions you obtain in excess of six thousand dollars ($6,000) shall go in diminution of our guarantee.

Our general idea of the purpose of Harvard House is that we should have large rooms and good opportunities for meetings of Harvard men, and that it should be a Harvard House where everything in the interest of the College should be looked after rather than a strictly social club, but this guarantee is without condition, we relying upon the good judgment of the Committee and the Club.

Three nights after this, at the annual dinner, President King's announcement of the anonymous guarantee and of the plan to purchase the plot on West 44th Street touched off a tumultuous display of enthusiasm. But the diners' glee over the prospect of acquiring a spacious, made-to-order clubhouse—the first to be built in the city by any group of alumni—was tempered by sadness over the recent death of a fellow member long revered and even loved for his simple humanity and goodness, Bishop Phillips Brooks of Massachusetts. Joseph H. Choate, speaking extemporaneously, found a way to link the two subjects. "I have been of late," he said, "connecting in my mind the names of John Harvard and Phillips Brooks, two centuries and a half apart in time and in culture, yet each representing the best attainments of the age in which he lived. . . . Last summer I visited Stratford-on-Avon, and went to the most beautiful of all the ancient houses of the place—the home of the mother of John Harvard. As we are about to build a Harvard House in New York, I trust that the committee in charge will study the facade of the house in Stratford as a fit front for our house here."

Harvard House, Stratford-on-Avon

On May 3, 1893, the subcommittee having the matter in charge purchased from their owners, one George H. Penniman and his wife Mary, the two lots at Numbers 27 and 29 West 44th Street, measuring between them 50 feet east and west and 100 feet north and south. The treasurer paid Mr. Penniman $72,000 for the deed, part of that sum, presumably, borrowed against the authorized $40,000 future mortgage. (The new subscriptions drive had by then brought in about $3,000 more.) And at a meeting on May 24 the Club House Committee ratified, confirmed and approved the purchase. The instrument of that purchase, by the way, contained interesting details regarding the Club's predecessors on West 44th Street: It provided that the leases of the tenants then occupying the Club's new property be extended to July 1 "upon condition that the lessee of the saloon shall take good care of, and generally look after, the empty stable on the premises, free of cost to the Club."

With the question of the new clubhouse's width finally settled and the increased mortgage approved by the membership, construction plans were needed. But who would draw them up? Their abandonment of a projected architects' competition suggests that the Building Committee had already decided they wanted Charles F. McKim to design Harvard House, and it is easy enough to understand why. McKim was already known to and very much liked by several prominent members of the Club (he had created country houses for C. C. Beaman and Joseph H. Choate, among others, in the eighties, and more recently had done likewise for both of the men whose names had headed the first list of subscribers, Edwin D. Morgan '77 and Hamilton McK. Twombly '71, the latter of whom would incidentally be revealed in time to have been the anonymous letter-writer whose offer of cash had emboldened the Club to purchase the lots at Numbers 27 and 29). A few years earlier, McKim had designed the Johnston Gate at the western entrance to Harvard Yard, between Harvard and Massachusetts Halls, a construction that, remarkably, had delighted the alumni without exception, after which the University, in recognition of his oeuvre, had conferred an honorary master of arts degree on him. (Of the Johnston Gate, McKim's biographer, Charles Moore '78, writes that "the color and texture and form of the New Hampshire brick were the subject of experiment and repeated trials, with results finally so satisfactory that the term 'Harvard brick' came to be applied to them.") In the area of club architecture—specifically, New York club architecture—he had helped to design the Century Club (completed 1891) and in the last year alone collaborated on architectural jobs for the Knicker-

Charles F. McKim

bocker Club, the Union Club and the University Club. For the Columbian Exposition, better known as the Chicago World's Fair, running that very year, he had designed the colossal Agriculture Building and the exquisite New York State Building, based on the Villa Medici. And McKim was widely regarded as belonging, with his brilliant partner Stanford White and the much older Richard Morris Hunt, in the foremost rank of American architects. (His onetime employer, former Club member H. H. Richardson, had died in 1886.)

McKim readily agreed to undertake the task, in which he would be assisted by two younger men in his office, Henry Bacon and Henry Davis Ives. On September 7 the Club House Committee accepted his plans, with thanks. (The architect declined to accept any payment, asking that the committee consider his plans a contribution to the clubhouse fund.) On that same day the committee approved a contract with one Charles T. Willis, a contractor, to build the clubhouse, "in accordance with the Drawings and Specifications of Messrs. McKim, Mead & White," for $31,010, to be finished on or before May 1, 1894.

When McKim's drawings went on exhibit in the clubhouse it was evident that he had not taken up the suggestion put forward by his friend and quondam client, Joseph H. Choate, regarding the proposed building's facade, but was sticking to his original intention to make it of "Harvard brick," so as to "preserve . . . the characteristics of the old colonial buildings in Cambridge."

That was in October; a month later, on the evening of Saturday, November 11, the Club once again welcomed a visiting Harvard football team with food, drink, speeches, cheers and singing. The young athletes had come to the city not to play, but to watch others play: In line with the same principle of equidistance that had prompted Harvard and Yale to schedule games in Springfield, the Yale and Pennsylvania elevens had clashed that afternoon in New York, with the visitors from Cambridge looking on, studying their archrivals' tactics in preparation for the season's last, climactic gridiron encounter. (In 1893 Harvard would, as usual then, bow to Yale, 6–0.)

When May Day 1894 arrived, Harvard House was not, after all, ready for occupancy, but everyone could see that it soon would be, and on May 12 Club members assembled at 11 West 22nd Street for their last meeting in the first clubhouse. With the election of officers, "the announcement of the names of Messrs. King and Blagden were received with enthusiasm and prolonged applause," according to the minutes. While they and Secretary Wendell remained in office, Treasurer Russell stepped down and was replaced by Frederic Cromwell '63.

# 6

# HARVARD HOUSE (1894–1902)

Late in the evening of June 12, 1894, as darkness fell along 44th Street west of Fifth Avenue, members converged on the new building at Number 27, its windows ablaze with light. Inside, they greeted friends and glanced around curiously, then swarmed upstairs to inspect the upper stories and finally crowd together in the fifty-foot-long room on the second floor, overlooking the street, where President King called the meeting to order. Henry Van Duzer '75 of the Building Committee recounted how the clubhouse had come into being; his audience applauded

Harvard House, 1894

mentions of the mighty King and Blagden, of the architects, and of Van Duzer himself, in appreciation of his and Sherwood's labors in furnishing and decorating the place. And they clapped after each item as Van Duzer read out a list of objects people had donated: tables, chairs, fire screens, andirons, clocks, candelabra and pictures. One notable gift, from Mrs.

King, Mrs. Blagden, Mrs. Beaman and Mrs. J. H. Choate, was a huge crimson flag bearing the name "Harvard" in white capitals; another, from Dr. W. S. Seamans '77, was a subscription of $200 to pay for turfing over the fifty-by-fifty-foot yard behind the clubhouse and covering the building's rear wall with creepers.

Van Duzer concluded his remarks with the announcement that the Building Committee was now turning over to the Club, in the person of its president, Edward King, the clubhouse (which would officially open on November 11)—the work of Edward King. And when King rose to reply he was, the minutes record, "unable to speak for several minutes owing to the enthusiasm of his greeting, and was conclusively shown that the Club members fully appreciated all that he omitted to say in his few words of his own share in their beautiful new house."

Charles F. McKim's nephew, Lloyd McKim Garrison '88 L'91, then read some dedicatory verses he had composed:

> Throw back the doors! Up windows all!
>   Now nature is atune,
> Waken our slumbering house to life
>   And flood it full with June!
>
> Then slyly shut the summer in,
>   So, through the changing years,
> We shall keep sunshine in the house
>   Though streets run wet with tears.
>
> Oh! Shrine whose very pattern mounts
>   To those red temples there
> In our dear Attica grown sweet
>   With centuries of prayer,
>
> Thou movest us even as are moved
>   Sojourners in strange seas
> Beholding their lost country's flag
>   At the Antipodes.

Next, Overseer Beaman read a letter from President Eliot expressing his satisfaction that the members had built "a good house in New York, not merely as comfortable quarters…but as a visible sign of their brotherhood and unity," and his hope that it would become "a center of all public-spirited activities on behalf of the nation and the city, as on behalf of science, literature, art and good fellowship."

Austen G. Fox moved that the members "express their thanks to the Club House Committee for their labors during so long a time, and at such personal inconvenience, in the perfecting of the club house," whereupon Overseer Wetmore delivered an emotional speech seconding the motion, which was promptly and unanimously carried. The members, rising, then sang "Fair Harvard" and gave three cheers for President King, upon which, Secretary Wendell recorded, "the most successful meeting in the Club's history ended, with the wish in everyone's heart that was so fittingly expressed in the end of Mr. Wetmore's address: 'That this beautiful club house remain to be a bulwark of Harvard's increasing power and glory in our city of New York as long as the name "Veritas" remains above the door, and "until the stock of the Puritans die." ' "

Compared to this euphoric gathering, the next regular meeting in Harvard House, held in October, was a humdrum affair in which the main business was the election of new members, including, among eighteen in the resident category, Charles F. McKim, and among eleven nonresidents, a young Harvard teacher of English who had just been made a professor, George Lyman Kittredge '82.

By this time, for the edification of all Harvard men, the *Harvard Graduates' Magazine* had published, in its September number, a detailed account of Harvard House by its bardic panegyrist, Lloyd McKim Garrison, prefaced by a photograph of the building's facade. Because the interior of this oldest part of the present clubhouse has since been greatly altered, particularly on the ground floor, Garrison's description deserves to be quoted in full.

> The house is a three-story building, whose simple and sincere exterior of "Harvard brick" (laid, like that of the Harvard gates, in Flemish bond) and Indiana limestone, is reminiscent of Holworthy, the Gates, and of the old Tudor and Hancock houses which used to adorn Beacon Hill. Our frontispiece needs little comment, except that the three dates carved beneath the Harvard arms—1636, 1865, 1893—are respectively the dates of foundation of the College, Club, and House; that behind the solid columns of the portico is a white door opening into a white colonial vestibule; and that the final door admitting the visitor to the club is of dark mahogany, with single panels of great beauty.
>
> Within is a broad hallway finished in red with a big fireplace at one end, and an ample staircase, with slender white balusters surmounted by a heavy mahogany rail. The hallway is full of light, from the windows on the street, from another window above the stairs which lead into the basement, and from those in the grill-

room. Its floor is of hard wood, and a big red rug is spread over it, which accords with the loyal color scheme of all the rooms on the ground floor.

The grill-room opens from the hall to the right of the stairs, and its windows look upon the little lawn at the rear of the building, which will one day be built upon. A pantry connects with it by a swinging door. At the eastern end of the hall is a reception room, fronting upon the street. To the right and left of the vestibule are little official rooms; and the western end of the hall, in proportion with the reception-room, is extended to the outer wall, and is also lighted from the street, which runs, speaking roughly, east and west, the house being on the northerly side of the street.

Half a flight up the staircase is a broad landing, with a fine great window looking out on the green yard. A tall eight-day clock adds to the dignity of the stair. At the next half-flight one enters the western end of the library, which is a stately room, running the whole fifty feet along the front of the club, very high ceiled, and furnished simply but richly in oak and dark green, in refreshing contrast to the prevailing reds of the club's interior.

The windows upon the street, which open upon balconies of wrought iron, are of great height, and flood the room with light and, when opened, with air. A supper-room, corresponding to the grill-room, above which it is, leads from the library, from which it is separated only by folding doors—a device which adds to the spaciousness of the larger rooms, as the smaller rooms on the first floor add to that of the hall. Tall and well-filled bookcases run along the walls of the library, from the top of which look down two cheery busts of Emerson and Holmes, presented by Mr. Evert J. Wendell '82. Above the eastern fireplace is a large painting of President Eliot; an inferior one of the late Dr. Peabody hangs opposite.

The third floor has a similar air of amplitude gained by wide doorways and the connection of rooms, and comprises a large billiard-room, a committee-room and two smaller cardrooms. Here are hung several pieces of varying value and interest, placards and other souvenirs of the College, which will now no doubt be greatly added to.

The woodwork of the interior of the building is white, and the general effect of the interior is one of age, refinement and tranquility.

Harvard House, one of McKim, Mead & White's first essays in Georgian architecture, was also one of the firm's best, and its facade is generally ranked among McKim's minor masterpieces. Inside the building, however, the architect was limited in what he could do by the Club's modest construction budget, wherefor the members had to be content with white woodwork and walls plainly finished in crimson material. On the other hand they almost certainly were not merely content but delighted with their spare and simple new environment. If any of them secretly yearned for opulence and grandiosity they kept it to themselves, and the grumbling about the clubhouse that would soon be heard would focus on its lack of sufficient space rather than aesthetic considerations.

By 1894 Charles W. Eliot had been president of Harvard twenty-five years, and many Club members responded to an appeal for contributions toward a gold medal launched by Bishop William Lawrence '71 STD (hon.) '93 of Massachusetts, three eminent laymen and a brilliant lawyer and future Supreme Court justice, Louis D. Brandeis L'77. That year, too, the "Annex," with about 250 students, was chartered under the name of Anne Radcliffe, Lady Mowlson, a seventeenth-century benefactress of little, faraway Harvard College. Elizabeth Cabot Agassiz, widow of the great naturalist, became Radcliffe College's first president. Also, much to President Eliot's satisfaction, Harvard transferred its major athletic activities from Jarvis Field, north of the Yard, to Soldiers Field, the thirty-one-acre tract of land across the Charles River that Major Henry Lee Higginson AM (hon.) '82 had given the University in 1890, naming it in memory of six companions of his youth who had died in the Civil War.

A financial panic the year before had brought on an economic depression, the effects of which would continue to be felt for another three years. Some city clubs had already lost members through resignations and would lose more, but the Harvard Club kept on growing, its membership in 1894 reaching 703. Nevertheless it established, in October 1894, a committee "to inaugurate and maintain an organized effort to increase the membership of the Club," and the five men appointed to this Committee on New Membership promptly added twenty-seven more to their ranks. The Club also set up a Committee on Amusements. And the chairman announced, for a Saturday evening two weeks thence, a reprise of an event that had proved popular the previous August: a ladies' reception.

As before, opening the clubhouse to wives and friends afforded much pleasure all around. And the "amusements" that followed Club meetings that night and on another Saturday evening four weeks later—the first ones ever reported in the minutes—suggest that in those somewhat simpler days, Club audiences may have been easier to please than they have since become: On the first evening a young Princetonian told funny stories and sang comic songs, and on the second a professional musician "improvised most charmingly on the piano, his variations on the theme of 'Fair Harvard' arousing especial enthusiasm."

In May 1895 Edward King stepped down as president, having served five full years, longer, at a single stretch, then anyone else before or since. James C. Carter once again assumed the post, twenty-two years after relinquishing it. Henry S. Van Duzer became vice-president, Amory G. Hodges '74 treasurer and Walter Alexander '87 L'90 secretary.

Month after month the minutes of Club meetings recorded the receipt of gifts, most of them articles of furniture or pictures, but on November 9, 1895, the record noted two donations of a new kind: the stuffed and mounted heads of a moose and a caribou, presented by George W. Green '76, the city's aqueduct commissioner. Soon after this, newly elected Mayor William L. Strong appointed another hunter-politician Club member, Theodore Roosevelt, a police commissioner; Roosevelt soon became president of the police board, and set out, with zeal and energy, to reform the department. For a start, he insisted that the police begin enforcing a law that forbade the sale of liquor on the Sabbath. This move earned Roosevelt considerable attention in the press—and a tongue-in-cheek rebuke, at the 1896 annual dinner, the Club's thirtieth, from a guest speaker, Rev. Dr. Richard S. Storrs STD (hon.) '59 of Brooklyn. "I don't altogether approve of him," Dr. Storrs said. "He has disturbed the moral equilibrium of this part of the universe. We always knew that New York was greater than Brooklyn, but we used to think that Brooklyn was better than New York. Now, when a New York man wants to get drunk on Sunday, he has to cross to Brooklyn. But I rejoice in the man and his work. He stands as a representative of courageous manhood, the highest ideal of education at Harvard."

Meanwhile, other developments of interest to members had been occurring far from West 44th Street. In early November of 1896, to the satisfaction of most, Republican Governor William McKinley of Ohio was elected president, and later that month the Club's oldest member, Thomas White, Law School '28, who had joined at the rather advanced age of ninety-two, died at ninety-four. In February 1897 the annual dinner, still costing six dollars a head, was held, exceptionally, at the Waldorf-Astoria Hotel, Fifth Avenue and 34th Street. On March 4, President McKinley was inaugurated, and soon afterward Theodore Roosevelt went to Washington to serve as assistant secretary of the Navy under another Club member who had once been governor of Massachusetts, John D. Long.

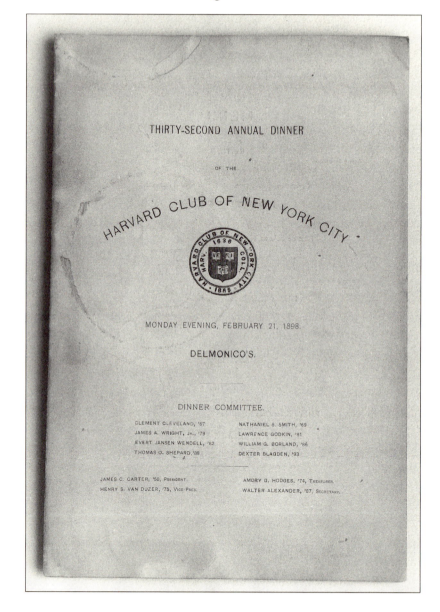

THIRTY-SECOND ANNUAL DINNER

OF THE

HARVARD CLUB OF NEW YORK CITY

MONDAY EVENING, FEBRUARY 21, 1898.

DELMONICO'S.

DINNER COMMITTEE.

CLEMENT CLEVELAND, '67          NATHANIEL S. SMITH, '69
JAMES A. WRIGHT, Jr., '79       LAWRENCE GODKIN, '81
EVERT JANSEN WENDELL, '82       WILLIAM G. BORLAND, '86
THOMAS O. SHEPARD, '88          DEXTER BLAGDEN, '93

JAMES C. CARTER, '50, President.        AMORY G. HODGES, '74, Treasurer.
HENRY S. VAN DUZER, '75, Vice-Pres.     WALTER ALEXANDER, '87, Secretary.

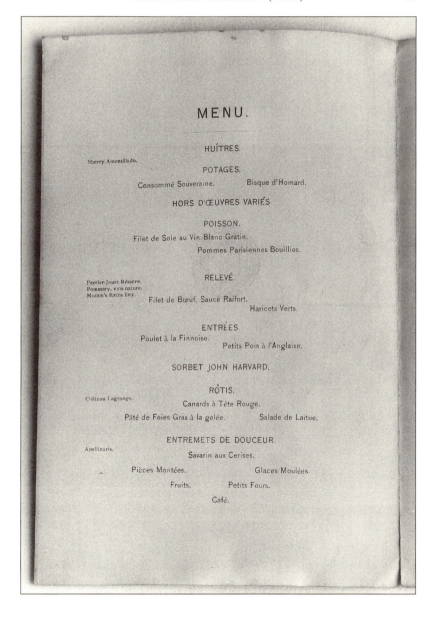

## MENU.

HUÎTRES.

Sherry Amontillado.

POTAGES.

Consommé Souveraine.     Bisque d'Homard.

HORS D'ŒUVRES VARIÉS

POISSON.

Filet de Sole au Vin Blanc Gratin.

Pommes Parisiennes Bouillies.

RELEVÉ.

Perrier-Jouet Réserve.
Pommery, vins nature.
Mumm's Extra Dry.

Filet de Bœuf, Sauce Raifort.

Haricots Verts.

ENTRÉES.

Poulet à la Finnoise.

Petits Pois à l'Anglaise.

SORBET JOHN HARVARD.

RÔTIS.

Château Lagrange.

Canards à Tête Rouge.

Pâté de Foies Gras à la gelée.     Salade de Laitue.

ENTREMETS DE DOUCEUR.

Apollinaris.

Savarin aux Cerises.

Pièces Montées.     Glaces Moulées.

Fruits.     Petits Fours.

Café.

In May 1897, the governor of New York signed into law an act creating a Greater City of New York of the five present boroughs, under a charter that would take effect the following year. Roosevelt not being available, reform-minded Republicans picked Seth Low, former mayor of Brooklyn and now president of Columbia University, as their candidate for mayor of the consolidated metropolis. But Senator Thomas Platt, "boss" of the regular Republicans, refused to accept Low and nominated another man, with the result—foreseen by Platt and quite acceptable to him—that the Tammany Democrat was elected.

On January 8, 1898, the Club held a reception for the Yale Club, founded just months before, and for Yale graduates generally: "The Club House was filled to overflowing," according to a Yale Club historian, "members of both clubs were choked with food, drink and songs, and gave each other countless long cheers." But it didn't end there: "Invigorated by that experience," the same writer continues, "the Yale guests immediately decided they must have a bigger, better clubhouse to return the compliment."

Next month, on February 21, the Harvardians again repaired for their annual dinner to Delmonico's—at its new location, about 150 paces east of their clubhouse on the corner of 44th Street and Fifth Avenue. There the banqueters, standing, drank a solemn toast offered by President Carter to the memory of the 260 officers and enlisted men who had perished six days earlier in the explosion and sinking, in Havana harbor, of the battle-ship *Maine*, a disaster that had shocked and shaken the nation.

As S. E. Morison was to observe in *Three Centuries of Harvard*, the college might well claim the Spanish-American War as her own, inas-much as all of the "three political musketeers" who did most to bring it about were sons of hers: Senator Henry Cabot Lodge; yellow-press lord William Randolph Hearst, a dropout member of the Class of 1886; and New York's own Theodore Roosevelt. Secretary John D. Long, moreover, would run the Navy, and Colonel Leonard Wood MD'84 would command the Rough Riders. On the other hand, President Eliot came out forthright-ly against invading Cuba, his name heading a list of eighty-six Harvard administrators and professors opposed to fighting, and Professor William James MD'69 attacked the moral cowardice of war in a speech to his students that ended with the memorable injunction "Don't yelp with the pack."

In March, as war fever mounted, the Club received two distinguished visitors, Major Higginson and Dean of the College Le Baron R. Briggs '75, who addressed the members on matters relating to the Corporation. By the end of April the country was at war. At least 62 members of the Club took some part in what Secretary of State John Hay would call "this splendid little war," at least nine as Rough Riders under Colonel Wood and Lieutenant Colonel Roosevelt; about 100 Harvard students enlisted, and ten paid the supreme sacrifice. The armistice, coming in August, left Colonel Wood military governor of Cuba. And in November Lieutenant Colonel Roosevelt, an authentic war hero thanks to his having led a charge up San Juan Hill, was elected governor of New York.

On January 11, 1899, President McKinley named Joseph H. Choate ambassador to the Court of St. James's, and the night before he sailed for England, February 21, 451 of his fellow Harvard alumni assembled at the Waldorf-Astoria to bid him farewell. According to the *Times*, "the evening was perhaps the most enjoyable ever experienced by those who have attended Harvard Club dinners." It may also have been the noisiest, "enlivened by college and patriotic songs and a tremendous amount of cheering. The rah-rahing was deafening to speakers and auditors nearly half the time."

After the Club's March meeting the members present were treated to an entertainment of a kind that was becoming a staple at men's clubs: a talk by a big game hunter back from Africa illustrated with stereopticon views of the hunt. Then they heard two professors discourse on the new American Academy in Rome, an outgrowth of the American School of Architecture that Charles McKim had founded there in 1894. Next month, a development of enormous importance to the Club took place very quietly when four well-to-do members jointly bought up, for $121,000, all of the property directly behind the clubhouse's backyard, including three houses standing in a row, facing north, on the south side of West 45th Street. The purchasers were Hamilton McK. Twombly, Francis R. Appleton '75, Robert Dudley Winthrop '83 and Robert Bacon '80, and their purpose, as they told the Managers, was to offer the Club the option of acquiring the property any time, at cost.

**University Boathouse**

At a stroke, the space available to the Club for horizontal expansion had trebled.

Meanwhile Austen G. Fox had been pursuing a private obsession aimed at putting up a building on the banks of the Charles River. Ten years earlier New Yorker George W. Weld '60 had given the University a boathouse, and Fox, inspired recently by a talk by Harvard crew coach R. C. Lehmann AM (hon.) '97, had decided that the Club should do as Weld had done. With an ad hoc committee he raised $27,500 from clubmates and sent it to the University treasurer. A new University boathouse began to rise on the Brighton side of the Charles just upstream from the Larz Anderson bridge, but on December 27, 1899, the nearly complete structure burned to the ground. Fox would appeal anew to his fellow donors at the Club, and construction would recommence.

The Club's first act of the twentieth century was to hold a reception, on January 13, 1900, for the Princeton Club of New York, incorporated just thirty-eight days earlier. Incidentally, the Yale Club of New York would shortly acquire two stables diagonally opposite Harvard House, at Number 30.

As usual, the annual dinner, at the Waldorf-Astoria, produced torrents of oratory from the likes of President Eliot, President Arthur Twining Hadley of Yale, Governor Roosevelt and Secretary Long. Roosevelt praised Judge William Howard Taft, a Yale man, whom President McKinley had just appointed head of a commission to organize civil government in the Philippines, while Long speculated that a distant member of the Harvard Club of Havana, "Doctor Colonel General Governor Leonard Wood," might well be "the coming man." But the high point of that evening in terms of its lasting significance for the Club was the unveiling of three-quarter length oil portraits of two former Club presidents, Joseph H. Choate and James C. Carter, by the leading portrait painter of the day, John Singer Sargent ArtD (hon.) 1916.

Years before, a modest amount of money had been raised and pledged to pay Sargent for a picture of Choate, but until the lawyer was posted to London, where Sargent lived, all efforts to bring the two men together had failed. By September 1899, however, Choate's portrait was finished and Sargent was completing a companion portrait of Carter. Chairman Wendell of the committee on the portraits had appealed for contributions to pay the portraitist's fees, and the members' response had been more than adequate.

Choate was, of course, in London, but Carter was on the scene, and at the behest of President Wetmore, who couldn't resist alluding to Sargent's "speaking likeness" of him, he delivered a brief speech of thanks.

That spring, members entering and leaving the clubhouse could observe the demolition of the stables across the street and the excavation on the site of a huge hole, fifty feet wide, that extended some eighty feet south. Clearly, the Yale Club's future home would cover a lot more territory than Harvard House did, and rumor had it that it would rise a lot higher as well. In mid-July, as its foundation was being laid, the newspapers reported that the Republican delegates, convening in Philadelphia, had nominated Governor Roosevelt to run for vice-president with the renominated President McKinley—and that New York's Republican "boss," Senator Thomas Platt, wanting the reformist Roosevelt out of the state, had backed his nomination. And on October 4, members of the Club were shocked to learn of the death of their talented and greatly liked fellow member Lloyd McK. Garrison, of typhoid fever contracted on a visit to Cuba. He was just thirty-three.

Later that month, President Wetmore appointed five men, headed by Edward King, to consider acquiring the 45th Street property and enlarging the clubhouse. On November 3 Austen G. Fox headed a New York delegation at exercises dedicating the new University boathouse (now also called the Newell boathouse), paid for entirely by members of the Club. And three days later, McKinley and Roosevelt triumphed at the polls.

Before that year was out C. C. Beaman died, and at the January 1901 meeting Edward King offered a resolution, recalling that the dead man had "endeared himself to us by his lovable character, as young as the youngest in his enthusiasm, yet always wise and temperate in counsel." Secretary Alexander then read aloud a letter from Beaman's widow presenting the Club with a bronze bas-relief portrait of her husband by his friend Augustus Saint-Gaudens LLD (hon.) '97.

A week later, on January 19, 1901, the Princeton Club, reciprocating the Club's hospitality the previous year, held a reception for Harvard men at its clubhouse, a former Vanderbilt residence at Park Avenue and 39th Street. By this time, the Yale Club's new clubhouse at 30 West 44th Street was nearing completion. An eleven-story behemoth, it towered over Harvard House and every other building on the block. (In anticipation of its opening the New York *Tribune* quoted one Yale man as saying that "It will be an easy matter to look down upon the Harvards and throw bouquets to them when there is an occasion for doing so.")

In April, more than three years after Greater New York City came into existence, the Club's bylaws were at last amended to reflect this development, references to "the City of Brooklyn" and "the cities of New York and Brooklyn" being changed to "the City of New York." And the following month, the Club elected new officers: President Charles S. Fairchild, Vice-President Austen G. Fox, Treasurer Amos T. French '85, and Secretary Francis H. Kinnicutt '97 L'00.

On May 10, with much fanfare, the Yale Club's upward-soaring new home across 44th Street opened in its ascendant glory: oak-paneled ground floor grill room, double-height library and lounge one flight up, six stories of bachelor apartments, ninth floor banquet rooms, a double-height dining room seating 400 on the tenth floor and a top-floor kitchen. The contrast it presented to little Harvard House, opposite, must have

occasioned some chagrin in the latter camp, but the report that Edward King and his fellow committeemen now submitted showed that they, at least, were not about to be stampeded on that account into precipitate and ruinous overbuilding. They recommended, first, that the Club buy the land fronting on 45th Street, leaving the houses thereon intact for the time being to bring in revenue, and second, that the clubhouse be extended northward to fill the vacant part of the Club's present property, in the process enlarging the dining area and the room used

**President Theodore Roosevelt**

for meetings, and providing much-needed bedrooms, all of this building to be done more or less in accordance with plans that a committee member had commissioned from Charles McKim at his own expense, and that were now on display in the clubhouse. The committeemen estimated the cost of this construction at about $75,000.

Before the Club met again, the death on September 14 of President McKinley, shot by an assassin eight days before, propelled Vice-President Theodore Roosevelt into the White House, the fourth Harvard graduate and first member of the Harvard Club of New York City to become president of the United States.

# 7

# ENLARGING THE CLUBHOUSE (1902–1905)

$A$t the Club's annual meeting on May 10, 1902, the Building Committee called for the erection of a large addition to the clubhouse, from designs by Charles F. McKim, to cover all of the vacant and built-on land north to 45th Street. Then, after duly electing the candidates nominated for office (Fairchild and Fox for the top spots, Thomas W. Slocum '90 for secretary and David I. Mackie '83 for treasurer), the members present were regaled by a chorus of undergraduates belting out comic numbers from the 1902 Hasty Pudding show, *Hi-Ka-Ya.* A week later, preparatory to an extraordinary meeting on May 24, all 1,659 members of the Club were sent copies of the Building Committee's report. In it, the committee called particular attention to a vast enclosed space, designated "Harvard Hall" on the plans, which would extend from the centerline of the city block 100 feet north to the property line on the south side of 45th Street, a space 38 feet wide and between 35 and 40 feet high. "It is contemplated," the report stated,

> that the interior will be finished after the manner of the commons in English Universities, or the large hall in the Harvard Union, but with stone floors and stone walls above an oak wainscot. With such splendid proportions, lighted at the 45th Street end and by windows opening on the 10 foot passageway shown on the plans, and with its two large fire places, the Committee are confident that members will take much pleasure in using the hall for general Club purposes and will also take great pride in the possession of a Club Room particularly appropriate in style for college men, and unequalled in this country for architectural beauty.

The Club accepted the architect's plans, authorized the purchase of the 45th Street lots, and referred the matter of the proposed addition to the Board of Managers and the Building Committee, with power to construct the building as they deemed best. Conferring together, the members of the two bodies quickly realized that the limited addition they had settled on would not meet even the Club's immediate needs, and so decided to erect, instead of a tall, square tower, a building four stories high extending north from the present clubhouse all the way to 45th Street, the northern two-thirds of it consisting of Harvard Hall and a single story atop it. By the terms of the contract President Fairchild had signed in November the total cost of altering the present clubhouse, tearing down the existing buildings on 45th Street and erecting this addition would come to $184,000, and the work would be completed on or before February 1, 1904.

In December 1902 laborers began excavating the grassy plot behind the clubhouse, and on the thirty-first the Club took title to the 45th Street lots. In January 1903, however, as workmen started to demolish the houses on these lots, the Building Committee and the Board decided to add on an extra floor of bedrooms, doubling the number of these to twenty, and a third squash court. A new contract called for a structure five stories high (exclusive of the squash courts), to cost $219,078.

Once the Club's newly acquired land was clear of buildings, excavation commenced. Before long the diggers came upon an underground stream that flowed across the property; this unanticipated obstacle, together with intermittent strikes, caused delays, but by May the foundations were laid and a framework of steel girders was about to rise from them.

In charge of construction was Harry Lindeberg of the McKim, Mead & White office. Although he was not a Harvard man, the Building Committee members and others keeping track of progress would come to feel that he could just as well have been, as, over the next two and a half years, they would admiringly observe his tireless, determined, never-flagging efforts to translate his employer's vision into reality.

If McKim's plans for the enlarged clubhouse inspired general enthusiasm and his lieutenant's implementation of them confidence, awareness of the burgeoning cost of the enterprise would weigh increasingly on the minds of President Fairchild and his associates.

One possible target for cost-cutting was the annual dinner. The Club's biggest expense, year after year, had been making up the difference between the income from the sale of tickets and the cost, always greater, of putting on the dinners. Why not, someone suggested, eliminate this heavy annual charge by dropping the event from the Club calendar? At a Board of Managers meeting this proposal won considerable support and might even have carried had not an objector produced figures showing, first, that losses from the annual dinner had been decreasing of late (1900, $1,044; 1901, $957; 1902, $575) and second, that the fixture remained enormously popular with the rank and file (of the 285 members listed on the program of the 1902 dinner, fully half, it turned out, entered the clubhouse no more than twice in the course of a year), so the members voted to raise the price of a ticket to $8 for members and $10 for nonmembers. Next month, however, the Board decided on second thought to leave things as they were, and on February 20, 1903, at Delmonico's, 300 alumni came together for the Club's thirty-seventh annual dinner.

This show of traditional fraternity notwithstanding, the future of the annual dinner remained uncertain, and two factors—first, the prospect of the Club's soon having a dining room, Harvard Hall, big enough to accommodate the event on the premises and second, growing sentiment, on the part of some members, in favor of scheduling the dinner earlier in the year—would ensure that it continued to be an uncertainty.

Even as they tried to contain expenses, the Club's governors strove to strengthen its financial condition by soliciting gifts of cash from its members, with, as a rule, meager results. Hardly less disappointing than the fund drive's results was the members' participation in it. In June 1902, in a circular, President Fairchild had noted that only a little more than a third of the 1,659 members had contributed to the building fund and expressed the hope that many more would now do so; but two years later the record would show that of some 2,031 members just 756—again a little more than a third—had contributed.

One scheme for raising money did succeed, however. This was the introduction of a new category of membership. It occurred on April 11, 1903, when, in line with a suggestion from Francis R. Appleton, the Club amended the bylaws to provide that any member or candidate for membership five years out of the University could, on payment of $300, be elected a member for life, exempt ever afterward from annual dues. Life members were limited to 100, and although 17 men took out life memberships in the first month they were available, the one hundredth would not be claimed until 1906.

What with the din and dust of the construction next door and the ever denser human traffic within it resulting from increased membership, the little brick clubhouse at Number 27 could no longer be counted on to provide a quiet haven from the busy metropolis, but the Club itself continued to evolve apace, not always in ways that could have been foreseen.

January 8, 1903: The Board considers: Should the Club create the office of chorister, to be held by a member with a good voice who could lead the singing of "Fair Harvard," "Auld Lang Syne," etc., sing appropriate airs himself when called on to do so and arrange musical programs for the members' entertainment?

February 11: John B. Embick '91 is elected chorister. To avoid the necessity of amending the bylaws the office is not made official, and its holder is understood to enjoy a status equal to that of the librarian.

March 12: Committees are appointed to look into two matters: (a) acquiring portraits of presidents and former presidents of the Club and (b) joining or not joining the Associated Harvard Clubs.

May 1: The annual report. Membership is 1,862, up 203 in the last year. The entire library, 6,500 books and pamphlets, has been catalogued. In the past year 598 volumes have been received, 224 of them donated by James J. Higginson '57. Gardiner M. Lane '81 has given the Club a bust of his father, Harvard classics professor George M. Lane '46. (Lane was long remembered at Harvard for his mock-epic poem, "The Lay of the Lone Fishball" [1853], which inspired a comic opera, *Il Pescoballo*, and J. R. Lowell's playful ballad "One Fish Ball.")

June 11: The Board, noting that the Club's popular forty-five-cent dinner actually costs forty-eight cents to prepare and serve—and that the Yale Club has long since raised its fifty-cent dinner to sixty cents—votes to raise the price of the table d'hôte dinner to fifty-five cents.

September 10: The House Committee reports that in spite of the price increase attendance at dinner has held steady and that there have been no complaints; also, that whereas in July 1902 the restaurant had lost $152, in July 1903 it had shown a profit of $26. A record 102 members are dropped for nonpayment of dues (but most will pay up and be reinstated within a month). The Club formally thanks Lawrence E. Sexton '84 for his gift of the stuffed and mounted head of a Rocky Mountain goat.

October 8: Max L. Scull '95, a nonresident member, has given the Club a medal he received from the government in recognition of his service in the war with Spain. Scull is the only Harvard man who served throughout the war on board the cruiser *Harvard*.

November 12: Secretary Slocum informs the Board that Delmonico's has only one evening available for the annual dinner: Wednesday, January 27, 1904. Treasurer Mackie proposes amendments to the bylaws rescheduling the monthly meetings and fixing the time of the annual dinner as the last Wednesday in January "or the nearest practicable day."

November 23: Secretary Slocum reads aloud the constitution of the Associated Harvard Clubs and names their constituent organizations, the Harvard Clubs of Chicago, Cincinnati, St. Louis, Minnesota, Indiana, Omaha, Milwaukee, Louisville, and Central Ohio, and The Rocky Mountain Harvard Club. He moves that the Club join the A.H.C. Several Board members speak on each side of the question and Slocum's motion is voted down, 7–5.

December 12: The Club adopts amendments to the bylaws rescheduling the monthly meetings and annual dinner. And so, the Club's thirty-eighth annual dinner, the first ever not to take place on or around Washington's birthday, is held at Delmonico's on January 27, 1904.

The featured speaker that evening was President Nicholas Murray Butler of Columbia, but the diners probably listened more attentively to two speakers from Cambridge: Byron Hurlbut '87, the successor to Dean Le Baron R. Briggs, and Professor of Government A. Lawrence Lowell. Both men talked about the undergraduates, and about the financial disparities dividing them. Dean Hurlbut praised the courage of students paying their way through Harvard, asserting that the price of the dinner his hearers had just consumed, six dollars, would pay the board of many undergraduates for as much as three weeks. And he told of one youth, thin and pale, who earlier that month had reluctantly confessed to having eaten no meat whatever since the beginning of the college year, one of several privations he was stoically enduring in order to procure a coveted education.

Professor Lowell, himself a wealthy man and a member of a distinguished Boston family, deplored the tendency toward aristocracy evident at the College. "Too many of what we call rich young men come to Harvard," he said. "The lives of these men are too indolent and aimless." Then, in words that seem startlingly prophetic in the light of Lowell's role in bringing the house plan to Harvard a quarter century later, he set forth a program of action calculated to limit or eliminate the evil. "If you are to have a great college," he declared, "you must have a real community of learning. Class lines must be obliterated, the rich and the poor student must fraternize. All classes must mingle together in a single purpose. They must live in dormitories of the same standing as to comforts. The rich man must not have more sumptuous quarters than the poor. All must live on the same plane."

As of May 1, the annual report showed a membership of 2,031 (including life members). Later that month, at the annual meeting, President Fairchild and his slate were reelected for a fourth straight year, and John Embick was renamed chorister. And in June, in the first but unfortunately not last incident of its kind, Chairman Joseph A. Stetson '91 L'94 of the House Committee recommended that the Club's superintendent be discharged on the grounds that his usefulness had ceased and that he was "entirely incompetent."

It had always been understood that when the time came to integrate the existing clubhouse with the new extension the former would have to be vacated, and on the evening of September 15 the entrance to 27 West 44th Street was locked and barred. Until the clubhouse reopened, the Club would maintain an office at 500 Fifth Avenue, where members could receive their mail and settle their accounts. Eight clubs extended the hospitality of their clubhouses to Harvard Club members: the Calumet Club, City Club, Manhattan Club, New York Yacht Club, Princeton Club,

Republican Club, St. Nicholas Club and The Players. A week later the National Arts Club and Yale Club also welcomed them, and in mid-October, the Columbia Club and Democratic Club did likewise.

Most Harvard Club members who availed themselves of these clubs' hospitality behaved themselves on their hosts' turf, but a few did not: thus the first batch of vouchers to arrive in the Club office revealed that one man who had been suspended from membership had nevertheless signed for food and drink at at least two clubs, and that other members who were posted at the Club and whose credit had been stopped had also run up debts elsewhere. The first man was quietly dropped from the Club roster and the rest received "severe letters" from Secretary Slocum. The oddest instance of Harvardian misbehavior involved a member of the Class of '92 who, welcomed to the Yale Club by a trusting member thereof, proceeded to run up a bill for forty-eight dollars. On being shown the vouchers and informed that their signer did not belong to the Club, Treasurer Mackie nevertheless authorized payment of the bill, but on learning this the Yale Club's officers protested that they felt obliged to honor the debt themselves. Secretary Slocum was instructed to thank them for their "extreme kindness" in making the offer, but to state firmly that the Harvard Club would pick up the tab unless the Elis could collect it from their recent guest. This apparently settled the matter.

If, lacking a meeting place, the Club's members were dispersed, three events coming in quick succession tended to unite them in spirit.

October 27, 1904, saw the opening of New York City's first subway, running from City Hall north to Grand Central Terminal, west to Times Square and then north again under Broadway to 145th Street. As most resident members of the Club were aware, the prime mover behind this immensely significant development was their clubmate August Belmont '74, financier and organizer of the Interborough Rapid Transit Company.

On November 8, the Club's own Theodore Roosevelt was elected president of the United States with the biggest plurality ever accorded a victorious presidential candidate.

And on the afternoon of Saturday, November 19, the Harvard and Yale elevens clashed in New Haven. Members ordered 936 tickets, and 664 members traveled to and from the game in railway cars rented by the Club. (As usual, Yale won, 12–0.)

In November, laborers and craftsmen were at work daily on the old clubhouse and the new extension, the twenty bedrooms were painted and ready for papering and bookshelves were in place in the library, but December brought strikes, and while the tile setters soon came to terms the marble setters stayed off the job. Delmonico's wanted to know whether the Club would be holding its annual dinner there on January 25; the Board released the restaurant from that date but reserved its large room for Wednesday, March 26. By January each of twenty Harvard classes had opted to pay $210 to furnish a bedroom that would ever afterward be identified by its year of graduation. A committee appointed to set up subcommittees in various cities to recruit nonresident members reported that it had made a promising start. In March, Nicholas Biddle '00, a young man associated with managing the Astor Estate who had been monitoring the Club's construction, told the Board that all of the new building except Harvard Hall would be completed by mid-May, and that the great hall would require another month or two.

Confronted by a request from Radcliffe College for permission to give entrance examinations at the Club, Secretary Slocum cited his earlier turndown of an identical request from Harvard, stating that the clubhouse was unusable just now for any function—and noted, in addition, that having prospective Radcliffe girls in a men's club could "complicate matters." Finally, the Board decided that in view of the enormous expense the Club had incurred in building the new addition, no annual dinner would be held that year after all.

In April, a House Committee spokesman estimated that the Club would need seventy-five servants and an annual payroll of $38,000 to operate the expanded clubhouse properly and that the Club's telephone bill might run as high as $1,000 a year, making it advisable to charge members five cents for local calls. The Board spent $150 for a fireproof safe in which to store important Club papers after deciding not to buy a costlier one that was also burglarproof. In May, the Board voted to thank Secretary Slocum and former Secretary Nathaniel Smith for enabling the Club to buy at wholesale the commodities each man dealt in as a businessman, textiles (sheets, linen, towels) and glassware, respectively. Four bedrooms facing on 45th Street were assigned to the Classes of 1853, 1857, 1863

John Harvard Window, Southwark Cathedral

and 1875. It was agreed that the remaining bedrooms would be assigned to other classes by lot. And on May 25, without ceremony, the entire expanded clubhouse, except Harvard Hall, was declared open.

Two days before then, in London, Ambassador Choate had realized a long-cherished ambition with the dedication by the Archbishop of Canterbury, in St. Saviour's Church (Southwark Cathedral), of a stained-glass window he had had the artist John La Farge create honoring John Harvard, who had been baptized in that church in 1607 and grown up nearby. This act of piety accomplished, Choate was ready to conclude six highly effective years as ambassador to Great Britain: On May 29 he called at Buckingham Palace to say good-bye to King Edward and Queen Alexandra, and the next day he and Mrs. Choate sailed home.

On the evening of the day, June 8, that the Choates arrived back in New York, the Board met for the first time in the remodeled old clubhouse, in a room that Robert Bacon, since joined by others, had refurbished and furnished for just such a purpose. (Replacing what had formerly been a billiard room, this long, wood-paneled chamber, on the third floor over-looking 44th Street, is the Mahogany Room, and a plaque at its eastern end lists the members of the Mahogany Club who that year presented it to the Club—as does a bronze plaque on the door.)

Suddenly back at the center of things after nine months of enforced marginality, the House Committee produced a spate of reports and pro-posals, among the former the facts that more than half of the 164 lockers on the squash courts floor had already been rented; that as the bedrooms, lacking transoms over the doors, were rather close, lattice doors had been ordered for them; that a pegboard would shortly be set up just inside the entrance on which the doorman would peg members in and out; and among the proposals, that on the completion of Harvard Hall the price of the table d'hôte dinner be raised to sixty-five cents and that the Club's office be empowered to cash members' checks of up to fifteen dollars. The library now numbered more than 8,000 volumes, and the Club's art collection was also growing, having recently been augmented by a por-trait photograph of the president of the United States, accompanied by a jaunty autograph letter expressing his best wishes to the Club.

On June 14, at a belated annual meeting, President Fairchild announced that within weeks Harvard Hall would be complete in all respects but one: the windows on 45th Street would be of plain glass rather than colored or tinted glass, a "deficiency" he hoped would soon be remedied by members' subscribing the needed funding. Next, the members present elected Austen G. Fox president and Henry S. Van Duzer vice-president, retaining Messrs. Slocum and Mackie as secretary and treasurer.

That summer, the often bellicose President Roosevelt turned peacemaker, bringing together representatives of the warring empires of Russia and Japan in Portsmouth, New Hampshire, for consultations that resulted in their signing the Treaty of Portsmouth (September 5), ending the Russo-Japanese War—an act that was to earn him the Nobel Peace Prize in 1906.

Late in September, when the Board met again after the summer hiatus, they found heartening evidence of improved financial discipline among the members: Although they numbered 2,205, only 52 had to be dropped for nonpayment of annual dues. A first-time-ever inventory revealed that 538 pictures of various kinds were hanging on clubhouse walls. And yet another stuffed and mounted animal head, of a moose shot by Donald Scott '00, joined the other hunters' trophies thereon.

That month Secretary Slocum persuaded the Board to establish an Entertainment Committee, including himself and the chorister, to handle this important aspect of club life. And in October, at Treasurer Mackie's suggestion, a Finance Committee was appointed, including three officers and two ex-presidents, to deal with the Club's pressing fiscal problems. After rejecting proposals to assess the members and to increase the $10 entrance fee, these committeemen came up with a solution that would win the approval of the Board and the members: The Club would borrow $5,000 from each of ten wealthy members, issuing them two-year notes in return, and it would raise the dues, to a top of $40 for resident members seven years out of the University.

The new Entertainment Committee confronted a crisis of sorts when a Club member, one Edward J. Ware '81, requested that W. E. B. Du Bois '90, AM'91, PhD'95, of Atlanta University, be invited to address the Club. Booker T. Washington, the well-known champion of vocational education for Negroes, would presumably have been acceptable in that role—after all, President Roosevelt had had him to dinner in the White

House—but Dr. Du Bois, an outspoken advocate of full equality for Negroes and a future co-founder of the organization that would become the National Association for the Advancement of Colored People, was another matter. Secretary Slocum, referring to himself in the third person in the minutes of a Board meeting on November 9, related in dry, detached language how he had deflected the momentary threat to the Club's decorum:

> The Secretary stated that he had told Mr. Ware that while he would bring the matter to the attention of the Board he considered it extremely doubtful if it would be considered desirable for the Harvard Club to grant this request. The Board voted that the position taken by the Secretary was in accordance with its wish.

The formal opening of the clubhouse addition, on the evening of Thursday, December 7, was a grand affair. In the presence of more than 1,000 members—five times the number that had attended the opening of Harvard House eleven years before—and to the accompaniment of flourishes and fanfares supplied by a hired band, Buildings Committee Chairman Higginson turned the building over to the Club in the person of President Fox. Then came speeches by President Eliot, Ambassador Choate and former President Wetmore. Finally, a collation was served, with champagne and other wines, while the band played a medley of college airs, old favorites and show tunes by, among others, Victor Herbert—all paid for, as the celebrants would learn, by a handful of resolutely anonymous members.

# 8

# INTERNAL IMPROVEMENTS (1905–1910)

$A$s altered and enlarged, the clubhouse was still just 50 feet wide (38 feet, north of the recess in the eastern wall of Harvard Hall), but it was now 200 feet deep—four times deeper than Harvard House had been and about six times bigger. To picture its ground floor interior in terms of the present clubhouse one should imagine its west wall beginning just past the old cigar counter and extending north alongside the front stairs, then crossing the Grill Room to join the west wall of Harvard Hall. On the second floor the library occupied both the present Cambridge Reading Room and the present library, ending in the broad, long balcony (the Gallery) overlooking Harvard Hall, while on the third floor the Club's one private room (now the Mahogany Room) and an adjacent kitchen (now the banquet manager's office) occupied the southern end, with, north of them, stairs leading down, a broad hallway, card rooms, and, finally, a capacious billiard room, which at that time opened onto the small balcony giving out on Harvard Hall above the Gallery. The fourth and fifth floors above Harvard Hall—much narrower, of course, than the present ones—each contained ten bedrooms, which were still being decorated with group photographs, commencement programs and other memorabilia of the sponsoring classes, together with what was then considered an appropriate number of bathrooms. And above these were three squash courts, with showers and locker rooms.

Although Harvard Hall then lacked the massive leather-upholstered

The Library (Note windows in the east wall, at right)

furniture it now contains, most of the portraits now lining its lower walls, the elephant head and the tapestries adorning the upper walls, it looked otherwise much as it does today. It functioned primarily as a restaurant, with breakfast, lunch and dinner served daily, but it also could be and on occasion would be converted to other uses. To a man, it seems, the members found the great hall, with its spectacular forty-foot ceiling and its two massive, ornate chandeliers of finely worked German silver, inspiring and spirit-lifting rather than overpowering, and agreed that the architect had succeeded brilliantly in preserving the homelike simplicity of the old clubhouse. This consensus was nicely summed up in a letter sent to a friend by a visiting graduate of the Class of 1841: "I stopped in New York over Sunday," the octogenarian wrote, "and was able to look in on the Harvard Club for the first time, and was perfectly delighted with it. Hearing much about the new building, I had supposed that it was something rather grand and formal, whereas I entered upon this mellow dark picturesque homelike place, which made me feel as if I had been there many times before."

Harvard Hall. "London has no such splendors."

H. G. Wells in *Harper's Weekly* (July 14, 1906)

With, for a second year, no annual dinner in prospect, the Club sought other ways to dispel the winter doldrums. Thrice in February 1906, at intervals of two or three days, the clubhouse was given over for the afternoon to ladies' days, and at the last of these, on a Saturday, more than 2,000 people showed up. The Club provided music, flowers and refreshments, but since the increased business these open houses generated usually more than offset these expenses, the Board tended to look upon them favorably.

That evening Chorister Embick informed the Board that he had arranged with three professional singers to give recitals at the clubhouse on successive Sunday afternoons—at, his listeners were delighted to hear, no expense whatever to the Club. These events proved popular, and at the next Board meeting, in March, Embick announced that he had scheduled more musical Sundays. Again these recitals and concerts drew good crowds, but on Thursday, April 5, members were stunned to learn that Embick had died suddenly of a heart attack the day before, aged thirty-six. That Sunday afternoon, when the soloist came to an air that had been a particular favorite of Embick's, his auditors rose to their feet and remained standing in silence after the song ended.

In other developments, W. J. Farquhar '91 loaned the Club a stuffed moose head and the College authorities again asked permission to give entrance examinations in the clubhouse in June, a request that was instantly granted. But their Radcliffe counterparts, having apparently taken to heart Thomas Slocum's assertion that the presence on the premises of nubile young women could "complicate matters," did not renew their parallel request.

Meanwhile, President Fox had taken the unprecedented step of asking the Nominating Committee not to follow custom and renominate him but instead to designate Joseph H. Choate its candidate for president in recognition of his "great and lasting service to Harvard and the Club." The committee complied, but before Choate could be elected a number of unrelated developments suggested, in various ways, that the Club was, if somewhat strapped, nevertheless a going—and growing—concern. The Board's annual report put the membership at 2,605 (including 100 life members), up exactly 400 since May 1, 1905. In response to an increasing demand from squash players, the Club built thirty new lockers, bringing the total to 194. The widow of a member, Mrs. Prescott Hall Butler, gave the Club a pool and billiard table. And a certain member had to be asked to stop using 27 West 44th Street as his business address in newspaper advertisements, several women having innocently entered the clubhouse on their own under the impression that it was the man's office.

On Saturday, May 12, the Club's annual meeting took place in Harvard Hall. Joseph H. Choate, aged seventy-four, was elected president, with

Austen G. Fox assuming the vice-presidency and Langdon P. Marvin '98 L'01 the secretaryship. As always, the urbane former ambassador found words to suit the occasion: "This is," he proclaimed, "the finest club in the world. I saw nothing better anywhere abroad. Think how much it has done for you and for New York. Every member should be much more of a man because of the Club." Then, after remarking on the amazing proliferation of Harvard men in the metropolis since he had arrived here more than half a century before, the new president addressed the central problem of the hour: "As to our indebtedness," he said, "I feel like Mr. Daniel Webster in speaking of the National Debt. 'It must be paid; I'll pay it myself.' I will do all I can to pay it off. It won't do for us to have a splendid hall like this, and have a debt hanging over it."

That debt, as President Choate's hearers were aware, had mushroomed in less than four years from a mere $10,000 on June 2, 1902, to $439,500, the annual interest charges on it having simultaneously skyrocketed from $400 to $17,580.

That summer, as had happened yearly during the Club's occupation of its rented clubhouse on West 22nd Street and as would happen virtually every summer thereafter, the demand for bedrooms slackened; so did the use of the clubhouse and its facilities, with the result that throughout June, July, August and early September the Club operated at a loss. Other than financially, however, the Club was prospering. Membership was up by another 200, to about 2,800. One new member was Felix Frankfurter L'06, and one of the committeemen who elected him would thirty-three years later appoint him to the Supreme Court, namely, Franklin D. Roosevelt '04. Tournaments in squash, backgammon and pool during the past year had involved the participation of well over 200 members.

With regard to presidential portraits, there occurred, that fall, a remarkable flurry of activity. Mrs. Mabel Osgood Wright gave the Club an oil painting of her father, its first president, Reverend Samuel Osgood; a portrait of Edward King was reported ready for delivery; Amos French promised a likeness of his late father, Francis O. French; Austen G. Fox offered to present a portrait of himself, and the Committee on Literature and Art asked Edmund Wetmore to do the same. In addition, Evert Wendell gave the Club a pastel portrait of President Choate, F. Tilden

Brown '77 an engraved likeness of former Governor (of Massachusetts) William E. Russell '77, Arthur M. Sherwood a portrait, medium unspecified, of Charles F. McKim, R. Buckminster Fuller '83 an enlarged photograph of an oil painting of his father, Rev. Arthur Buckminster Fuller '43 and Jacob Wendell '91 a likeness, in oils, of his dead friend, John B. Embick. And at its last meeting of 1906 the Board again voted, for the third year in a row, not to hold an annual dinner, scheduling instead a monthly meeting of the Club in January.

On January 10, 1907, the Board heard cheering news: the Club's operating costs since the end of May 1906 had been between $12,000 and $13,000 lower than those for the corresponding months of 1905. The Board extended the privileges of the Club to Professor George Santayana '86 PhD'89, down from Cambridge. Then the meeting took up the curious case of a certain nonresident member, as spelled out in correspondence between former Secretary Slocum and the chairman of the Committee on Admissions. According to information in the candidates' book, "Abel Caine," who had attended the College for four years, had been proposed by his fellow-Bostonian Fred Joy '81 and seconded by George F. Baker, Jr. '99, the future chairman of the First National Bank. Upon investigation, however, it turned out that Caine had not received any degree and that neither Joy nor Baker had ever heard of him. As well as forging the signatures of his pretended proposer and seconder, Caine had apparently forged proposing and seconding letters from both and so nominated himself. This could not be positively confirmed, since, on Caine's election to the Club, these letters had, as was customary, been destroyed, but as the Admissions Committee would not have considered Caine's candidacy without such letters, they had to have existed. In the end, the Board charged Caine with obtaining his membership by fraud and deception, and had the secretary write him to that effect. Not surprisingly, Caine opted not to reply, and on February 9 the Board expelled him.

Just a month later, having in the meantime raised the cost of a life membership to $500 and voted to continue the existing dues schedule for another three years, the Board had to deal with an outbreak of somewhat more conventional misbehavior. The previous Saturday night two young members had come to the Club a quarter hour before midnight, when four Club servants were still in attendance, and had gone up to the sixth floor; breaking open a mutual friend's locker, they played squash for an hour. One of the young men had left his coat in the locker room, and after showering he discovered that $50 in bills was missing from it; rushing downstairs, the pair demanded that the four servants be brought to the office and summoned a detective by telephone. The detective arrived, but before he could search anyone an older member intervened and the detective left. Some heated discussion followed, but finally everyone went home.

After deliberating, the Board had Secretary Marvin inform the young men in writing that they stood accused of "conduct unbecoming a member of the Club" in summoning the detective and insisting that the Club employees be searched. House Committee Chairman Francis G. Caffey '91 urged that in view of the offenders' youth their punishment be light, and as both promptly wrote the secretary letters of frank and full apology, the incident was forgotten.

Meanwhile, progress was made toward procuring portraits of both physician former presidents: In February it was revealed that a daughter of Dr. John O. Stone, the president in 1868, would soon be presenting a likeness of him and that member John Greenough '65 had arranged to have a portrait of Dr. Francis M. Weld painted for the Club. And in March a group of members who were friends of Edward King gave the Club an oil portrait of him by Ellen G. Emmet. The Fox and French portraits were again promised, and word came that Edmund Wetmore had selected an artist to paint him.

On March 7, the Board voted unanimously to join the Associated Harvard Clubs, and a few days later the membership ratified the decision.

Late in May, President Choate, reelected for a second year, sailed for The Hague, President Roosevelt having picked him to head the American delegation to the Second International Peace Conference there.

During the fall of 1907 no other development can have pleased members more than the announcement, in November, that the Board was at last prepared to restore the annual dinner to its central place in the Club calendar. As in years past the charge would be six dollars, including wine and cigars, but for the first time the dinner would be held in the club-house. And since there were limits to the capacity even of vast Harvard Hall, attendance would have to be restricted to members.

Somehow, on the night of January 31, 1908, room was found in Harvard Hall to seat 406 men in evening dress—not black tie, but white tie and tails. And although the gallery on the hall's south wall could easily have accommodated a dozen or so wives dining apart while watching the festivities below, it remained empty, as it would thereafter on such occasions, women being marginally less welcome in the clubhouse, apparently, than they had been in the big dining room of Delmonico's. The fact that both President Choate and President Eliot were in their seventies did nothing to dampen the banqueters' enthusiasm. Then as now, the Club's members were considerably younger on average than those of most New York clubs, so that when thirty-eight-year-old Thomas Slocum was called on to speak for the younger men present he said he could no longer do so inasmuch as some 2,500 men had joined the Club since he had—which went to show, he added, "what will happen by giving a good example." Noting that would-be Harvard freshmen now took entrance exams on the premises, Slocum speculated on what that experience might mean to such a boy: He "comes here, and walks up three flights of stairs between pictures of Harvard dignitaries and, as he glances from side to side, he says, 'I must get into this College so that I can join this Club.' "

That winter and spring the House Committee had to cope with mysterious noise and vibration emanating from Harvard Hall; even after a clattering exhaust fan was moved up to the roof and the steam pipes carefully separated from contact with the building walls the rattling continued. This problem was never solved; in time it simply "went away." Hardly less challenging was the question of what to do about a respected member who, on entering the hall one evening for dinner, spat twice on the stone floor, and then, sitting down at a table beneath the Sargent portrait of former President Carter, leaned over and thoughtfully spat again. He was sent "an unusually severe letter," and two disgusted witnesses brought charges against him. Then there were the complaints of card players that they could find no place to play, especially on those nights, and there were many, when the Club's one private dining room, the

Mahogany Room, was in use. To these complaints Nicholas Biddle, now chairman of the House Committee, responded in decisive fashion: he had the pool and billiard tables taken down to the basement and set up there, transforming what had been the third-floor billiard room, thus vacated, into another card room. He also announced that a barber shop would shortly open in the basement.

By then, the pensive expectorator's apology had been accepted and the charges against him dismissed.

Meanwhile, most other developments had been more conventional. Late in February the Committee on Literature and Art received a letter from Blair Fairchild '99 requesting that the $1,000 check accompanying it be used to set up a fund in memory of his brother, Nelson Fairchild '01, killed in a gun accident in Manchuria while serving as a vice-consul there. Interest income from the fund was to be spent on books for the library. Modest though it was, this fund would, over the years, finance the purchase of hundreds of volumes, supplementing those donated by members, including, more and more often, author members. (Among men of letters who had recently joined the Club were poet, novelist and future biographer of Theodore Roosevelt Hermann Hagedorn '07, Philadelphia bibliophile Harry Elkins Widener '07, future editor Maxwell Perkins '07 and the great psychologist and philosopher William James. The literary historian Van Wyck Brooks '08 would join in 1909.)

Since October 1907 Chairman Biddle had regularly presented to the Board figures showing how many members had made use of the Club's various facilities during the previous month and what revenues had accrued therefrom, together with similar data for the same month the year before. Apart from unpredictable restaurant receipts, which occasionally registered a slight decline, the Club's income from other operations almost invariably posted gains, the biggest money-spinners being the rental of bedrooms and the sales, in Bar and Dining Hall, of wines and liquors. As surpluses steadily mounted from these and other sources (such as sales of cigars and cigarettes, fees charged for playing squash and billiards, and for the rental of lockers and letter boxes) it became increasingly clear that the lean years were over.

Nor was this improvement in the Club's financial health merely temporary: Indeed, a pattern of ever-increasing receipts (and expenditures), reflecting a growing membership, which in turn reflected ever larger enrollments in the College and graduate schools, was to repeat itself every year, with only a brief interruption during the country's participation in the First World War, until the Great Depression.

At the annual meeting, Joseph Choate having declined renomination, Austen G. Fox was elected to resume the presidency of the Club for a second year, with Camillus G. Kidder '72 L'75 as vice-president and with the incumbent treasurer and secretary retaining their posts. And on June 11 the Board elected Francis Rogers '91 chorister. At the same meeting Chairman Biddle promised, on behalf of the House Committee, to look into the feasibility of laying out a roof garden atop the clubhouse to afford members some relief, after sundown, from the city's oppressive summer heat.

Just one week later word came from Chicago that the Republicans in convention had nominated President Roosevelt's handpicked successor, Secretary of War William H. Taft, to be their standard bearer, Governor Charles Evans Hughes of New York having come in a distant second in the balloting. In July, in Denver, the Democrats for a third time chose W. J. Bryan as their candidate, and in late September (when Chairman Biddle told the Board his committee had found the roof garden "unpracticable") the presidential race began in earnest. A solid majority of members of the Club supported Yale graduate Taft, and on Wednesday, November 4, when their man's electoral victory was assured, the prevailing mood at 27 West 44th Street was surely one of quiet satisfaction.

The next day, however, the Grill Room and Harvard Hall buzzed with other news. In Cambridge, President Eliot had submitted his resignation to the Overseers, who had accepted it. As few members under age sixty had ever known any other president of Harvard, many found this development unsettling, and just about everyone perceived that it signified the end of an extraordinary era.

Who would succeed Eliot? As speculation mounted, the Club noted, with sorrow, the passing on November 19 of Edward King, who, as its president from 1890 to 1895, had done more than anyone else to bring into being its first clubhouse on its own property. And some notable

Colonel Wilder Dwight

works of art and literature made their way into the Club's collections: Thus Mrs. Eastman Johnson, widow of the distinguished painter, gave the Club her late husband's portrait of Colonel Wilder Dwight '53 L'55 in Civil War uniform, and the Class of 1883 presented a marble bust of James Russell Lowell, by Daniel Chester French AM (hon.) '17, while the library expanded by seventy-two volumes and some fifty scholarly pamphlets presented by Sara Norton as a bequest from her recently deceased father, art historian and Harvard professor Charles Eliot Norton '46, who had wanted the Club to have them. Meanwhile, apparently on his own initiative, financier J. Hampden Robb '66 had arranged to have a copyist paint a replica of the portrait of former president C. C. Beaman then hanging in the University Club, and was energetically drumming up subscriptions to pay for it; early in 1909 the Committee on Literature and Art would gratefully receive the portrait, and at about the same time would have workmen place the Lowell bust on the southern mantel in Harvard Hall, where it remains to this day.

That winter, as in the last two, intramural tournaments were held in squash, bridge, backgammon, dominoes and checkers, but for the first time the Club's leading squash players, among them Dr. Alfred Stillman '03, Grenville Clark '03 L'06 and George Whitney '07, also competed extramurally, within a league including the Yale, Princeton and Columbia Clubs as well as the Brooklyn Casino. They would finish the season league champions.

On January 13, 1909, in Cambridge, the Harvard Corporation elected Professor A. Lawrence Lowell '77 L'80 president of the University, and on the twenty-seventh, the Club tendered a reception to President Eliot.

More than 1,000 members turned up to show their esteem and affection for the man who, over four decades, had led their alma mater through the greatest expansion in her history. Then or soon after J. J. Higginson, an ingenious hatcher of good ideas, hatched another: that the Club create a class of honorary members, with Eliot the first person named to it. He put this suggestion in writing, and when Secretary Marvin read it out at the next Board meeting the reaction was instantly favorable.

A. Lawrence Lowell

In May the Club elected a slate headed by James J. Higginson and Francis R. Appleton, with Langdon P. Marvin for secretary and Frederick R. Swift '99 L'02 for treasurer. And the 250-odd members present endorsed their new leader's idea by approving an amendment to the bylaws making all living past and present presidents of Harvard honorary members.

That summer, mysteriously, the Club's business, apart from the renting of bedrooms, declined hardly at all. Dinners served, for example, including the ever-popular sixty-five-cent table d'hôte, amounted some nights to as many as 120.

On September 14 Charles F. McKim, the designer of Harvard Hall and, indeed, the entire clubhouse, died, at age sixty-two. Nine days later the members of the Board, noting his passing, also noted receiving from John Greenough the long-awaited portrait of former President Weld. And they extended the privileges of the Club to members of the Cornell Club, then moving their clubhouse.

On October 6 President Lowell was inaugurated in Cambridge, and three nights later Jerome D. Greene '96, secretary to the president and fellows, treated the Club to an eyewitness account of the event. The following week Thomas Slocum, as president of the A.H.C., requested the use of Harvard Hall for a dinner for representatives of the various Harvard clubs, which request the Board instantly granted. (Almost from the moment the great hall was thrown open in late 1905, Harvard-related organizations, including College classes and groups like the Harvard Engineers' Club, had sought to rent all or part of it for dinners, and the Club, welcoming the extra income, agreed to most such requests.) Among recent donors to the library had been the new Harvard president's elder brother Percival Lowell, now a professor of astronomy at M.I.T., and lawyer James Byrne '77 L'82, who had been asked to investigate how the Club was being managed and rule on whether a member could be put in charge of managing it. Byrne's report affirmed that a member could indeed act as superintendent, and that the House Committee had the power to hire him.

J. Otto Stack '05, who had spent two years running a nearby hotel, the Knickerbocker, promptly resigned from the House Committee, and on November 1 began work as superintendent. (Stack was to carve out a distinguished career in hotel management, serving as general manager of the St. Regis in 1935 and five years later as president of the Ritz-Carlton.)

The previous Saturday afternoon, in the course of a football game played up the Hudson between Harvard and host West Point, Cadet Eugene Alexis Byrne had suffered injuries from which he died, and on November 2 some thirty members of the Club traveled north for the funeral. From Cambridge, President Lowell, noting in a letter that the captain of football and head of the student council had also attended the ceremony, wrote President Higginson: "I feel that you have done much to cement the good feeling between these institutions, which is of vast importance to our common welfare."

If, of a Sunday morning, most Club members either went to church or stayed home before putting away a big midday family dinner, some, particularly the young unmarried, repaired thereafter to the clubhouse, as can be inferred from a news item that appeared in the *New York Times* for Monday, December 6, 1909:

## HARVARD CLUB BARS PRINCESS
### Russian Portrait Artist Not Permitted to Enter Its Doors

The Princess Lewoff Parillagney of Russia, who stays at the Plaza and paints portraits, met with a rebuff yesterday from the Harvard Club on West 44th Street. She made a sensation when, in her landau with its gilded and colored crests, she drew up in front of the club in the early afternoon. The young men coming to the windows saw her epauletted and cockaded footman jump from the box and approach the door. He was met by a bellboy, who, after much expostulation, sent in for a member of the House Committee.

This member took from the hands of the Princess the visiting card of a club member, on which was written:

Please allow the Princess to inspect the portraits in Harvard Hall.

The House Committee member said that was impossible. "If you come on a ladies' day, Princess," he began.

"But," she said, "I have come to-day, and I am introduced by the card of a member."

"This is a man's club," said the member. "There are only men here."

"I understand," returned the Princess, "but I have not come to see the—I have come to examine the portraits."

By this time people had stopped on the other side of the street to watch the incident. Children were gazing in wonder at the brilliant coachman and footman, and people were looking from all the windows, so the Princess gave the word to her coachman and the glittering landau wheeled about and rolled off up the avenue.

Like the Russian princess, Chairman Appleton of the Committee on Literature and Art found himself, around that time, at a frustrating impasse anent the Club's wall decorations. That nemesis of East African wildlife, William G. Sewall '97, who had previously given the Club several hunting trophies, now wanted to present fifteen more heads of small and middle-size creatures, along with the heads of a lion and an elephant. The lesser heads, which could be mounted in the Grill Room, the card rooms, the Billiard Room or any of a number of other locations, were no problem, but the clubhouse contained only one interior space large enough to house the two big ones, and Appleton was loath to clutter majestic Harvard Hall with anything so bulky and awkward as the head of a trumpeting African elephant. (The lion head, it seemed, could not be displayed on a wall but only in a glass case.)

McKim, Appleton knew, would have backed him up, but he was gone: In his stead, the chairman set out to enlist the support of William Kendall '76, an associate of the great architect's since 1882. And he deliberately left the elephant's head and lion's head lying on the floor of Harvard Hall, confident that members passing them on their way to meals would come to feel, as he did, that such gross objects did not belong in such a stately setting.

Unable to attend a Board meeting on January 6, 1910, Appleton urged his colleagues in writing to postpone accepting the two large heads until the next meeting so that more members would have an opportunity to see them, but House Committee Chairman Biddle said this was not possible as Sewall was leaving the country on January 12 and had to have an answer by then. And on motions by Biddle and Secretary Marvin respectively, the Board voted forthwith to accept the elephant head and the lion head.

Within days the lion head was boxed in glass, but before the elephant head could be hung architect Kendall submitted the expert aesthetic appraisal Appleton had asked him for:

> It is with great regret that the conclusion has been forced upon me of its unsuitableness as a decoration for this room. The head is remarkable and certainly deserves a fitting home, but its very merits as an elephant's head make it, in my opinion, distinctly unadapted to the proposed location. In other words its enormous size and the exaggeration of its dimensions by the unusual position of the trunk render it in the first place out of scale with its surroundings, and in the second place, out of decorative relation to the wall. To go perhaps further than has been asked of me, I venture to hope that the policy of the Club with regard to this hall will be to exclude all animal's heads in view of the fact that portraits and busts already form the key to the decoration, and with the addition of tapestries on the masonry above the wainscotting would eventually give the proper and dignified character which the proportions of the room seem to demand.

Soon after its donor left New York for foreign parts the head was raised by block and tackle and attached to the wall in the position it still occupies. Kendall again wrote Appleton:

> I have already seen the elephant's head since it has been hung in Harvard Hall, and I think it looks as well as such a head could in that hall. I am still of the opinion, however, that it should not be in the hall at all, and I am in favor of having no heads in the dining room. I think its position in the recess makes it less objectionable than it might be in another place.
>
> When you speak of the possibility that the hall "might be flooded with incongruous and objectionable things" you express exactly what my fear is. The hall seems to me too noble an apartment to be decorated with animals' heads. The head itself is certainly a remarkable one.

The elephant head

Undismayed at being overruled, Chairman Appleton, in a special committee report on February 10, expressed faith that a reassertion of common sense and good taste was bound, sooner or later, to correct the error of the moment, recalling

> McKim, who designed the Hall, frequently expressing himself that only oil paintings, tapestry or sculpture would ever find a fitting place there. Your committee have always adapted that creed as the best and safest.
>
> We do not believe that the heads of wild animals should ever be part of the permanent decoration of the Hall.
>
> The elephant's head was not at once rejected for reasons generally governing the Committee but was hung on the wall in order that no decision should be reached before a view might be had of the result and effect after the head was in actual place.
>
> We now, after this head is in place, are strong in our opinion that it is not suitable, however magnificent and superb. Aside from the inherent nature of it as a decoration it is too dominant and overpowering and entirely out of keeping with the objects and purposes of the Hall.
>
> After this head has remained on the wall for a reasonable period of novelty it will, in our opinion, become a monstrous blemish and should then be removed and returned to the donor under the terms of the gift. The same is to be said of the lion's head, which in its necessary glass case is essentially a museum piece.

Irish elk antlers

Four weeks later the Board solemnly resolved that in the selection of objects of art or decoration for the great hall the Club would be governed by the general principles laid down in the report of the Committee on Literature and Art made on February 10—only minutes after noting, with evident satisfaction, that a huge pair of Irish elk horns just given the Club had been placed on view on the western side of Harvard Hall! (In fact, the implied contradiction was not quite as blatant as might appear, since no one, presumably, expected the very large palmate antlers of the extinct giant European fallow deer, commonly called Irish elk, the gift of Edwin D. Morgan, to become part of the hall's *permanent* decor.)

While some members undoubtedly shared Appleton's distaste for its placement, there can be little doubt that the elephant head, its great ears flung back and its trunk thrust dramatically forward between magnificent tusks, was a solid and instant hit with most members, of all ages.

On January 28, 1911, accompanied by band music, singing, cheers, speeches and the reading of verses by Edward S. Martin, '77 AM (hon.) '16 (a founder of both the *Harvard Lampoon* and *Life*) the Club welcomed Harvard's new chief to its annual dinner. Besides President Lowell, the speakers included Secretary of the Navy George Von L. Meyer '79 and Major General Leonard Wood, now Army Chief of Staff.

In September, Nicholas Biddle resigned from the House Committee, and on his recommendation Anton Schefer '03 was appointed chairman in his place. That fall, Schefer would take steps to enlarge the bar off the Grill Room and renovate the second-floor reading room, and in December would suggest that the College classes originally furnishing the bedrooms now refurbish them. A proposal by Thomas Slocum that the Club follow the example of the University Club and set up a system for pensioning its employees was referred to Schefer's committee. Meanwhile, Chairman Appleton announced that a bronze tablet commemorating Charles F. McKim had been mounted at the entrance to Harvard Hall, that a portrait of former President William G. Choate, painted at the Board's request, had been delivered, that portraits of former Presidents Bellows and French had been promised, the first by a group of members and the second, again, by the late banker's family, and that still more hunting trophies had been received: the head of a wart hog, on loan from E. Hubert Litchfield '99, and as gifts from Paul J. Rainer '97, a musk-ox head and a large polar bear skin.

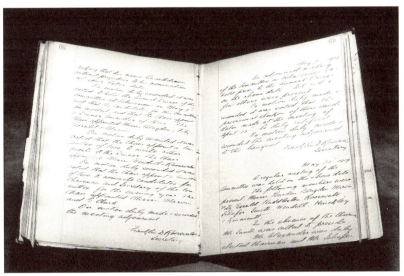

Admissions Committee minutes written by Franklin D. Roosevelt, secretary, March 1909

# 9

# THE CLUBHOUSE DOUBLES IN SIZE (1911–1915)

Nineteen-eleven was just five days old when President Higginson suddenly died of heart failure, at age seventy-four. The clubhouse was draped in black crepe for four days, until after his funeral in Grace Church. The Board postponed the annual dinner and notified all other Harvard clubs of Higginson's death. A minute prepared at its request recalled his service in the Civil War, his career as a stockbroker, and his numerous philanthropies; it told of his devoted labors as chairman of the Building Committee and of his generosity in giving the Club copies of five Memorial Hall portraits (of John Winthrop, Nicholas Boylston, John Adams, Charles Chauncey and Samuel Eliot) and nearly 1,000 books, and it ended by enumerating his endearing personal qualities. Acknowledging this document, Higginson's brother, Major Henry Lee Higginson of the Harvard Corporation, the donor of Soldiers Field and the Harvard Union, commented: "I do not think I ever read anything more simple or graceful or affectionate than these notes, and I do not know whether to be prouder of my brother or of you gentlemen . . . and of my association with you. I really never read anything that pleased me more."

Vice-President Appleton usually took the chair at meetings of the Board and of the Club pending the election of a new president.

At the delayed annual dinner in May, both of the Club's honorary members, Presidents Eliot and Lowell, spoke at length. And five days later, at the annual meeting, a new—or, rather, half new—slate of officers was elected: Peter B. Olney '64 L'66 for president and Amory G. Hodges for vice-president, with Marvin and Swift continuing as secretary and treasurer. Recruits to the Admissions Committee included one so closely in touch with the undergraduates that he was still one himself: George Whitney's younger brother, Richard Whitney '11.

In June, the Associated Harvard Clubs (A.H.C.) accepted the Club's invitation to hold their annual meeting the following year in New York City. In October, the Club sent "hearty congratulations" to Joseph H. Choate on his and Mrs. Choate's golden wedding anniversary. And on December 9 James Byrne, as chairman of a committee appointed in 1910 to investigate the entire subject of dues, submitted to the Club an exhaustive report, a model of the genre, thousands of words long and containing numerous tables, which concluded with the recommendation that "for the present, there would be no change in the dues."

On January 2, 1912, word reached the Club of the death in Bermuda of Robert Taylor Campbell, "for 23 years a loyal employee and friend of successive generations of Harvard men." The flags in front of the clubhouse were lowered, and "a floral piece" sent to the funeral site.

Nine days after this, at a meeting of the Board, John W. Prentiss '98 outlined the difficult situation confronting the Club's squash players. The three courts, he reported, were in constant demand, with between thirty and forty men using them daily except in the summer and with ten to fifteen others having to be turned away. About three squash players in five competed in the tournaments. Having earned $1,600 to $1,800 in fees every year since 1906, the courts were obviously profitable; wouldn't it make sense, Prentiss asked, to construct two more, at an estimated cost of $12,000?

Whereupon, at the Board's request, President Olney set up a committee to consider, not just Prentiss's proposal, but the entire future expansion of the clubhouse.

For some months a committee had been studying needed alterations to the second floor of the clubhouse; plans had been drafted, and at a Board meeting on February 8 the committee called for the erection of two marble fireplaces in the reading room. In the meantime, however, the newly formed committee to consider future expansion had made a disturbing discovery: that the foundations under Harvard Hall were not strong enough to support additional stories, although the walls of the hall could withstand the downward pressure on them and although it was generally assumed that the foundations had been laid with the eventual erection of additional stories in mind. Committeeman Franklin Remington '87, an architect, estimated that it would cost $12,500 to strengthen the foundations, while the McKim, Mead & White office put the total cost of strengthening the foundations, building three stories of bedrooms and four new squash courts and installing an elevator at $110,000. The Board appropriated $12,500 to reinforce the foundations.

At the next Board meeting a letter from Edgar H. Wells '97 of the Harvard administration was read, in which Wells suggested granting a scholarship of $150 for 1912–13 to a certain boy in his last year at Brooklyn Manual Training School; a Board member volunteered to subscribe the money, but instead of leaving it at that his colleagues voted to look into the feasibility of the Club's offering scholarships to needy city schoolboys on a regular basis.

A meeting of the Board on April 18, mainly given over to considering how the clubhouse should expand, resulted in a decision that divided the ordinarily united leadership.

Thomas Slocum, for the expansion committee, began by presenting some facts. The property just west of Harvard Hall—lots 32, 34 and 36 West 45th Street, each 20 feet wide by 100 feet deep and consisting of a house and backyard—could be bought for about $256,000. Mortgages on it came to $200,500, leaving $55,500 in cash to be raised before title to it could be taken; however, certain members had already agreed to put up $30,000, and the balance could easily be obtained. Total carrying charges would amount to about $15,000 a year.

The plan, Slocum went on, was to erect on the whole of this property, at a cost of about $75,000, a building six stories high, with squash courts on the top floor and bedrooms on the fourth and fifth. The three lower floors, rising to the height of Harvard Hall, would, for the next few years, be rented out as stores and lofts, bringing the Club, by Slocum's estimate, an annual income of about $36,000.

But would this be legal? President Olney thought not. Citing the passage in the Club's certificate of incorporation defining as "the particular business and object" of the Club "to promote social intercourse" and "for that purpose to establish and maintain . . . a club house, having a library, a reading room, a gallery of art and such other appurtenances and belongings as are usual in clubs and club houses," he expressed doubt that the Club had either the right or the power to lease any of its premises for commercial use.

The Board members now turned their attention to the 25-by-100-foot built-up lot adjoining the clubhouse on West 44th Street, Number 31 West, currently being held for the Club by Slocum and a few other members. This property was rented until 1914; there was a mortgage of $100,000 on it, and its price was $130,000. The stable lot west of it at Number 33, also 25 by 100 feet, could probably be purchased for about $110,000; it had been leased long term, until 1926, but the lease might possibly be bought.

Perceiving that most of his fellows favored acquiring the 45th Street property only, Secretary Marvin warned that doing so would deprive the Club for years to come of further space on 44th Street; even so, the Board, in the end, recommended that the Club purchase only the three adjoining lots for $256,000, with Olney and Marvin dissenting.

That day, as on the three preceding days, the newspapers were full of stories stemming from the sinking, south of Newfoundland on the night of April 14–15, after colliding with an iceberg, of the *Titanic*, claimed to be the world's fastest ocean liner and just about unsinkable, on her maiden voyage, with 2,224 people on board. Each day, fuller and more accurate lists appeared of the survivors, most of them picked up by a passing liner, and of the victims; in the end they would show 711 of the former and 1,513 of the latter. One passenger who drowned was a nonresident member of the Club, twenty-seven-year-old Harry Elkins Widener of Philadelphia; a scion of a family of great wealth, he was a passionate collector of rare books, and was last seen in the icy North Atlantic waters clutching a leatherbound volume thought to have been a 1598 edition of essays by Francis Bacon. The lost youth's mother would give Harvard the funds to build, as a memorial to him, the magnificent library that bears his name.

On June 6, J. P. Morgan, Jr. '89 was taken onto the Board of Managers in place of the late Nathaniel Smith, and on the tenth, Anton Schefer having resigned as chairman of the House Committee, E. Gerry Chadwick '04 was elected to the post.

Late on Thursday, June 13, the advance guard began arriving at 27 West 44th Street of what the next day would swell to a mighty host: 1,635 Harvard alumni of all ages, converging on the clubhouse from every corner of the land for the sixteenth annual gathering of the A.H.C. On Friday afternoon Harvard Hall was given over to business meetings, and that evening some 1,400 registrants and others trooped over to the Hotel Astor, in Times Square, for the Association's annual dinner. Joseph H. Choate presided, and President Olney welcomed the out-of-towners; other speakers included the president of the A.H.C., the dean of Harvard Medical School, Major General Wood, and President Lowell.

The following morning, so the *Times* would report, 1,200 alumni, most from faraway places but with some members of the Club tagging along, boarded a Hudson River steamer, behind a forty-piece brass band, heading north to West Point. There, after the cadets had paraded, the call went up for games, and while a small number of polo-playing graduates followed the post's officers off to a nearby field, Crimson football coach Percy Haughton '99, once the captain of Harvard's varsity baseball nine, quickly organized a team to face the cadets' nine out of various former heroes of diamond and gridiron. At the bottom of the sixth inning, with the Harvard veterans at bat, the bases loaded and the score 9–6 in the cadets' favor, Dr. Alfred Stillman, squash champion of the United States, knocked out a home run, transforming the score to 10–9 for Harvard. Captain Haughton sought out the West Pointers' captain. "We'll have to quit now," he told him. "You know, old chap, we've got a smoker on tonight at the Astor." A friendly argument ensued, which former Ambassador to France Robert Bacon was called on to adjudicate, but just then it was learned that the West Point officers had decisively defeated the Harvardians at polo; good feelings were restored all around, particularly after Haughton said he would be glad to play out the last three innings of the game at any time. And with a hearty three times three for their hosts the visitors straggled back down to the dock and boarded their waiting steamer.

Reaching West 42nd Street around 8:00 P.M., the holiday-makers, not bothering to wash up and change or even to shave, surged en masse, behind their hired band, to the Hotel Astor and its grand ballroom, still decorated with Harvard flags for the previous night's dinner, there to spend a festive evening with no set speeches but abundant food, drink, cigars and song.

On Friday, June 21, at New London, Harvard oarsmen outrowed their Eli rivals, and the next day, in Chicago, President Taft, Yale '77, narrowly survived the challenge by former President Roosevelt to win renomination on the Republican ticket. Roosevelt led his followers out of the convention to form the Progressive Party, which would nominate him, and on July 2, the Democrats picked New Jersey Governor Woodrow Wilson, Princeton '77, to run. So began a three-way race for the presidency unique in American annals in that it pitted against each other graduates of three old universities then and now regarded by their alumni, if not necessarily by anyone else, as the nation's three premier institutions of higher learning.

The annual meeting in May had authorized the purchase of lots 32, 34 and 36 West 45th Street and the drawing up of plans for additions to the clubhouse covering those lots and 31 West 44th Street as well. In September Thomas Slocum, for the Building Committee, presented tentative plans prepared by McKim, Mead & White, and in October the Board directed that copies of the committee's report be sent to all members. In it, the committee pointed out that in the decade since the Club had acquired the site of Harvard Hall its membership had more than doubled, from about 1,800 to about 3,700. "In view of the present crowded condition of the Club," the report went on, "and of the likelihood of a steady and large increase in membership owing particularly to the size of the classes now graduating from College, the Building Committee is convinced that this additional space is needed at once."

On November 9, four days after Woodrow Wilson was elected president, the Club voted to buy the property at 31 West 44th Street, and on November 21 it took title to all four lots. Thomas Slocum revealed that he had discussed with the owner of the Webster Hotel, at 40 West 45th Street, the possibility of the Club and the hotel jointly owning Number 36, but that both men had agreed, finally, that such an arrangement would not be practical. And two days later, a Saturday, following a 4–0 football victory over Yale, exuberant members in New Haven rounded up Crimson players and coaches and brought them to New York, willing captives, in their special train, to celebrate with them at the Club into the wee hours.

The next month, a brief entry in the minutes noted a tragedy of a kind that occurred often back then, when medical knowledge was still relatively limited. A certain graduate of 1900 had been dropped from membership in October for nonpayment of dues and charges, and a month later had died; his young widow had since paid up his debt, wherefor the Board moved to rescind its earlier act and expunge all mention of it.

If more members than usual attended the Club's December meeting, some presumably came to hear the featured speaker, new member Vilhjalmur Stefansson GS '06. The thirty-three-year-old Stefansson, a Canadian of Icelandic extraction, was beginning to win fame as an Arctic explorer. Although he had a New York address—the Explorers Club—he was, for obvious reasons, classified as a nonresident member. Having recently returned from a four-year expedition along the coasts of Canada's Northwest Territories, where he had come

Club flag at the South Pole, 1971

upon a group of indigenous hunter-fishermen with "European-like characteristics," Stefansson spoke on "The Eskimos of Coronation Gulf," illustrating his talk with magic lantern views. Only a month later, members would be able to attend another illustrated lecture about a journey to the other end of the earth, when Sir Ernest Shackleton would talk about the late Robert Falcon Scott's ill-fated expedition to the South Pole November 1911–January 1912. (Six decades after this, then-Secretary George P. Kramer '50 L'53 would reach—and return safely from—the South Pole, where he planted a Harvard Club flag.)

In February 1913 the Board was confronted by an awesomely brazen demand. Having lost money sponsoring a lecture by former president Eliot, the Civic Union wanted the Club either to make up its loss or, at the very least, help defray it. While excitable Board members may have been provoked by this to a state close to apoplexy—or hysterics—in the end they would decide simply, with their colleagues, that "the Club could not accede to this request."

Soon after President Wilson took office in early March, the appearance of the Club's entrance hall was altered—and not for the better—when a cigar stand was installed in the well under the stairs leading up to the library. One outraged member, Robert Wheelwright '06, collected seventy-eight signatures to a petition calling for its immediate removal. For Edward S. Martin of the Committee of Literature and Art, this latest desecration was the last straw: Deploring the impairment of the lobby's "academic atmosphere," he urged that the huge pegboard by the door be abolished, the sale of cigars relegated to "one of the smaller rooms on the side of the entrance to the dining room" and the posting of notices on the walls be stopped altogether. The Board accepted Martin's indictment, but then voted to keep the cigar stand where it was and explain to Wheelwright that it had been moved there to relieve congestion in the office and because there was no better place to put it.

The Club formally took over its new property on the somewhat equivocal date of April 1. On May 16, a Friday, 1,500 people came to a late-afternoon reception honoring the remarkable Choate brothers, William G., aged eighty-three, and Joseph H., eighty-one, and the next evening members elected Amory G. Hodges president and John W. Prentiss treasurer, retaining Francis R. Appleton as vice-president and Langdon P. Marvin as secretary. That year, exceptionally, the Nominating Committee had something more to set before the annual meeting than a list of recommended candidates for office, to wit, a resolution to elect Joseph H. Choate president emeritus of the Club, "to perform from time to time such functions as may be agreeable to him upon the suggestion of the President or the Board of Managers." As former Treasurer Mackie commented, the resolution was unique in the history of the Club. The Nominating Committee did not, he said, intend to create a new office, but merely to honor for the rest of his life the Club's "most distinguished and beloved member" with "an honor as distinguished and unique as it is possible for the Club to confer upon any of its members." Seconded by retiring President Olney, the resolution was adopted forthwith.

On May 22 an important national society was founded in the clubhouse, probably in the Board or Mahogany Room, at the initiative of Clement Cleveland, an eminent gynecologist who had been one of the Club's incorporators in 1887. Concerned about the growing menace of cancer, Dr. Cleveland brought together nine distinguished physicians and five prominent laymen for the purpose of organizing what would in 1945 become the American Cancer Society.

On November 12, to mark the opening of the Harvard Club of Boston's splendid clubhouse on Commonwealth Avenue, Secretary Marvin sent its president, Major Henry Lee Higginson, the Club's congratulations, with, by special messenger, a very large letter H made up of red roses. Many members attended the Boston club's gala reception on November 21, the eve of the Yale game. And after the New York club's December meeting members took in an illustrated talk by University librarian William Coolidge Lane '81.

Among contributors to the Club's library that month were President Lowell, Walter Lippmann '10 and Oswald Garrison Villard '93, as well as, apparently by coincidence, three members of a single illustrious clan: Charles Francis Adams '56, Henry Adams '58 and Brooks Adams. Meanwhile, the House Committee, promising to move it to the basement very soon, installed a bulky news ticker in the already cluttered entrance hall.

Since the Lane dinner of 1866 nearly all speakers at Club functions had been Americans, but banqueters at the annual dinner on January 30, 1914, heard a talk by a Frenchman, Ambassador Jean Jules Jusserand LLD'07, while the March meeting, in another curious foreshadowing of the catastrophe about to engulf Europe, was addressed by a German exchange professor at Harvard, Ernst von Dobschütz. A few weeks after that hundreds of members turned out to welcome back their favorite speaker of all, Charles T. Copeland '82. "Copey," as he was universally known, was unlike any other professor of English, at Harvard or elsewhere, before or since: Not a scholar, like his classmate, Shakespeare authority George L. Kittredge, he possessed instead an uncanny ability to communicate to others the profound enjoyment he derived from good writing. His method consisted largely of reading aloud passages of his own choosing from works of the imagination. Copey's annual appearances at 27 West 44th Street, dating from 1906, were red letter days on the Club calendar, eagerly awaited and always well attended.

Early in May workmen at last began tearing down Numbers 32, 34 and 36 West 45th Street, but the building at 31 West 44th Street remained standing as the Mooney-Maxwell Company's owners declined to vacate their premises in it. After negotiations they agreed to move two doors west into Number 35, owned by Cornelius Vanderbilt, the Club agreeing in return to pay Mooney-Maxwell a forfeit and reimburse Vanderbilt for the alterations he made adjusting the building to its new tenant's needs. Not until July 15 could the demolition of Number 31 begin.

On July 4, racing at Henley in England, the Harvard second crew, captained by Leverett Saltonstall '14 L'17, pulled ahead of the Union Boat Club of Boston's shell and stayed ahead to win the coveted Grand Challenge Cup. Harvard men everywhere rejoiced, even as they followed, in their newspapers, the ever more ominous diplomatic maneuvering among various European states that had been set in motion by the assassination a week earlier of the heir to the Austro-Hungarian throne. At the beginning of August war would break out between the Central Powers

Harvard wins at Henley, July 4, 1914

(Germany and Austria-Hungary, soon to be joined by Turkey) and the Allies (France, Britain, Russia, Serbia and Belgium).

In New York that summer the opening act was played out of a drama that would bring the Club in conflict with one of America's leading painters. At the suggestion of Charles C. Burlingham '79, a well-known lawyer keenly interested in art, the commission to paint a portrait for the Club of former President Olney had been awarded, with the sitter's approval, to George Bellows, whose famous prizefight picture, *A Stag at Sharkey's*, magnificent views of the Hudson and realistic depictions of city life and scenes had earned him both critical and popular acclaim. In June the artist's latest canvas went on temporary display in Harvard Hall, and although the members who saw it differed as to how well he had captured Judge Olney's craggy features, none could ignore the painting's polychromatic glow. Olney himself disliked the picture, and said so, but Bellows wasn't entirely happy with it either; well before it came down, the two men agreed to try again some time.

During these months laborers were excavating the land west of the clubhouse. Near 45th Street they encountered, as expected, the western continuation of the underground stream beneath Harvard Hall, and elsewhere massive rock formations that had to be broken up with dynamite. In August the Building Committee decided to carry out the architects' plans in their entirety. And in October, when excavating ceased and construction began, the architects retracted their earlier warning that the foundations under Harvard Hall might not be able to bear the weight of added floors above it. Having looked into the matter thoroughly, they reported that these foundations would be fully adequate so long as the ground water remained high enough to cover the piles completely, preserving their soundness.

All of the thirty-four new bedrooms would have running water and twenty-four would have adjoining bathrooms; these last rooms were up for adoption, and '90, '93, '94, '96 and '98 had each already claimed one. As Secretary Marvin remarked, this adopt-a-bedroom scheme was a sure winner: While sparing the Club the expense of fitting out the bedrooms it enabled members to commemorate, permanently and publicly, their cherished College classes.

Construction, 1914                    The New-York Historical Society

The previous March, with many Harvard graduates out of work, President Hodges had, on the Board's instructions, appointed a committee on appointments to help them find employment, and now, seven months later, that committee filed its first report. Of seventy-six men who had sought its assistance the committee had placed sixty-three in paying jobs, thirty-one permanent and thirty-two temporary. This appears to have been the very first of many efforts by the Club to procure jobs for unemployed members and Harvard alumni generally.

Over the next eight months a tall, narrow building mantled in brick and extending north from 44th Street through the entire block rose along the western wall of the existing clubhouse, inside which workmen broke through that wall to make the two structures one. In the evenings club life could continue as before, but during the day the noise must sometimes have tried members' nerves.

Although Germany's invasion of Belgium at the start of the war aroused indignation in the United States, most Americans backed President Wilson's policy of neutrality. This was even the case, no doubt, within the Club, where anglophilia and, to a lesser extent, francophilia were entrenched, and it remained true even after the receipt of two items that abruptly brought the remote conflict into focus: an appeal from Christ College, Cambridge, for used clothing for Belgian refugees and the news that George Williamson '05, an officer in the British Army, had been killed in France on November 12, the first member of the Club to die in the war. But some Americans, including some

Major General Leonard Wood

in the Club, foresaw the possibility of their country's one day being drawn into the struggle, and as they observed the desperate efforts of the British authorities, in particular, to mold hundreds of thousands of civilian men into a disciplined force, they felt that the United States must prepare for the same eventuality while there was still time. This could best be accomplished, many thought, by training volunteers in close order drill, the manual of arms, the use of rifles and sidearms and the entire repertory of modern combat techniques, so that if and when the country were to go to war they could, as officers, swiftly transform hordes of recruits into fighting men.

Such, in essence, was the doctrine of national preparedness, and its leading proponent was the Club's own General Wood. After the annual dinner on January 29, 1915, Wood, speaking in his usual direct, sincere manner, made the case for preparedness and sat down to thunderous applause. (With him at the head table, besides President Lowell, were Major General George Washington Goethals LLD (hon.) '12, governor of the Panama Canal Zone, and Assistant Secretary of the Navy Franklin D. Roosevelt.)

On May 8 Americans were stunned to learn that the British liner *Lusitania* had been sunk by a U-boat off Ireland; of the 1,195 men, women and children who perished 128 were American citizens, including four Harvard graduates. The torpedoing of the unarmed passenger vessel caused an immediate falling off of sympathy for the German cause. Two days later, with the world still waiting for President Wilson's reaction, fifteen prominent New Yorkers, all but two of them members of the Club, sent him a telegram urging that measures, "however serious," be taken "to secure full reparations and guarantees." The next day, without addressing the sinking, Wilson declared in a speech that "There is such a thing as a man being too proud to fight." But the signers of the telegram, undeterred, summoned about fifty or so friends of like mind to the Club "to talk about the *Lusitania*." Out of their discussions emerged the idea of a military training camp for adult men, and General Wood promised that if 100 men registered for it he would hold a "business man's camp" at Plattsburgh, New York, in August, after a scheduled camp there for college students.

The War Department in Washington showed no interest in their project and declined to support it. Former President Roosevelt offered to help raise money for the camp, but his help was not needed: Bernard Baruch gave Wood $10,000 and persuaded others to contribute.

As lawyers, bankers, stockbrokers and others, most well past their first youth, began to sign up for Plattsburgh, the Board convened, on May 20, to hear from Secretary Marvin about an important art transaction. On the recommendation of an adviser concerning such matters, William M. Kendall of McKim, Mead & White, the officers had accepted the loan, from one Martin van Straaten of London, of the eight splendid Flemish

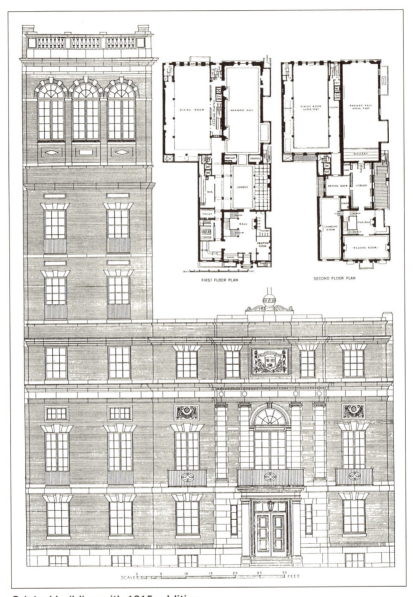

Original building with 1915 addition

tapestries already adorning the stone upper walls of Harvard Hall. The terms of the loan, as spelled out in a letter from Marvin of April 24 and in van Straaten's reply, dated April 30 and written in New York, where he had been visiting, were straightforward: The tapestries would remain van Straaten's until and unless they were purchased by the Club, its members or anyone else, and the Club, meanwhile, would insure them against loss by fire in the sum of $50,000, and keep them so insured. Everything was in order, Marvin told his colleagues, except one thing: Martin van Straaten was dead, having embarked on the *Lusitania* the day after signing his letter to Marvin and gone down in her six days later.

Pending developments, the Board voted to ratify the officers' action in accepting the loan.

In June, George Bellows's new portrait of Judge Olney was temporarily hung in Harvard Hall, and Secretary Marvin announced happily that certain College classes had by now assumed responsibility for furnishing and decorating every one of the twenty-four new bedrooms with baths. But recruiting for the Plattsburgh camp was lagging, so badly that it looked as if the project might have to be abandoned. Grenville Clark called a mass meeting of business and professional men for mid-June in Harvard Hall and saw to it that people came. As he had hoped would happen, General Wood's earnest appeal turned the tide, inspiring dozens of his hearers to register on the spot, and when the campers would assemble two months thence on the shore of Lake Champlain they would number 1,200.

On June 14 a self-contained section of the clubhouse addition just under its roof, consisting of a swimming pool, a solarium and dressing rooms, was opened. These amenities were to vanish forever during World War II, the space allocated to other uses, but the image of them that remains in the memories of older members is a vivid one, imbued with nostalgia. A description of them written by architectural critic John Taylor Boyd, Jr., for *The Architectural Record* of December 1915, helps explain why. The swimming pool or plunge, Boyd wrote,

> is placed on the very top of the building to derive the full advantage of light and air. It is this fine situation, as well as its interesting arrangement and architectural treatment, that makes the Harvard Club plunge so successful. The average pool in

**The Plunge**

clubs, gymnasiums, and Y.M.C.A. buildings is usually subterranean, ill lighted and ventilated, and certainly most uninteresting architecturally. It is usually as utilitarian as the barber shop. But the Harvard Club pool, while extremely simple, impresses one as a most genial, cheerful, pleasant sort of place, where one likes to linger and enjoy the lingering as much as the swim. For this purpose of tarrying after the exercise, the adjacent "solarium" is provided, separated from the pool only by a little lobby, which contains a tiny hot room and a winding staircase to the dressing rooms below.

The unusual charm of the plunge and solarium, which were treated together as a whole, is further enhanced by the color. The solarium has white trim, walls and ceiling of light grayish yellow, mantelpiece of Belgian black-and-gold marble, with a floor of very rich deep green of the battleship linoleum. The plunge has much the same effect. White marble bands are used, white mosaic for the pool, and gray terrazzo is found on the floor and as a dado on the side wall. The side of the pool itself is formed of small inch squares of white mosaic, with dark green bands. To set off this delicate color, which might tend otherwise to be insipid, there are little hedges of bay trees, set in the recesses of the casement windows. Extremely simple as it is, this arrangement of the plunge is as perfect a bit of architecture as one often sees. It bears the stamp of style in every part of it.

The Dining Room

On July 1 both Harvard Hall and the new dining room west of it were closed off as massive kitchen fixtures were installed in the greatly enlarged basement below. On August 12 a western extension of the Grill Room and a new bar beyond it were opened, and four days later Harvard Hall was reopened. Simultaneously, the new dining room was thrown open for business. Two stories high, covering even more floor space than Harvard Hall and with a gallery around it, the majestic hall excited the admiration of, among others, John T. Boyd, Jr., who was particularly pleased that the architects had so contrived that at a certain point a person approaching either Harvard Hall or the dining hall from the front of the clubhouse could glance into both, "a striking instance of how the limitations of the situation have not only been surmounted but actually turned to advantage."

> Quite different from the graceful, cozy plunge is the great new dining hall on the ground floor. Its bold fine treatment, its virile character, its rich striking color express admirably its purpose—a dining hall in a club with Harvard traditions in

the background. One can see at a glance that the architectural antecedents of the room are the old English halls, yet the treatment is original, the detail is free, and the adaptation is in no way slavish or mechanical . . . What a straightforward, manly quality it has! The slight looseness of the room, which results from the conditions imposed by the old work and which cannot be helped, is frankly faced. For instance, three of the walls of the room are not exactly symmetrical, and the needs of the service require that almost half the space under the galleries be blocked off. Yet the splendid ceiling is designed to hold all this together, and prevent the eye of the beholder from contemplating too closely these minor irregularities. The arrangement of bedrooms and light courts above causes the wide column-spacing of the three central bays of the galleries, which does not seem too wide, however, for wooden construction. Incidentally, the general dimensions of the hall are as follows: The ceiling is some 95' long and 35'8" wide, and the total height of the room is 28'7". The height from the first floor to the gallery floor is 12'5".

While members whose jobs kept them in the city could cool off after work with a dip in the plunge (twenty-five cents) followed by dinner in the new dining room (sixty-five cents and up, the table d'hôte dinner at the old price having been restored by popular demand), many were spending their vacations that August undergoing military training 300 miles north. Their regime was identical with that followed at the student camps, and while it presented no problem to athletes like Devereux Milburn L'06 and recent all-American Hamilton Fish '10, it was hard on men like former Secretary of State and Ambassador to France Robert Bacon. But the spectacle of celebrities and millionaires drilling, exercising and doing KP alongside policemen and lumberjacks intrigued the press, and when, in late August, former President Roosevelt arrived to address the campers, platoons of reporters descended on Plattsburgh. A few publications, including Oswald Garrison Villard's New York *Post*, poked fun at the campers as rich men playing childish war games, but most portrayed them as latter-day Rough Riders and exhorted readers to emulate their patriotic example.

Many would: As more and more colleges and universities went in for compulsory military training, camps for older men would proliferate. Thus the campaign for preparedness hatched at 27 West 44th Street and launched therefrom would burgeon into a national movement. Still, it should not be assumed that the Club was made up exclusively of fire-eating Progressive Republicans. Villard, after all, was a member, as were

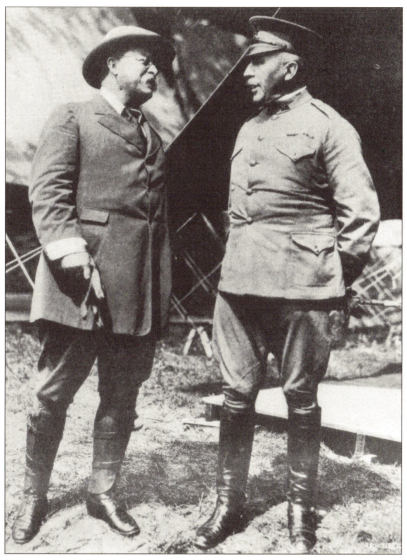

Roosevelt and Wood at Plattsburgh

Heywood Broun '10 of the New York *Tribune*, whose dispatches from France two years later, criticizing General Pershing and the American war effort, were to land him in hot water, and Robert C. Benchley '12, whom the same paper would dismiss in May 1917 as failing to sound sufficiently bellicose in print. By an amusing irony, moreover, the largely conservative and firmly capitalistic Club would shortly—on November 12, 1915—welcome as a lecturer member and war correspondent John Reed '10, who in the next five years would witness the Bolshevik Revolution, make friends with Lenin, return home briefly to found the Communist Labor Party, be tried twice for treason, write propaganda for the Soviet Union, report on its civil war and at last, dying of typhus at thirty-two in 1920, be buried in the Kremlin.

In October Chairman Chadwick of the Executive Committee reported that the addition, very nearly doubling the size of the clubhouse, was complete. The cost of building it came to $525,000, bringing the Club's mortgage indebtedness to $1.25 million, which suggested redoubling efforts to attract new members. Finally, noting that the Yale Club had moved east from across the street to its new home on Vanderbilt Avenue, Secretary Marvin stated that the Club could not accept George Bellows's second portrait of Olney, particularly as the judge hated it, and he asked C. C. Burlingham to convey the bad news to the artist.

Bellows was shocked, but not entirely surprised. The previous June, observing how the somber setting and discreet lighting of Harvard Hall altered the colors of his newly hung canvas, he had confided his misgivings to a friend in a letter: "I have just finished one of the best things I've ever painted," he wrote. "It's a blow to see a thing hung in a place not suitable for pictures. . . . But it's so rich it can't be altogether killed, and it doesn't look quite so musty as the rest of the coal cellar portraits." In September, many members returning from the Berkshires, Newport, Southampton—and Plattsburgh—were disturbed by the picture's high color. "There's an awful how-de-do about the portrait of Olney," Burlingham wrote the artist. "He [the judge] has now come out in the open and said he cannot bear to have it hung on the walls of the Club. . . . Of course those chaps up at the Club don't know the difference between a portrait and a Uneeda Biscuit advertisement." Later, the lawyer informed the painter that "The Committee of Art and Literature, so-called, has recommended . . . that the portrait of Mr. Olney not be accepted. . . . As was said by a famous lady to a strong man of old, 'The Philistines be upon thee.' . . . Meanwhile I think the portrait had better go back to your studio."

Burlingham, feeling responsible, offered to pay the artist's fee, but Bellows, hurt and angry, would not hear of it. "This would not satisfy me," he wrote Secretary Marvin, "for the shoddy respect in which my work has been held by the Art Committee of the Harvard Club. Nor do I wish to have my work pass into the possession of anybody who holds it in slight regard. But when I am solicited as a distinguished painter to under-take the commission of a portrait, when after months of earnest consider-ation bringing all my energies and ability to bear on the matter, and when the result in my own judgment and in the judgment of the men most com-petent . . . to judge is a most unusual success then I feel and rightly that the matter has been successfully concluded.

"The Harvard Club owes me fifteen hundred dollars. . . . I will settle for seven hundred and fifty dollars, if I am also allowed to retain the painting, and I will not deviate from those terms."

In the end, however, the Club would pay George Bellows nothing.

If Bellows's admirers saw the Club's governors carrying philistinism to new heights—or depths—in this affair, most members were probably unaware of what had happened. And even if they had been aware they might well have been too busy exploring the new parts of their expanded clubhouse to give the matter much thought.

The inventory was impressive. In the basement—seldom visited by most members—the kitchen had been enlarged, and space found for addi-tional offices. On the ground floor more offices had been added, together with a coatroom, a lavatory, a barroom and the new dining room, two sto-ries high, while the Grill Room had been extended several feet westward. On the second floor, additional reading and writing rooms had been pro-vided, and on the third floor, a good-sized billiard room and three private dining rooms. Thirty-four new bedrooms had been constructed on the fourth and fifth floors, while the sixth floor contained two new squash courts and two others that had been enlarged to standard size; it also boasted new dressing rooms, showers, baths, lavatories and a barber shop. And on the seventh floor, finally, the plunge and the solarium had been installed. But what pleased many members most was that in creating all of these additions the architects had managed somehow—almost miracu-lously, some thought—to keep the atmosphere of the clubhouse as warm, welcoming and homelike as it had been before.

The three new private dining rooms on the third floor could open out into a single long hall, and on the evening of Wednesday, November 3, 1915, they were so combined for a dinner party of eighty men. Around host Amory G. Hodges sat both of the Club's honorary members and its one and only president emeritus, while at other tables were seated three former presidents of the Club, a former secretary of the Navy and a future one, representatives of the new extension's architects (McKim, Mead & White) and builders (Marc Eidlitz & Son) and assorted dignitaries. Their dinners consumed, these select four score descended to the dining room, where a thousand members had assembled for what President Hodges would call a "hyphenated celebration," with the dual purpose of dedicating the enlarged clubhouse and observing the Club's semicentennial.

First came the dedication. After Secretary Marvin recounted how the Club's western addition had come into being, Executive Committee Chairman Chadwick handed the president canceled vouchers to show that all payments for it had been made. Odin Roberts '86 of the Harvard Club of Boston gave Hodges a silver bowl with thanks for the Club's having provided his organization with the example it had followed. And the president read aloud a poem by the absent Edward S. Martin that closed with

> Thanks for this generous pile that so
> > Completely meets our creature needs!
> Blest be its use and may it grow
> > To seem to us as time proceeds
> A statelier mansion of the soul
> > Of Harvard, whence shall always come
> Wisdom ready at call of roll,
> > Valor at tap of drum.

Then it was Joseph H. Choate's turn to speak:

> One little incident shows the difference between the President of the time when I entered College in 1848 and the Presidents that we have known since. Mr. Edward Everett was the President, and after I had been in College about a week—I came from the antiquated city of Salem, which was not remarkable for its knowledge of etiquette—I received a message from Mr. Alexander Everett, the President's secretary: "Wouldn't I please come to his office." I went there in great apprehension; I did not know but what I had committed the unpardonable sin. He looked very solemn, and he said, "Mr. Choate, the President has directed me to say

to you that you passed him in Harvard Square yesterday without touching your hat. I trust that this offense will never be repeated."

It has made me think of Eliot—Eliot, stalking through Harvard Square, through the whole College Yard, and no notice taken of him. And I have thought what a wonderful change had come over the manners of the University.

The wide-stalking former president of the University, still vigorous in his eighties, rose to praise the Club for having taken such good care of young graduates coming to live in the metropolis. Next, President Lowell declared, to loud cheers, that he felt his audience had assembled not only to celebrate the opening of the new clubhouse and the Club's first half century but also to honor the man, President Eliot, who had guided the amazing growth of the University during practically the whole of that time. And he wondered aloud what the University would be like fifty years thence, in the almost unimaginably distant year of 1965.

A corner of the Reading Room

# 10

# THE CLUB IN WORLD WAR I (1915–1920)

With the Club now obligated to come up with $5,312 every month to service its two mortgages, Treasurer Prentiss stressed the need to economize. The Board imposed a dime surcharge on meals and introduced a dime charge for cashing checks, both of which moves caused grumbling. But economizing had its limits: That fall, the Board happily approved spending $43 a week on renting an Irwin Football Reproduction Board, a device that enabled a person to follow action on a distant playing field while he listened to reports of that action, telegraphed in from that field, as they were read aloud.

The clubhouse continued to function as an active center of the preparedness movement. Before 1915 was out, Grenville Clark helped to found the Military Training Camps Association and became its secretary; over the next year and a half the MTCA would train, at Plattsburgh and thirteen other locations, more than 16,000 future officers. (According to one estimate 80 percent of the American officers who saw combat in World War I were products of these camps.)

While the oratory at a banquet on February 17, 1916, commemorating the Lane dinner fifty years before was presumably of the usual high order, the talk that evening that would mean most to the Club was a private chat between two banqueting members: William M. Kendall and George Leland Hunter '89, a connoisseur and the author of *Tapestries: Their Origin, History and Renaissance*. The two men agreed to effect a major change in the decor of the Club's two great ground floor halls, rehanging the van Straaten tapestries in the dining room and hanging in their place a suite of early seventeenth-century Brussels tapestries which Hunter would supply. Two months later, before an attentive audience in Harvard Hall, Hunter described in detail the large and colorful hangings overhead, on loan from P. W. French & Company, which depicted episodes from the life of Cyrus the Great, founder of the Persian Empire in the sixth century B.C.

In May, the annual meeting saw the election of Francis R. Appleton as president and Evert J. Wendell as vice-president, with Langdon P. Marvin continuing as secretary and John W. Prentiss as treasurer. For the first time, membership exceeded 4,000, but since the enlargement of the clubhouse had increased the cost of operating the Club, more members were urgently needed. To bring them in, a special committee was appointed, with lawyer William E. Chadbourne '00 as its secretary.

On June 7 the Board named a new Committee on Appointments to help out-of-work Harvardians find jobs, and, at the instigation of Grenville Clark, Edward S. Blagden '08 and Philip J. Roosevelt '13, a Committee on Civic and Social Work to assist Harvard men wishing to volunteer for such tasks. Meanwhile, in Harvard Hall, Assistant Navy Secretary F. D. Roosevelt was addressing a large gathering of men who were thinking about signing up for a naval training cruise in August and September.

On that very day Republican delegates convened in Chicago, where they would nominate former New York Governor and U.S. Supreme Court Justice Charles Evans Hughes for president; the following week, in St. Louis, the Democrats renominated President Wilson, and on June 15 the Club opened its doors to members of the neighboring New York Yacht Club, whose kitchen and restaurant were closed down for repairs. Even with these gentlemen in attendance, however, the seasonal drop in activity was more pronounced than ever that summer, what with the absence of so many members, not only on vacation but at Plattsburgh, on a naval training cruise—or on the Mexican border. (A raid into New Mexico by partisans of the guerrilla fighter "Pancho" Villa in which American citizens had been killed had prompted President Wilson to order a punitive expedition under General John J. Pershing to capture Villa. Pershing would not succeed in this, but in the meantime many New York Harvard men, notably those belonging to the very social National Guard unit Squadron A, would experience their first taste of military life in the field with him that summer.)

In October Treasurer Prentiss announced that in the five months since May 1 the Club had grown by 10 percent, taking in 418 men to reach a total of 4,483. He credited most of this growth to the efforts of the special committee, whose secretary and sparkplug was now, it turned out, serving on the Mexican border; the Board directed Secretary Marvin to write William Chadbourne seeking his advice on how to keep up his good work. The Board members were relieved to learn that the Committee on Art and Literature had judged Ellen Emmet Rand's oil painting of Peter B. Olney "a portrait of great artistic distinction"; then, at their president's bidding, they rose and drank a silent toast to the Harvard men who had fallen in Allied service.

Having campaigned on the slogan "He kept us out of war," President Wilson won reelection, but while some Club members, naturally, favored Wilsonian neutrality, sentiment for intervention in the war was far stronger at 27 West 44th Street than in the nation at large. Thus two days after the election, in a darkened Harvard Hall, A. Piatt Andrew, AM'95, PhD'00, inspector general and de facto head of the American Ambulance Field Service, showed movies (silent, of course) as he described how his men, volunteers all, transported wounded *poilus* to field hospitals, often saving their lives. When the lights came on again Colonel William Cary Sanger '74 proposed that the Club buy and equip an ambulance for the A.A.F.S., and within the next few minutes Secretary Marvin, who was present, collected $129 for this purpose.

No purchaser having been found for the van Straaten tapestries, their owner removed them from the dining room and clubhouse. Member R.A.F. Penrose, Jr. '84 PhD'86 gave the Club a bronze replica of a bust of the great geologist Nathaniel S. Shaler '62 SD'75 LLD'03 by sculptor Robert Ingersoll Aitken. Early in December Chorister Rogers announced the formation of a glee club. Then, on December 8, something unexpected happened: A large, flat stone in the ceiling of Harvard Hall tore loose and plummeted down to shatter on the stone floor. No one was hurt, but the hall was immediately closed and experts on the staffs of the original architects and builders brought in. They determined that the accident had been caused by the drying up of the plaster surrounding the stone, and proceeded to go over all of the hall's stonework, foot by foot.

While they were at it, the men from Marc Eidlitz & Son, the builders, drilled test holes under the east, north and west walls of Harvard Hall deep enough to permit them to inspect the tops of the nearest piles, leaving the holes open for several days in order to observe the action of the underground water. They discovered that the average water level was several inches below what it had been when the piles had been sunk and the foundations built, presumably because in the course of erecting a new building just east of the clubhouse on 45th Street a deep cellar had been excavated that was drained by sumps; they also noted that the water level fluctuated in height by as much as seven inches. They concluded that under present circumstances the wooden tops of the piles, permeated with capillary moisture, were not in danger of deteriorating, but warned that more construction in the vicinity could further lower the water level, leaving the tops of the piles high and dry. (A report from McKim, Mead & White would corroborate these findings.)

On February 1, 1917, came news of the German government's decision to resume unrestricted submarine warfare, and two days later President Wilson broke off diplomatic relations with Germany. Over the next weeks several American vessels were sunk, and on March 9, responding to a petition issued by thirty-five of their colleagues, hundreds of members assembled half an hour before their monthly meeting to adopt a resolution urging that Congress be recalled to make provision for the national defense. On March 22 a "patriotic mass meeting" was held in Madison Square Garden under the auspices of the Club and other college clubs, and on March 28 the Board appointed a Committee on Military and Naval Service, with Langdon P. Marvin as chairman, to inform members of opportunities to train and serve in the armed forces and in ancillary services, and to represent the Club in all matters pertaining to the war.

By April 6, when Congress declared war on the Central Powers, many members had already taken up arms or were participating in the global

French officers at the Club

struggle in noncombatant roles, and the Committee on Military and Naval Service had already launched an effort, which it would carry out largely by means of frequent mailings of questionnaires, to keep track of them. Now, more members rushed to enlist. Not all were young and fit: Colonel Roosevelt—as the former president now preferred to be called—was almost blind in one eye from an old boxing injury and often weak from the aftereffects of a tropical disease, yet he wanted to raise and command a volunteer force in France. And his friend General Wood confidently awaited posting overseas. But both old men would be disappointed: President Wilson was to deny Roosevelt's request, and, naming General Pershing to head the American Expeditionary Force, deprive General Wood of a combat role.

By then, incidentally, Colonel Sanger had raised sufficient funds to purchase and maintain not one ambulance but two, and to endow a bed in the American Hospital at Neuilly as well.

On the twentieth the Club welcomed six French officers who would be its guests before proceeding to Cambridge to teach undergraduates in the Harvard regiment the fine points of infantry and artillery warfare. On hand to greet them personally was President Lowell, who had procured their transfer, not through American and French government channels but by negotiating it directly with his friend and fellow scholar Ambassador Jusserand: Replying for the newcomers were their commandant, Major Paul Azan, and Second Lieutenant Jean Giraudoux. This rather senior junior officer (he was in his midthirties), who had twice been wounded and twice decorated for bravery, was the future diplomat-dramatist who would one day give the world *Amphitryon 38, Tiger at the Gates, Electra, Ondine* and *The Madwoman of Chaillot*. As he told his hearers at the Club, he had already spent a happy year at Harvard in 1906–07 as a teaching fellow and was eager to get back to the Cambridge he remembered with affection.

Ten days later about 500 members attended a farewell reception at the Club for General Wood, who would entrain that night for Charleston to assume command of the Southeastern Department. And on the afternoon of Friday, May 4, Harvard Hall was the scene of a mass meeting to promote the officers' training camps, at which the speakers were Colonel Roosevelt, former Secretary of War Henry L. Stimson PhD'89 and. . . Joseph H. Choate.

Choate was now eighty-five. Since August 1914, while serving on various civic, professional, cultural and philanthropic boards and as president of the Century Association, he had taken upon himself the task of alerting his countrymen to their duty of going to the aid of the Allies.

His speeches carried weight, thanks to his reputation and to the fact that audiences found the spectacle of a man of his years speaking with such passion strangely moving.

America's entry into the war gratified Choate's dearest wish, and when thereafter Britain and France sent a joint top-level mission to the United States he was the obvious choice to greet its chiefs, British Foreign Secretary Balfour and, for France, former Premier Viviani and Marshal Joffre. He gladly accepted the chairmanship of the New York reception committee. Sunday, May 6, initiated a week of ceremonial appearances that a man half Choate's age might have found tiring, culminating the following Sunday in ceremonies at the Cathedral of St. John the Divine. The service over, Choate said to Balfour, in parting, "Remember, we meet again to celebrate the victory," and the next day he died at home, of heart failure.

In April, Treasurer Prentiss declined renomination, explaining that he had been named treasurer of the Harvard Endowment Fund, whereupon the Nominating Committee picked Harold B. Clark '01 for the post. Secretary Marvin informed his colleagues about momentous goings-on in Albany. The recent so-called February Revolution in Russia, accompanied by civil unrest, had triggered a "red scare" in this country, and a conservative legislator named Stivers had introduced into the New York State Senate a bill prohibiting the carrying of red flags in parades; on learning of this, Greene had consulted with State Senator Ogden L. Mills '05 L'07 and Assemblyman Robert McC. Marsh '99 AM'00, who, after huddling with Senator Stivers, had assured the secretary that the bill would be amended so as not to affect the public bearing, waving or flaunting of Harvard flags or banners.

Among the distinguished guests at the annual meeting on May 25 was General Wood's successor in command of the Department of the East, Major General J. Franklin Bell, and a young aide of Bell's named Captain George Catlett Marshall. Following the reading of a letter from President Wilson expressing gratitude for the Club's "generous pledges of cooperation and support" came ratification of the official slate: Appleton and Wendell again for president and vice-president, Jerome D. Greene for secretary and Harold B. Clark for treasurer. Days after this, however, in the first of several such incidents, Clark received an Army commission and had to resign. (In July, Thomas Slocum would be elected treasurer.)

On June 6 the Board voted—as it would many times thereafter—to extend the privileges of the Club for a given period of time to certain Allied officers, in this instance five British officers ranging in rank from captain to brigadier general. Then President Appleton read aloud a letter from an unnamed  young member which could hardly have left his hearers unaffected:

> In arranging to have my will redrafted, as many of us, in view of the possibility of active service in the war, are doing, I have planned to leave a small legacy of $1,000 to $2,000 to the Harvard Club of New York City. Since many members of the Club are no doubt so situated that were the matter brought to their attention they could and would be glad to provide in their wills for a bequest to the Club, I am venturing to inquire if some way could not be found to suggest to members that they consider this step.
>
> Many of us feel that we owe a great deal to the Harvard Club, which beyond peradventure is the most effective and useful activity connected with the University outside of Cambridge and its immediate vicinity. In view of the financial problems which, by reason of the war, the Club must face, problems which are more serious for clubs such as ours where so large a percentage of the membership will go to the front, it seems to me that the present may be a particularly appropriate time to take up the matter. Any bequests of this sort could be treated as a permanent endowment fund, the income from which could be expended at the discretion of the Board of Managers. In this way those of us for whom the Club has done so much could have a permanent memorial of our appreciation and affection, and thereby make the Club even more useful than it is at present to those who come after us.

The Board agreed that the letter writer's suggestion be brought to the members' attention, whereupon President Appleton raised a matter of more immediate concern. It was now illegal, he noted, to serve liquor to officers in the armed forces, and the Club was complying with this law: Shouldn't all the members contribute to the law's stated objective—of conserving alcohol for war production—by denying themselves the pleasures of the bar?

For a week, members of an ad hoc committee checked around town; they found that some college clubs were complying with the law and that some were not, but that none was considering going dry. In the end, their spokesman, Thomas Slocum, recommended that the question of whether or not to restrict alcoholic beverages not be submitted to the members.

On behalf of the House Committee he revealed, however, that a counter would shortly be installed somewhere in the clubhouse at which soft drinks would be served, and that a tea table would be set up in the Grill Room every afternoon.

At a reception in Harvard Hall on August 15 for newly commissioned graduates of the R.O.T.C. program in Cambridge, Colonel Roosevelt lamented the fact that not a single American rifle had yet been fired at the enemy. Two weeks later, word reached the Club of the death in Paris, following an operation, of Vice-President Wendell, who was in the French capital representing Harvard at the foundation of the American University Union and working to establish a fund for American aviators in France. Had he lived, Wendell probably would one day have headed the Club, but as it was, his myriad, various and selfless services to it over decades left his fellows much in his debt.

In mid-September, at the behest of the War Department in collaboration with the New York City Police Department, the Board agreed to maintain a clubhouse for enlisted men, to be known as the National Service Club No. 1 for Soldiers and Sailors, in a three-story building at Seventh Avenue and 33rd Street, opposite Pennsylvania Station. A few well-to-do members put up the $1,500 needed to keep the facility going for a month, and the Board resolved to seek further contributions from all of the members; then the call went out for volunteers to serve, a few hours a week, as hosts at the service club, helping to make lonely doughboys and swabbies feel at home.

But what about officers? Early in November, with the service club going full blast, Police Commissioner Arthur Woods '92 AM (hon.) '16 told the Board that the War and Navy Departments were hoping that the principal clubs in the city would extend a welcome to officers in their respective branches. He suggested that the Harvard Club take the lead by opening its doors to as many as it could accommodate. In the meantime, however, the Club had apparently acted on its own, for later that month President Appleton announced that 352 officers stationed at Camp Upton had received cards entitling them to its privileges. At the Board's next meeting House Committee Chairman Stack reported that 569 cards had been issued to Army officers, adding that in his, Stack's, opinion, it would be wise, for the sake of the Club's financial health, to distribute many more of these cards.

That month, some friends of the late vice-president bought, from The Players, a fine pastel portrait of Evert Wendell by Albert Sterner, and at the Club's request Secretary of War Newton D. Baker sent an auto-graphed photograph of himself for display in National Service Club No. 1, expressing "apprecia-tion for all the Harvard Club of New York is doing in the interests of the Army and Navy." In Russia, meanwhile, the new Bolshevik rulers, brought to power by the October (i.e., November) Revolu-tion, concluded a separate peace with the enemy: This would enable the Germans to concentrate their forces along their western front, dashing Allied hopes that the arrival on the scene of half a million fresh American troops would suffice to ensure victory.

Evert J. Wendell

In 1918 the annual dinner was again omitted, "postponed indefinitely due to war conditions." Just before the extra monthly dinner that was sub-stituted for it, on January 26, 1918, an incident occurred at the bar that would have embarrassing consequences for the Club. A certain member ventured some disparaging comments on President Wilson; another member, incensed, called the first speaker an insulting name; and in sec-onds fists were flying. Other imbibers quickly separated the antagonists, but by then a third member was on his way downtown to the Associated Press office on Chambers Street, where he blurted out an account of what he had witnessed; told that the AP wasn't interested, he hurried over to the City News Association on Church Street, where someone took down his story, together with copious details about the informant himself, and the following morning several dailies, including the least savory, carried gleeful reports of a squalid barroom brawl breaking out over the president's actions and character in the ultra-respectable Harvard Club. Naturally, the Club brought charges against the informant, but when, at his hearing three months later, he offered sincere apologies all around, he was neither expelled nor even suspended, but merely reprimanded.

In the volatile circumstances of wartime, the slate of officers elected at the annual meeting on May 24—Appleton for president, J. P. Morgan for vice-president, Greene for secretary and George Whitney for treasurer— proved even less durable than its predecessor: within days Greene would cable from London, where he was with the American Shipping Mission, to say that he expected to be away at least another year and could not possibly serve. Anton Schefer was elected in his place, but then—again within days—he, too, resigned to enter government service. Finally, Chorister Rogers, back in New York after several months in France with the Y.M.C.A., would be pressed into service as secretary.

In a special report, Chairman Marvin of the Committee on Military and Naval Service presented the best available information on the Club at war. Of the Club's 4,857 members, 1,247, about one-quarter, were on active service, 976 in the American and Allied armies, 203 in the Navy and another 68 in Europe with the Red Cross, Y.M.C.A. and American Ambulance Field Service. In addition, committee records showed another 731 members engaged in other war-related work, including members of the diplomatic corps and men in service with the Red Cross and on war commissions and missions, so that, altogether, 1,978 members, about two in five, were rendering war service of some kind.

So far as was known, twenty-seven members had, until then, died in the service of the United States or its allies or in consequence of war conditions, but with American troops being shipped abroad in the tens of thousands and rushed to the front, that figure was bound to increase.

On June 12 the Board, despairing of finding decent help and determined to cut costs, discontinued all service in the Grill Room and Harvard Hall, decreeing that all meals be served buffet style in the dining room. Meanwhile, the Squash Committee had reluctantly concluded that not enough members were using the courts to justify retaining the well-liked pro, Stephen Ferron; thereafter, the courts would be in charge of a marker.

In mid-July, with Americans in and out of uniform avidly following developments in the newspapers, General Ludendorff launched what would prove to be the last phase of Germany's 1918 offensive. In three days the assault played itself out, and on July 18 Marshal Foch, the Allied commander-in-chief, ordered a counterattack. This offensive, as General Pershing would write, "turned the tide of war." On August 10 Pershing obtained Allied consent to an independent American army commanded by himself, with Colonel George C. Marshall as his operations officer; in mid-September an American-led force of ten American and three French divisions captured the Saint-Mihiel salient; and on September 26 the Meuse-Argonne campaign, involving 896,000 American officers and men, began. Everywhere, the Allies were pressing forward and the enemy under siege. On September 30 Bulgaria, smallest of the Central Powers, capitulated, and a few days later a new German chancellor was addressing peace overtures to President Wilson.

At the Club, as October began, Treasurer Whitney resigned to enter national service; the Board replaced him with Winthrop Burr '84, confirmed Francis Rogers as secretary and elected Gardner Lamson '77 chorister. And Chairman Percy S. Straus '97 joked that his Committee on Appointments would soon be buttonholing returning Harvard veterans on the docks as they disembarked, to start finding them jobs without delay.

On the subject of employment, American women had been holding down jobs previously reserved for men ever since the country had entered the war, thereby earning the nation's gratitude and respect, but in spite of this—and of the prospect that with the imminent adoption of the Nineteenth Amendment to the Constitution they would shortly have the vote, and, in principle, political parity with men—many men clearly preferred to keep them at a distance. Thus when, on October 9, Secretary Rogers read aloud a letter by member J. P. Hazen Perry '03 proposing that some privileges of the Club be extended to women, the Board decided that "any such radical departure from the customs of the Club was at the present time inexpedient." Were these men misogynists? They would undoubtedly have denied the charge, perhaps citing in their defense the assistance several of them were rendering just then to the National League for Women's Service. The N.L.W.S. ladies feared that they would need another ambulance in which to transport wounded servicemen from incoming ships to hospitals and convalescent sites; informed of this, Acting Chairman Lawrence E. Sexton of the Committee on Military and Naval Service approached a few well-off members, who promptly subscribed $1,800 for the vehicle—to be known, incidentally, as the Harvard Club ambulance.

At 11:00 A..M. on November 11, by the terms of an armistice signed in Marshal Foch's dining car on a siding in Compiègne, France, the most terrible war of all time ended. At the Club, the reaction appears to have been one of inexpressible relief. Two members of the Club—Colonel Charles W. Whittlesey, L'08 and Captain George G. McMurtry '99, had been awarded the country's highest decoration for valor, the Congressional Medal of Honor, and in December President Appleton formally acknowledged, in letters, the Club's pride in them.

With peace restored, the 1919 New Year's Day open house would have been a cheery affair, but six days later sadness may well have pervaded the clubhouse as members noted the passing, early that morning in his beloved Oyster Bay home, Sagamore Hill, of their illustrious fellow member Theodore Roosevelt, felled at sixty by a heart attack. But if the man himself was gone, the spirit he had incarnated of life as a perpetual quest lived on in certain members, for example Vilhjalmur Stefansson, back in New York after five and a half years in the Arctic, who three nights later would address the Club on "The Value of Northern Exploration."

Another adventurer, as it happened, had recently come to the attention of the Club's governors. Twice in December John Reed, still a staff writer for the radical weekly *The Masses*, had cashed personal checks at the Club, for $15 and $15.10, respectively. Both checks had bounced. The treasurer had written the journalist seeking an explanation, and a few days later he received his letter back annotated as follows:

> My dear Mr. Burr:
> The explanation is that my salary was not sent to the bank as it should have been until four days late. Naturally I have remedied the mistake. But I object very much to the tone of this letter.
> 
> John Reed.

By then, however, Treasurer Burr had received from the Fifth Avenue Bank a check made out to the Club by Reed in the amount of $30.10. It was stamped, in block capitals, INSUFFICIENT FUNDS.

Hearing nothing more from Reed, Burr charged him in a letter with "conduct prejudicial to the interest of the Club" and invited him to respond in person to the Board; Reed wrote back defending his actions but failed to appear at the next meeting of the Board, which thereupon suspended him for six months. In fact, Reed was both too busy and too far distant to attend the meeting. In late February he and his wife, Louise Bryant, testified before a Senate committee in Washington, and a few days later, in Philadelphia, he gave an "incendiary speech"; he was arrested, but then released. During that year of 1919 he would publish *Ten Days That Shook the World*, widely considered the best eyewitness account of the Bolshevik Revolution.

Meanwhile, in January, Chairman Marvin presented updated figures—still, he warned, not necessarily final—of the Club's participation in the war: of 4,960 members, 1,487 had served in the armed forces of the United States and its allies and 54 had died, wherefor the Club's service flag would display the numeral 1,487 and fifty-four gold stars. On the sixteenth, Nebraska became the thirty-sixth state to ratify the Eighteenth Amendment to the Constitution, prohibiting the manufacture, sale and transportation of intoxicating liquors, which, having thus been approved by the legislatures of three-quarters of the states, would become law a year to the day thereafter.

That, obviously, was going to be a development of major concern to the Club, and indeed to all clubs.

While the Club still lacked a portrait of the late Amory G. Hodges, president 1913–16, such a painting did exist and would go on display as soon as its creator, a Peruvian artist named Bacaflor, could be talked out of certain reservations he had about it. But the Club possessed no likeness of its second president, Frederick A. Lane, donor of the precedent-setting Lane dinner. At the Board's request, William M. Ivins '01 of the Committee on Literature and Art, a lawyer who two years before had given up his practice to join the Metropolitan Museum as its curator of prints, inquired into the matter. In a month of research he uncovered numerous details of Lane's life but no picture of him, and to this day Lane remains the only president of the Club whose image is not to be found anywhere in the clubhouse.

At the annual meeting on May 24 Robert P. Perkins '84, a onetime oarsman who had until recently been the commissioner of the American Red Cross to Italy, was elected president and Thomas Slocum vice-president; Francis Rogers stayed on as secretary, while Francis M. Weld '97 began what would turn out to be a thirteen-year stint as treasurer. (Weld, a banker, was the son and namesake of the physician who had served, 1881–83, as the Club's ninth president.)

In June, the Club finally closed down the enlisted men's facility at Seventh Avenue and 33rd Street and returned the building to its owners. During its twenty months of existence upward of 60,000 soldiers and sailors had made use of it and at least 8,000 had stayed overnight; its paid staff, moreover, had often been supplemented by volunteers from the Club.

Clifford M. Holland

That month, though few men at the Club other than his friends were aware of it, Clifford M. Holland '05 SB'06, a civil engineer and a member of the Admissions Committee, took on the biggest challenge of his unusual career. After thirteen years with the Rapid Transit Commission and its successor the Public Service Commission, working on both the first Battery Tunnel and on four double subway tunnels under the East River, Holland quit the P.S.C. to become chief engineer of both the New York State and New Jersey interstate bridge and tunnel commissions, with a mandate to design and construct a vehicular tunnel under the Hudson River.

Holland started working on this very ambitious project on July 1. One week later, in the Club's public rooms, several members were scandalized by the presence among them of Eamon De Valera, head of the militant Sinn Fein and president of the self-proclaimed Republic of Ireland, who had escaped from a British jail and come here to raise funds and solicit support for an independent Ireland. They protested, but as De Valera had been brought to the clubhouse by a member and conducted himself circumspectly enough therein, the Board took no action.

Meanwhile, the Club's thousand-plus veterans of land warfare, finding the spectacle of younger men in uniform scrambling for territory on their behalf much preferable to their own recent experience contesting for turf in France, rejoiced in the resumption, after two autumns without a game, of a full intercollegiate football schedule. The 1919 Harvard team gave them plenty to cheer about, winning its first six encounters without once being so much as scored on. On November 8, at Princeton, before a crowd that included no fewer than 1,484 Club members and their guests conveyed there in three special trains, the Crimson and Tiger elevens tied, 10–10, but two weeks later Harvard defeated Yale 10–3, to finish the season with the cumulative score, against nine opponents, of 232–13.

To the astonishment, no doubt, of more than a few older members of the Club, the Harvard footballers, judged the best in the East, entrained to California at the end of 1919, and on New Year's Day 1920, in the Rose Bowl at Pasadena, eked out a 7–6 victory over the University of Oregon. The news of that epochal win, which presumably reached 27 West 44th Street via the ticker (by then installed in the Bar) must, for the members huddled around it, have made for a thoroughly agreeable introduction to the new decade.

On January 16 the country and the Club went dry, and two weeks later, for the first time, no wine flowed at the annual dinner.

In February, for the Committee on Military and Naval Service (still in existence fifteen months after the end of the war), Chairman Marvin submitted to the Board a design, from the drafting tables of McKim, Mead & White, for a memorial to members who had died in the conflict. The memorial was to be set up in the alcove near the southeastern corner of Harvard Hall, under the trumpeting elephant head, and its central feature was to be a tablet of red marble, covering most of one side of the alcove, to which would be affixed bronze capital letters spelling out the names of the fallen. Above this would hang a tapestry copied from a cartoon by the well-known mural painter and designer-weaver of tapestries Albert Herter, whose son, Sergeant Everit A. Herter '14, had died of wounds in

France. The ensemble would be completed (and unified) by one or two figures to be created by sculptor Robert Ingersoll Aitken. While no one present found fault with the proposed memorial, several were dismayed by its estimated cost—tablet, $6,000; cartoon and tapestry, $6,000; sculpture, $5,000—so the Board put off dealing with the matter.

Looking ahead to the Club's March meeting, the officers and Board members steeled themselves for a rebellion in the ranks over the proposal to raise entrance fees and dues, but in the event the members approved the necessary changes to the bylaws without demur. And at the annual meeting in May President Perkins announced with satisfaction that the Club had finally acquired a portrait of former President Hodges, the artist having at last agreed to let Mrs. Hodges present it. Meanwhile, the Club's governors had been relieved of a nagging worry. They knew that before the Club year ended on April 30 some members would resign rather than pay the increased dues, and the question was, how many? The final figure, 109 resignations, must have seemed reassuringly low, though it contrasted rather starkly with the number of resignations the previous May, to wit, eleven.

One member who resigned around then, but not over money, was Robert C. Benchley. Having long served on the Admissions Committee, he had been present at a meeting of that body in October 1919 at which a certain John A. Macy '99 AM'00 had been proposed for membership but held over pending investigation of a charge of radicalism. (In 1916 Macy had published *Socialism in America*, and although he found much in that social system to criticize, he clearly preferred it to capitalism.) At successive meetings that winter and spring Macy's candidacy had been repeatedly held over, but with fewer committee members opposing him each time.

Macy had much to recommend him. Entering Harvard almost totally unknown, he had acquired top academic honors and achieved considerable extracurricular success (editor-in-chief of the *Advocate*, an editor of the *Lampoon*, elected to the best clubs, class poet). Thereafter he had taught English at Harvard for two years and worked on *Youth's Companion* for eight, meanwhile publishing *Edgar Allan Poe* and *A Child's Guide to Reading;* in 1913 his book *The Spirit of American Literature* had come out and he had become, briefly, literary editor of the Boston *Herald*. Although he often gently reproached his fellows for their narrowness of outlook, he had long been a valued member of Boston's very respectable St. Botolph Club, and it was there that he had composed a poem, "France," that had deeply moved its hearers when read aloud at a banquet honoring the French military mission to Harvard. As to his personal qualifications for membership, his fellow journalist, Ernest Gruening '07 MD'12, was to describe him in a *Dictionary of American Biography* entry as "impulsively warm-hearted" and "generous," adding that "a genial sweetness, a deep kindliness, pervaded his personal contacts."

Benchley was a liberal, a registered Republican, and no socialist, but he felt strongly that a man's political opinions should not bar him from membership in the Club. So, it turned out, did other, solidly conservative, members: Thus as Macy's case remained, awkwardly, unresolved, the committee received letters making this very point from such pillars of the Establishment as Thomas W. Lamont '92, Eliot Wadsworth '98 and Edgar Wells '97. At last just two holdouts—the committee's "intellectual pygmies," Benchley called them—still blocked Macy's election; they were, however, unbudgeable, and what was more could, in a formal vote, deny the majority its every wish. Once more, then, a vote was postponed, and Benchley, finally perceiving that the cause was lost, dashed off a furious letter to Secretary Rogers, declaring that if Macy could not belong to the Club he, Benchley, should not, and was therefore resigning.

Absurdly, there were complications: Because he owed the Club money Benchley could not resign, and because he had incurred charges after being posted for nonpayment he had been suspended for a year. Just before that year was up Benchley would pay his bill in full and resign definitively. His many friends at the Club would miss him, the more so as when, approaching the clubhouse on foot around lunchtime, they would often spy him strolling happily westward toward the Algonquin Hotel. They took some comfort, however, in the fact that the Club was now so large and diverse in its membership that a member arriving on his own at the clubhouse door could be reasonably sure of finding congenial company within.

Since the start of the year and decade much had happened. Chairman Straus's efforts to disband his Committee on Employment, formerly on

Appointments, on the ground that it had completed its postwar mission of finding work for former servicemen, had found support in an unexpected quarter when President Lowell embraced the idea of a single big intercollegiate employment agency. A peace treaty had been adopted by the Allies in Paris and rejected by the Senate, and the New York State Assembly had denied five duly-elected socialist assemblymen their seats, an act the Bar Association had condemned in a strongly worded resolution signed by, among others, C. C. Burlingham, Grenville Clark, Ogden L. Mills and five other lawyer members of the Club. At the instigation of Attorney General A. Mitchell Palmer, Justice Department agents had rounded up thousands of allegedly subversive foreign nationals for deportation, but then a reaction had set in against these "Palmer raids." Americans in general seemed thoroughly sick of Europe's quarrels and eager to get on with the simple enjoyment of life. All signs pointed to a coming repudiation of the Democrats, the "war party." And the top contender for the Republican presidential nomination was the Club's own General Wood.

Model of the U.S.S. *Harvard*

# 11

# THE
# TWENTIES
# (1920–1929)

Shortly after noon on Saturday, June 12, 1920, members who had just completed their regular work week that morning began arriving at the clubhouse. After lunch, those who stayed on made frequent trips to the bar—not necessarily for refreshment, although by then the Club had, like most such institutions, found ways to get around the new draconian ban on liquor, but to check the news ticker there for late word from Chicago, where the Republicans were in conclave. In the balloting, which had begun the night before, General Wood had led from the start, but Governor Frank Lowden of Illinois had gained on him until, on the sixth ballot, he and Wood were tied at $311^1/_2$ votes apiece. When two more ballots produced little change it was clear that the convention was deadlocked; Governor Lowden released his delegates from their pledges of support and a two-hour recess was called during which the party chiefs conferred and agreed on a compromise candidate. That evening, on the ninth ballot, Senator Warren G. Harding of Ohio received $374^1/_2$ votes and on the tenth he was nominated, whereupon the delegates picked Massachusetts Governor Calvin Coolidge to run for vice president.

If General Wood was thus out of the running, the Club would nonetheless have a major party candidate in the race, for on July 6 the Democrats chose Franklin D. Roosevelt to run with their standard bearer, Ohio Governor James M. Cox. But in November, after what the distinguished journalist and member of the Club Mark Sullivan '00 would call an "extraordinarily unexciting" campaign, the Harding-Coolidge ticket won handily.

Just as Sullivan was to chronicle the American experience through the first quarter of the twentieth century in *Our Times* (six volumes, published 1926–35), another journalist-author in the Club, Frederick Lewis Allen '12, would, in *Only Yesterday* (1931), recount the history of this country and its people from the end of the Great War to the onset of the Great Depression. During these last years relatively few members of the Club occupied high positions of power in government, but a remarkably large number of them contributed importantly to the cultural life of the time.

Among politicians, the most consistently successful was W. L. Mackenzie King AM'98, PhD'09, LLD'23, prime minister of Canada, except for a few months in 1926, from 1921 to 1930 (and later, 1935–48). Even more durable in office was Congressman Hamilton Fish, who represented an upstate New York district continuously from 1921 to 1945. And in 1928 Franklin D. Roosevelt, Fish's neighbor and future fierce political opponent, was elected governor of the state. In contrast, Theodore Roosevelt, Jr. '09 ably filled appointive posts (assistant secretary of the Navy 1921–24, governor of Puerto Rico 1929–32 and governor general of the Philippines 1932–33), but failed to win election in 1924 as Republican candidate for governor of New York. (His half-brother-in-law Nicholas Longworth '91 was speaker of the House of Representatives 1926–31, but by then he had resigned from the Club.) Member Ogden L. Mills, a congressman from New York 1921–27, became assistant secretary of the Treasury 1927–32 and secretary 1932–33, and Hanford MacNider '11, national commander of the American Legion 1921–22, was named assistant secretary of war 1925–28 and minister to Canada 1930–32. Toward the end of the Twenties, Harvard Corporation treasurer Charles Francis Adams '88 L'92 became secretary of the Navy, to serve 1929–33; meanwhile, Dwight F. Davis '00 was assistant secretary of war 1923–25 and secretary 1925–29 before becoming governor general of the Philippines. Incidentally, Davis had been, as an undergraduate, intercollegiate tennis champion and (with Holcombe Ward '00, also a member) national doubles champion. In 1900 he had established the Davis Cup, an international tennis challenge cup that has since come to signify world team championship.

During the boom years of so-called Coolidge prosperity, 1925–29, it almost seemed as if membership in the Club was a prerequisite for a top diplomatic post, with the ambassadorships to Great Britain, France, and Japan held by, respectively, industrialist Alanson B. Houghton '86, political leader Myron T. Herrick LLD (hon.) '15 and lawyer Charles MacVeagh '81. (Herrick had already been America's envoy to France, 1912–14 and since 1921, and Houghton our man in Germany, 1922–25, while two other members, lawyer-author Richard W. Child '03 L'06 and career foreign service officer Joseph Clark Grew '02, had been, respectively, ambassador to Italy [1921–24] and minister to Denmark and Switzerland, in 1920 and 1921.) In 1927 Grew was named ambassador to Turkey, and in 1930 former Governor General of the Philippines W. Cameron Forbes '92 LLD'12 became ambassador to Japan, to be succeeded two years later by Grew, who would remain in Tokyo until the outbreak of World War II. Among jurist members of the Club, Felix Frankfurter, a professor at the Harvard Law School since 1914, helped to found the American Civil Liberties Union in 1920, and in that year was appointed to the new chair of administrative law established by a gift of the Club's own James Byrne. Augustus Hand '90 L'94 was a conspicuous ornament of the New York bar, and beginning in 1924 his cousin, Judge Learned Hand '93, L'96, illuminated the Second Circuit, soon beginning to acquire, through his opinions and frequently cited appellate decisions, a national reputation as a defender of free speech.

The Club certainly did not lack professional practitioners of free speech. Conservative Mark Sullivan commented regularly on current issues in the New York *Herald Tribune*, as did liberal Oswald Garrison Villard weekly in *The Nation*, while Walter Lippmann offered penetrating appraisals of leading political personalities and passing events in the New York *World*—published, incidentally, by a group headed by Ralph Pulitzer '00, whose brother and fellow member Joseph Pulitzer, Jr. '07 published the St. Louis *Post Dispatch*. Historian Archibald Cary Coolidge '87 LLD'16 edited *Foreign Affairs* from 1922 to 1927. Edward S. Martin, who had founded *Life* in 1883, was still writing for that magazine, while contributing a monthly "Easy Chair" column to *Harper's*, on the staff of which Frederick Lewis Allen, its future editor, began in 1921 an association that would last for a third of a century. Robert E. Sherwood '18, having earlier shared an office with Robert Benchley at *Vanity Fair*, worked and wrote for *Life*, becoming its editor from 1924 to 1928. At the *Times*, following a stint on the *Harvard Alumni Bulletin*, Brooks Atkinson '17 edited the paper's Sunday *Book Review* from 1922 to 1925, when he turned drama critic and was replaced by fellow member J. Donald Adams '13. Meanwhile, Roy Larsen '21 was rising fast on *Time*, and in 1927 Ernest Gruening bought a newspaper, the Portland (Maine) *Evening News*, which he would edit into the 1930s. Finally, H. V. Kaltenborn '09 of the Brooklyn *Eagle* pioneered, starting in 1922, as a news analyst with the infant medium of radio, becoming a full-time broadcaster-commentator for CBS in 1929.

During the War-to-Depression period several of these journalists produced outstanding histories, biographies and other works of nonfiction— e.g., Walter Lippmann's *A Preface to Morals* (1929)—but so did other Club members, among them John Jay Chapman '84 (in Edmund Wilson's view the best writer on literature of his generation), who published, notably, *Letters and Religion* (1924). A year before that Henry James '99 brought out a life of former Club president Peter Olney's brother Richard Olney, attorney general and secretary of state in President Cleveland's second administration, and in 1931 his two-volume *Charles W. Eliot* was awarded the Pulitzer Prize for biography. Literary criminologist Edmund Pearson '02 wrote *Studies in Murder* (1924), *Murder at Smutty Nose* (1926) and other books of the genre, while economist Stuart Chase '10 launched a remarkable career as an author of popular books on important topics with *The Tragedy of Waste* (1925, on the conservation of natural resources) and *Your Money's Worth* (1927, advice to consumers). Dutch-born Hendrik Willem Van Loon '06, a prolific producer of nonfiction bestsellers, turned out *Ancient Man* (1920), *The Story of Mankind* (1921), *The Story of the Bible* (1923), *America* (1927) and *Man, the Miracle-Maker* (1928); Vilhjalmur Stefansson published, between 1921 and 1924, four books about his Arctic explorations; and Mark Antony DeWolfe Howe '87 of the *Atlantic Monthly* won the 1924 Pulitzer award for biography for his *Barrett Wendell and His Letters*. Scholar members, including Harvard professors, were the authors as well as the subjects of important contributions to letters: thus George Lyman Kittredge published *Sir Thomas Malory* (1925) and *Witchcraft in Old and New England* (1929), and John Livingston Lowes AM'03 PhD'05 his extraordinary study of Coleridge, *The Road to Xanadu* (1927).

Publishers in the Club included future envoy to Greece Lincoln MacVeagh '13, president of the Dial Press; Cass Canfield '19 of Harper & Brothers; and George Palmer Putnam '10 of G. P. Putnam's Sons, who in 1931 would marry the aviatrix Amelia Earhart. Maxwell Perkins was the best known book editor of his and perhaps any subsequent time, nursing to print the novels of, among other authors, F. Scott Fitzgerald, Ernest Hemingway and Thomas Wolfe G'22.

Of the Club's own living fiction writers the first to have attained national fame was Owen Wister '82 L'88, whose classic Western novel *The Virginian* (1902) would several times be made into a movie. Also dramatized and filmed was *Seven Keys to Baldpate* (1913) by Earl Derr Biggers '07, who was even better known for his novels, also adapted for the screen, about Chinese detective Charlie Chan. Another creator of a celebrated fictional character was attorney Arthur Train '96, whose shrewd country lawyer Ephraim Tutt figured in numerous stories in the *Saturday Evening Post* that were reprinted in collections. Although banker Edward Streeter '14 wrote little for publication during the Twenties he was gratefully remembered for his hilarious *Dere Mable: Love Letters of a Rookie* (1918) and its sequel, *That's Me All Over, Mable* (1919). Meanwhile, John P. Marquand '15 turned out stories for the *Saturday Evening Post* and several novels of romance and adventure— trial runs, as time would show, for the gently satirical novelistic studies of well-born New Englanders that would, in the coming decade and later, win him critical acclaim, many readers and a Pulitzer Prize (for *The Late George Apley*, 1937). Thomas Wolfe, a member by virtue of a graduate year studying drama, taught English at New York University from 1924 to 1930 and published four autobiographical novels, including *Look Homeward, Angel* (1929) and *Of Time and the River* (1935), before dying in 1938. F. Van Wyck Mason '24 started publishing his popular detective stories and historical romances. And two talented brothers—grandsons of the John La Farge who had created stained glass windows for Memorial

Hall and John Harvard's boyhood church in London and sons of architect Christopher Grant La Farge, the designer of New York's Cathedral of St. John the Divine—began testing out the possibilities of literary genres that each could ultimately almost claim as his own. In *Laughing Boy* (Pulitzer Prize, 1929), anthropologist Oliver Hazard Perry La Farge '24 produced the first of several novels about American Indians, while Christopher La Farge '20 conducted private experiments in poetic storytelling that would lead him to compose, in the 1930s, two novels entirely in verse.

Other poets in the Club included Hispanic scholar Archer M. Huntington AM (hon.) '04, Witter Bynner '02, Percy Mackaye '97 and Ogden Nash '24. Among artist members were portraitist and aquarellist Charles Hopkinson '91, painter and sculptor George Biddle '08 and painter Waldo Peirce '07, living in Paris but soon to return to his native Maine. Paul J. Sachs '00, a member of Harvard's fine arts faculty since 1917, became a full professor in 1927. At least one member, expatriate Samuel L. M. Barlow '14 of Eze, France, was a composer.

Thanks to Harvard's 47 Workshop, a playwrights' course and production laboratory set up in 1906 by Professor of English George Pierce Baker '87, the Club numbered in its ranks such giants of American dramaturgy as George Abbott G'12, Eugene O'Neill G'15 and Sidney Howard G'16, as well as Robert E. Sherwood, who had managed—just barely—to get through College after serving in France with the Canadian Black Watch and writing a Hasty Pudding show. Abbott, starting out as an actor, began to co-write and direct plays in 1919, scored a hit in 1925 with *The Fall Guy*, and after directing motion pictures 1927–30, became, increasingly, a theatrical producer; at this writing (1994) he is, reportedly, still going strong at age 106. O'Neill, still accounted by some America's greatest playwright, turned out 18 Broadway plays between *Moon of the Caribbees* (1919) and *Mourning Becomes Electra* (1931), including *Desire Under the Elms* (1924) and *The Great God Brown* (1925), winning Pulitzer awards for *Beyond the Horizon* (1920), *Anna Christie* (1922) and *Strange Interlude* (1928). Howard wrote, among other dramas, *Swords* (1921), *Yellowjack* (1928) and *They Knew What They Wanted* (1925, Pulitzer Prize), as well as the screenplay for *Gone With the Wind*, while Sherwood, belatedly discovering his true calling as a playwright in *The*

*Road to Rome* (1927), became thereafter a frequent contributor to Broadway, destined to collect three Pulitzer awards.

The Club's dramatists were not its only members who made their livings from Broadway theaters, most of them conveniently located just a short stroll west of the clubhouse. Others included actors Walter Hampden '00 and Osgood Perkins '14, set designer Robert Edmond Jones '10, producer Vinton Freedley '14 and two young drama critics, Brooks Atkinson and John Mason Brown '23. And as the Club's roster included one man who had explored vast tracts of Arctic tundra and another who was building a tunnel under the Hudson, it contained at least one landscape architect—Frederick Law Olmsted '94, the able son and namesake of a more famous one—and several architects, the best known of whom was probably Henry Ives Cobb '81. On it, too, were notable men of science, among them physicist Theodore Lyman '97, psychiatrist Carl Binger '10 and neurologist and psychologist Morton Prince '75, founder and editor (until his death in 1929) of the *Journal of Abnormal Psychology*. Notable educators were also members of the Club: e.g., Professor of English Robert Morss Lovett '92 of the University of Chicago, President Frank Aydelotte, PhD '03 of Swarthmore and biologist Clarence Cook Little '10, president of the University of Maine 1922–25 and the University of Michigan 1925–29, and after 1929 managing director of what is now the American Cancer Society.

Meanwhile, certain Club members racked up noteworthy records at various sports and games. In 1920, off New York Bay, Charles Francis Adams piloted the yacht *Resolute* to a 3–2 win over Sir Thomas Lipton's *Shamrock IV*, retaining the America's Cup for the United States. And at three-year intervals, in 1921, 1924 and 1927, Devereux Milburn captained U.S. polo teams in successive defeats of teams representing Great Britain.

Having fielded four national champions of squash tennis during the previous decade (Alfred Stillman '03 in 1911, 1912 and 1914; George Whitney '07 in 1913; Fillmore Van S. Hyde '16 in 1918; and John W. Appel, Jr. '06 in 1919), the Club continued to dominate the sport, with Hyde ranking first in the nation in 1921, 1924 and 1926, and William Rand, Jr. '17 in 1925. But although younger squash players at the Club opted increasingly for squash racquets, only one of them, W. Palmer Dixon '25, attained top national ranking—twice, in 1925 and 1926. In two other indoors sports played with racquets, Club members excelled with fair consistency: thus in 1926 and 1928–29 the country's top-seeded court tennis players were, respectively, C. Suydam Cutting '12 and Hewitt Morgan '17, while in racquets Clarence C. Pell '08, rated by some experts the greatest American player of all time, was America's number one player in 1920, 1921, 1922, 1924, 1925, 1927 and 1928.

If court tennis and racquets were arcane activities indulged in by a few rich men, the same could hardly be said of bridge, the card game played often and avidly in millions of homes, most of them modest, across America, and indeed around the world. The phenomenal popularity of contract bridge, the form of the game that largely supplanted auction bridge in the last years of the Twenties, resulted from important innovations introduced to it in 1925 by Club member Harold S. Vanderbilt '07. A railroad executive, Vanderbilt was also a keen yachtsman, and in 1930, off Newport at the helm of the *Enterprise*, he scored a memorable victory: having outsailed Navy Secretary Adams for the honor of defending the America's Cup, he defeated Lipton's last challenger, *Shamrock V*, in four straight races.

Finally, what about Harvard? In the midst of their active lives members did not forget their club's reason for existence; during the 1920s, indeed, they not only responded more generously that ever before to financial appeals from Cambridge but gave the University no fewer than six endowed chairs. In addition to the Byrne Professorship of Administrative Law (1920), these were:

The George F. Baker Professorship of Economics, established in 1920 in the name of the banker-philanthropist who, having given Harvard funds with which to found a graduate school of business administration, would donate another $5 million for the construction of a group of buildings to accommodate it, south of the Charles River and east of Soldiers Field, that would be completed in 1927. The chair was the gift of Baker's son, George F. Baker, Jr.

The Nathan Littauer Professorship of Jewish Literature and Philosophy, established in 1925, honoring his father, from a gift of Lucius

N. Littauer '78, the donor as well of $2 million, which would ultimately go to founding a graduate school of public administration (1935).

The Theodore William Richards Professorship of Chemistry, established in 1925 in honor of his old teacher—a Nobel Prize–winner (1914) and father-in-law of future Harvard president James B. Conant '14 PhD'16—from a gift of Thomas W. Lamont.

The Charles Eliot Norton Professorship of Poetry, established in 1925 by a gift of Charles C. Stillman '98 in honor of his Harvard mentor, Professor (of art history) Charles Eliot Norton.

The Isidor Straus Professorship of Business History, established in 1927 from gifts of Jesse I. Straus '93, Percy S. Straus '97 and Herbert N. Straus '03 in memory of their father—the co-owner, with his brother Nathan, of R. H. Macy & Co.—lost in the *Titanic* in 1912.

A seventh chair with a New York provenance that would be given to Harvard during the decade was the gift, not of a member of the Club, but of the widow of one: the Charles Stebbins Fairchild Professorship of Comparative Public Law, established in 1928 by a bequest of Mrs. Fairchild in memory of her late husband, the onetime secretary of the Treasury, president of the Club 1901–05.


Out for a good time, avid of novelty, impatient with moral and legal constraints, the Roaring Twenties (jazz, flappers and hip flasks, raccoon coats and rumble seats, bootleg whiskey and bathtub gin) were hardly staid or static—not for relatively well-off young white American males, anyway. Yet throughout that turbulent decade the Club—in which, as usual, the young abounded—remained surprisingly stable. Year after year it grew—but gradually, so that its facilities were rarely overtaxed. And year after year it made money, enabling its financial managers to pay off more and more of its mortgage debt. To produce a profit while the cost of living was creeping upward they would again have to raise the dues and some charges, but at the same time the cost of a Harvard education was simultaneously increasing much more rapidly: Tuition for one year, with four courses, which had remained fixed at $150 throughout President Eliot's long tenure and gone up to $200 in 1913, would rise in 1922 to $250, in 1925 to $300 and in 1928 to $400.

In the spring of 1920 former Secretary Greene, determined that the Club have a copy of John Singer Sargent's portrait of President Roosevelt, wrote the artist, asking him to suggest a copyist. Sargent recommended Alexander R. James of Cambridge, a son of William James. Because Sargent's picture hung in the White House, permission to copy it had to be obtained from the Federal government, but instead of encountering bureaucratic delays the project sped through, as nonresident member Charles Moore, chairman of the National Commission of Fine Arts (and future biographer of McKim), was on hand in Washington to negotiate on the Club's behalf. In September Sargent's portrait was moved to the Corcoran Gallery; painter James went to work, and in November his copy arrived at 27 West 44th Street, where President Perkins pronounced it excellent.

In February 1921 Edgar Wills, the new chairman of the Committee on Literature and Art, reported the delivery to the Club of a portrait of former President Appleton by Joseph De Camp, and he informed the Board that certain well-to-do members were talking about establishing five annual Club scholarships to Harvard for city boys.

That winter so many members made use of the squash courts that sixty new lockers had to be installed, and the squash season itself was, so the Board's annual report would claim, "the most successful in the history of the Club," with the Club's team defeating the Yale Club's in its final match to wind up as number one in the metropolitan league. Meanwhile, devotees of billiards and backgammon, chess and bridge held their intramural tournaments; members took in a variety of musical programs and illustrated talks; the library and the plunge were much resorted to; the dining hall and the private dining rooms did a brisk business; and the bedrooms upstairs were regularly occupied. But although the Club appeared to be thriving, the Admissions Committee's Gilman Collamore '93 worried about a trend that in time could, he feared, seriously vitiate its character. Among recent candidates for admission, he informed the Board solemnly, nearly a quarter were lawyers—and, worse, the majority of these Harvard Law School products did not hold Harvard AB degrees.

(Collamore, a portly, mustachioed bachelor importer-broker of comestibles, was an authentic "character." Over many years he interviewed countless prospective members, most often standing with them by the counter west of the Grill Room, which today functions as a waiters' serving station but which was then, within the restrictions of Prohibition, a working bar; on meeting a candidate there he would invite him to take turns rolling dice to determine which of them, as the loser of the greater number of throws—typically, two out of three—would pay for the drinks. "Colly" would quickly put nervous young graduates of the College at their ease, but although he held the (mildly) advanced degree of AM, he could be witheringly chilly toward any graduate of a professional school he suspected of entertaining a high opinion of himself, addressing him sarcastically as "Doctor" at every opportunity. But if he deplored the steady (and inevitable) increase in the proportion of graduate school men among the candidates for admission, he did not let this predisposition affect his judgment of individuals. The metal plaque sunk in the top of the onetime bar identifies the site of his interviews as "Colly's Corner"; while the inscription below these words—"10 out of 19?"—refers to the fact that when luck happened to favor him in successive throws of the dice he would insist on continuing the play until he lost, thereby becoming obliged to pay for all the drinks that he and his interviewee had consumed.)

At the annual meeting in May 1921 the bylaws were amended to add 100 life memberships at $750 each and to divide the Committee on Literature and Art into two bodies. For the Committee on Scholarships, Edgar Wells announced with evident pleasure that five members of the Class of 1925, due to matriculate in September, were young New Yorkers holding Harvard Club scholarships. And in October George Whitney suggested shifting the start of the Club's fiscal year from May 1 to the beginning of the calendar year, a suggestion the Board would soon adopt. In the meantime, Admissions Chairman Collamore declined to excuse a certain member from having to pay the initiation fee and first year's dues of a candidate whom that member had successfully proposed for admission without the candidate's knowledge or consent.

For many months now the nation's economy had been in recession: unemployment was widespread, and at the November Board meeting Chairman Chadbourne of the Social and Civic Work Committee talked about the "pitiable condition" of former servicemen in the streets, inhibited from seeking work by the threadbare state of their clothes. Chadbourne readily won the Board's consent to inform resident members by mail about agencies in the city that would accept their old clothes for distribution to these unfortunates. Many members would respond to his appeal. An extra spur to compassion, no doubt, was the knowledge that among the city's estimated 75,000 jobless veterans were a number of Harvard graduates, surely including members of the Club.

Percy Straus had long represented the Club in talks with alumni groups from other institutions aimed at creating an intercollegiate employment bureau, and early in 1922 it began to look as if that bureau might actually come into being. In April, accordingly, House Committee Chairman Phillips B. Thompson '97 moved to discontinue the Committee on Employment. Chadbourne objected, insisting that the committee's efforts were sorely needed, and on May 11 he returned to this theme with gusto: Pointing out that President Lowell was now saying he would not call a meeting of college presidents on the matter until Harvard, Yale and Princeton were agreed on terms for the projected bureau, Chadbourne predicted—accurately, as things turned out—that that amenity would never be established. While the Club was, he acknowledged, a social organization, he maintained that it bore an inescapable responsibility toward the New York Harvard community, which included, just then, individuals who were truly destitute. Further, he urged that the Committee on Employment, bolstered by a budget of $1,000, be charged to do nothing whatever for men merely seeking a better job but concentrate on helping those with no work at all.

Chadbourne's sincerity and eloquence carried the day, and the Board adopted his proposal. Thus one problem was resolved, for the time being at any rate. But another long-standing problem—how best to honor those members who had died in the war—was no closer to a solution than it had been when the war ended, the design for a memorial the Club turned down that day as inappropriate being the third in a row from McKim, Mead & White it had rejected. Strange to say, the memorial problem would not finally be solved until six years later!

Apropos of persistent problems, a member of the House Committee had, earlier that year, raised anew an old spectre in the minds of a few impressionable Board members. Reminding his hearers that Harvard Hall was supported on wooden piles standing in water, he had warned that if a proposed 42nd Street subway were built the excavation could easily draw off the water, whereupon the piles would quickly rot and the entire northern half of the clubhouse would collapse. This apocalyptic prospect was not completely dispelled until Clifford Holland, arguably the world's leading authority on subterranean submarine construction, visited the Club's engine room and nethermost reaches. Holland felt no concern, he said, about the foundations of Harvard Hall, as there was plenty of water around the piles. He did not believe that the subway, if built, would affect these piles, and he was confident that the piles would last indefinitely.

At the annual meeting on May 19, the last one to be held at that time of year, James Byrne was elected president, with Thomas Slocum, John Elliott '12 and Francis M. Weld continuing as vice-president, secretary and treasurer.

The monthly meeting (until 1887 the only occasions apart from the annual dinner at which members came together) had naturally dwindled in importance since the existence of a clubhouse had permitted Club life to go on almost without interruption. Attendance at the meetings had waned, to the point that no objections were raised when Vice-President Slocum proposed doing away with all of the monthly meetings except the two at which the bylaws called for (1) the election of two members of the Nominating Committee and (2) the report of that body. The Board took Slocum's proposal under advisement, but in October Langdon Marvin topped it by proposing that the annual meeting and annual dinner be held consecutively on the same evening. The Board approved both proposals, and at the Club's October meeting—its last such meeting, of course—By-Law VII (Meetings) was amended so as to limit meetings of the Club to three a year: the annual meeting on the fourth Friday in January and the monthly meetings in November and December.

On January 26, 1923, for the first time, the Club's annual meeting and annual dinner were held consecutively; at the former, the officers, having served a "year" of eight months, were reelected. Three weeks later Nicholas Biddle died after a long illness. In March, Charles C. Stillman gave the Club 450 books from the private library of his undergraduate mentor, Professor Charles Eliot Norton. And a nonresident member, Theodore T. Scudder '11 of Boston, sparked excitement within the Board by proposing in a letter to give the Club a portrait of one of its founders, James H. Fay '59. Scudder was, it seemed, the only godson of Fay, a life-long bachelor, and his intention was to use a legacy from his godfather to have the latter's likeness painted in oils from a photograph for presentation to the Club. He also offered to arrange for the execution, at the Club's expense, of portraits of the four other founders, Amory, Haseltine, Kilbreth and Kinnicutt.

The next month, the library acquired at auction the earliest broadside catalogue in its collection, the *Catalogue Eorum* of 1751, in which the graduates' names were listed, in Latin, in order of their social standing. And in May Phillips B. Thompson urged his colleagues to consider refurbishing the private dining rooms, saying that many potential users were unwilling to hire any room except the Board (Mahogany) Room. Soon after this, Vincent Astor '15 offered to have one of the banquet rooms in the northern part of the clubhouse redone and redecorated in memory of Nicholas Biddle, and his offer was accepted with alacrity.

In June, the real estate firm of Douglas Gibbons, Inc., notified the Club that the Hotel Webster, next door on 45th Street, was for sale, at an asking price of $650,000. Although there was little sentiment at Number 27 for annexing that very large neighbor, the thought of acquiring all those bedrooms nevertheless made the prospect tempting. For the Club's shortage of bedrooms was acute: During the first four months of 1923 it had to spend hundreds of dollars on hotel accommodations for guests it had had to turn away, and on most nights the solarium dormitory (in which a bed cost $1.50) had been full. In late July, then, a special committee met to consider possible moves:

• Purchasing the Hotel Webster. (This suggestion was promptly rejected as impractical, a costly kind of overkill.)

• Leasing adjacent rooms in the Webster, cutting through the walls of both buildings to communicate with them and sealing them off on the hotel side. (But would the hotel's owners permit this?)

• Buying one of two nearby buildings—either the former Yale Club, now occupied by the D.K.E. Club, which was thinking of moving, or a small apartment house just east of the clubhouse on 45th Street, which had recently been on the market. (Either alternative would be prohibitively expensive.)

• Adding on two floors to the clubhouse above the squash courts. (This would not only cost a good deal but might also harmfully affect the squash courts' lighting and ventilation.)

• Leasing rooms in the new Hotel Shelton (Allerton House), nearing completion at Lexington Avenue and 48th Street, whose management was looking for organizations in need of extra space. (This alternative would provide a means of expanding the Club's facilities at comparatively little cost—but at too great a distance from the clubhouse.)

In the end, the committeemen decided that the Club's best bet would be to subdivide its existing bedroom space, redesigning the large rooms on the fourth and fifth floors of the old (1905) building so as to create three rooms where there were now two, thereby adding a total of ten new bedrooms the size of those then renting for $2.50 a night.

When, at summer's end, the Club resumed its usual rituals and rhythms, the country had a new chief executive, President Harding having died suddenly on August 2 and been succeeded by his vice president, Calvin Coolidge. In October Art Chairman George B. de Gersdorff '88 and the Board managed to pass up a rare opportunity to fill a conspicuous gap in the Club's portrait collection. Recalling Theodore T. Scudder's offer to arrange for likenesses of the Club's four founders besides James H. Fay, de Gersdorff said he felt a question of Club policy was involved here, and that the Board should consequently decide how to deal with the offer without any recommendation from his committee. Given no guidance, the Board, after the briefest of discussions, voted . . . to take no action. (True, it could have accepted Scudder's offer at a later meeting, but it did not.)

In November, Board member Jesse Straus advanced a timely suggestion: that the Club use oil for fuel instead of coal. The Sports Committee reported that a springboard had been installed in the plunge, and the Squash Committee that the National Squash Association's fall scratch tournament had been held at the Club and won by Hewitt Morgan, who had defeated the national champion in the final round. The Board approved plans for the Biddle Memorial Room drawn up by the distinguished architect Charles A. Platt. Art Chairman de Gersdorff declared that his committee favored the latest concept for a war memorial being circulated: a large stained glass window at the northern end of Harvard Hall. He also noted being offered, for $500, the largest bison's head on record, which he had turned down. (More often than not, de Gersdorff's habitual caution served the Club well, as when, after making a show of checking the would-be seller's claims for it, he declined to buy a small pew said to have been used by John Harvard in the church he attended in Charlestown.)

Early in the new year of 1924 Theodore T. Scudder came to the club-house to present a framed portrait by artist Kleber Hall of his late godfa-ther, James H. Fay, and receive the thanks of Chairman de Gersdorff. In anticipation of Thomas Slocum's customary participation, representing the Club, in an annual ceremony on January 17 on Park Row, at the foot of a statue of a great American—a ceremony marking, that year, the 218th anniversary of the birth of that man—a card was engraved with the following inscription:

Harvard
honors the memory of
Benjamin Franklin
Honorary Master of Arts, 1753
The Harvard Club of New York City

Eight days after this Slocum was elected president of the Club and Howard Elliott '81 vice-president, with John Elliott and Francis M. Weld staying on as secretary and treasurer.

A notable passage in the Club's never-ending struggle to maintain decorum grew out of an incident at a Ladies' Day reception in early March. On the evening of April 16, in the Mahogany Room, seventeen Board members working their way through the agenda came to the case of a celebrant at the reception who, it was alleged, "while intoxicated did accost two ladies with whom he was not acquainted . . . in an objection-able manner unbecoming a member of the Harvard Club, asking these ladies to come to the bar and have a drink with him." After reading out this charge Secretary Elliott read aloud letters from the culprit himself, from a friend of his and from two witnesses; then the balding, forty-six-year-old miscreant appeared, looking drawn and tense, to recount the circumstances leading up to his misstep and to answer questions. On his withdrawing, his letter-writing defender came in to ask for leniency, then left, whereupon the Board members took up for consideration the House Committee's recommendation that the man be expelled. That recommendation had been unanimous, but only seven of the men present approved it, six short of the thirteen needed for a decision.

There followed a "straw ballot," in which each man wrote out on a piece of paper the punishment he felt most appropriate.

Votes for expelling the man totaled..........................................................................6
for requesting him to resign...................................................................................1
for suspending him for five years..........................................................................2
for suspending him for two years..........................................................................1
for suspending him for one year............................................................................5
for suspending him for six months........................................................................1
for issuing him a letter of censure ........................................................................1

So began a marathon debate, punctuated by frequent voting, without any parallel in the annals of the Club, one that demonstrated rather conclusively that the individuals making up the Board of Managers—that board, anyway—drew very fine distinctions indeed.

A motion to send the accused member a "severe letter of censure" and suspend him for a year obtained nine votes; another, to suspend him for two years, seven; yet another, to suspend him for five years, five. At 10:48 P.M. all parties agreed to a five-minute recess, but at 10:53 the making and seconding of motions and the balloting thereon recommenced.

A motion for expulsion received ...................................................................7 votes
One for a two-year suspension .....................................................................6 votes
for a one-year suspension with letter of censure ...........................................9 votes
for a five-year suspension............................................................................10 votes
for a one-year suspension ............................................................................8 votes
for a three-year suspension...........................................................................7 votes

At this point, Jerome D. Greene, recalling his experience disciplining undergraduates in Cambridge, suggested imposing a period of suspension

along with the right to apply for reinstatement at the end of a shorter period. Greene's suggestion was twice put to a vote, but to little purpose:

A motion to suspend the accused man
for five years with the right to apply
for reinstatement after three received ...............................................................8 votes
A motion for a five-year suspension
with the right to apply for reinstatement
after one year received.....................................................................................2 votes
A motion for a five-year suspension received.............................................8 votes
for a one-year suspension .................................................................................8 votes
for a three-year suspension................................................................................6 votes
for a five-year suspension .................................................................................9 votes
for a three-year suspension ..............................................................................10 votes
A compromise motion for a four-year
suspension accompanied by a letter of
censure received ...............................................................................................8 votes
And a motion to adjourn received just ..........................................................6 votes

Now, well after midnight, Jerome D. Greene read aloud the draft of a
letter of censure and moved that the Ladies' Day Lothario be censured in
these or similar terms and suspended for a year; his motion drew just nine
votes. With the Board hopelessly deadlocked, President Slocum appointed a five-man panel to interview the accused man more thoroughly, and
at 12:48 A.M. on April 17 the conferees adjourned at last.

Promptly at noon on Monday, April 21, the five-man committee convened in the offices of Lee, Higginson & Company on Exchange Place.
The accused man appeared and submitted to questions; then, after relating the Ladies' Day incident in even greater detail than before, he left.
Over lunch, the quintet agreed by a vote of 4-1 (the dissenter preferring a
harsher punishment) on a one-year suspension accompanied by a severe
letter of censure.

Three days later—again in the evening and again in the Mahogany
Room—the five reported to the full Board. President Slocum read aloud
a letter of apology from the accused (who by now had clearly suffered a
good deal—almost, some might say, enough) and moved that the committee's recommendation be ratified. Amazingly, his motion lost, garnering
only ten votes! Following more discussion, some of it acrimonious,
President Slocum insisted on the necessity of taking some definite action.

The rejected motion was put again, and this time it received . . . the bare minimum of thirteen votes needed for approval. Thus was settled, at long last, a question that may have been more resistant to resolution than any other the Club would ever confront—and at the same time one of the most trivial.

On June 24 Democratic delegates from across the nation assembled in Madison Square Garden, a mile south of the clubhouse, for the first major party convention held in New York since 1868. From June 30, when balloting began, the contest for the presidential nomination was between former Secretary of the Treasury William G. McAdoo and New York Governor Alfred E. Smith, whom Franklin D. Roosevelt had memorably likened, in a speech putting his name in nomination, to the poet Wordsworth's "happy warrior." Day after day the balloting continued, with neither rival coming close to obtaining the two-thirds of the delegates' votes required for nomination, and at last—on July 9 and on the 103rd ballot—the weary convention chose a compromise candidate, John W. Davis, a prominent corporation lawyer well known to many attorneys, financiers and others in the Club.

All that summer carpenters, plasterers and electricians were at work upstairs, and by mid-October they had almost finished reconstructing the older (1905) large bedrooms in such a way as to add four new rooms on the fourth floor and three on the fifth and refurbishing both the North Room and the Biddle Room. However, not all developments were so positive: thus, although business conditions had improved substantially since 1921, the Committee on Appointments (so restyled) had received forty-five applications for employment and found jobs for only twenty applicants. Even worse, perhaps, of the five boys selected for Club scholarships only two had passed the College entrance examination! While no one considered him responsible for this debacle, Edgar Wells quietly resigned as chairman of the Scholarships Committee.

At that meeting, on October 16, Clifford M. Holland, away in Michigan at the Battle Creek sanitarium recovering from a breakdown brought on by overwork, was named to the Nominating Committee, but eleven days later, while waiting to be notified that the two teams of sandhogs tunnel-

The Biddle Room

ing toward each other from Manhattan and New Jersey had come together, he suffered a heart attack and died. He was forty-one. By the time the mid-Hudson linkup occurred days later, the authorities had agreed that his creation should bear his name, to remain, as the Holland Tunnel, his memorial.

Meanwhile, Harvard's great former football coach, Percy Haughton, also died suddenly, also on October 27, aged forty-eight. Some members attended both funerals, and the Club sent flowers to both.

On Election Day—to the satisfaction, no doubt, of most members of the Club—President Coolidge routed his Democratic challenger. And on the evening of November 20, the Club's governors, in formal attire, gathered for their monthly dinner—not, as had so long been their custom, in the Mahogany Room, but about sixty paces north of it in the new Biddle Memorial Room, where they were joined by the architect, Charles A. Platt. In a brief speech, Vincent Astor formally presented his splendid gift to the Club. While they dined, the men admired the stately apartment, paneled in French walnut, with chandeliers and wall brackets of silver,

Nicholas Biddle

and, above the mantel over the fireplace in the west wall, a portrait by Ellen Emmet Rand of their longtime colleague Nicholas Biddle, the gift of a number of his friends and classmates of 1900.

On December 18 the Board, apparently for the first time, came to grips with a problem which must often have arisen in the past—and almost as often, no doubt, been discreetly taken care of by individual members.

Informed that a certain well-liked member in his sixties, hard pressed for cash, had reluctantly submitted his resignation for financial reasons, the Board voted never to accept it, and Treasurer Weld extended the privileges of the Club to the man for six months, during which time, it was hoped, a special dues-free category of membership could be created for older members in financial difficulties.

A week earlier, a colorful member of the Club, August Belmont, had died, whereupon the *New York Times* had hailed him, in an affectionate editorial, as both the banker who had had the vision to back the city's first subway and the Cape Cod Canal (1910–14) and the sportsman who had successfully bred and raced Thoroughbred horses, leaving Belmont Park, the racetrack, as his memorial. Pointing up Belmont's penchant for innovating, in very diverse fields, the editorial noted that even as an undergraduate he had purportedly founded a society of art appreciators while, as a sprinter, he was introducing the wearing of spiked shoes to college track. These remarks inspired an exchange on the paper's editorial page that would amuse Club members. It led off, on Christmas Eve, with a letter to the editor headed "The Founding of the Harvard Club":

> In reading an editorial last week upon the late August Belmont I was quite a bit amazed to find the statement that "he was said to have founded the Harvard Club." As it happened, on the wall just above my desk hangs a framed copy of the original statement concerning the foundation of the Harvard Club (New York) with a full list of the officers and organizing members. The date of its organization was 1865, at which time Mr. Belmont would have been 12 years old. Samuel Osgood, DD (my father) was the first President, and such men as George Bancroft, Joseph H. Choate, Willard Parker, M.D., John O. Sargent, Francis Howland, George Blagden and Henry Whitney Bellows were among the charter members. It is after all a matter of slight importance perhaps, but the statement seemed to me so farfetched that as I looked above my desk the evidence spoke for itself, and so I write.
>
> MABEL OSGOOD WRIGHT<br>Fairfield, Conn., Dec. 17, 1924.

Left thus with the exhilarating impression that the lordly *Times* had, in printing her letter, acknowledged its error and credited her with spotting it, Mrs. Wright must have felt not a little deflated to read in her paper the following morning, Christmas Day, an editorial titled "Failing Attention":

> Social philosophers and educators have long deplored the many distractions of modern life which tend to destroy the power of close attention. The difference

between a great scientist and one only mediocre has been said to be that the former excels in minute and sustained observation. The common failing today is double: we do not look at a thing long enough nor examine it in detail intently.

　　With all respect and gratitude for those who write letters to the *Times*, we are bound to say that they sometimes illustrate rather vividly this defect—in which all of us share to a greater or less extent. Yesterday, for example, a communication was printed from a correspondent who declared that she has been "amazed" to find in an editorial upon the late August Belmont the statement that "he was said to have founded the Harvard Club." Thereupon she adduced a list of the real charter members. But the singular thing is that her amazement did not suggest to her the need of looking carefully at the words which startled her. In plain print they were simply that Mr. Belmont was said to have founded "The Harvard Art Club"— certainly a horse of another color.

During the year now drawing to a close an era had ended in Cambridge with the shutting down of the commons in Memorial Hall, obliging the majority of upperclassmen who did not belong to a final club to take their meals at eating places in and around the Square. In the Yard four new buildings were either in place or nearing completion: three dormitories— Mower, Lionel and Straus Halls—and, on the site of old Dane Hall, Lehman Hall, housing the University's financial offices.

At the 1925 annual meeting, President Slocum, Vice-President Elliott and Treasurer Weld were reelected, and William G. Wendell '09, son of Barrett and nephew of Evert, became secretary. The next month, the Board remitted the new year's dues of the impecunious older member who had sought to resign, in effect creating an informal category of membership exempt from dues. In March the Board decisively rejected, 8–3, the stained glass window memorial that both Marvin's and de Gersdorff's committees had by then endorsed.

In May came arresting news about Board member Charles C. Stillman: he had, it seemed, bought up several privately held lots between the Yard and the Charles River to present them to the University, and had endowed the Charles Eliot Norton Chair of Poetry. (Its first holder would be Oxford professor Gilbert Murray, probably the world's foremost classical scholar.)

Although radios were becoming standard fixtures in American homes and broadcast reports of college football games were already standard fare on Saturday afternoons, the Club continued, for some reason, to bring Harvard games to its members by telegraphic means. To the Club's squash players, almost one resident member in ten, the available facilities for that sport seemed similarly antiquated and inadequate. Most players wanted to play not squash tennis, but squash racquets, and the one court in which they could do so was below standard size. In a postal poll they voted overwhelmingly in favor of the Club constructing at least two new courts, both designed for squash racquets play.

At the Board's first meeting of 1926 Langdon Marvin, still doggedly pursuing his quest for an acceptable war memorial, presented two designs therefor from McKim, Mead & White; his colleagues approved one of them and empowered Marvin's committee to raise the money to manufacture and install it. And a few nights later, at the annual meeting preceding the Club's sixtieth annual dinner, all four officers were reelected.

In March, the Committee on the Reception of Allied Officers was at last, mercifully, abolished, and the Committee on Military and Naval Service was renamed the Committee on the War Memorial. And in April the Board, possibly reflecting a shift in popular taste, passed up the offer of a perfectly good moose head to concentrate on two perennial concerns: the condition of the bedrooms and the viability of the table d'hôte dinner. As to the former, oversight would soon be transferred from the House Committee to the Art Committee, while several older College classes responsible for decorating particular bedrooms were reportedly more than eager to cede their responsibilities to younger classes. As for the repast, a great favorite with the members, Chairman Henry Sedgwick '04 of the House Committee would reveal in May that in providing it for a dollar plus a dime cover charge the Club was losing 13 cents, asking whether the price should not be raised to $1.25.

On August 17 members read in their newspapers of the dramatic end, at sea, of Charles C. Stillman, forty-eight, who had suffered a ruptured appendix on board the liner *Aquitania*. In addition to continuing the generous giving to Harvard initiated by his father, James Stillman, the donor inter alia of Stillman Infirmary, the deceased had been a singularly dedicated alumnus and Club member, holding, at the time of his death, half a dozen Harvard-related posts, as well as being a candidate for Overseer. And less than a week after this came news of the death—at his home in Maine, at ninety-two—of Charles W. Eliot. In the next days tributes to him would pour in to University and Massachusetts Halls from around the globe, while editorialists across the nation eulogized the remarkable citizen who had, by his example, transformed American higher education. Representing the Club, a delegation of prominent members would attend Eliot's funeral in Memorial Hall and follow his coffined corpse to Mount Auburn Cemetery for burial.

As the football season neared, Chairman Sedgwick, with the Board's assent, purchased a new display board capable of communicating more information than its predecessors had, and arranged to install a "radio apparatus," together with loudspeakers, on the ground floor of the clubhouse. He reported that two bakers had been let go, and that the Club would thenceforth buy its bread daily instead of baking it. Additionally, he noted, cryptically, that a certain quinquagenarian attorney had been charged with "improper use of a bedroom."

Big changes were in the offing: throughout September workmen installed cables and switches, pipes and valves, and on or about October 1 the Club ceased forever generating its own power, to depend thereafter on the Edison Company for electricity and the New York Steam Company for steam. Like the switch from kitchen-baked to commercial bread, this change represented a retreat from self-sufficiency, but it saved the Club money, and on October 19 the Board hailed the development, which it credited to the initiative of the House Committee's Frank T. James '08. Then, almost as an afterthought, it raised the price of the table d'hôte dinner to $1.50.

In the midterm elections New York's Governor Al Smith, who two years before had defeated Theodore Roosevelt, Jr., beat back a challenge from another member, Ogden L. Mills. And on Saturday, November 13, in Harvard Hall, reports of the Dartmouth game, which Harvard won 16–12, were received simultaneously via both radio and telegraph, with the new display board also in play. (This mixed-media experiment apparently succeeded, as it would be repeated next year.)

That fall, the library again subscribed to *Moody's Manual*, increasingly in demand as more and more members were drawn to invest in the ever-rising securities market. Langdon P. Marvin disclosed that photographs of the members who had died in the war, with brief biographies of them, had been bound together in a handsome volume. But the most welcome development, surely, in terms of future generations, was that William B. Kendall—by then reconciled, presumably, to the trumpeting elephant head in Harvard Hall—presented the Club with a magnificent pair of chandeliers of ornamental bronze that would hang in the dining room.

During 1926 the Club had, in spite of resignations and deaths, gained 133 members, but to read the year-end reports of some of the committees one might think it was heading straight into a winter of discontent:

Entertainment: It is hard to secure interesting speakers. The proposal to put on bi-monthly movie-and-radio nights won't do as such entertainment can all too easily be purchased in the city.

Scholarships: The marks scored by current holders of Club scholarships are "not remarkable."

Literature: The library has acquired 479 books during the year—but 16 of them have since been stolen.

House: The Grill Room, Harvard Hall and dining room are receiving insufficient heat, and are "almost uninhabitable" in very cold weather.

Appointments: In the year just ending, sixty-five Harvard men had sought help in obtaining employment and forty-nine employers assistance in filling vacancies, but the total number of positions filled was . . . nine.

By New Year's Day 1927 improvements to its heating system had made the Grill Room snug again, and the Board's first meeting of the year brought more warming news: nine members had together given the Club almost $50,000 for the purpose of reducing its first mortgage indebtedness. (They were J. P. Morgan, Jr. '89, Thomas W. Slocum '90, Thomas W. Lamont '92, Jesse I. Straus '93, Percy S. Straus '97, Langdon P. Marvin '98, John W. Prentiss '98, George Nichols '00 and Herbert N. Straus '03.) Then came a chilling aftermath. Secretary Wendell reported that Nelson Dougherty '09, a member, had written him requesting permission to bring Chief Amoh of the Gold Coast, British West Africa, to the Club for lunch. How should he reply? Wendell was instructed to inform Dougherty that in the Board's opinion "the best policy would be to refrain from bringing a Negro to the Club."

On January 26 Howard Elliott was elected president and Thomas Lamont vice-president, with Wendell and Weld retaining their posts.

In February, the Board voted to replace the windows in Harvard Hall with new ones, equipped with storm windows for better heat retention. And it created a new committee of senior advisers, made up entirely of former presidents of the Club. Then, confirming rumors that had been circulating for some time, came the revelation—in a letter from former President Slocum, read aloud—that a syndicate of members had bought the property at 33 West 44th Street and were holding it for the Club's possible future use. These men, who would soon incorporate themselves as the H Club Holding Corporation, were, again in descending order of seniority, Dwight P. Robinson '90, Thomas W. Slocum '90, Thomas W. Lamont '92, Francis M. Weld '97, Samuel L. Fuller '98, John W. Prentiss '98, George F. Baker, Jr. '99, Thomas Crimmins '00, Samuel A. Welldon '04, and George Whitney '07.

During January and February the Club's bridge team matched wits with teams representing the Yale, Princeton and Columbia Clubs to emerge victorious, "thus once more," as the minutes of the Board's March meeting put it, "upholding Harvard's supremacy in intellectual pursuits." A spokesman for the Literature Committee reported that, throughout that winter, every chair in all three library rooms had been filled on Saturday afternoons, and often in the evenings. On the other hand there had been a disturbing falling off in attendance at the Sunday afternoon concerts. Should women be invited to them, then? Not a man present, apparently including the one who had raised the question, spoke up in favor of the idea.

On April 15 a special committee appointed by President Elliott recommended that the Club add on two squash racquets courts, funding their construction by issuing $30,000 in notes. And Treasurer Weld, encountering strong opposition to an assessment, recommended raising the dues of all but the youngest members, the new schedule to range from $10 to a top of $60. The Board approved all of these suggestions, but turned down another: a request from filmmaker Robert Flaherty, creator of the documentaries *Nanook of the North* (1922) and *Moana of the South Seas* (1925), to shoot footage of the elephant's head in Harvard Hall for a film about impressive sights of New York City.

On May 22, Americans were electrified to learn that young Captain

Charles A. Lindbergh, having taken off two days before in a monoplane from Roosevelt Field, Long Island, had managed to fly, in 33$^{1}/_{2}$ hours, all the way across the Atlantic to Paris. On his return to New York in June, the city gave Lindbergh a hero's welcome, and at the Board's next meeting there was much excited talk about tendering a dinner to him. The conferees finally decided, however, to put off any decision on the matter and instead to honor the Club's own General Wood, due back soon from the Philippines.

Wood returned to the United States on schedule in failing health, and on August 7 he died.

On September 16, however, as things turned out, a gala dinner was in fact held at the Club—for Harvard's director of athletics, William J. Bingham '16. Most of the city's and, indeed, the country's leading sportswriters came. That event, the brainchild of the well-known publicist and Club member John Price Jones '02, was a frank attempt to induce the press to present Harvard's participation in various sports in a more sympathetic light.

In October, the managers' first concern was the dwindling attendance at the Sunday afternoon concerts; by the narrowest of pluralities—a single vote—they opted to let women attend them, as an experiment. The following month, they worried about a marked falling off of restaurant business. Could it be due to the higher price of the table d'hôte dinner? Chairman Sedgwick thought not, but his committee, to be on the safe side, had instituted a one-dollar self-service dinner.

Since women would be attending the concerts starting in January, the Board abolished the regular Ladies' Day.

At its November meeting, the Club amended the bylaws in line with the Board's recommendation, modestly raising the dues as of January 1, 1928, whereupon the Club's governors instantly began fretting over resignations. They need not have, however: in the event, year-end resignations totaled 109, by coincidence the same number as had resigned after the previous raising of the dues in 1920.

The experiment of admitting women to the Sunday afternoon concerts proved an immediate success, as the attendance at the first two concerts demonstrated:

| Jan. 8: New York String Quartet | Members | 183 |
|---|---|---|
| | Women guests | 157 |
| | Total | 340 |
| Jan. 15: Mischa Mischakoff, violinist | Members | 239 |
| | Women guests | 183 |
| | Total | 422 |

With women on the scene, many more teas than usual were ordered, bringing in welcome extra income. In the general euphoria that greeted this innovation one member, Edgar Mills '91, suggested doubling the scheduled concerts to twelve, gallantly offering to pay for the additional six, but the Board declined his offer, with thanks.

At the annual meeting on January 27, 1928, all four officers were reelected, and a speaker noted the recent death of an honored member, Major General George W. Goethals, the great engineer who had guided the construction of the Panama Canal to completion.

In February, the War Memorial Committee at last set a firm date for the dedication: April 6, the eleventh anniversary of America's declaration of war on the Central Powers. And on March 8 Commander Richard E. Byrd, who had flown over the North Pole with Floyd Bennett two years earlier, addressed the Club on his flights of discovery, showing films he had shot himself.

In 1928, the Club offered four freshman-year scholarships funded by, respectively, James Byrne, Harold Vanderbilt, George Whitney and the Board; the Scholarships Committee was hoping to come up with funding for a fifth. To publicize these grants-in-aid and encourage applications, the committee sent copies of Rollo Brown's biography of Dean Briggs to fifteen high schools in the city, to be awarded to the academically outstanding junior in each. But this well-intentioned effort fell short of producing the desired results: few of the principals bothered to acknowledge Chairman Welldon's gracious accompanying letter and four returned the books rather than award them. "On the whole," Secretary Wendell concluded in the minutes, "probably the book award has been worth the expense and trouble, although there is some doubt."

By then, moreover, in June, two of the four boys selected for Club scholarships had failed the entrance exam.

The Club finally achieved an important undertaking with the dedication —late in the afternoon of April 6, Good Friday, in Harvard Hall, in the presence of several hundred people, including a number of widows of the honored dead—of a permanent memorial to the sixty-three members of the Club who had fallen in the Great War. (These included Joseph H. Choate and Evert J. Wendell, who, though not combatants, had died while furthering America's and the Allies' war aims.) The ceremony, presided over by President Elliott, was impressive. The memorial tablet, affixed to the wall at the center of the alcove and covered by the Club's war service flag, bearing 1,333 silver stars for those members in the armed services and 63 gold ones for the dead, was unveiled by Lawrence G. White '08 of the Art and War Memorial Committees and of McKim, Mead & White. The Rev. William T. Crocker '84, a former Army chaplain, offered a prayer. Francis R. Appleton, president of the Club 1916–19, during America's participation in the war, delivered a stirring speech. Chairman Marvin of the War Memorial Committee called the roll of the dead and formally transferred title to the memorial to President Elliott, representing the Club. At intervals, the assembled company sang "The Battle Hymn of the Republic," "The Star-Spangled Banner" and "Fair Harvard." At the conclusion of the roll call a bugler sounded taps.

In their first full season, the two new squash racquets courts saw plenty of action: the Club's team played six outside combinations and won all six matches. Ultimately, three members of the Club played on a four-man New York City team which took the national championship. Meanwhile, after consulting with Kermit Roosevelt '12 (like his late father, a mighty slayer of large quadrupeds), Art Committee Chairman W. Rodman Fay '07 told the Board that the Club's forty-four mounted animal heads were in deplorable condition and extracted $800 to have them restored. And a House Committee spokesman, attempting to explain why the one-dollar self-service dinner had not caught on, observed that most diners at the Club were older men, willing to pay more for a better meal.

For months the House Committee discussed cutting through the west wall of the clubhouse, on the third floor, to 33 West 44th Street, and converting the vacant apartment there into additional bedrooms—until it learned that doing so would steeply increase the Club's insurance premiums. In June, however, the committee came up with a project that would benefit everyone without affecting insurance rates: moving the barber shop to the basement, making it readily accessible from the ground floor while greatly enlarging the space on the sixth floor available for changing. The barber was quite ready to have his yearly rent increased to $1,500 so long as he could charge a quarter for a shave and half a dollar for a haircut.

On June 14 Republicans in convention chose Secretary of Commerce Herbert C. Hoover as their presidential candidate. Two weeks later New York Governor Alfred E. Smith, again placed in nomination by Franklin D. Roosevelt, became the Democrats' standard bearer. And on July 8, President Elliott succumbed to a heart attack at his place on Cape Cod, the second head of the Club to die in office. Days later, Vice-President Lamont summoned the Board to his Wall Street office: he would act as president, he told them, but not assume the title.

On October 2 New York State Democrats drafted Franklin D. Roosevelt to run for governor, and on November 6 he was elected, although Governor Smith lost both the state and the nation to Hoover. That night, incidentally, a number of members stayed at the Club until midnight or later listening to the election returns on the radio.

That fall, whenever Harvard men came together, they were likely to talk about the astonishing gift that Yale man Edward S. Harkness had made to their alma mater. Failing to interest the administrators of his own alma mater in building a super-college for exceptionally promising students, Harkness had taken his idea to President Lowell, who had enthusiastically embraced it and then persuaded Harkness to modify it so as to conform more closely to his own cherished ideal of an undergraduate community in which rich and poor students would coexist on a more or less equal footing. The outcome was, of course, the house plan, calling for the erection of seven huge dormitories for upperclassmen, each with its own common room, dining room and well-stocked library.

One day after the Club ushered in the year 1929 with the usual festivities, word came that former President Francis R. Appleton had died in his Murray Hill home nearby. Most members knew of him as the Club's

Harvard Hall, by Chester B. Price

leader throughout the country's involvement in the Great War, but older ones recalled an even more important service he had rendered the Club earlier in the century when, over the vehement objections of his fellow members of the Building Committee, he had insisted that Harvard Hall rise three full stories high. As the Club's memorial minutes put it, "We all realize now that this grand hall—the finest of its kind in the country, if not in the world—is a lasting monument to his prophetic vision."

On January 28 Thomas W. Lamont was elected president and Langdon P. Marvin vice-president, with William Wendell and Francis M. Weld remaining in their respective posts. But three days later President Lamont took ship for France, with J. P. Morgan, Jr., and General Electric Chairman Owen D. Young LLD (hon.) '24, to represent the United States in an international conference on German reparations to the victorious Allies. On February 9 Young was named chairman of the conference, and later that month the three men were joined by a fourth delegate, Thomas N. Perkins '91 L'94.

Even before the departure of the Lamont group, the Club's remaining governors had been upset about a snide and singularly unfunny attack on Harkness and the house plan in the *Harvard Lampoon*. At the Board's direction, Secretary Wendell wrote President Lowell to ask whether something could not be done to "prevent such unwarranted discourtesy as that which has bitterly incensed a large number of Harvard men in New York." By return post Wendell received a note addressed, in avuncular fashion, to "Dear William":

> The editors of the *Lampoon* have been chastised by the most efficient body, to wit, the graduates who are former editors; and they have sent to Mr. Harkness an apology approved, and practically dictated, by those graduates.
>
> A. Lawrence Lowell

Langdon Marvin, presiding over a Board meeting in February, positively glowed with pride as he reminded his hearers that all four of the American delegates to the ongoing reparations conference, including the conference chairman, were members of the Club. Throughout the late winter and spring the conference would be front page news, and on June 8 Club members would be able to read in their papers complete details of the Young Plan for a new reparations schedule, with certain concessions by the Allies. Reaction to the plan by leading figures in American government and business was uniformly favorable, and on the fourteenth Young and his colleagues, docking in New York, came home in triumph.

On Thursday, October 17, at the initiative of Vice-President Marvin, the Board would formally congratulate Young, Morgan, Lamont and

Perkins for having ably executed "an all-important duty." Then, a week
later, came "Black Thursday," October 24, when, as the *Times* would
report the next morning, "The most disastrous decline in the biggest and
broadest stock market of history rocked the financial district." Billions of
dollars of market values vanished in an avalanche of sell orders as an
incredible 12.9 million shares changed hands. Never had the Stock
Exchange known such frenzied hours. Yet at the closing gong there
remained in the minds of those present on the scene the memory of a big,
broad-shouldered man who, with the selling madness at its height, had
dramatically restored a measure of calm.

That man, well known by sight to all traders as vice-president of the
Exchange, was a Harvard man and longtime member of the Club,
Richard Whitney. At about 1:30 P.M., after conferring with a handful of
leading bankers, including Thomas Lamont, Whitney strode out onto the
floor and headed for Trading Post Number 2, where U.S. Steel shares
were traded, to call out, "I bid 205 for ten thousand Steel"; then he had
proceeded on to other trading posts, placing further large orders at prices
well above the going ones. Fortunately, the bold ploy worked: the panic
subsided, prices firmed, and the worst was, for the moment, averted. The
hard-pressed brokers had found a hero.

On Friday and Saturday, stock prices rallied, but on Monday "the second hurricane of liquidation within four days hit the stock market," and
on Tuesday "Stock prices virtually collapsed . . . swept downward with
gigantic losses in the most disastrous trading day in the stock market's
history." Disastrous indeed: an unbelievable 16,410,030 shares were liq-
uidated at whatever price they could fetch.

On November 5, New Yorkers overwhelmingly reelected Mayor James
J. Walker, and at the end of the month Commander Byrd, in Antarctica,
thrilled the nation by flying over the South Pole and back. But the much-
heralded recovery of stock prices stubbornly refused to materialize, and
as the 1920s passed into history the suspicion grew in some minds—
including, surely, some accustomed to taking their exercise at 27 West
44th Street—that the future held something a good deal more difficult,
not to say threatening, than just a new decade.

# 12

# FROM THE CRASH
# TO PEARL HARBOR
# (1929–1941)

In its sixty-five years of existence the Club had weathered four periods of severe economic turbulence, those beginning in 1873, 1893, 1907 and 1920, on each occasion contriving not only to avoid the sad depletion of its ranks that many New York clubs had had to undergo but actually to grow, taking in more than enough new members to replace those who resigned or were dropped. But the Great Depression would prove to be another matter: with businessmen being laid off or forced to accept salary cuts and with professional men seeing their earnings fall off steeply, the Club would for the first time contract, its numbers diminishing over five years by fully one-fifth.

With President Lamont in the chair, distinguished guests at the 1930 annual dinner included, in addition to President Lowell, Acting Secretary of State Joseph P. Cotton '96 AM'97 L'00 and the three other delegates to last year's reparations conference besides Lamont: Messrs. Young, Morgan and Perkins. (Two months later the Reichstag would ratify the Young Plan, but no sooner would it go into effect, in May, than Germany would feel the full impact of economic depression, necessitating a moratorium in fiscal 1931–32. Adolf Hitler, on taking over Germany in 1933, would repudiate the unpaid reparations debt, rendering the plan a dead letter.)

In March, House Committee Chairman Stuart D. Preston '06 reported an arresting discovery: thanks to falling prices, the Club was now paying

**Charles Townsend Copeland**

eight cents less for food per dollar of restaurant sales than it had just a year earlier. His committee was granted an appropriation for the construction of an amenity that appears to have been a first: a women's rest room in the basement. In April the Board voted to buy 33 West 44th Street from the H Club Holding Corporation.

Secretary Bill Wendell's many friends knew him to be mildly eccentric but highly meticulous in carrying out his secretarial chores, so it can only have been due to a rare lapse of attention on his part that he signed the typed minutes of that meeting without noticing the statement, prefacing the usual list of members who had died since the previous board meeting, that

> The following deaths were approved.

A dinner on April 26 for Professor Copeland, marking both his twenty-fifth successive yearly visit to the Club and his seventieth birthday, was a gala affair, which culminated in the unveiling of a portrait of him by longtime member Charles Hopkinson of Boston. Two weeks after this, Harvard College announced the retirements of both "Copey" and another giant of the English department, Bliss Perry LittD (hon.) '25. Saluting the former, a *New York Times* editorial had this to say about the soon-to-be-emeritus Boylston Professor of Rhetoric and Oratory:

> As for "Copey," the social solitary of Hollis, he has become a legend, a genial and whimsical god whose cult is practiced yearly at the New York Harvard Club. A Yankee from the St. Croix River, the dry wit of his origin ever breaking out from the highly cultivated surface; celibate but far from cloistered; original, perhaps a bit "queer," if he is not, rather, amusing himself at the expense of his audience: a sharp observer and epigrammatist —"Copey" is a great deal more than the old pompous title of his present chair indicates. He is professor of Life and Literature and Things in General. He has made a school. He has taught young

men and women to seek eagerly the meaning and beauty of the things of the spirit. By reading aloud himself and inculcating the habit in his students, he has done much to widen love of lovely sounds and the mysterious incantation of poetry and great prose.

If, by now, some members were finding big game hunting in Africa a bit of a bore, most remained susceptible to the lure of remote and wild places in a world that, with aviators darting across entire oceans and continents, seemed to be shrinking almost daily. Among the topics of the talks, most accompanied by motion pictures, available to them that year were hunting in Tibet (with members C. Suydam Cutting and Kermit Roosevelt), travels in subarctic northern Ontario and explorations in the jungles of British Guiana and the Malay peninsula. For the evening of May 3 the Committee on Entertainment scheduled an illustrated lecture on mountain climbing; members who turned up at it without reading the notice carefully must have been startled to find that the speaker was a mere freshman, one Henry Bradford Washburn, Jr. '33. Despite his youth, Washburn, a native of Cambridge and graduate of Groton, was entirely at home with his subject, having climbed peaks in the Alps and the White Mountains and even written books for children about his ascents. In his senior year he would head the Harvard Mountaineering Club and after graduating would lead expeditions in Alaska, scaling mountains and measuring the movement of glaciers. He would become an expert cartographer and photographer and a frequent lecturer on geography and geology, eventually being tapped to head Boston's Museum of Science. For many years, Washburn was a member of the Club, and today, in his eighties, he continues, with his wife of more than half a century, to go on expeditions and conduct surveys and mapping projects in the world's great mountain systems—and, in aircraft of various kinds, above them.

At the end of May, the Club took title to 33 West 44th Street. The total cost was $198,317.07. Of this amount $48,000 was paid out of general funds; in August another $35,000 would be paid out, and at the end of the year $10,000 would be paid on the mortgage and a new mortgage of $100,000 taken out.

On Friday, July 18, as they had for a good many Julys now, the Harvard and Yale Clubs of New York held a joint outing at the Rockaway Hunting Club at Cedarhurst, Long Island. As usual, the Elis won the baseball game, but in the tennis tournament Hoffman Nickerson '11 AM'13, the most consistent winner in the last decade, again took the honors. That summer, however, golf was to command the public's attention as never before when Robert Tyre Jones, Jr. '24 became the only golfer ever to win the "Grand Slam," both the amateur and open championships of both Britain and the United States. Modest and likable, Bobby Jones became an instant national hero—and the best living advertisement for his alma mater to come along in years.

At summer's end Lowell and Dunster Houses opened, the first completed dormitories of the house plan to admit upperclassmen. On October 3 came the dedication of the Dillon Field House at Soldiers Field, the gift of member Clarence Dillon '05, whose son, C. Douglas Dillon '31, was manager of football. By then, incidentally, Harvard alumni were becoming familiar with the names of the Crimson eleven's two principal spark plugs, Captain Ben Ticknor '31, a lineman, and quarterback Barry Wood '32.

At 27 West 44th Street the Board members pondered a proposal from the Harvard Placement Service in Cambridge that the Club establish an office under its auspices. They appointed a committee to raise $10,000, the estimated cost of operating such an office for two years, after which the central office would presumably be able to fund the Club office's work out of fees collected from men who had obtained their jobs through its efforts. Also, they decided to tender a dinner to Bobby Jones, instructing Secretary Wendell to invite him to pick a convenient date. On November 1 Rear Admiral Byrd, as he now was, talked, with movies to match, about "Flying to the South Pole," the most important (and, at $1,000, most expensive) entertainment of the year. On the fifth the members learned, with little surprise but also, for most, little joy, that the Democrats had swept the country in the previous day's elections.

Although Harvard's football team had, so far that season, outscored its opponents 2–1, it went into the Yale game with just three victories and a tie to four defeats—and the Eli eleven included, in diminutive Albie Booth, a.k.a. the "Mighty Atom," a player already recognized as one of college football's all-time greats. Harvard's hopes rested offensively on Wood's passing and defensively on Ticknor and his mates stopping Booth. And so it worked out, the Crimson eleven triumphing 13–0 in an appropriate parting gift to their retiring coach, Club member Arnold Horween '20.

Great was the rejoicing, after so many losses to Yale, in the Harvard stands in the Yale Bowl—and, of course, at 27 West 44th Street.

Learning that the Club barber was barely making expenses, House Committee Chairman Preston persuaded the Board to cut his yearly rent in half, to $750. Revenue from both the bedrooms and the private dining rooms was down, but on the other hand the Club had spent twelve cents less on comestibles per dollar of restaurant sales in November than it had in November 1929, thirty-six cents compared to forty-eight cents. On discovering this, the House Committee restored the one-dollar table d'hôte dinner. This proved popular, as did the installation in the Grill Room of new backgammon tables, which were soon in almost constant use.

As well as Copey's, likenesses joining the Club's portrait collection included those of former presidents James J. Higginson, given by his widow, and Howard Elliott, presented by his children. The Board, at its December meeting, delightedly accepted a gift from H. C. Armstrong, former Australian high commissioner, who had recently enjoyed being a temporary member: a set of eighteen authentic boomerangs.

Finally, Bobby Jones's reply to the secretary's letter was read aloud. He was grateful, that most self-effacing of champions declared, for the offer of a dinner in his honor, but he seemed to have gotten himself a little overbooked. Would November 21, 1931, do? That date, almost a year in the future, must have struck the managers as too distant for serious consideration; in any case, the Jones dinner, like the Lindbergh dinner before it, was apparently abandoned.

By the end of 1930 the Club's head count came to 6,368, down imperceptibly for the year from 6,370. It was, of course, something quite new for the membership to decline at all, but with President Hoover assuring the nation that prosperity was just around the corner or somewhere equally accessible, one could at least hope that the coming year might bring renewed growth.

At the annual dinner on January 29, 1931, that followed the reelection of President Lamont and the other officers, the speakers were President Lowell, Governor Roosevelt and Paul Claudel, the poet and dramatist who was also the French ambassador to the United States. Apart from Presidents Charles A. Coolidge '81 ArtD (hon.) '06 of the Harvard Alumni Association and Joseph L. Valentine '98 of the Associated Harvard Clubs, both members, the remaining guests of honor testified by their presence to a marked resurgence of interest in Harvard football among the alumni. They were Director of Athletics Bingham; onetime Harvard football great E. L. Casey '19, Arnold Horween's successor as head coach; and Captain Ben Ticknor.

In February, Thomas Slocum, speaking for the Advisory Committee of former presidents, raised the possibility of the Club's expanding even further westward by acquiring the small brick building at 35 West 44th Street from the New York Yacht Club. Vice-President Marvin reported that the organizers of a new eating club at 83 Water Street wanted to know how the Board would feel about their calling themselves the Downtown Harvard Lunch Club, and the Board, after mulling over the question, produced a recommendation with which it would be more than a little difficult to comply: that the new club assert its Harvardian character without using the work "Harvard" or any derivative thereof in its name! Secretary Wendell revealed that almost all of the $10,000 needed to support a reorganized employment bureau had been collected.

With resignations greatly outnumbering admissions and business off, the Club's governors moved aggressively to cut costs and increase revenues. They approved renting out bedrooms by the month at reduced rates, added an appetizer to the one-dollar table d'hôte dinner and slashed the price of the basic Sunday night dinner to a dollar. Furthermore, they reluctantly let three employees go and put a fourth on part-time. Paradoxically, that spring season of austerity witnessed a proliferation of decorative and ornamental works within the clubhouse. The Board accepted a portrait by Charles Hopkinson of former President James Byrne, a gift of the sitter's son and daughter, and then, at the urging of Art Committee Chairman Lawrence G. White, it commissioned etcher Chester B. Price to make a drypoint of Harvard Hall, 100 proofs of which would be sold to benefit the Club. At the initiative of one of the officers, moreover—which one is not clear from the record—and with the blessing of Chairman White, the Board agreed to buy half a dozen very large drawings of New England scenes, full-scale cartoons for murals recently executed for the Addison Gallery at Phillips Academy, in Andover, Massachusetts, from their creator, a renowned mural painter, Club member Barry Faulkner '03. They would be mounted on the walls of the Card Room.

The most notable development of this kind was a wholly unexpected offer from Pierre Lorillard, a well-known manufacturer of tobacco products, to lend the Club a set of six tapestries, each about eleven feet high, depicting the conquests of Alexander the Great. Lorillard was not a Harvard man, but both of his sons—Pierre, Jr. and Griswold, of the Classes of 1904 and 1908 respectively—had belonged to the Club for many years. To this day these glorious panels of woven fabric contribute welcome color and a pleasing contrast of surfaces to the walls of Harvard Hall.

By that time, the Club's efforts to procure work for jobless Harvard men were on track and forging ahead, still under the supervision of the Appointments Committee but coordinated now with the efforts of the Harvard Alumni Association and of two agencies in Cambridge, the Student Employment Office and the Alumni Placement Service. Directing these efforts from his fourth-floor office, a commandeered bedroom, was an energetic young man named Lee M. McTurnan '28.

On Saturday, September 26, 1931, Harvard graduates, including many at the Club, must have felt a twinge of regret on reading newspaper accounts of a development that drastically reordered the College they had known. As the *Times* headlined it,

HARVARD FRESHMEN
CLOSE TO THOUSAND
Lower Class Takes Possession
of Yard for First Time in
University's History.

The article stated that freshmen would thereafter be housed in twelve dormitories in the Yard, including the new file of low brick buildings paralleling Massachusetts Avenue collectively known as Wigglesworth. And it reported that at a forthcoming meeting of the Class of 1935 Athletics Director Bingham, Assistant Football Coach Ticknor and football captain Barry Wood would speak.

That fall, the Club's governors could congratulate themselves on having ignored budgetary constraints and installed amplifying equipment in Harvard Hall: for radio listeners as for spectators in the stands that season was, as Harvard's quasi-official sports history, *The H Book*, put it, "a continuous delight through seven straight victories, the greatest a 14–13 victory over Army." Thus Harvard went into the Yale game, on Saturday, November 21, undefeated and untied for the first time since 1913.

Throughout the first three periods, as a throng in Harvard Hall listened raptly, the Crimson and Blue elevens struggled up and down the Stadium field, neither managing to score. Then, in the last quarter, Yale blocked a punt by Captain Wood and recovered on the Harvard forty-five; soon thereafter a pass from Captain Albie Booth to Herster Barres took Yale to Harvard's twelve. On the fourth down "Booth finally got his revenge after two years of frustration, booting the winning field goal to wreck Harvard's undefeated state and bring his career to a happy conclusion." (As for Wood's career, it easily survived this setback: named to the all-American team, like Ticknor the year before, he proceeded to complete an incredible undergraduate sports record that brought him nine major letters—three each in football, hockey and baseball—plus a minor one for playing on the Harvard-Yale tennis team that was to defeat an Oxford-Cambridge team the following summer.)

At half-time during the Yale game broadcast a collection was taken up in the hall for unemployment relief, the Board having decided not to launch a formal solicitation for that purpose until the Club's annual appeal for the employees' Christmas fund had run its course. The previous May the Empire State Building, the world's tallest, had opened, half a mile south of the clubhouse, and now the George Washington Bridge, New York's only trans-Hudson span, had opened to traffic. Meanwhile the Club received a commissioned portrait of President Lowell by Charles Hopkinson, the mounted heads of a buffalo and a dik-dik (a very small African antelope) from W. P. Draper '13 and a bronze plaque inscribed

"Harvard University bed" that had adorned that bed in the American Hospital at Neuilly. The gift of Wendell Baker '86, it was placed in the war memorial alcove.

Breadlines, panhandlers and apple-sellers were now familiar sights in the city streets, and although by the end of the year Lee McTurnan's office had placed fifty men in permanent or temporary positions (charging them $1,660 in fees on a total of $71,048 in earnings), more members than that had been laid off or suffered loss of income. In 1931 membership fell by 323, to 6,045. At the Board's direction, Treasurer Weld wrote those members who had not yet paid their annual dues asking them to do so, and if it was clear from their replies that they could not, Secretary Wendell was authorized to accept their resignations, thereby entitling them to be readily reinstated once their fortunes improved.

At the 1932 annual meeting new officers were elected: Langdon P. Marvin as president, Francis M. Weld as vice-president and Samuel Welldon as treasurer, with William G. Wendell staying on as secretary. The dinner that followed, priced at just $2.75, attracted an extraordinary 770 banqueters. But this show of solidarity, however gratifying it must have been to everyone present, did nothing to slow the pace of resignations. In February, in response to the urgent need to economize, the plunge, little used and operating at a loss, was temporarily closed down, and the Board decreed reductions in the employees' wages—10 percent for those paid more than $100 a month and 5 percent for those paid less.

In March, with the last of the upperclassmen's dormitories rising in Cambridge, the Board elected Edward S. Harkness an honorary member.

As of May 1, revenues had fallen by 14 percent since the beginning of the year but expenses by only 11 percent. Ever greater frugality was called for. Entertainment Chairman Curt E. Hansen '12 vowed to sign up only speakers who would charge no fee, like pundit member Walter Lippmann or Judge Samuel Seabury, whose ongoing probe into municipal corruption would earn him an honorary LL.D. at Commencement and in September drive Mayor Walker from office. Also, former President Lamont paid Charles Hopkinson in full for his portrait, saving the Club a considerable amount.

In view of the shortage of available funds, what happened that year regarding scholarships seems surprising—and exemplary. Samuel Welldon, still Scholarships chairman as well as treasurer, could count on collecting $800 each from Chauncey D. Stillman '29 and George Whitney, plus $400 from Harold Vanderbilt and another $400 from 100 or more other members. That added up to three full scholarships of $800. On interviewing the applicants, however, the committee decided that two more deserved a shot at Harvard. How an additional $1,200 was raised, and whose arms got twisted, the record does not say, but the matriculating Class of 1936 would include four holders of full Club scholarships and one of a half scholarship. The last youth, credited by one interviewer with "a brilliant mind," was sixteen-year-old Simon Michael Bessie '36, who would become a celebrated book publisher and remains active in the field to this day.

Hoping thereby to keep wavering members from resigning and to lure back some of those who had left, the Board eased the terms for paying dues and scrapped an entrance fee for ex-members reinstated after less than two years away. If the Club's governors clearly perceived the need for new members, they were not yet ready, it seemed, to relax their own rather rigid standards of eligibility: in December, a spokesman for a new Committee on Increase in Membership would report having discreetly sought recruits in Cambridge within the undergraduate social clubs and the staffs of the publications, groups which together made up no more than a fraction of the senior class. (In a similar vein the squash courts would be available on weekday mornings during the Christmas holidays to sons of members—and to boys attending boarding schools.)

Before then, 1932 had proved to be a decisive year for both the country and Harvard University.

On July 1, Governor Roosevelt became the Democratic Party's choice to challenge President Hoover in the coming election, and the next day he called for "a New Deal for the American people." The liberals among his fellow members of the Club were not impressed: Oswald Garrison Villard wrote in *The Nation* that "it is an unearned honor that has gone to Franklin Roosevelt," while columnist Heywood Broun dubbed him "the corkscrew candidate." Some members recalled, too, that Walter Lippmann had recently characterized him in print as "a pleasant man who, without any important qualifications for the office, would very much like to be President."

One member of the Club, however, lawyer Adolf A. Berle, Jr. '13 AM'14 L'16, had long been an "idea man" in the candidate's entourage, and would be part of his post-inaugural "Brain Trust" of advisers.

On November 8, Roosevelt outpolled Hoover in a landslide, while the Democrats, pledged to end Prohibition, won control of both houses of Congress. And on November 22 President Lowell of Harvard announced that he was stepping down.

In the first nine months of 1932 costs had been reduced by $10,535— $8,000 in wages and the rest by such expedients as discontinuing Club bookmatches ($235) and orange sticks ($250), for a total reduction of 12.55 percent. But revenues had simultaneously declined by 14.63 percent. In the course of the year, the library's collection had grown by 456 volumes, including a romantic historical best seller, ideally suited to helping readers escape the Depression blahs, titled *Mutiny on the Bounty*, by Charles Nordhoff '09 and James Norman Hall G'11. But 725 members had resigned, been dropped or died, and membership was down to 5,469. Since Director McTurnan's arrival in April 1931 his office had placed 122 men in permanent and temporary jobs, but the Committee on Appointments' original funding was by now almost exhausted.

Members alert to historic occasions would have thought twice in January 1933 before discarding their invitations to the annual dinner, at which the principal speakers were the retiring president of the University and the president-elect of the United States. In any case, the event was well-attended, and it brought the Club a modest profit.

Early in February, the press reported, President-elect Roosevelt went fishing off Florida in the yacht *Nourmahal*, the guest of her owner, Vincent Astor. On the fifteenth, shortly after he came ashore in Miami, a would-be assassin fired a pistol at him but missed, instead mortally wounding Mayor Anton J. Cermak of Chicago. A week later, Club members were amused to hear about the *Crimson*'s "scoop," revealing the selection of a fictitious Midwestern businessman as the University's new president, a hoax so successful that the Associated Press sent the story out around the world. And on March 4 Franklin D. Roosevelt was inaugurated president of the United States, the second member of the Club to reach that exalted office.

The presidentially decreed "bank holiday," during which every citizen had to make do with whatever cash he or she happened to have on hand, cannot have greatly affected life at 27 West 44th Street, where all transactions were on a credit basis. By March 13, most banks had reopened; on the sixteenth, at the Club, workmen began installing tanks, tubing and pumps in the Bar, and on April 7 beer, on draft and in bottles, flowed openly at 27 West 44th Street for the first time since 1920.

With the Appointments Committee down to its last $426, the Harvard Alumni Association took over the operation of the New York employment office, retaining Lee McTurnan in charge.

In April, Literature Chairman Edmund Pearson reported that member Samuel Williamson '16, the editor of a magazine called *News-Week*, which the chairman described as "somewhat similar to *Time* but written in English," had given the Club a year's subscription to it. Pearson also noted the purchase of several books by or about Harvard men: *Looking*

Drawing by Gluyas Williams; © 1933, 1961 The New Yorker Magazine, Inc.

*Forward,* by President Roosevelt; *Justice Oliver Wendell Holmes,* by Silas Bent; *Henry Adams,* by James Truslow Adams; *Adventures in Ideas,* by Alfred North Whitehead SD (hon.) '26; and a novel of contemporary Harvard undergraduate life, *Not to Eat, Not for Love* by George Anthony Weller '29, a former editorial chairman of the *Crimson.* (Weller's book would soon be in greater demand than any other title.)

The second-floor reading rooms, with their deep armchairs and wide sofas, continued to attract both readers and post-prandial nap-takers—as captured in line to perfection by member Gluyas Williams '11 in a drawing that appeared in the May 11, 1933, issue of *The New Yorker,* and which, framed and always on display somewhere, has since delighted countless members and guests. There were, to be sure, rare occasions in which the Library ceased to be a quiet refuge, as

James B. Conant

when, on May 9, following the announcement in Cambridge that chemistry professor James Bryant Conant would succeed Lowell as president of the University, it was suddenly overrun by reporters seeking data and color on Conant and Harvard.

With the coming of summer a three-way contest for mayor of New York began to shape up in which three lawyer members would participate importantly on behalf of Fiorello La Guardia, a former Republican Congressman of decidedly progressive views. Adolf A. Berle, Jr., organized support for La Guardia among leading citizens like Judge Seabury, who hated Tammany Hall and yearned for honest government. Charles C. Burlingham, a revered elder statesman of civic reform, presided adroitly over a turbulent meeting of reformers that named La Guardia the candidate of the City Fusion Party. Finally, the redoubtable William E.

Chadbourne became campaign manager for La Guardia, who also ran as a Republican.

In October, with the mayoral race heating up, the Board elected President Roosevelt an honorary member. The House Committee revealed that while revenues had fallen almost 11 percent during the year to date, operating costs had decreased by 14 percent, netting the Club that almost forgotten entity, a profit. The committee requested and obtained funds to set up an oyster bar in the Dining Room and to purchase a "beer-and-beverage wagon" for use in serving dinners in the private dining rooms. (With one state legislature after another ratifying the Twenty-first Amendment to the Constitution, repealing the Eighteenth Amendment, it was clear that the days of the "noble experiment," Prohibition, were numbered.)

On Election Day, November 7, La Guardia defeated his two opponents, independent Democrat Joseph V. McKee and Tammany stalwart John J. O'Brien. He would take office in January. The new mayor would include several liberal Republican members of the Club in his government. Berle, whose financial judgment he valued, would become city chamberlain, Langdon W. Post '23 commissioner of housing and William C. Chanler '19 L'22 corporation counsel. Burlingham—the one man living, it was said, to whom the fiery, feisty mayor invariably deferred—was usually around to offer sage advice. Among other Club members in the La Guardia administration were Fulton Cutting '09 AM'11 MEE '12 SD'15 and Goodhue Livingston, Jr. '20, who, after filling lesser posts, would become the mayor's executive secretary.

When the Harvard Hall broadcasts of football games resumed, members found they could follow the gridiron action perfectly well without the indicator board, which had been retired—permanently, it would turn out. For some reason, however, a falling off of interest in football seems to have occurred: so few members applied for tickets to the Yale game, to be played on Soldiers Field, that for the first time in memory plans to hire a special train were scrapped and arrangements were made instead to attach a special car to a regular Boston-bound train. It was a pity, for Harvard won handily, 19–6.

In November Lee McTurnan, having been offered an executive position with a blue-chip firm, resigned, amid a chorus of praise for his good work; in his place, the Cambridge office appointed Blodgett Sage '17. And at 5:32 P.M. EST on Tuesday, December 5, Utah became the thirty-sixth state to ratify the Twenty-first Amendment, which, with three-quarters of the states thus concurring, thereupon went into effect. The Club was prepared, having purchased—not, strictly speaking, legally—liquor worth $1,500. As the legalization of beer had, Repeal caused an immediate upsurge in attendance at the Club, but the plunge, which had reopened, remained largely unfrequented.

Three days before Repeal, longtime member Travis Howard Whitney L'03, a partner in a prestigious Wall Street law firm, took on the task of directing the Civil Works Administration's program for the city, an undertaking that would end tragically. He had been appointed by presidential adviser Harry Hopkins at the suggestion of Mayor-elect La Guardia. The C.W.A., a brainchild of Hopkins's, aimed to provide temporary employment for millions through the winter of 1933–34—in New York, clearing the city's parks, rebuilding its rotting docks, setting up shelters for the homeless, constructing covered municipal markets and repairing public buildings.

On assuming his new post, Whitney became a man possessed, driving himself unsparingly to help the hundreds of thousands of desperate men and women wandering the streets. One day, as Thomas Kessner relates in *Fiorello H. La Guardia and the Making of Modern New York*, Whitney telephoned Heywood Broun and said that if the columnist would give him a list of jobless reporters he would place them in C.W.A. projects. When should he come over? Broun asked. Now, Whitney replied. Before long Broun was facing a tense, utterly serious individual who asked to see his list, and on learning that Broun had none told him brusquely, "That won't do at all. You don't understand. This is a rush job, every day counts."

He meant it. In just over five weeks, Whitney placed thousands of unemployed New Yorkers in jobs, but on January 8, 1934, he collapsed in exhaustion on his desk. He was rushed to the hospital, but it was too late. "Killed in action," wrote Heywood Broun.

In 1933 artist Chester Price had turned out another elegant etching of the clubhouse facade, for sale to members, and the Scholarships

Committee, citing a lack of "really first-class material among the applicants," had awarded only three freshman grants-in-aid. The membership had contracted again, to 5,228, but expenses had been drastically reduced. In its first act of 1934, the Board showed its high regard for the Club's hard-working manager, Frank J. Melia, by voting him $1,000 and insisting that he take a vacation. The Sunday afternoon concerts were mobbed, but as more bodies meant more revenue the Board ignored complaints of overcrowding. And the 1934 annual dinner, affording members a chance to see and hear their alma mater's new chief, attracted more than 500 members.

That winter, the coldest in decades, witnessed the usual tournaments in backgammon, bridge and squash, with Beekman Pool '32 again capturing the metropolitan squash racquets championship. Apart from the July outing with the Yale Club, from Copey's yearly visit (his twenty-ninth) and from talks by unpaid volunteers, including Professors Samuel Eliot Morison and Harlow Shapley '10 SD (hon.) '33, not much of great importance transpired at the Club in 1934, although Blodgett Sage's office did place sixty men in permanent jobs, a new record for a single year. But the efforts to stem the exodus of members continued. In October, House Committee Chairman Ralph Blaikie '14, a restaurateur by occupation, boldly offered a complete lunch for 55 cents and a dinner for 75; in December, however, acknowledging that his experiment had not boosted attendance in the Dining Room after all, he ordered a retreat to the old prices.

As 1935 began the Club's membership stood at 5,080, down 1,290 since the onset of the Depression. While no one could yet say the decline was over, it was clear from the new faces at the clubhouse—and old faces that hadn't been visible for some time—that a recruiting drive launched the previous fall by a special committee on membership, under Chairman Thomas W. Lamont and Secretary Grinnell Martin '10, with the participation of representatives of College classes and the graduate schools, was beginning to bear fruit. Waiving entrance fees helped, as did reducing to one year the requirement that former graduate students spend two years at their school to be eligible for membership.

Chances are that simple curiosity drew a number of members, particularly those in the financial community, to the 1935 annual dinner, at which a featured speaker was the newly appointed first chairman of the recently created Securities and Exchange Commission, Joseph P. Kennedy '12.

One night, a certain member in his forties got drunk and started behaving in an abusive manner; in February the Board suspended him for five years. Disorderly conduct was becoming a problem, and in March Chairman Blaikie successfully proposed that member Theodore L. Turney, Jr. '24, a former football player who happened to be unmarried, be engaged to enforce discipline in the clubhouse nightly from 9:00 P.M. until 1:00 A.M. closing time in return for free lodging and meals at half price. Turney's tour would last from April 1 through July.

On April 3 the Club gave a dinner honoring Harvard's new football coach, Richard C. Harlow. At a Board meeting later that month a central concern was a portrait, not actually there in the Mahogany Room, of President Roosevelt, showing him in profile, seated at a desk. It had been painted at the request of Roger A. Derby '05 (who, though an investment banker, admired the president) by Margaret White, a daughter of the well-known physicist Robert W. Wood '91 of Johns Hopkins and sister of member Robert W. Wood, Jr. '16. President Marvin, who had seen it, pronounced the canvas an excellent likeness of his onetime law partner, but said the Club had no funds with which to buy it, and the Board consequently left it to Derby to raise the painter's $1,000 fee.

Night after night that spring, watchman Turney conscientiously—and as inconspicuously as he could—patrolled the Club's public rooms, but there was little for him to do. The one instance of someone stepping out of line occurred early in May when a middle-aged party, mellow, perhaps, but hardly intoxicated, treated two Club servants to drinks. (Summoned later to account for this act, the man declared, with perfect ingenuousness, that he had not realized that what he had done was against the rules!)

At the Board's May meeting the news could not have been more encouraging: 289 new members had been admitted since the start of the year, compared to 88 during the same period in 1934, and 105 old members readmitted. Meanwhile, Roger Derby had collected Margaret White's fee from other admirers of the chief executive, paid her and presented the portrait to the Club. It had been hung in the entrance hall. Within a day or

President Franklin D. Roosevelt, by Margaret White

two President Marvin received a letter, the first of several in similar vein, demanding that the image of the hated "man in the White House" be taken down at once. Marvin replied in a tactful note, and the Board, to whom the matter was referred, took no action.

By early summer business at the bar was up, the restaurant was making money, and demand for the bedrooms was such that for the first time in years there was sometimes a waiting list for would-be overnight guests. At the end of July, Theodore L. Turney, Jr., completed his tour as what would now be called a security guard and moved out. Whether or not his experience had soured him on the single life or club life or both, Turney would get married in September.

For some reason, few members availed themselves of the newly refurbished plunge that summer even on the hottest days, prompting House Committeeman James H. Ripley '14 MCE'15 to advise that the facility be discontinued, thereby effecting important savings.

On his own initiative Ripley, an engineer, made a study of the Club's infrastructure, and in December the Board invited him to present his findings and recommendations. To circumvent the legal requirement to keep qualified (and costly) engineers on hand to service the brine system then in use for refrigeration and ice-making, Ripley suggested (a) installing a Frigidaire system to keep food cool and (b) buying ice, as needed, from suppliers. The Board appropriated funds for freezers. With regard to heating and lighting the clubhouse Ripley proposed that the Club install its own equipment for making electricity and steam, and President Marvin appointed a committee to consider the proposal. No one, apparently, remembered that the Club had depended on its own generator until 1926, when an earlier member of the House Committee had convinced the Board it could save money by purchasing power from outside.

(Today, the Club makes its own ice and buys both electricity and steam from Consolidated Edison; still, the suggestion is periodically raised that the Club economize by generating its own power.)

For some time the College authorities had been trying to persuade the Club to yield up (or return, as they may have construed the matter) one of its greatest treasures: a master of arts degree awarded in 1701 to Samuel Mather AB 1698, son of Cotton Mather '78 and grandson of Increase Mather '56, president of Harvard 1685-1701. Now, with Harvard's tercentenary looming, the Board voted to have the document photographed and the original framed for presentation to President Conant at the forthcoming annual dinner (the Club's seventieth).

Nineteen thirty-five produced the first annual growth in the Club's membership in six years, from 5,080 to 5,276. This increase was duly credited to those volunteers who had labored to recruit new members, coax former members back into the fold and persuade resigning members to reconsider. Their efforts undoubtedly helped, but the probability that the turnaround had come about largely as a result of improving business conditions was underscored by year-end data from the Committee on Appointments. During 1935 the club's employment office had found permanent or temporary jobs for 115 men and for the first time had been able to help undergraduates find summer work. Altogether, the office had placed one out of every three men who sought its assistance in a salaried position, and with the economy continuing to pick up its success rate in 1936 would rise to one applicant in two.

In January 1936, at the annual meeting, three new officers were elected, Francis M. Weld becoming president, Frederick Roy Martin '93 vice-president and Sheridan A. Logan '23 treasurer, Secretary Wendell alone continuing in his post.

That winter, as usual, the crowds attending the Sunday afternoon concerts taxed the capacity of Harvard Hall, the two balconies and adjacent rooms. Each concert was followed by the serving of tea and cocktails, with numerous members, many escorting woman guests, staying on for dinner. This routine had been standard for some years, but in January and February 1936, it worked out so well for all concerned—not excluding the Club's treasury—that the Board decided to continue encouraging woman guests to dine at the Club beyond the concert season into March and April. This innovation would, in turn, prove so popular that it, too, would become standard.

But even as the Club thus opened its doors a little wider to the opposite sex, two Sunday evening incidents demonstrated that the introduction of women into a normally monastic environment could produce unforeseen consequences. Curiously, both incidents featured members in their forties born and raised in the South. On January 26 a drama critic from Texas incensed a member twenty years his junior by speaking slightingly of his wife, and on entering the Dining Room sat down at a table occupied by two younger men and their woman guests; he was asked to leave, which, the minutes relate, "he took with ill grace." And on February 9, in the Grill Room, a lawyer from Mississippi, the host of a party that included women, struck a waiter in the mouth.

The puncher was summoned, as the earlier offender already had been, to a special meeting of the Board on March 18. Before that date, however, some brisk legal skirmishing occurred. Acting for the assaulted waiter, a lawyer member brought proceedings in magistrates' court against his client's assailant, who then, on the advice of Grenville Clark, sought an interview with him; this meeting proving futile, Clark telephoned the waiter's lawyer to propose a financial settlement. The man said his client would accept $2,000, which Clark rejected as excessive. The case came up on February 28 but was adjourned until March 10, when it was settled out of court for $600, a sum that included the cost of a new plate or set of false teeth for the waiter.

At the Board's special meeting the Mississippian read a statement explaining the incident from his perspective and expressing sincere regret therefor, whereupon Grenville Clark read letters extolling his friend's character from three well-known and widely respected members of the Club: Elihu Root, Jr. L'06, Howard Reid '12 L'15 and Robert P. Patterson L'15. Clark then read communications from two men who had been dinner guests of the Mississippian the night of the incident; both recalled believing at the time that the waiter—who had struck their host before the latter struck him—had been drunk. Further testimony established a consensus within the Board that the dinner host had not been intoxicated; that the waiter had not been drunk either, but had recently taken aspirin or some other medication that had affected his behavior; and that the waiter had landed the first blow.

Notwithstanding these conclusions, the Board censured the Mississippian, leaving to the House Committee the question of whether or not to reinstate the waiter in his job, and at its regular meeting the next day, following discussions that "became at times highly animated, although entirely within the bounds of friendly decorum," voted to suspend the denture-smashing lawyer from membership for three months, which punishment it imposed on the boorish drama critic as well.

The Club library now contained more than 20,000 books—20,102—and the Club's portrait collection was growing. At the joint request of President Lowell and Charles Hopkinson the Club exchanged its portrait of the former by the latter for another—and, in the opinions of both men, better—representation. It bought, with Club funds and private funds raised by Langdon P. Marvin, a likeness of General Wood by Stanley G. Middleton. And it acquired, by gift of member Walter T. Rosen '94, a crayon portrait by Alexander Iakovleff of C. C. Burlingham.

Since late 1930, when Langdon P. Marvin and Archibald G. Thacher '97 had initiated informal discussions about how best to celebrate the completion of Harvard's first three centuries, other members of the Club had joined them, and of the fourteen men, drawn from the Corporation, the Board of Overseers and the alumni generally, who made up the Tercentenary Committee, under the chairmanship of President (and honorary member) James Bryant Conant and in association with Tercentenary Historian (and nonresident member) Samuel Eliot Morison, no fewer than ten belonged to the Harvard Club of New York City. They were Charles Francis Adams '88, Henry S. Grew '96, Archibald G. Thacher '97, Langdon P. Marvin '98, Joseph L. Valentine '98, Henry James '99, Nathaniel F. Ayer '00, Alfred M. Tozzer '00, Henry L. Shattuck '01 and Grenville Clark '03. Since September 1934, moreover, primary responsibility for coming up with a program and organizing the proceedings had rested with still another Club member, whom the Corporation had appointed director of the Tercentenary Celebration on the committee's recommendation: Jerome D. Greene '96.

In May, President Weld appointed a committee of members to represent the Club at the Tercentenary, and at the invitation of the Tercentenary Committee about twenty-five Harvard graduates in the city, members and nonmembers, made up the New York contingent of the Tercentenary Chorus. Until mid-July they would rehearse frequently in the clubhouse under the direction of Lowell P. Beveridge '25.

In Cambridge, meanwhile, after the conclusion of Commencement on June 18, an extraordinary series of conferences, institutions and summer schools had begun; they continued all summer, culminating in the Tercentenary Conference on Arts and Sciences, August 31–September 12, to which a number of the country's and the world's leading scholars submitted papers. During the three final days of the celebration, September 16–18, emissaries from the foremost centers of learning of the Old and New Worlds were joined by many thousands of alumni, and among these, members of the New York Harvard Club were particularly conspicuous. The central feature of the second day of the celebration, a huge meeting, open to all Harvard men, of the Associated Harvard Clubs, was presided over by that body's president, nonresident member Elliott C. Cutler '09 MD'13, whose remarks followed an invocation by the Rev. Minot Simons '91 STB'94 of New York, himself both a resident member of the Club and a former president of the A.H.C.

That meeting was held in the open, in that part of the Yard bounded by

*Harvard Tercentenary*, by Waldo Peirce

Widener Library, Sever Hall, Memorial Church and University Hall, which area, with a platform of tiered seats extending in a slight arc across the south portico of the church and facing out on seats for 16,000 spectators, had been designated the Tercentenary Theater. The next morning, on the final and climactic day of the celebration, this quadrangle, under threatening skies but gay with crimson gonfalons, was the scene of a colorful academic procession, much oratory and the awarding of honorary degrees. But before noon the heavens opened. Following a break for lunch, the concluding exercises were therefore confined to Sanders Theatre, with loudspeakers outside it and in the Yard conveying the proceedings to the thousands who had to be excluded.

It was then, after a brief turn by a distant foreign leader, that three longtime members of the Club set their respective seals on the historic occasion. Following opening remarks by Presidents Lowell and Conant, the assembly heard "a message from the University of Cambridge": the voice of Stanley Baldwin, speaking via radio from England, not as prime minister but as chancellor of the ancient institution that, as the alma mater of most of Harvard's founders, was effectively her own foster mother. When President Lowell thanked Baldwin, another message was read aloud from another chief of state: Canada's—and the Club's—W. L. Mackenzie King, who regretted being prevented from attending by his duties as a Canadian delegate to the Assembly of the League of Nations, scheduled to meet momentarily in Geneva. Next, after the singing of a psalm, came an address, remarkable for its thoughtfulness and profundity, by New York's Learned Hand, judge of the Second Circuit and president of the Harvard Alumni Association. Finally, the moment arrived to hear from tophatted Franklin D. Roosevelt, who, to the amusement of his largely conservative and Republican audience, recalled, apropos of the College's bicentennial celebration 100 years before, that

> At that time, many of the alumni of Harvard were sorely troubled concerning the state of the nation. Andrew Jackson was president. On the two hundred and fiftieth anniversary of the founding of Harvard College, alumni again were sorely troubled. Grover Cleveland was president. Now, on the three hundredth anniversary, I am president.

No one in the laughing crowd needed to be reminded that Jackson and Cleveland had both been Democrats!

After the president spoke, the Tercentenary Chorus sang "The Shores of Harvard," with words by yet another member of the Club, Mark A. DeWolfe Howe. And finally, on a proposal by President Conant put to the assembled graduates by President Lowell and unanimously approved by them, the meeting of alumni was adjourned to September 18, 2036.

On November 3—to the satisfaction of some members but the chagrin of many more—President Roosevelt was reelected, by a lopsided tally of 523–8 in the Electoral College, over Governor Alfred M. Landon of Kansas. Meanwhile, with the encouragement of Appointments Committee Chairman John Price Jones, the well-known sportswriter John R. Tunis '11 had launched a course of instruction for members aspiring to write for publication, meeting weekly with an average of twenty men to criticize their work and advise them on how to market it. On alternate weeks Tunis brought in professionals to meet and talk with his writers' group, among them, during his workshop's first three months, editors on the staffs of the *Saturday Evening Post* and *Cosmopolitan*, member (and former squash tennis champion) Fillmore Hyde of *To-day*, and writers George Frazier '32 and George Weller.

As to words in print, that month saw a notable development at the Club library. Since its beginnings in the 1880s the facility had exclusively served readers on the spot, but although members were forbidden to make off with books some did, rarely bringing them back. In the hope of at least slowing this continuous depredation, the new librarian, Richard S. Currier '32, ordered a pair of rubber stamps made and began stamping each new acquisition, as it came in, HARVARD CLUB LIBRARY on its outer edge and PLEASE DO NOT TAKE THIS BOOK FROM THE HARVARD CLUB OF NEW YORK CITY inside.

With 1936 ending the Board felt (as it would state in its annual report) that due recognition should be paid to the achievement of Robert Grant III '34 in winning five of the Club's eight squash tournaments: the Class A squash racquets championship and all four of the squash tennis championships. It was a feat that had never before been equaled.

Once again the Club had grown in 1936, to 5,413. But the outlook ahead was not promising: after a gradual and partial recovery the national economy was about to slide into recession, with the result that during the rest of the decade and beyond the Club would continue to lose members, though not so precipitately as in 1930–34.

On the afternoon of Wednesday, January 20, 1937, a chamber music concert by the Stradivarius Quartet was said to have broken all records for attendance, and on Sunday, March 14, Harvard Hall was again filled to overflowing, for a lecture by *Herald Tribune* columnist Dorothy Thompson. Her topic was a plan President Roosevelt had asked Congress to approve, empowering him to appoint up to six associate justices to the Supreme Court in case all six of the sitting justices aged seventy and older declined to retire. While Miss Thompson's celebrity undoubtedly helped to swell her audience, hers was just one of several so-called entertainments being offered by the Club that were, in fact, serious explorations of contemporary political and social issues. By the late 1930s Harvard graduates were clearly tending, in common with other thoughtful Americans, to be more concerned about important developments in the national and international news than they and their like had been just a few years before.

Of the twenty-one nonmusical entertainments presented at the Club in 1937 only four were of the familiar hunting-fishing-mountaineering variety. Three dealt with science and technology, one was an old standby (Copey's thirty-first reading), another parochial (two short films about Harvard) and still another just fun ("Nickelodeon Nights," old silent movies plus homegrown amateur talent). All the rest, starting in January with a talk and film about the ongoing Spanish civil war by member Arthur von B. Menken '25 and ending in December with a lecture by Harvard Professor Samuel Hazzard Cross '12 AM'15 PhD'16 on "Soviet Government by Trial and Error," treated aspects of a world become, with Nazism and Fascism in Europe and ruthless Japanese military aggression in Asia, ever more menacing.

In May, completing their course after twenty-eight meetings, John R. Tunis's aspiring writers agreed that their experiment had succeeded: one had contracted with a publisher to write a book, a number had sold articles to national magazines and virtually all had submitted prose or verse to periodicals or publishing houses. Meanwhile, Literature Chairman Pearson reported that new books had practically ceased disappearing from the library, the stamped identification on them rendering them next to useless to collectors and dealers, and almost guaranteeing their return.

That spring, two evolving news stories dominated the headlines—as well, no doubt, as much conversation at the Club. One told of mounting opposition to Roosevelt's latest scheme, even among his friends: thus C. C. Burlingham, who had supported him in 1932 and 1936 and would again in 1940, informed his class secretary that "my absorbing passion has been to help beat the President's plan to enlarge the Supreme Court." The other recorded a titanic struggle being waged by John L. Lewis's Congress of Industrial Organizations, through the novel tactic of the sitdown strike, to force the makers of America's automobiles and steel to recognize the C.I.O.'s constituent unions as the sole representatives of their workers in collective bargaining over labor-management disputes.

In late April or early May the Club itself became the target of an attempt by outsiders to organize its work force, but unlike the sitdown strikers in the Midwest these would-be organizers—affiliates of the C.I.O.'s older and less militant rival, the American Federation of Labor—were not at all confrontational. As Secretary Wendell recorded the incident, Manager Melia "received communications from a person or persons who represented that they spoke for certain employees of the Club in requesting various changes in working arrangements, conditions, wages, etc." The callers asked for a conference, whereupon President Weld, on the Board's recommendation, authorized the chairman of the House Committee and others to meet with the employees' representatives; when they did, Chairman Curt E. Hansen and his colleagues found, no doubt to their relief, that the Club could readily grant all of the employees' requests (including improved ventilation in their working areas) except those relating to wages, which they promised to study carefully.

On the question of recognizing the A.F.L. union—the Hotel, Restaurant and Cafeteria Employees' Organization—as its employees' sole bargaining agent, however, the Club's governors balked: on hearing the union's terms read aloud, the Board instructed Chairman Hansen to tell its leaders the Club would not sign the contract in the form presented.

In June the Board viewed—and accepted—a portrait of Langdon P. Marvin, acquired by subscription, by Ellen Emmet Rand. Marvin, as it happened, was present, with some mildly upsetting news: the Mississippi-born lawyer who had been suspended for striking a waiter, and who had since resigned, was prepared to sue the Club for libel and breach of contract over its having posted a public notice of his suspension. It would be, Marvin believed, the first time anyone had ever sued the Club. The former president said he thought the matter could be settled with a diplomatic letter to the complainant over Secretary Wendell's signature, whereupon the Board asked him, Wendell and President Weld to compose and dispatch such a communication. As the minutes of subsequent meetings of the Board contain no further mention of the threatened lawsuit, it seems likely that Marvin's hunch proved correct.

On June 24 Thomas Slocum, a lifelong bachelor whose services to the Club exceeded those of any other member before or since, succumbed at seventy to a wasting illness. His colleagues recalled that he had, uniquely, held every Club office (secretary 1902–07, treasurer

1917–18, vice-president 1919–24, president 1924–27), chaired the Admissions Committee (1916–17) and twice served as an Overseer (1914–20 and 1923–29). Slocum's timely acquisitions of property for the future expansion of the clubhouse were gratefully remembered, as was his delightful penthouse a few paces east, overlooking 27 West 44th Street, where he had dispensed hospitality to countless Harvard men. (He had been able to live atop an office building, technically in violation of the zoning laws, by having himself designated the building's resident janitor.)

Around then, workmen moved the portrait of President Roosevelt from the north wall of the entrance hall, left of the door to the Grill Room, to a spot above the first landing of the main staircase, in its place hanging the new likeness of former President Marvin. With anti-Roosevelt sentiment peaking over the court-packing plan, some people saw this as a downgrading of the president's image; rumors flew, and on July 12 the *New York Times* weighed in with ROOSEVELT CANVAS/REPLACED AT CLUB, acknowledging that the presidential portrait was still on view but adding that "one must climb three stairs to see it." A Club spokesman was quoted denying a report that some younger members had tried to bear the portrait out into the street and destroy it, "regardless of the fact that some members may not see eye to eye with him politically." And two days later the same paper ran a caustic epistolary comment headed "Harvard Club Portraits":

> Very unimportant, but behold how misunderstandings are started in this world. Your reporter creates the impression that the economic royalists of the Harvard Club have insulted the President of the United States by putting his picture where you have to climb three stairs to see it. Will you kindly take that reporter to your Webster's and show him the difference between stairs and steps? . . .
>
> Furthermore, who said that the pictures to the left of the grill . . . are placed there as a token of honor? I am under the impression that all the latest arrivals go to that spot for a little while until they are buried decently in more secure places. Which is as it should be, for most of the portraiture of the Harvard Club is abominable.
>
> HENDRIK WILLEM VAN LOON

Eight days after this the Senate killed the president's court-packing bill, 70–20.

During that summer more meetings were held with representatives of the A.F.L. local, Local 6, but the Board, having raised the employees' wages and increased payments for unemployment and old-age insurance, was less inclined than ever to accept the union as the workers' sole bargaining agent. In November it accepted, from the sitter's family, a portrait of the late incorporator Clement Cleveland. And in December it returned to the donors, as unacceptable, contributions to the Employees' Christmas Fund which had been made contingent on the employees' voting not to unionize.

On Saturday, December 5, in an election held under the supervision of the New York State Labor Relations Board at the Bar Association building, diagonally across 44th Street, most of the Club's personnel opted to designate the Hotel, Restaurant and Cafeteria Employees Organization, A.F.L., their exclusive agent in collective bargaining. The vote was 69 for the union, 21 against and 1 ballot blank. (Four months later, on March 29, 1938, in a second N.Y.L.R.B. election, a large majority of the Club's culinary and maintenance workers would follow suit, making the Club a union shop.)

Finally, House Committee Chairman Hansen and his colleagues, particularly James H. Ripley, could pride themselves on a remarkable achievement: reducing the Club's bill for electricity, water and steam, in just two years, by a third, from $42,124 in 1935 to $28,544 in 1937.

Before the 1938 annual meeting both President Weld and Secretary Wendell declined renomination. Small wonder: Weld had served as an officer continuously since 1919, for nineteen years, breaking his father's record of fifteen years (1868–83), while Wendell had held his post for thirteen years, longer than anyone else. In the event, only Treasurer Logan stayed in office. Vice-President Frederick Roy Martin, assistant general manager of the Associated Press, was elected president, surgeon Eugene H. Pool '95 vice-president and lawyer Francis Kernan '24 L'27 secretary.

In February John Price Jones reported that an ad hoc group considering ways to honor the late Thomas Slocum were agreed that the Centre Room, on the third floor north of the Mahogany Room and southeast of the Biddle Room, would be converted, with funds to be raised privately, into a memorial to Slocum. Next, a two-man "inspection committee" (St. John Smith '98 L'01 and John Elliott '12) suggested that a "cheap dinner" be introduced "for the convenience of younger members." But Chairman Hansen declared that it would be impractical to offer a dinner for under a dollar. His stand seems to have sparked a rare revolt within the committee, for in April Hansen announced the debut of a two-course dinner, with meat, potatoes, vegetable, dessert and coffee, for 85 cents. This meal would have many takers, helping the restaurant department to realize, according to the annual report, an exceptionally good year.

Meanwhile, a prominent member of the Club had become embroiled in a highly public scandal. He was stockbroker Richard Whitney, the man who on "Black Thursday" in October 1929 had temporarily halted panic selling on the floor of the New York Stock Exchange and had since been rewarded with five consecutive one-year terms as president of that institution. There, at the beginning of trading on Tuesday, March 8, 1938, had come the stunning announcement that his firm had been suspended for insolvency; Whitney had filed for bankruptcy protection, and thereafter had been indicted by New York County for embezzling $105,000 from his father-in-law's estate and by New York State for misusing $120,000 in bonds belonging to the Club's West 44th Street neighbor, the New York Yacht Club, of which he was treasurer. Having resigned from that club— and from the Board of Overseers' visiting committee to the Department of Economics—Whitney had pleaded guilty to combined charges of grand larceny; on April 11 a judge had sentenced him to five to ten years behind bars, and the next day, handcuffed to two other prisoners, he had been escorted by train up the Hudson to Sing Sing prison.

Nine days later the Board, having solemnly considered a letter of resignation from Whitney, voted to accept it "with regret."

At the start of that summer the Board accepted a portrait by Robert Brackman of former President Weld, who donated it, and on Chairman Hansen's assurance that the facility would soon pay for itself in increased efficiency, voted funds to construct a kitchen pantry next to the Dining Room. While this work went forward on the ground floor, workmen on the third floor were creating a handsome but also eminently usable shrine to Thomas Slocum, among other things installing paneling from his penthouse apartment. And in November Manager Melia organized three special trains to New Haven. Harvard won, 7–0. Later, Treasurer Logan jubilantly lauded Melia for his enterprise, which netted the Club $3,300.

Ordinarily, the return to the fold of a strayed member was of interest only to his friends and the Admissions Committee, but in December one such event was deemed to be of such exceptional interest that it was brought to the attention of the Board, to be dealt with as that body's first item of business:

> The application of Mr. Robert Benchley, Class of '12, for readmission to the Club, was read and discussed.
>
> It was unanimously voted that Mr. Benchly [*sic*] should be reinstated on payment of the $25 enclosed with his letter.

Eighteen years after resigning in disgust from the Admissions Committee and the Club, Bob Benchley was back!

During the year now ending membership had again declined, to 5,194, but gross revenues were, gratifyingly, up. For the third straight year Germain G. Glidden '36 had won the national squash racquets championship, together with the New York State and metropolitan titles. The library was richer by 585 volumes, many from Thomas Slocum's collection. And the new kitchen pantry was in constant use, speeding food to diners' tables sooner and hotter.

But the most important amenity the Club acquired in 1938 was the Slocum Room, toward the construction and decoration of which more than 400 members had eventually subscribed. Arthur C. Jackson '88 had overseen the architectural work, while George Nichols and Slocum's older brother, William H. Slocum '86, had provided gifts and loans of both cash and valuable memorabilia. Together with the Board Room, furnished by the Mahogany Club, and the Biddle Room, presented by Vincent Astor, the Slocum Room now offered, as John Price Jones wrote, "a third fine place for general enjoyment and private entertainment."

On January 5, 1939, President Roosevelt appointed to the Supreme Court, replacing deceased Justice Benjamin Cardozo LLD (hon.) '27, his longtime confidential adviser, a Club member for a third of a century, Harvard Law Professor Felix Frankfurter. Before that winter was out a third great jurist who had himself once belonged to the Club, Justice Louis D. Brandeis, would step down from the Court, whereupon the president would pick S.E.C. Chairman William O. Douglas to fill the vacancy.

For some reason fewer Sunday afternoon concertgoers than in past years were staying on for tea and dinner; to diversify these weekly programs Chorister John K. Watson '23 decided to extend the "winter" concerts into April, alternating them with entertainments. Some of the latter were lighthearted (e.g., Helen Howe portraying "Characters and Caricatures") but in the wake of the Anglo-French capitulation to Hitler at Munich the previous September more programs reflected concerns that were troubling many members: thus in February Graham Hutton spoke on "British Foreign Policy Since Munich" and the Countess of Listowel on "What Munich Means to Europe"; in March, colonial administrator Sir Ronald Storrs discussed "The Problem of Palestine"; and in early April Harvard Professor Bruce C. Hopper '18 AM'25 PhD'30 lectured on "Comintern and Fascintern versus Democintern—the Impending Division of the World?"

On the evening of March 23, before an overflow audience in Harvard Hall, the Club presented three University professors—historian Crane Brinton '19, economist Sumner Slichter LLD (hon.) '49, and Carl J. Friedrich AM (hon.) '42 of the government department—in a colloquium on "Social Science and the Future of Democracy." Was Professor Slichter aware that his hosts, confronted by a union, were determined never to let their club become a closed shop? It would seem unlikely, but the officers and Board members present doubtless heard with considerable interest what he had to say on the subject. Slichter spoke of the almost universal belief among managers that a closed shop gave organized labor a stranglehold over employers, but then went on to cite a recent study of 300 actual labor-management agreements which showed that in practice open shops imposed restrictions on employers' rights to lay off employees far more often and more rigorously than did closed shops.

As W. Roger Burlingame '13 noted in a report on the colloquium in the *Harvard Alumni Bulletin*, none of the speakers betrayed misgivings regarding "the future of democracy." But events in Europe hardly appeared to justify such confidence: less than a week after the speechmaking, for example, Madrid fell to Franco's Falangists, ending Spain's civil war in total victory for antidemocratic forces allied to Nazi Germany and Fascist Italy.

In America, meanwhile, not many miles from the clubhouse, another, apolitical vision of the future had taken form, and at the end of April President Roosevelt officially opened the biggest international exposition ever put on anywhere, at Flushing Meadows, Queens, site of the first New York World's Fair. During the weeks and months that followed, hundreds, perhaps thousands, of members made their way out to "The World of Tomorrow." There they found, extending outward from the Theme Center, with its symbolic Trylon (a slender, three-sided pyramid) and Perisphere (an enormous sphere), low buildings of various curious configurations, unlike anything they had ever seen before, housing various exhibits. Did the sight of these futuristic structures remind certain visitors from midtown Manhattan of the Club's own building project and suggest they get on with it?

In fact, preparations to construct a two-story western extension of the clubhouse had been going forward for months. Lawrence G. White had drawn up plans for a ladies' dining room and other rooms, and for an extension of the bar, all of these spaces to be provided with that marvelous new amenity, air-conditioning. Simultaneously, a scheme had been worked out to finance the project independently of the Club treasury, with proceeds of the sale of ten-year bonds and a sizeable bequest that Thomas Slocum had left the Club; the necessary funds were in hand, and demolition of 33 West 44th Street could begin at any time.

Before long, however, events overseas put all such undertakings in doubt. On August 24 Germany and the U.S.S.R. signed a pact of mutual nonaggression; on September 1, German forces invaded Poland; on September 3, Poland's allies, Britain and France, their ultimatums to Berlin ignored, declared war on Germany; and on September 17 Soviet forces began to occupy eastern Poland. Thanks to the enterprise of Entertainment Committee Chairman Howard Reid, the first speakers to address the Club following these momentous developments were former heads of state of the two aggressor powers: former chancellor and foreign minister Heinrich Brüning of Germany, now teaching at Harvard, and onetime (July–November 1917) prime minister of Russia Aleksandr Kerensky.

Still, the outbreak of a second great European war did not immediately affect Club activities. In October, after discussing a proposal to order a plaque honoring Gilman "Colly" Collamore, who had just died, the managers heard a detailed report of the cost of constructing the proposed addition. In the end, however, they put off acting on the matter, and by November, having come to agree with President Martin that the element of uncertainty introduced by the war in Europe demanded that they defer the project indefinitely, they voted to return all subscriptions for the new building to their donors.

With Poland defeated and partitioned, hostilities had been suspended in Europe until, at the end of November, the Red Army invaded Finland on a trumped-up pretext. Americans rallied to the support of little Finland, long enshrined in their affections as the one country that had unfailingly repaid its previous world war debts. Most, of course, also hoped that Britain and France would somehow prevail against Nazi Germany, but a large majority were determined, this time around, to stay out of the war.

In December, Treasurer Logan regretfully informed the Board of what might almost be called perfidy on the part of that highly respectable institution, the New York, New Haven and Hartford Railroad. The Club had earned considerably less in November 1939, Logan reported, than during the previous November—partly because restaurant and bedroom receipts were down, but mainly because the railroad had taken back for itself the liquor concession on the special football trains.

By 1940 the Club's membership was down to 5,054, and parts of the clubhouse were looking a little shabby. In March, House Committee Chairman Hansen presented a list of ten long-overdue repairs and replacements that would cost $3,660; Treasurer Logan gave him a quick verbal rundown of the Club's financial situation, whereupon Hansen revised his wish list to just three items costing $500: slipcovers for Harvard Hall, two typewriters and ventilation for the new Dining Room pantry. The Board obliged. Incidentally, President Martin pointed out that the Club was benefiting greatly from the continuing movement of business firms into midtown Manhattan, as a result of which, at lunchtime most weekdays, the Bar and Dining Room were very busy places.

By May the Soviet Union had annexed part of Finland, and the "phony war" of waiting had exploded in *Blitzkrieg*, "lightning war," as German mobile units overran Denmark and invaded Norway. On May 11, a day after Winston Churchill replaced Neville Chamberlain as Britain's prime minister, with the German war machine rolling inexorably across the Netherlands and Belgium, the World's Fair re-opened. Next day, the *Times* and *Herald Tribune* reported that over the coming weekend the Club would be host to the Associated Harvard Clubs, and on the morning of Friday, May 17, delegates representing 123 Harvard clubs across the country and around the world, some 1,200 of them, started converging on 27 West 44th Street.

That three-day meeting, memorialized in the clubhouse in two framed drawings done at the time by the famous illustrator James Montgomery Flagg showing Father Knickerbocker, in tricorn and knee breeches, cordially welcoming a gawky John Harvard in Puritan garb, was an important event in the annals of the Club, then just months shy of its seventy-fifth anniversary. The A.H.C.'s forty-third annual meeting was only the second ever held in New York City.

Harvard Comes to New York

On Friday evening the Metropolitan Opera House was the setting of a symposium, presided over by President Conant, on "Our Expanding Horizons"; the proceedings, explorations of the theme by four Harvard professors in relation to, respectively, science, industry, foreign policy and public education, were transmitted by wire to Boston and thence broadcast internationally by shortwave radio. The following night, the association's annual dinner was held at the Hotel Astor, and as the diners lighted up postprandial cigars, toastmaster Marvin read aloud a communication from an old friend in Washington who may well, in the act of composing it, have called to mind that joyous evening twenty-eight years before, in the same place and under the same auspices, when he himself had been among the merrymakers:

> What this weary old world, worn with strife and discord, most needs is more laughs, something that will afford escape from the tumult of the time disconsolate. I hope the meeting of the Associated Clubs will do just that. Please give all the Harvard family my hearty greeting.

President Roosevelt's words prompted some handclapping, but also hoots, jeers and catcalls, inspiring Mayor La Guardia to observe that any Harvard graduate could be sure of getting a warm welcome at any Harvard gathering "unless the particular alumnus happens to become President of the United States"; which remark elicited, the *Times* reported, "sportsmanlike applause."

Sunday was officially Harvard Day at the World's Fair, and at the appointed midafternoon hour the delegates assembled on a lawn formerly occupied by, until it was recently torn down, the Soviet pavilion. "I am gratified," Board Chairman Harvey D. Gibson of the Fair Corporation told them, "to greet the crimson of Harvard on this American Common here today rather than the red of Russia. The contrast could not be greater, since we all know that the crimson of Harvard stands for decency and honesty. I hate to think what the red of Russia stood for during the last few months."

Before long the A.H.C. delegates were heading home, and their meeting in New York became a memory.

One week after this, the evacuation to England, from Dunkerque in northern France, of about 335,000 Allied troops began, in vessels large and small. On June 9, as German soldiers thrust westward into France, their comrades took Norway; next day, Italy declared war on France and invaded, and on the twenty-second the French government capitulated, first to Germany and then to Italy, leaving Britain standing alone against the all-conquering Axis powers.

At this point, on schedule, America's presidential electoral machinery whirred into action. The Republicans nominated Wendell Willkie, a Wall Street lawyer, for president. Roosevelt kept his intentions to himself, but when the Democrats renominated him he accepted. This flouting of the hallowed tradition, based on George Washington's example, of limiting presidents to two terms outraged many citizens, including many members of the Club, who, in the Bar, Grill Room, Dining Room, locker rooms or elsewhere, roundly denounced this latest offense to decency by their least favorite fellow member.

On July 10, the Soviet Union seized the three small Baltic republics of Lithuania, Latvia and Estonia. And in August the German air force, preparatory to an amphibious invasion of England, intensified its attacks on British coastal defenses and shipping. So began the Battle of Britain. On August 24 the Germans shifted their attacks inland to Royal Air Force installations and aircraft factories, but on failing to gain air control over southern England they began, on September 7, night bombing of London and other cities. Although the Luftwaffe greatly outnumbered the R.A.F. it lost far more planes and pilots; gradually the German high command gave up hope of invading England any time soon, and toward the end of October its attacks tapered off.

This first major check to Germany's plans of conquest convinced many Americans—undoubtedly including many Club members—that the beleaguered British might yet stave off defeat, and engendered in some a positive willingness to help them do so. Even as the great air battle raged, moreover, our government, which in June had approved the sale of surplus war material to Britain, announced the transfer to the Royal Navy of fifty overage destroyers in exchange for the use of British naval and air bases in the Western Hemisphere. (C. C. Burlingham played a key behind-the-scenes role in arranging this historic deal.) And Congress passed legislation that set in place the first peacetime conscription in the nation's history, calling for the registration of all men between the ages of twenty-one and thirty-five and the induction into the armed forces of 800,000 draftees.

This measure affected the Club directly, of course, and at the Board's October meeting Chairman Hansen proposed that employees who were drafted or who volunteered to serve be given bonuses. The Board decided that for the time being Manager Melia should refer individual cases to President Martin and Chairman Hansen for action, and it authorized Martin to appoint a committee on military and naval affairs. Meanwhile, members could hear journalist John Wheeler-Bennett speak on "Four Recent Weeks at Home in London" and the noted biographer and novelist André Maurois try to answer the question "What Happened to France?"

On November 5 most members stoically accepted as regrettable but unavoidable the reelection of President Roosevelt to an unprecedented third term, and three weeks later the Board dealt with sundry matters, for one thing approving the sale at the cigar counter, during the pre-Christmas season, of items labeled BUNDLES FOR BRITAIN, for British war relief. Finally, at the conclusion of scheduled business, President Martin spoke of the remissness of the Club in not providing more and better "facilities for the ladies." The Club was, he said, lagging behind comparable organizations in this respect, and would sooner or later have to catch up. He asked Marvin, Hansen and Reid to look into the matter.

Beginning the following evening, this trio sought the advice of four architect members—Lawrence G. White, C. Kenneth Clinton '12, William E. Shepard '12 and William H. Russell '18—who willingly focused their imagination and talents on the project. Their common objective, all agreed, was an attractive and adequately capacious suite of rooms within the existing clubhouse that would require minimal structural changes and a relatively small operating staff. Over three weeks, the seven men met often. By degrees, they arrived at a consensus, expressed in drawings by Clinton, Shepard and Russell. And at the Board's December meeting the three-man panel submitted an amply illustrated report.

Their initial problem (the planners wrote) was to decide how people were going to get into the ladies' facilities from the street. A lady could, of course, enter by the main entrance, turn right and proceed into the Visitors' Room, her view of the Club's interior (and members' view of *her*) blocked off by walls or screens boxing in an area of about fifteen by fifteen feet. But having to share the entrance hall with women might well, the planners feared, provoke resignations by enough "crotchety" members to cost the Club dearly in lost dues and charges. It seemed important, too, to be able to state forthrightly, in printed material aimed at recruiting new members and luring back old ones, that the ladies' quarters were "completely isolated from the rest of the Club." (The members who had had the plan explained to them had liked all of its features except the common entrance lobby: "A separate one, by all means!" almost all had urged.)

The committeemen had consequently decided to build a separate ladies' entrance just east of the main entrance by transforming the window there into a proper doorway, reached by a couple of steps. They recommended this facility, even though it would cost a good deal to construct and would require an additional woman attendant, in order, they said, "to keep intact practically all of the first floor space for males only, except, of course, on approved Sundays."

Just inside the new ladies' entrance, part of the Visitors' Room would become a small entrance lobby, while the remainder, together with the space beyond, then occupied by the telephone operators, would be converted to "a prinking room [sic] for ladies," equipped with "powder puff tables, toilets, basins, a shower, one or two dressing rooms, etc." (The telephone operators would be moved back downstairs.) A staircase would be built in the rear of the entrance lobby, rising to the second floor and giving access to "the front or red room, now in use by relatively few members, some of whom nap and snore there." This "red room" (now the Cambridge Reading Room) would become a ladies' lounge, with a cocktail service bar either there or in the adjacent dining room. The west wall of the future lounge would be broken through to the Card Room (now the lower Cambridge Dining Room), which would be transformed into a ladies' dining room seating at least fifty people, with an adjacent kitchen and pantry.

As to operating costs, the planners posited a need for two women attendants downstairs and four new employees upstairs (cook, pantry woman, busboy and night cleaning woman). To finance the project they recommended offering members a ten-year 5 percent note issue. And in summing up, they declared, accurately enough, that their proposal amounted, not just to rooms for ladies, but to a complete ladies' clubhouse, insulated from and independent of the Club itself.

It was a lot for the Board members to take in all at once. For the present, they agreed that facilities of some sort for ladies were desirable, if not essential.

As of January 1, 1941, the Club had 4,968 members, some of whom were entering the armed forces; on the fourteenth, the Board excused thirty new servicemen from paying dues. It also scrapped provisions in the ladies' quarters plan to convert the reference library into a kitchen-cum-pantry and the main library into a new boardroom. And a week later the special committee (Marvin, Hansen and Reid) mailed copies of its revised plan to the members, for their comments.

At the annual meeting Eugene H. Pool became president, Samuel A. Welldon vice-president and Howard Reid secretary, while Sheridan A. Logan stayed on as treasurer. Although the annual dinner was, in theory, the Club's seventy-fifth, no notice of this fact seems to have been taken.

By February 20 most of those members who had bothered to reply to the special committee's mailing—a minority, of course—had approved the plan. The Board adopted it forthwith, and announced a wholesale reshuffling of committee chairmanships. (The new chairman of the Sports Committee, Benjamin H. Ticknor II, was the first all-American footballer to join the Club since Hamilton Fish.)

The minutes of the Board's meeting on March 18 contain a terse entry under the rubric "Absent Membership" that reads "Varian M. Fry '30 as of 1/1/41." This is the only allusion in the Club's archives to a remarkable episode of World War II. Fry had, in fact, left New York the previous summer, for Marseilles, where, representing the Emergency Rescue Committee, he had since worked tirelessly to smuggle refugees via Spain to Lisbon or onto cargo vessels bound for Algeria. By September 1941, when the French authorities would expel him, Fry would have engineered the mostly clandestine departures for the United States of at least 1,200 artists, writers, scholars, statesmen and others, including Hannah Arendt, André Breton, Marc Chagall, Marcel Duchamp, Max Ernst, Wanda Landowska, Jacques Lipschitz, Heinrich Mann, André Masson, Franz Werfel and Alma Mahler Gropius Werfel. Fry would return to New York, and the Club, early in 1942; he would enlist, but the Army would reject him because of his chronic stomach trouble. He would tell his story in a book, *Surrender on Demand* (1945), and die in 1967.

At the March 1941 Board meeting President Pool described his recent negotiations with representatives of the employees' union over a new contract, copies of which had been distributed to everyone present. After reviewing the document carefully the Board members authorized the officers to sign it, whereupon the Club would soon, for the first time, function in accordance with a compact acceptable to both members and employees.

In April, as German forces overran Yugoslavia and Greece, a team of skilled workmen started reconstructing the Visitors' Room and the second floor Red Room and Card Room in conformance with the special committee's plan, while other workmen, armed with picks and sledgehammers, attacked the front wall of the clubhouse, a few feet to the right of the entrance, to open up a second door. In May the Board, avid for new members, disregarded the bylaws to take in two young applicants who had not yet completed a full academic year at the University. Incidentally, Membership Committee Chairman Morgan D. Wheelock '31, dispatched to Cambridge to interview New York–bound seniors, discovered that many or most of his prospects expected to join some branch of the service upon graduation.

As for scholarships, the days of a few deep-pocketed donors were over, and the Club's grants-in-aid now came, for the most part, from the shallow pockets of several hundred small contributors. That year, the Club awarded just four freshman half scholarships of $400, together with two Slocum scholarships of $400 and $800 respectively. (These last stipends, established in memory of the former president, an ardent supporter of Harvard football, were supposed to reward in particular qualifications other than academic excellence.) The Club's total commitment came to $2,800—not bad, except in comparison with the Yale Club's long-standing practice of awarding, year after year, ten scholarships of $600 each.

For the Appointments Committee, Chairman Roy E. Larsen warned that the University might soon discontinue its New York employment office, and in June Harvard did in fact withdraw its support of the long-established agency. Reluctantly, the Board accepted the resignation of its executive head, Blodgett Sage. The officers and managers were loath to shut down this vital service, but with the Club operating at a deficit it could not and should not, they felt, take on the additional expense.

As it turned out, however, this was not the end after all: several members volunteered to help carry on placement work part time, and in July Ferdon Shaw '09, a banker, offered his services full time, for nothing. Shaw's enthusiasm, energy and ability rekindled interest in the enterprise: both registrants and placements increased dramatically, to the point where a certain member, who chose to remain anonymous, guaranteed Shaw $3,600 for one year, starting in September, providing that the Club furnish him with office space and secretarial help, which it did.

The war in Europe had taken a spectacular turn on June 22, when Germany, joined by Italy, Romania, Hungary, Slovakia and Finland, had invaded its supposed ally, the U.S.S.R. By the end of 1941 German mechanized divisions would have destroyed much of the Red Army and overrun much of European Russia, but had been brought to a halt by the Russian winter and a Soviet counteroffensive. Meanwhile, at 27 West 44th Street, Chairman Weld's Committee on Military and Naval Affairs formulated plans for civil defense and called for volunteers to serve perhaps, one day, as air raid wardens.

At 5 P.M. on Wednesday, October 15, came the eagerly awaited opening of the section of the clubhouse to be known thereafter as the Ladies' Club Rooms. Hundreds of couples and numerous men and women on their own trooped through the second-floor suite, checking out the wallpaper and pictures, the furniture and rugs, the discreet lighting—all adding up, most agreed, to an ambiance that was agreeably clublike without being oppressively masculine.

Within weeks the Club's governors knew they had a winner in this new facility. The overall cost of creating the Ladies' Club Rooms came to $45,990, slightly more than a third of what the Board had been prepared to spend two years earlier for ladies' quarters next door. From the outset, moreover, the new venture succeeded brilliantly: in its first ten weeks about 1,400 women would apply for and receive signing privileges, and gross receipts would amount to $22,874.

Hardly less impressive was the amazing expansion of job placement that took place under the leadership of Ferdon Shaw. By the end of 1941 about 1,800 job-seekers would have registered with his office, and steady employment found for 246 of them. (In retrospect, Shaw is a rather

**Ladies' Reception Room**

touching figure. As only his close friends were aware, he had suffered a tragic blow in 1934 with the death of his only child, Ferdon Shaw, Jr. '36. "Mine is not a saga of success," he would write in his class's fortieth anniversary report a few years before his own death, "but there has been joy in the effort to aid others and pride in the achievements of classmates and other splendid examples of the men Harvard sends forth into the world of affairs.")

In the Far East, events had begun to move toward a crisis in late July, when Roosevelt, retaliating against Japan's assuming a protectorate over French Indochina, had frozen Japanese assets. Britain and the Netherlands had followed suit, cutting off Japan's sources of credit and of rubber, scrap iron and oil. The United States wanted Japan out of China, but the Japanese military chiefs were not about to be dislodged from their vast continental conquests. In late October War Minister General Hideki Tojo became Japan's premier; on November 20 he presented the United States with an ultimatum, the terms of which were clearly unacceptable, and on December 7. . .

Only a handful of members happened to be in the clubhouse that Sunday afternoon when word came via radio of the devastating Japanese surprise attack by air and sea on the fleet in Pearl Harbor and nearby military installations, but during the next days the Bar, Grill Room and Dining Room teemed with men earnestly discussing late developments, striving to guess what was coming and comparing notes as to how best to cope with the drastically altered circumstances. By Monday afternoon the United States was at war with Japan, and by Friday with Germany and Italy as well. Little was certain beyond the obvious fact that the country was in for a difficult time—and with it, of course, the Club.

**Board of Managers silver**

# 13

# WORLD WAR II (1941–1945)

With the country at war, the Club's dues-paying base was sure to erode. Many members would enter the armed forces along with many graduates who would ordinarily have joined the Club. Shortages of manpower and goods would simultaneously drive prices up. So much was already clear, but the consequences would turn out to be quite different from what one might have confidently predicted. Although the Club's expenses would indeed escalate, its revenues would rise faster. And its membership, contrary to all expectations, would increase substantially.

With respect to one of the Club's chief functions, providing overnight accommodations, the war would prove a boon from its onset. Because of New York's paramount role in the war effort—as the country's principal port for the shipment of food and supplies, war materiel and, ultimately, troops to Britain and the North African and European Theatres, as headquarters of the Third Naval District, as the metropolitan center for outlying aircraft factories and shipyards, airfields and Army bases, Coast Guard and merchant marine installations—it would attract so many people that finding a place to stay there would become a problem. Soon, and thereafter throughout the war, the Club's bedrooms would nearly always be filled to, or near, capacity.

Meanwhile, if the proliferation of khaki and navy blue in its ground-floor public rooms altered its atmosphere somewhat, the clubhouse would remain a refuge from care and a center of fraternal camaraderie. And if certain traditional events went by the board—the July field day with the Yale Club, the autumnal broadcasts of Harvard football games (intercollegiate sports having been suspended) and Professor Copeland's readings (canceled because the old man was no longer up to making the trip)—the Club's routine would continue to be followed almost as in peacetime. Each fall members would be asked to give to the employees' Christmas fund, and just before the holiday each employee would receive a share, determined by seniority, of the first distribution of it (the final one coming the following March), together with a Christmas turkey. Through nearly four years of war squash players (increasingly senior, to be sure) would represent the Club in metropolitan matches, while devotees of bridge and backgammon competed in intramural and extramural tournaments. The Club would put on between seven and eleven concerts on winter Sundays, culminating in the Harvard Glee Club's April visit and alternating with talks by invited speakers, mostly on war-related topics. The Scholarships Committee would interview promising students and help to stake four to seven of them annually to a year at Harvard; the Membership Committee would strive to recruit members; and successive curators of the Club's book collection would lament the persistence of bibliophilic kleptomania among the local sons of Harvard.

On the subject of books, President Conant, in Cambridge, revealed on January 12, 1942, that member Arthur Amory Houghton, Jr. '29 was the donor of a building going up in the Yard which would house rare books and manuscripts. The Houghton Library would be dedicated on February 28, and two months later Houghton would resign as the president of Steuben Glass and curator of the Library of Congress's rare books to join the Army. Meanwhile, the Art Committee discussed moving the more valuable portraits to a safe place but decided finally to leave them where they were, and the Entertainment Committee resolved to put on "programs of an informative and stimulating nature bearing on the national crisis" in place of those aimed only at entertaining. The Board (aware, of course, that the Japanese had sunk HMS *Prince of Wales* and HMS *Repulse* off the Malay Peninsula and seized Hong Kong) granted guest privileges to British officers on shore duty in and around the city. Finally, the Committee on Military and Naval Affairs shortened its name to the

Committee on War Affairs, and its chairman, former President Weld, invited all members to a "war meeting" on February 4.

That evening, several hundred members solemnly approved a resolution offered by Chairman Weld to the effect that

> We, members of the Harvard Club of New York City, in our Harvard Hall in mass meeting assembled, do pledge our unremitting efforts toward establishing a fair and lasting peace, and we are resolute to serve our country to the best of our abilities in the accomplishment of these great purposes.

A few days later President Pool gave the Club an outsize American flag which in 1871 had flown from the USS *Franklin*, flagship of the European fleet, then under the command of Pool's grandfather, Rear Admiral Charles Stuart Boggs. It would thenceforth hang at the north end of Harvard Hall. And the Board extended guest privileges to American officers stationed in New York whose names had been presented in writing by their commanding officers or members of their staffs, provided that each officer, unless sponsored by a member, pay cash.

On March 19 Treasurer Logan informed the Board that if the losses incurred to date in 1942 persisted at the same rate the Club would lose $40,000 on the year's operations. Logan, a scholarly banker from Missouri not given to hyperbole, startled his hearers with his next statement: "Such a result would," he told them, "cause bankruptcy of the Club, and most drastic steps must now be taken to avoid this danger." He called for continuing to cut back on staff, extending buffet service while reducing the number of dishes offered and, most drastic of all, imposing a $7 \frac{1}{2}$ percent surcharge on members' house accounts.

Without debate, the Board approved these recommendations.

Next month (with the Japanese occupying Southeast Asia and taking the Philippines and the Dutch East Indies) House Committee Chairman C. Kenneth Clinton questioned whether members of the Radcliffe Club of New York should enjoy signing privileges in the Ladies' Club Rooms. The Board asked him and the officers to work out an arrangement with Radcliffe Club President Dorothy Coit R'11 by which members of her club approved by her could be issued signing privileges.

In May (after the Navy had scored a major victory over the Japanese in the Coral Sea) Chairman Clinton came up with further ideas for saving money, all, interestingly, involving female labor. One was to have the Club's laundry done in the clubhouse; another was to employ women cooks instead of chefs. And a third, somewhat startling to read about today, was to "substitute chambermaids for the men on the bedroom floors."

Most members apparently accepted the need for the war emergency surcharge and paid it without protest. Now, Treasurer Logan won permission to try two more cash-raising gambits: first, life members were invited by letter to emulate the example a few of their number had set by paying sums equal to the dues they were exempt from paying, and second, enclosing with all members' bills for the second half of their annual dues a request for a voluntary contribution of 10 percent of those dues. Finally, the treasurer gave the Board an accounting of the nonmembers who currently held cards entitling them to use the Club's facilities. They amounted to 552, evenly divided into 276 civilian guests of members and 276 officers in the Army (including the Army Air Corps), Navy, Marine Corps and Coast Guard, 142 of them sponsored by members.

Just weeks, then, after pronouncing the dread "b" word out loud in the presence of the Board, Treasurer Logan had a solid bulwark in place against bankruptcy. But would the tax on house charges, the voluntary tithing and the practice of encouraging outsiders to use the Club bring in enough revenue to offset the loss of income from members and would-have-been members gone to war? No one could say.

Since Pearl Harbor, Ferdon Shaw's employment bureau had outstripped even its prior performance, arranging 6,000 interviews for 2,000 applicants and placing hundreds of men as commissioned officers or in civilian war work. Roy Larsen had accordingly merged his Appointments Committee into the War Affairs Committee, but that body had run out of cash to pay Shaw and his expenses; with the Board's blessing Vice-Chairman Larsen launched an appeal to the membership. And when Games Chairman Philip H. Robb '25 reported that no one in the Yale Club leadership seemed eager to continue the clubs' joint outing the Board voted to discontinue it for the duration.

By June, thanks to the $7 \frac{1}{2}$ percent surcharge, the Club was operating in the black. Responding to the treasurer's appeal, thirty-seven life members had contributed $1,490 and other members almost as much to support the employment bureau's work. Although the Club had, until then, concerned itself exclusively with officers in relation to the services, it was going to stage a vaudeville show in Harvard Hall the following month for 200 invited soldiers. And the brothers Pierre and Griswold Lorillard formally gave the Club the tapestries their father had loaned it eleven years before.

These developments, coming on the heels of Admiral Nimitz's victory at Midway Island, must have cheered the Club's governors. But trouble was brewing. One day in mid-July, at 12:30 P.M., Club employees quit their posts in the bedrooms, the kitchen and points between to spill out onto the sidewalks in front of and behind the clubhouse, having left, on the Dining Room and Grill Room tables, copies of a statement claiming to show disparities between their wages and those paid Yale Club employees. Hurrying outside, Manager Melia urged representatives of Local 6 to send their people back indoors, which they did, once Melia assured them that the Club's officers would soon review their grievances. By 1:05 lunch was once again being served. The officers convened that very afternoon, but, lacking the Board's authorization to take action, they simply called a special meeting of the Board for July 20.

At that meeting (in the Mahogany Room), Melia, present at his own request, confirmed that in numerous job categories the Yale Club did indeed pay higher wages. A consensus quickly formed that the Club should match the pay scales of other clubs, especially the Yale Club. By that organization's standards for compensation the Club's deficit added up to $10,000 per annum, and since the year 1942 was half over, President Pool recommended appropriating $5,000 to raise the Club's employees' wages at once to parity with those of the Yale Club. The Board complied, in all likelihood averting a strike.

As soon as Melia left the room, President Pool produced a typescript, which, as he explained, Secretary Reid had compiled, on his own initiative, from the financial records of the Harvard and Yale Clubs. Listed in it was every expenditure each club had made for operations from 1937 through 1941, and a comparison of the two clubs' figures revealed, Dr. Pool went on, substantial differences, all to the Club's disadvantage. At his suggestion the Board empowered the officers to hire a competent person to look into the Club's operations. So began, seemingly with little or no thought to the likely consequences, a process that would embitter a considerable body of members, supporters to the end of that singularly popular individual, Frank Melia.

Earlier that month the Board had taken out insurance against damage from air raids in the amount of $1,000,000 (annual premium, $1,125). On August 4 the Club's hired investigator, a Mr. Gertenbach, began checking into day-to-day operations, with Frank Melia's full cooperation.

On October 15 (as the battle for Guadalcanal, in the South Pacific, entered its third month), the Club's governors named replacements for Board members and committee chairmen who had enlisted or accepted commissions, a ritual they would repeat periodically over the coming years. After conferring with both Gertenbach and Melia, together and separately, a special committee chaired by Langdon P. Marvin recommended that House Committee Chairman Clinton temporarily take over the management of the Club; that a search begin for a new manager; that Frank Melia nevertheless be retained with a new title, his many close ties with members making him a "valuable liaison" between them and the House Committee; and that Gertenbach continue his investigation. From these recommendations, which the Board duly approved, it seems clear that Gertenbach had as yet uncovered no evidence of actual wrongdoing—certainly not by Melia—but abundant indications of duplication, waste and inefficiency.

On November 4 former President James Byrne died, leaving the Club, as most of his predecessors had done, a sizeable bequest ($5,000). Four days later came bracing news of a massive American landing in North Africa, in which action, as his fellow members would eventually learn, member Pierpont Morgan Hamilton '20 played a key role (see page 241). And on the nineteenth, with U.S. forces under Lieutenant General Dwight D. Eisenhower in control of all Morocco and Algeria, the Board again took stock. The Club was still operating in the black, but this happy state of affairs could no longer be credited to the war emergency surcharge alone: another obvious cause was the patronage of the ever more numerous nonmembers. (By Chairman Clinton's latest count, fully 2,752 men without any connection to the College or University, in uniform and out, now held cards entitling the bearer to Club privileges, good for as little as three months and as much as the duration of the war, while 1,921 women could sign for drinks, meals or whatever in the Ladies' Club Rooms.)

For the first time since 1936—thanks largely to the exertions of Membership Chairman Chadbourne, who had pulled off a similar feat a quarter century earlier during another war—the Club grew in 1942, by 38 members, to 4,965. Although 225 of these were listed as "in military service," the actual number in uniform was much higher, many members having refrained from applying for exemption from dues to help the Club get through the difficult patch that was the war.

By December the four officers and Chairman Clinton had found just the man to run the Club in Clifford T. Howes, an experienced manager of hotels and clubs. He would take over on January 1, 1943, as managing director, with former manager Melia assistant director; to spare Melia embarrassment, however, no announcement was made of Howes's succeeding him.

Soon after the New Year began Harvard men around the world noted the passing on January 6 of former President Lowell, and on the fourteenth, opening a meeting of the Board, President Pool affectionately recalled the Club's longtime honorary member who over the years had graced so many annual dinners. Chairman Clinton reported that the Club's card players, whose Card Room had been converted into the Ladies' Dining Room, could thereafter pursue their pleasures at the north end of Harvard Hall. The Board again admitted an applicant who had attended the College less than a year—an "exceptional" procedure rapidly becoming routine. Regarding admissions, that meeting was most memorable, however, for admitting a candidate who was no longer living, an act prompted by a letter from two respected older members, Eliot Tuckerman '94 and St. John Smith, who wrote that

> We have the honor to request that the name of Robert Ludlow Fowler 3rd, Harvard 1941, Lieutenant junior grade, USNR, killed in action off Guadalcanal while serving as torpedo officer on the USS *Duncan,* be enrolled, posthumously, as a member of the Harvard Club of New York City.

The petitioners' ensuing account of their kinsman's last hours—severely wounded, then lashed to a mattress and set afloat when his ship was abandoned; his rescue by another destroyer, death and burial on a volcanic island—made an affecting narrative, and one can readily understand why the Board unhesitatingly elected the late Lieutenant (j.g.) Fowler to membership. That act was wholly unprecedented in the Club's annals, but it would be followed by several more posthumous admissions.

At the annual meeting six days later banker Samuel A. Welldon was elected president and Judge Augustus Hand vice-president, while Secretary Reid and Treasurer Logan were reelected.

In February (with the defeated Japanese evacuating Guadalcanal), Treasurer Logan revealed that between them card-holding male guests and women with signing privileges outnumbered the members, and that the Club now had more than 10,000 active accounts. But if the Club was thriving, it remained, like American society in general, impoverished with respect to race relations. This was highlighted when nonresident member Dwight P. Robinson of Braintree, Massachusetts, a retired banker and former Overseer and president of the Associated Harvard Clubs, proposed for membership his classmate W.E.B. Du Bois '90 AM'91 PhD'95, "a member," Robinson was careful to note, "of the colored race." The Board, the same body that had been routinely admitting youths after only a few months' stay at Harvard, referred the matter back to Robinson, advising him to follow standard admissions channels, but in language that made it plain that the candidacy of Dr. Du Bois, perhaps the greatest African-American between Frederick Douglass and Dr. Martin Luther King, Jr., was not one it would particularly encourage.

In an attempt to determine the extent of the members' participation in the war, the War Affairs Committee had sent out a questionnaire, and the first returns would shortly appear in the *Bulletin*:

| | | | |
|---|---|---|---|
| A. | Died in Service | | 8 |
| B. | In the Armed Services: | | |
| | a) COMMANDER-IN-CHIEF | | 1 |
| | b) ARMY: | 1. Brigadier Generals | 1 |
| | | 2. Colonels | 15 |
| | | 3. Lieutenant Colonels | 40 |
| | | 4. Majors | 52 |

|  |  |  |  |  |
|---|---|---|---|---|
|  |  | 5. Captains | 72 |  |
|  |  | 6. 1st Lieutenants | 64 |  |
|  |  | 7. 2nd Lieutenants | 53 |  |
|  |  | 8. Enlisted Men | 71 | 368 |
|  | c) NAVY: | 1. Captains | 2 |  |
|  |  | 2. Commanders | 3 |  |
|  |  | 3. Lieutenant Commanders | 32 |  |
|  |  | 4. Lieutenants | 120 |  |
|  |  | 5. Lieutenants (j.g.) | 58 |  |
|  |  | 6. Ensigns | 55 |  |
|  |  | 7. Ratings | 13 | 283 |
|  | d) MARINES: | 1. Colonels | 2 |  |
|  |  | 2. Captains | 4 |  |
|  |  | 3. 1st Lieutenants | 7 |  |
|  |  | 4. 2nd Lieutenants | 2 |  |
|  |  | 5. Enlisted Men | 1 | 16 |
|  |  | **Total in Armed Services** |  | 668 |
| C. | In Civilian War Work |  |  | 782 |
|  |  | **Grand Total** |  | 1450 |

("Now that college athletics are on the wane," *The New Yorker*'s "Talk of the Town" would observe, "the Yale and Harvard Clubs have been reduced to competing in the number and rank of the men they have in the services. The competition would seem to have been conclusively and triumphantly ended by the Harvard Club, which included a tabulation of members in the armed forces in the March issue of its *Bulletin*. At the top of the list . . . is a modest notation: 'Commander-in-Chief—1.'")

In March Chairman Clinton reported that keeping in line with new mandatory air raid precautions blackout shades had been installed in the Dining Room windows and blackout curtains hung on the great windows in Harvard Hall. The next month, he announced that a service flag showing the number of members serving in the armed forces would soon be hung in the entrance hall next to a board bearing the names of members who had died in military service. Meanwhile, the Club welcomed an unusual painting of George Washington; a bequest from Mrs. Eliza E. E. Richards, widow of member Edward Osgood Richards '86, it was a copy, painted on glass early in the nineteenth century by an unknown Chinese artisan, of the familiar portrait by Gilbert Stuart that adorned and still adorns the U.S. dollar bill. The Art Committee would quickly have the picture framed, with a plaque attached identifying the sitter by his Harvard honorary degree of LL.D. 1776.

Since the previous summer the library had received twenty-six books by Harvard men, including *Our Fighting Faith* by James B. Conant, *Thucydides* by John H. Finley, Jr. '25 PhD'33, *Report from Tokyo* by Joseph C. Grew, *Kaltenborn Edits the War News* by H. V. Kaltenborn, *The Wisdom of China and India* by Lin Yu-tang G'22, *Rivers of Glory* by F. Van Wyck Mason, *Admiral Sims and the Modern American Navy* by Elting E. Morison '32 AM'38, *All-American* by John R. Tunis, *What the Citizen Should Know About Submarine Warfare* by David O. Woodburn '18 and *Young Man of the World* by Thomas R. Ybarra '05.

Concluding that April meeting, the Board heard the reading of a letter from Wilder Goodwin '07 and Curtis N. Browne '12 requesting that John Horton Ijams, Jr. '40, First Lieutenant, Army Air Corps, be posthumously elected to the Club. Lieutenant Ijams, a son of longtime member John Horton Ijams '07, had been killed in action over North Africa while piloting a Flying Fortress bomber, and had been posthumously awarded the Air Medal. A motion to elect him carried unanimously.

In May a net was set up in a squash court for golfers wanting to practice their swings. Not that squash was moribund: while many players were off at war some were still around, and two, Germain G. Glidden and Donald M. Frame '32, ranked first and second that season in metropolitan squash racquets competition. Before long, however, both portrait painter Glidden and Frame, a professor of French at Columbia University, would be in uniform. Incidentally, with Southeast Asia and the Dutch East Indies, prime sources of rubber, under Japanese control, that commodity was in short supply, and a squash ball made of synthetic rubber had come into use. Though not as lively as the prewar ball it stood up well, and some players came to prefer it.

With the war dispersing members and prospective members to distant shores, Membership Chairman Chadbourne, defying its centrifugal effect, had been heading yet another membership drive, and in June, in his absence, Treasurer Logan reported the all-but-incredible result: the biggest short-term gain in the Club's history, from 4,965 members on January 1 to 5,504 just five months later. Also in June, the *Bulletin* printed some lines by Christopher Morley, from his *Mandarin in Manhattan, Being Further Translations from the Chinese*:

INCOGNITA

All afternoon I was plagued
By a strong sweet perfume,
An aroma of amour, unaccountable,
That seemed to be part of me,
On my fingers and in my clothes.
I, the old anchorite, wondered much,
And found myself thinking impossible thoughts.
At last I diagnosed this influenza of musk:
It exhaled from a casual folder of matches
Which I had picked up in a tea-shop.
It was inscribed *Harvard Club of New York Ve-Ri-Tas.*
O unknown Lucifer of Harvard,
Who is the lady who smells so sweet
That you keep her supplied with your matches?

What to do about Frank Melia? On July 29 the Board endorsed a recommendation of four special committeemen headed by Edward Streeter '14 who since May had carefully reviewed Melia's entire record: that he be retained until the end of the year and then let go. Word of this action spread slowly, but after Labor Day many returning members were dismayed to learn that their good friend was being fired: on September 15 the Board members spent two hours discussing the criticism their July 29 decision had engendered; on September 21 President Welldon read them letters denouncing that decision; and on September 27 a dozen of them, with the four officers, received a group of twenty-nine angry Melia supporters. At this proceeding, without any parallel in the Club's annals, President Welldon read aloud confidential material from the special committee's investigation, then turned the meeting over to the Board's critics, who extolled Melia's long and faithful service and promised to come up with suggestions for work he could usefully perform.

On October 4, then, again in the Mahogany Room, Adolf A. Berle, Sr. '91, St. John Smith and Percy Hutchinson '98 formally presented their suggestions to President Welldon and Treasurer Logan in a letter. "The dissent from the Board's action is steadily increasing in violence and angry comment," that document began, and "is likely to increase," while "the damage to the club morale" was to be deplored. "There is," the letter went on, interestingly, "good reason to believe that officers of previous administrations are deeply resentful of the implied criticism of their ineffectiveness and inefficiency," adding that "in the period of Melia's employment, from the bellboy's bench to the manager's title, the club was administered by some of the leading men of the nation in science, law, medicine, education and business," some of whom, "and their descendants, feel the [Board's] action precipitate and not in accord with the Harvard spirit."

The letter writers suggested, finally, "that Melia be made, with the consent and cooperation of your new manager, 'Assistant to the Manager' for the period of one year. Such action would involve no sacrifice of the Board's convictions or repudiation of their previous action. But it would eliminate all personal questions and probably within the year the matter would solve itself."

Two evenings later the Board decided to give Melia a further trial, for no fixed period, performing such duties as Director Howes might assign him. Subsequently, President Welldon obtained Adolf Berle's agreement to this plan, then Melia's and Howes's, and on the twenty-first he reported all this back to the Board. A threatened split in the Club's ranks had been averted. At that same meeting, however, the Board heard charges of misbehavior lodged against two members, quinquagenarians both, who, though too old for military service, evidently still enjoyed a good fight. One, an investment counsel, had tackled and knocked down a 75-year-old industrial chemist and "imposed himself in an objectionable manner" on members taking their ease in the Grill Room, while the other, an architect, had struck a bellboy. Unlike most such cases, theirs would be settled with dispatch: asked to resign, both men would promptly do so.

That fall, with the clubhouse mobbed at lunchtime and bellboys hard to come by, the House Committee reluctantly installed, for the time being only, an annunciator system with eleven speakers set at low volume and strategically placed in Harvard Hall, the Dining Room and the Grill Room to permit the paging of members and guests from the front desk. A far more important development, the most important physical change to be effected, surely, during the war years, grew out of a proposal by

Clifford Howes, that the seventh-floor swimming pool be drained and floored over, and cots be installed in the space thus created. Though widely praised on aesthetic grounds, the pool or plunge had never been much used, but its elimination, called for by successive House Committee chairmen over a quarter of a century, finally came about, not in an effort to save money but in response to the acute need, in the wartime metropolis, for accommodations. The Board appropriated $1,250 to floor over the pool, purchase cots and bedding and construct cubicles—to be known, for better or for worse, as "roomettes." In so doing, many or even most Board members may have assumed that once the war was over the pool would be restored, but it never would be.

Shortly before Christmas the new roomettes, twelve in the Swimming Pool Room and four more in the sixth-floor Squash Trophy Room, became available to transients. Though somewhat Spartan, they proved instantly popular—as well they might have, providing a comfortable night's lodging for just one dollar.

Too late for action at its December meeting, the Admissions Committee received from Secretary of the University David M. Little, Jr. '18 a proposal, properly seconded, to elect Radcliffe's president Wilbur K. Jordan AM'28 PhD'31 a member. The Board promptly did so. Ironically, the same men had, half an hour before, voted down a proposal to let women attend meetings and dinners in the third-floor private dining rooms.

Since his illuminating experiment in comparing the Club's receipts and expenditures with those of the Yale Club (an organization roughly comparable in membership, dues and plant), Secretary Reid had persuaded the Club's accountants to continue what he called "identical accounting," with the cooperation, needless to say, of their Yale Club counterparts. And at the last Board meeting of 1943 he produced figures showing that, disregarding the $7\frac{1}{2}$ percent war emergency surcharge, the Club had achieved a profit of $3\frac{1}{4}$ percent of gross income compared to less than 1 percent for the Elis. Meanwhile, knowing that Reid was retiring from his post, some senior employees had prepared a surprise for him, and on January 11, 1944, somewhere in the clubhouse basement, they presented him with a framed testimonial hand-lettered by Chief Engineer Frederick Ebeling. Above the signatures of ten men and two women, with their job titles and tenures of service (seven of them with more than twenty-five years with the Club and one with more than thirty), it read, "A token of appreciation by the department heads for your tireless efforts to improve the working conditions of the employees of the Harvard Club of New York City."

Reid was, naturally, touched by this gesture, and pleased two nights later when, after the dinner following the election of Samuel S. Drury, Jr. '35 to replace him and the reelection of the other officers, President Welldon held the testimonial aloft, read out the text and the signatures and declared that no retiring officer had ever before been thus honored by the employees. But if Reid appreciated the ensuing applause, he knew that certain members would never forgive him for bringing low their friend Frank Melia. (Of his years as secretary, Reid would recall, in his class's thirty-fifth anniversary report [1947], that "my list of friends and acquaintances grew, but I also acquired some severe critics, who expressed themselves freely on several occasions.")

On January 19 some of the Club's remaining squash players gathered in the Bar with their pro, John Jacobs, to mark the twenty-fifth anniversary of the day in 1919 when Jacobs, a veteran of World War I, had come to work at 27 West 44th Street. And they drank a toast in memory of an ace squash racqueteer, Lieutenant Alfred W. Paine '24, USNR, killed in action on New Year's Day. By then, arrangements had been initiated for a handicap tournament in Paine's name, open to members, to be held every year in March.

With C. Kenneth Clinton resigning in February, the Board named Phillips B. Thompson chairman of the House Committee, a post he had first held a quarter century before, 1919–21. Next month, Thompson reported that the ground-floor lavatory had been decorated with large framed travel posters, views of European cities that were the gift of President W. Harold White of Thomas Cook & Son, Ltd., of New York. "They have," Thompson wrote, "given this rather dreary room a much needed cheerfulness," and indeed, those walls, which would be expanded westward with the enlargement of the room after the war, have sported similar colorful displays ever since.

In a special report to the Board Chairman Thompson noted that a $500 donation would be spent, with the "hearty approval" of donor Edmund

Kerper '11 L'13, on new lampshades in the Grill Room, Dining Room and Harvard Hall. Regarding members' occasional lapses of behavior, moreover, he laid down a policy in words that would be remembered: "The House Committee is determined," he wrote, "that the Club House is not to be used as a nursing home for alcoholics."

On April 20, the Harvard Business School Club of New York announced that former President of the United States Herbert C. Hoover LLD (hon.) '17 would give an informal talk on the evening of May 1. Somewhat incongruously, then, in view of the speaker's solemn mien and conservative politics, May Day, celebrated elsewhere with fertility rites and parades of organized labor, was designated Herbert Hoover Night at 27 West 44th Street. Following private dinners in the Mahogany, Biddle and North Rooms, dinners in the Ladies' Dining Room and a buffet supper in the Main Dining Room, the former president spoke on "Problems of Political and Economic Rehabilitation of Occupied Countries" to hundreds of members and male guests in Harvard Hall, with amplifiers transmitting his words to a mixed audience in the Ladies' Club Rooms. Recalling the evening eighteen days later, President Welldon pronounced it a huge success. At present, he reminded the Board, the Club's only honorary members were Presidents Conant and Roosevelt, and as Hoover was the only living former American president, "it had been suggested" that he be made an honorary member.

Was there a hint of animosity against the incumbent chief executive discernible in the haste with which the Board elevated his political and philosophical archenemy to parity with him in the Club's hierarchy? Unquestionably—but who can doubt that it was mixed with nobler motives?

June 5 and 6 brought electrifying news of the capture of Rome and of Allied armies landing in Normandy; then, at 27 West 44th Street, the men directing the Club's affairs returned to their concerns. Among these was—still—unhappy Frank Melia, and in a frequently emotional session on June 15 the Board voted to terminate his services in September and pay him a bonus of $10,000 over three years. (Remarkably, between forty and fifty members would chip in to send Melia to Cambridge for a full academic year at the Business School.)

In September, a bizarre problem manifested itself on the sidewalk behind the clubhouse, where, for reasons known only to their bird-brained selves, pigeons began to congregate, inconveniencing passersby and people making deliveries to the Club's kitchen. As Mayor La Guardia's executive secretary, member Goodhue Livingston, Jr., obtained permission from the mayor himself for the Club to trap the creatures in boxes and hand them over to the A.S.P.C.A.

On learning that the Club was losing money, Treasurer Logan proposed raising the war emergency surcharge to 10 percent and the monthly fee charged card-holding civilian guests from three dollars to five; the Board adopted the first proposal and would soon adopt the second. Meanwhile, members had to endure sporadic walkouts by union waiters (the worst, lasting thirty hours, occurring, appropriately, over Hallowe'en) who resented seeing temporary workers, hired to help with the lunchtime crush, treated on a par with them. On November 7 President Roosevelt was reelected to a fourth term with a new running mate, Missouri Senator Harry S Truman, defeating New York Governor Thomas E. Dewey, on behalf of whose candidacy a number of members had toiled long and hard.

That month, the House Committee installed daybeds in each of six large bedrooms, bringing to 86 the total of overnight accommodations the Club could provide. The Art Committee hired experts to clean, reweave and reback the Lorillard tapestries. In December Chairman Candler Cobb '08 informed the Board that his Entertainment Committee was anticipating the celebration of Radcliffe Day, on January 7, 1945, "with some trepidation." Radcliffe President Jordan, now a member, wanted to give a tea party to alumnae in the Biddle and North Rooms, and asked that his guests be allowed to enter the clubhouse by the main entrance and proceed up the main staircase to the third floor. Failing to think of a graceful way to deny this request, the Board granted it.

In the opening two weeks of 1945, in southern Belgium, Allied forces, having sustained fearful casualties, routed the remnants of a once-formidable German army to win the Battle of the Bulge. On the eighteenth, in New York, Treasurer Logan resigned. As President Welldon observed, Logan's supervision of the Club's finances through the Great Depression, recession and war had been exemplary, and although the Club's labor costs had increased 41 percent over the past two years its gross income had tripled, to exceed, in 1944, a million dollars (putting it, as Logan declared, only half joking, in the "big business" category).

At that meeting William Chadbourne, who had long advocated collecting information for an eventual history of the Club, finally became the first (and, it would turn out, only) chairman of a History Committee. And Entertainment Chairman Cobb announced that his committee, while continuing to provide entertainment for wounded officers, would give a dinner in February, in one of the private dining rooms, for fifteen wounded sailors. This would prove to be the first of about a dozen such dinners the Club would tender, with members volunteering to act as hosts, to wounded and blinded enlisted men in the various services.

The following evening, Edward Streeter was elected treasurer, and throughout the ensuing annual dinner a slim Army Air Corps colonel at President Welldon's table was the object of curious glances. He was, the glancers knew, their fellow member Pierpont Morgan Hamilton, the Club's only recipient, during the present war, of the Congressional Medal of Honor. He had earned his exalted decoration at the American landings in French Morocco on November 7 and 8, 1942. A French-speaker had been needed to accompany General Eisenhower's envoy, a colonel, on a mission to seek out the French commander and arrange a cease-fire, and then-Major Hamilton, who had lived in Paris for several years after serving as a pilot in World War I, had volunteered. As the pair sped toward Port Lyautey in a jeep, flying a white flag of truce, a burst of gunfire had killed the colonel. On reaching French military headquarters, Hamilton had presented General Eisenhower's request; by chance, Admiral Darlan, Vichy France's foreign minister and minister of defense, had been in Algiers, readily accessible by telephone, and he had ordered a cessation of hostilities. Hamilton's act had thus had the effect of saving no one can say how many lives, both American and French.

Colonel Hamilton's after-dinner remarks were not recorded, but they may have contained surprises: his expressed views on capitalism, in any case, were hardly what might have been expected of a great-great-grandson of Alexander Hamilton and a grandson of the elder J. P. Morgan. "Between wars," he wrote for his class's twenty-fifth anniversary report, due to appear in a few months, "I participated in various forms of that plain and fancy swindling that goes under the general head of American business. I have made and lost money, learned a great deal and managed not to swell the ranks of Harvard men in jail." (After the war, Hamilton would stay in the service, finally retiring as a major general from what by then would be the U.S. Air Force.)

Another speaker, Marine First Lieutenant John Elliott, Jr. '42, late of the USS *Pennsylvania*, related his experiences three months before in the epochal battle for Leyte Gulf in the Philippines, which Harvard's (and the Club's) Rear Admiral S. E. Morison would call "the greatest sea fight of this or any war" and a tremendous American victory.

In February the Board established an Insurance Committee, and President Welldon named Clement L. Despard '08, the chairman of his own family insurance firm, to head it. Then the Board discontinued, as likely no longer needed, the War Affairs Committee.

On March 24 came the stirring news that General George S. Patton's Third Army had crossed the Rhine into Germany, and on the evening of April 12 the stunning intelligence that President Roosevelt had died suddenly, of a cerebral hemorrhage, in Warm Springs, Georgia. Chairman Thompson saw to it that a vase containing five dozen red roses was placed beneath the late chief executive's portrait, and that the bar was shut down during his funeral on the afternoon of the fourteenth. Five days later, when the Board next met, the president asked the members to stand and called on former president Langdon P. Marvin, once the dead man's law partner, who moved the adoption of a minute:

> The Board of Managers of the HARVARD CLUB OF NEW YORK CITY records with deep sorrow the death on the 12th day of April, 1945, of FRANKLIN DELANO ROOSEVELT, of the Class of 1904, a member of the Club since December 16, 1904, and an honorary member since January 1, 1934.
>
> The Board also records its pride in his courageous and inspiring leadership of our Country and of the World during this most critical period of History. The President of the Club is requested to convey to Mrs. Roosevelt and to her children the deep and affectionate sympathy of the Club and of all its members.

Marvin's motion was duly seconded and his minute adopted.

Throughout the extraordinary first week of May 1945, beginning with Hitler's suicide and ending with the unconditional surrender of Germany,

Club members near and far rejoiced, even while reminding themselves that another formidable enemy remained to be defeated. As the euphoria of V-E Day subsided, other matters surfaced: thus when the Board next met, on the eighteenth, lawyer James L. Derby '08 wanted to know whether the Club's bar price for a martini (then made only with gin and dry vermouth, three or four parts of the first to one of the second, and served chilled in a stemmed glass, with an olive but no ice) was in line with what other clubs charged. Clifford Howes said he believed the Club's martinis cost, if anything, less than those stirred or shaken elsewhere in Midtown. (Howes, no longer styled director of the Club but its manager, would confirm his belief by checking numerous club bar prices, discovering in the process that although the Club's martini glasses held the same volume of liquor as the Yale Club's they were larger, and therefore less likely to spill their contents when borne aloft on a tray.)

After announcing yet another imminent party for wounded servicemen, in this case twenty soldiers, Entertainment Chairman Cobb read aloud a letter from Vice-Admiral Ross T. McIntire, surgeon general of the Navy, thanking the Club for putting on these dinners.

In June, Chairman Thompson reported a threatened shortage of food in the city. Board member James O. Stack came up with an ingenious suggestion: that a notice be placed in the *Bulletin* asking members who owned farms to supply the Club with eggs, chickens, milk and so on at ceiling prices. By August, however, when the September *Bulletin* would go to press, the food shortage would have eased.

During the previous spring, while troops under General Douglas MacArthur secured the Philippines, Marine units had, at heavy cost, stormed and taken the island fortresses of Iwo Jima and Okinawa. Unable to strike back by sea because their navy had in large part been sunk, the Japanese sent flights of suicide pilots aloft to crash-dive their bomb-laden planes into selected targets. That summer these kamikaze attacks sank or disabled many American vessels, but suddenly, on August 6, word flashed around the world that the city of Hiroshima had been leveled by an explosion of unheard-of magnitude that killed tens of thousands of people. Three days later a second atomic bomb was detonated above Nagasaki with similar effect, and on the fourteenth Japan sued for peace.

Finally, on September 2, in Tokyo Bay, on board the USS *Missouri*, emissaries of Emperor Hirohito signed articles of surrender.

Americans were naturally curious about the mysterious superweapon that had unexpectedly brought the war to an abrupt and cataclysmic end, and Entertainment Chairman Cobb asked members to suggest a qualified person who could enlighten them. But the next month President Welldon would announce that President Conant—still chairman, as he had been since 1941, of the National Defense Research Commission—would cover the subject at the annual dinner in January. Before then, Welldon obtained the Board's consent to his appointing a War Memorial Committee. And History Chairman Chadbourne, after reading aloud some recollections by older members of the Club before the turn of the century, advanced a suggestion that scored an instant hit with his colleagues. Pointing out that the paneling of the room in which they were meeting had been donated by the long-vanished Mahogany Club, he proposed that the chamber no longer be called the Board Room, but the Mahogany Room.

In October, Library Chairman Robert B. Bradley '08 reported that the microfilming of the library's card catalogue, undertaken at the behest of his classmate, Insurance Chairman Despard, had been completed. The Board members took this news calmly enough, but responded with considerably more interest to an announcement by Secretary Drury that a football game had been arranged with Yale, to be played at the Yale Bowl. If the game was not broadcast, Drury added, someone with a carrying voice would describe it play by play, as in preradio days, from reports telephoned in.

The locus of this putative activity (or of a broadcast) would of course be Harvard Hall, and in November the House Committee imposed one new rule on the use of that space and set aside two old ones. Over the past summer workmen taking up the hall's rugs for cleaning had found more than 800 cigar and cigarette burns in them; the committee extended its prohibition against smoking during concerts to cover all entertainments. The house rules it waived, temporarily, forbade members from entering the clubhouse and frequenting the public rooms after 1 A.M. Given the acute shortage of accommodations in the city, the committeemen felt constrained to let a member into his club at any hour, and "if he desires to make use of one of the couches in Harvard Hall, he is not to be disturbed."

Thanks to Chairman Despard, a valuation had by now been put on each of the Club's hundreds of artworks. And architect Henry I. Cobb '04 accepted the chairmanship of the War Memorial Committee.

On November 21, members read in their *New York Times* or *Herald Tribune* of how their onetime president, Thomas W. Lamont, had given Harvard $1.5 million to construct a "reading library" for undergraduates containing perhaps 100,000 books, an amenity intended to relieve some of the pressure on Widener Library. On Saturday, December 1, in the first gridiron encounter between the ancient rivals since 1942, the Blue team murdered the Crimson eleven, 28–0.

The expiration of "the duration" on September 2 had automatically invalidated the 2,000-plus guest cards in the wallets of military and naval officers. Since then, uniforms had increasingly been replaced in the club-house by suits and casual combinations sporting a metal lapel button in the form of a stylized eagle. This parting gift from the government, iden-tifying the wearer as a discharged serviceman or servicewoman, had been or soon would be dubbed by irreverent young veterans the "ruptured duck," and male veterans returning to undergraduate study at Harvard (though not perhaps at most colleges) quickly learned to pocket their avian service badges to avoid being viewed as show-offs by their peers.

Very soon now, on December 31, the approximately 450 civilian guest cards in use would likewise become invalid, and if its governors were eager for the Club to resume its all-Harvard character, even so they may have regretted the departure of these "paying guests" who had con-tributed so much to its coffers and well-being.

Symbolizing the Club's transition from war to peace, the huge American flag in Harvard Hall was taken down, at the request of its owner, former President Pool, and the ensign of the USS *Harvard*, long on display in the entrance hall, was removed for repairs. The Lorillard tapestries were at last back in place in the great hall, glowing like new. Art Committee Chairman Beverley R. Robinson '98 reported the gift, from member Mark I. Adams '11, of a portrait of President Eliot done in his nineties, which the Board gratefully accepted.

# 14

# THE POSTWAR
# YEARS
# (1946–1952)

As the Club's last wartime civilian guest members departed, members returning from near and distant theaters of operations took their places; the clubhouse continued to be crowded at lunchtime Monday through Friday, but not on Saturdays, the five-day office week having become standard in the city. Over the next months and years, moreover, ex-servicemen who had never belonged would apply for admission, at least some, no doubt, consciously or unconsciously seeking the all-male camaraderie they had known at Cambridge and in the armed forces. So, too, in even greater numbers, would young men emerging from a Harvard College and University packed with veterans enrolled under the G.I. Bill.

In the years just after World War II, as relations between the United States and its erstwhile ally, the Soviet Union, deteriorated into mutual hostility and the Cold War, the Club would grow rapidly, surpassing the record of 6,370 members set in 1930 to reach 6,395 by the end of the 1940s. Its expenses would, naturally, grow with it. But its governors' outlook, reflecting the nation's, would remain confident and optimistic, leading it to resume its long-suspended *Drang nach Westen* and annex 33 West 44th Street, extending the clubhouse westward to fill out its present confines.

Having made Herbert Hoover an honorary member 20 months earlier, President Welldon used his last evening in office to propose another candidate for that honor: Winston S. Churchill LL.D. (hon.) '43. Without ado, the Board elected him.

Next evening, before the Club's eightieth annual dinner, the members present elected George Whitney president, Arthur W. Page '05 vice-president and Robert P. MacFadden '26 treasurer, reelecting Samuel S. Drury, Jr., secretary.

One month later former Prime Minister Churchill was still in this country (he would deliver his celebrated "Iron Curtain" speech at Fulton, Missouri, in March), but former President Welldon had not yet succeeded in luring him to the clubhouse to receive his certificate of honorary membership. He promised to keep trying. And President Whitney reported that Welldon's portrait by John Lavalle '18 had been accepted.

Finally, the Board addressed the question of where to put the projected memorial to those members who had died in the recent war, a work that, it was understood, would take the form of a plaque like the World War I memorial listing the names of the fallen. Common sense seemed to dictate moving the existing plaque to one side of its Harvard Hall alcove and installing the new one on the other side, but Library Chairman Robert B. Bradley had devised a more ambitious plan and persuaded War Memorial Chairman Henry I. Cobb to endorse it. Neither man was present at that February meeting, but both had submitted written recommendations, which President Whitney read aloud. Citing the Library's need for shelf space, Bradley called for breaking through the Library's east wall (to one's right on entering the Library from the second-floor landing of the main staircase, a wall which at that time contained three windows looking out on the roof of the Grill Room) and constructing there a spacious room that would be lined with books except where the memorial plaque would be placed.

Chairman Cobb stated in his message that placing the two plaques together in the same space "did not seem feasible."

While the Board members sympathized with Bradley's desire to enlarge the Library, they shrank from spending the funds required to build the new room, perhaps $40,000. As for architect Cobb's objection to their own preferred solution, many found it disingenuous. Several insisted that the memorial be situated on the ground floor, and a majority voted to ask the War Memorial Committee to reconsider its stand.

In March, through banker and Board member Bayard F. Pope '09, the

Club obtained, on loan from the Hotels Statler Company, a tapestry that was hung at the northwest corner of the Main Dining Room. The railing of the lower balcony at the south end of Harvard Hall was raised a few inches to lessen the possibility of someone's losing his balance and

falling. And the Club's racquet wielders won the Metropolitan Inter-Club League Tournament, taking thirty-nine matches and giving up six. Following this triumph, former national champion Germain G. Glidden offered to put up $100 for a silver bowl, to be known, after Harvard's great coach, as the Harry Cowles trophy, and to be competed for annually in an invitation tournament by Class A players of the Metropolitan Squash Racquets Association. On March 21, the Board accepted Glidden's offer, with thanks. Incidentally, the Alfred W. Paine

**Harry Cowles**

memorial tournament, then in progress, had attracted forty-three entrants, and the Club had rented out seventy-five new lockers—clear signs of a resurgence of interest in the sport.

All efforts to bring Churchill to 27 West 44th Street having failed, the Board directed Secretary Drury to send the great man formal notice of his election, together with his certificate.

A month after this, War Memorial Chairman Cobb submitted a report that met with more favor than his last one had. In line with the Board's wishes, he said, he had sought the best ground floor site for the memorial, and finally settled on . . . the alcove in Harvard Hall. He proposed to move the existing plaque to the left, install the new one on the right and relate the two to each other by means of artwork between them. Settees would be placed at either side, and a low railing would be erected that would partially enclose the alcove. Such an arrangement would, Cobb declared gravely, preserve the sanctity of the World War I memorial while providing a symbolic remembrance of both wars, in keeping with the traditions of the Club and the architecture of the great hall.

Inasmuch as Cobb's proposal embodied what almost all of his colleagues had had in mind from the first, it was instantly approved.

President Whitney now reviewed for the Board three requests for more room that had come his way since he had taken office:

- that of Chairman Bradley to replace space appropriated from the Library for a lounge and a kitchen for the Ladies' Club Rooms;
- that of Manager Howes for an expanded coatroom, washroom and bar on the ground floor;
- and that of certain members who complained that the ladies' quarters were too constricted.

To Whitney, this last complaint was of particular concern, for the ladies' quarters were a great drawing card and potentially an important means of holding on to members in bad times. If they could be extended westward, moreover, some of the space taken from the Library could be returned to it.

Chairman Bradley nonetheless remained committed to the concept of a large additional room east of the Library proper, plans for which were even then being drawn up by Henry Cobb (as an architect, not in any official capacity). It so happened, however, that Bradley had quit New York around May 1 for a long summer (Antipodean winter) in New Zealand, and therefore presented his case in a letter which was read aloud at a Board meeting on May 16. Bradley argued that the Library needed 8,000 to 9,000 more books for members starting out in business and the professions, together with tables at which these young men could work and more armchairs for older readers, all of which his proposed room could, he said, provide.

The reading of Bradley's letter completed, President Whitney called on the Library Committee's acting chairman, lawyer Frederick P. Delafield '24, for comment. But instead of echoing Bradley's words, Delafield took another tack: if the kitchen immediately west of the Library could be converted to the latter's use, he said, there would be no need to add a room to the east. Henry Cobb, who was present, did not challenge

Delafield's statement, and President Whitney turned to assessing the Club's options to the west. Pointing out that the building at 33 West 44th Street was fireproof on its first two floors but not above them, he opined that in consideration of the city's fire and building regulations the Club's wisest course would be to tear down the fifth, fourth and third floors of Number 33 and extend various activities horizontally westward from the clubhouse into its basement and ground floor, adding, on its second floor, a second ladies' dining room. Meals ordered in both upstairs dining rooms could be prepared in the main kitchen and sent up by dumbwaiter, and the existing second-floor kitchen could be cleared out and restored to the Library for its use.

While plans to enlarge and restructure the clubhouse were thus being formulated, volunteers continued to welcome wounded and blinded servicemen at dinners and to visit bedridden veterans at Halloran and St. Albans Hospitals. Asked to gauge the sentiment in favor of reviving the annual outing with the Yale Club, Frederick R. Moseley, Jr. '36 found much enthusiasm among young members. With the United Nations about to establish its world headquarters in New York, the Board braced itself for requests to grant special memberships to distinguished visitors. And Art Chairman Robinson reported that certain members were agitating to have the late President Roosevelt's portrait removed from the entrance hall.

These same individuals were upset afresh by rumors that their bête noire was going to be listed on the memorial to the Club's war dead. Could it be true? It could: in June, President Whitney read aloud to the Board a letter from President Conant affirming that Roosevelt's name would most certainly figure on the University's war memorial. Surely, Whitney observed, the Club should follow Harvard's lead.

On July 12, at the Rockaway Hunting Club in Cedarhurst, the Club's players won at golf and tennis but lost at baseball. And next month there arrived at the clubhouse a letter addressed to "Dear House Committee" documenting one man's experience of the Club during a trying time:

> I have been a member of this Club for 30 years (conventional beginning, look out, trouble coming!)—and for some time I have thought of resigning—(there it is, see!) partly because I have reached an age when college clubs do not make quite

the *appeal* they once did, and then partly there was the war, and the few times I looked in during the war the old H.C. seemed to be, may I say, well, a Center for Displaced Persons, and *such* Persons; but after all it was highly *meritorious* and so on, and you don't easily break a habit of signing checks for club dues—not after 30 years—but then how long was this thing going on, for I am not so young, etc., but anyhow—

Tonight I had dinner at the Club, and it is so long since that almost all the familiar faces are gone, but

The food was delicious,

The service was excellent, and I extend my congratulations to the Committee and the Steward, and am once again a *Loyal and Happy Member*, to wit,

Yours very truly,<br>T. Brooke Price (LL.B.'15)

Regarding historical documents, William Chadbourne's intention of compiling a history of the Club was temporarily stalled. Pointing out that the task would require assembling a very large mass of written, typed and printed papers, he had asked the Board in June for $2,000 to pay for collecting this material and the exclusive use of the Trophy Room off the Grill Room for storing it. Instead, the Board had asked him to submit an outline of his proposed book. In September, however, Chadbourne made no report, nor would he before, five months later, the History Committee would quietly go out of existence. Presumably, he came to realize, on analyzing the task, that it would take more time to complete than he could spare, and also, perhaps, more money than the Board would be willing to spend on it.

Throughout 1946 the Club found itself in the unwonted situation of having more applicants than it could conveniently admit. Most came to it from Cambridge, where, since September 1945, the start of each term had seen the arrival of a horde of ex-servicemen eager to complete work for a bachelor's or graduate degree and clear out. (This now occurred, incidentally, not twice annually, but three times, the University continuing, as it had since 1943, to operate year-round.) The end of each term, then, witnessed a massive exodus of new graduates, many of whom headed straight for New York—and the Club.

During the previous spring and summer, the Admissions Committee had often toiled late into the night without getting to the last quarter or third of the names on their swollen lists. In September Chairman James

Coggeshall, Jr. '18 observed that as a result the Club effectively had, for the first time in many years, a waiting list.

In October, Entertainment Chairman Candler Cobb announced that his committee would no longer sponsor entertainments for wounded and blinded servicemen, and in November President Whitney suggested that the War Memorial Committee, reorganized with J. Horton Ijams as chairman and Henry Cobb as vice-chairman, find a way to honor young Harvard men who had not had a chance to join the Club before entering the armed forces but would have become members had they survived the war. Chairman Ijams suggested that, as had been done for the dead of World War I, biographical records be compiled of members who had died in the recent war, then bound together and placed under the plaque for consultation. Go ahead, the Board replied in effect, so long as the memorial's total cost did not exceed $20,000.

The Board agreed to commission John Lavalle, whose recent likeness of former President Welldon had been much praised, to paint a portrait of President Conant for the Club. Noting recent increases in book prices, moreover, it increased its monthly subvention to the library—to the satisfaction of Chairman Bradley, who, reconciled to the defeat of his proposal to extend the Library eastward, now looked forward to its expanding in the opposite direction.

At the Board's December meeting, Bradley reported that thanks to the recently introduced practice of either a librarian's or an assistant's always being on hand when the Library was open, thefts had diminished dramatically. Some time after this Secretary Drury read aloud a letter from Anton H. Schefer about the only son of member Bernon S. Prentice '05, Lieutenant Commander Sheldon Ellsworth Prentice '36, who had been killed off Okinawa on board the USS *Wasp*. Shortly before his death, as Schefer related, the officer had written his father as follows:

> It was not until I got away from New York that I realized what the Harvard Club means to so many graduates in New York, and, especially, to those from out of town—it is their home. I believe all of us should support it. I would like so much to have my name proposed for membership.

On hearing Schefer's proposal and the contents of two seconding letters, also read aloud by Drury, from other members, the Board unanimously added the name of Lieutenant Commander Prentice to the Club's roster.

After reviewing, for the Board, plans to incorporate 33 West 44th Street into the clubhouse, President Whitney revealed that the latest estimates put the cost of this expansion at $120,000. The Board authorized the officers to commence demolition in April. Next, Whitney asked Henry Cobb to leave the room, and when he was gone asserted that the Club owed the architect a great deal for his contributions to both the war memorial and the expansion into Number 33. Cobb was being characteristically modest, preferring not to be paid, but Whitney felt the Club should at least pay him $1,500 for his work to date and $100 a month in 1947. The Board concurred.

On December 29, in a Harvard Hall festooned with bright paper streamers and gay with multicolored balloons, the Club threw a party for members' children complete with a brass band, clowns, a trained seal and a Punch-and-Judy show. From the volume of the shrieks, screams and squeals, it was clearly a smash hit. And as they left the hall, some of the parents must have noticed a shiny brass plate at the entrance, reading

TO THE
HARVARD CLUB OF NEW YORK CITY
IN GRATEFUL ACKNOWLEDGMENT
OF THE HOSPITALITY RENDERED
TO THE UNITED STATES ARMY
1941–1945
PRESENTED BY
ARMY EXCHANGE SERVICE

At the end of 1946, the Club's membership stood at just over six thousand, a figure not reached since 1929.

The first notable event of 1947 came on January 11–12 with the inauguration of the annual tournament honoring Harry Cowles, the legendary Harvard coach who was known far and wide as the Father of Squash Racquets. The entrants included the country's top players, and the winner was Charles Brinton of Philadelphia. Like the national championship, the Cowles tourneys would be dominated for years to come by Philadelphians, but that year the Club's Class A squash racquets team would retain its Metropolitan Inter-Club League championship in a thrilling Garrison finish. Prior to the next-to-last match, held on Princeton Club courts, the home team led the Club by four games and needed only one more to tie and two to win; instead, the Harvards (who included Germain Glidden and Donald Frame) ran up a 5–0 victory.

Four days later, Scholarships Chairman Donald F. Bush '23 asked the Board to rename the Slocum scholarships Slocum aids, so that under-graduates in the fourth scholastic group, more gifted athletically than aca-demically, might benefit from them. After studying the matter, the Board decided to do so. To complaints about the lighting of Harvard Hall por-traits, Art Chairman Robinson riposted that the hall was not a gallery, and that its pictures had to be illuminated so as to show off, not them, but the hall instead. And former President Welldon suggested a procedure that could spare some future president embarrassment: on a president's leav-ing office the Club would commission an artist to paint his portrait, but if the retiring president hired his own limner the Club would accept the resulting likeness as his gift. The Board promptly adopted Welldon's sug-gestion, which still guides the commissioning of presidential portraits.

At the annual meeting Volney F. Righter '26 B'28 was elected secre-tary, replacing Samuel S. Drury, who had resigned.

At 7 P.M. on February 20, the Board assembled in the Slocum Room to question an errant member who, while drunk, had invaded the ladies' room at the approach to the Ladies' Club Rooms. Seldom can these gen-tlemen have felt quite so helpless; not only did the accused youth not show up, but as Treasurer MacFadden revealed, he had, by failing to lift his suspension for not paying house charges, ceased, as of January 15, to be a member. This disclosure would seem to render any action of the Board nugatory, but the men had summoned the fellow to a hearing, so they waited until 7:30 before adjourning for dinner.

Reconvening at 9:00, the Board members learned that the History Committee had been absorbed by the Library Committee and the Insurance Committee by the Auditing Committee. They elected Thomas W. Lamont '46, a son of Thomas S. Lamont '21 and grandson of Thomas W. Lamont '92, to posthumous membership. (Young Lamont, a sub-mariner, had been lost at sea in the USS *Snook.*)

Around the middle of March, Manager Howes started negotiating with representatives of Local 6, and on the twentieth he informed the Board that while the union had initially sought wage increases amounting to $160,000, the new contract increased the payroll by $51,000. At President Whitney's behest, the Board rechristened the Entertainment Committee the Activities Committee, and named Goodhue Livingston to head it, with Richard H. Dana '34 as both its vice-chairman and chorister. Anent the war memorial, Vice-Chairman Cobb described a scale model that sculptor Gleb Derujinsky had shown him, its central panel a side view bas-relief of the John Harvard statue. The Board, clearly uninterested in speeding up admissions, amended the bylaws to double the time an applicant had to have spent in some department of the University to be eligible for membership, from one year to two.

Early in April, John Lavalle delivered his portrait of President Conant; Chairmen Robinson (Art) and Thompson (House) pronounced it first-rate. Treasurer MacFadden persuaded the Board to apply the 10 percent usage charge (formerly, the war emergency charge) solely, thereafter, to income from the bedrooms, the restaurant and the bar. Meanwhile, although April 1 had come and gone, 33 West 44th Street stood intact, two lawyer tenants having, at the last minute, declined to vacate; inevitably, the Club sicced its own lawyers on the pair.

In mid-May the Board elected to posthumous membership two members' sons who had died in the war. They were Harrison Tweed Blaine '42, son of Graham B. Blaine '17, and William Temple Emmet II '42, son of Richard Stockton Emmet '19. The Board then reinstated, posthumously, three former members who had been killed in action: Edward Hutchinson Robbins '35, Lucius Townshend Wing '35, and Ashley Gordon Trope '37.

Further checking of Club and University records would bring to light the names of three other former members who had died in service a few months after being dropped from membership for nonpayment of dues. As these men had presumably never learned of the Club's policy of dues adjustment for members on active duty, the Board would in June posthumously reinstate Franz Ferdinand Colleredo-Mannsfeld '32, Robert Perkins Post '32 and Stratton Christensen '40, whose names would be inscribed on the honor roll.

With the coming of the first hot days of summer, some members wanted to know whether the swimming pool might not soon be reopening. President Whitney, Chairman Thompson and Chief Engineer Ebeling discussed this possibility, but as members learned from a notice in the *Bulletin*, they decided it could not be done that year, because the pumps and pipes were clogged and rusted and because new equipment was unobtainable just then. "However," the *Bulletin* notice concluded, in words allowing for lit-

W. L. Mackenzie King

tle doubt as to the anonymous writer's preferences, "a decision will [one day] have to be reached on whether to spend a substantial sum of money on installing pumps and running pipes from the basement to the sixth floor to put the pool back in operation, or whether this space could be used to more advantage to the members for some other use, such as improved squash facilities."

The Lavalle portrait of President Conant was now in Cambridge, in the Fogg Museum, on view to Commencement visitors. That Commencement, on June 5, would go down in history for a brief address in which Secretary of State George C. Marshall, there to receive an honorary doctorate of laws, urged that the war-devastated nations of Europe decide on their economic needs so that material and financial aid from the United States could be integrated on a grand scale. Out of his suggestion would come the vast project, unprecedented in kind and in scope, known as the European Recovery Program, or the Marshall Plan.

Eleven days after this, the Board elected Prime Minister W. L. Mackenzie King of Canada an honorary member. Unlike Winston Churchill, King would accept the honor with alacrity.

The following week, members were saddened by the death of doorman

Jimmy Redmond, and on July 7, with the Club's lawyer tenants evicted at last, the demolition of 33 West 44th Street began. The wreckers would pull down not just the top three stories, but the entire building, exposing details that would enable knowledgeable passersby to trace the evolution of the lower floors from a luxurious stable in the 1890s to a rooming house, a store and finally a restaurant.

On July 30, the Club lost another popular employee of long standing, head clerk John O'Malley. By then construction had begun in the broad excavation extending north halfway through the block along the club-house's western wall.

In September, the House Committee reluctantly raised restaurant prices, but Manager Howes said he would try to keep an 80-cent or 90-cent luncheon special. Former President Welldon warned that raising the dues could antagonize the many members who paid their annual fees faithfully but never came near the Club. Sculptor Derujinsky started carving, in teakwood, the war memorial's central panel. With the New York Yankees and the Brooklyn Dodgers capturing the pennants of their respective leagues, moreover, baseball aficionados welcomed that rarest of contests, a "subway Series"—and the prospect of watching the drama unfold on the Club's new television set.

Dramatic that series would certainly prove to be, the Bronx Bombers barely edging out "Dem Bums," four games to three. But Harvard's football season, Coach Harlow's last, would be disappointing, with losses to Dartmouth, Rutgers, Princeton and, finally, by a score of 21–31, to Yale.

On the night of Friday, October 31, the Biddle Room was the setting of a gala dinner at which President Whitney conferred on Mackenzie King the status of honorary member; then, after Judge Learned Hand had recalled King's most notable achievements as Canada's longest-running chief executive, the new honorary member spoke feelingly about Harvard's role in shaping his career. The next morning, King sailed for England in the *Queen Elizabeth*. Over the weekend, however, his thoughts evidently strayed back to that Friday evening, for on Monday President Whitney received a cablegram from midocean reading STILL WEARING HARVARD DINNER CARNATION—LETTER FOLLOWS. In the promised communication, the prime minister regretted that he had not spoken "more

The War Memorial

particularly of the Club itself, and what I owed to its open door," and asked that his letter be read aloud at the next meeting of the Board.

> For some thirty-three years [King wrote] I have enjoyed the Club's hospitality, in times of war and peace. It has been my home in New York on journeys from Ottawa to Washington, to London, and to other Capitals in Europe, and at more conferences than one. Having regard to letters written from the Club and to persons with whom I have had conferences while there, the Club has been, for me, at all times, in the course of my public life, a centre of international understanding, friendship and good will.

As for his honorary membership, it was, King said,

> an honour which I shall ever regard as one of the highest expressions of friendship, and one of the richest of the rewards of my public life.

In late November, the Activities Committee, citing the expense, chose not to hold another children's Christmas party, and Chairman Delafield said the Library was so pinched for shelf space it was being forced to decline offers of valuable books. President Whitney reported that the late Thomas Slocum's closest friends agreed that his $25,000 bequest could be appropriately spent on constructing, furnishing and decorating the new Bar. The Board voted that this be done. Before adjourning, it granted exempt status to Francis B. Allen '81 of Walpole, New Hampshire, a cofounder in 1904 of New York's Allen-Stevenson School for boys, who had belonged to the Club more than sixty-six years—two-thirds of a century!

That year, as it last had in 1941, December 7 fell on a Sunday, and at five o'clock that afternoon several hundred people, among them families and friends of members who had died in the war, gathered in Harvard Hall for the unveiling and dedication of the war memorial. President Conant spoke, as did former Club President Welldon. The ceremony—"impressive and dignified," Langdon Marvin was to call it—concluded with the singing of "Fair Harvard" and a bugler blowing "Taps."

Just before Christmas, as usual, an employees' party was held in the North Room, with the customary distribution of bonuses and turkeys. On Christmas Day, again as usual, eggnog was served in the Grill Room to members and guests, and on New Year's Day, 1948, this cheery scene was reenacted. By then, a neat little two-story building stood to the left, or west, of the clubhouse, its bricks, like those of the older structure, laid in Flemish bond. Inside, crews of skilled workmen were bringing into being rooms, corridors and other spaces on three levels: basement, ground floor and second floor.

Before the annual meeting, at which all four officers would be reelected, the House Committee, moving to ease the overcrowding at lunchtime, issued a directive communicated to the membership via a notice in the *Bulletin*:

> The Bar will open at 11:45 a.m. rather than at 12 noon as in the past. The reason for this is not necessarily to lengthen the period for stomachics but to stagger the lunch hour in the main dining room.

*The New Yorker*, reprinting this notice, commented:

> If it were the Yale Club, we'd put it down to sheer caprice—or the craving for one more stomachic before staggering in.

At a meeting on February 19, the Board noted the recent deaths of former President Lamont and former Secretary Reid. House Committee Chairman Thompson reported that the Employees' Christmas Fund had once again reached a new high—$40,112, from no fewer than 3,421 members. Thompson called this "a great compliment to the management and to the service the Club is giving the members," but in light of the labor crisis that would soon erupt, it could equally be seen as an indication of the affection and regard with which most members held most employees.

On or around the dread Ides of March the Club was hit by a strike. What precipitated it? The record is unclear, but on March 18, Treasurer MacFadden reported that while the Club's gross revenues were holding steady, its operating profits had fallen substantially, in large part because of increased labor costs; it seems likely, then, that when Manager Howes started negotiating with the union earlier that month he was under instructions to hold the line on wages even though living costs were going up fast. If that was indeed the case, the Board members could hardly have been surprised when the talks broke down and the union pulled its members off the job, leaving the Club to make do with its nonunion employees plus casual labor available for hire. By April 15, the strike had cost the Club around $8,000.

On May 10, the new Bar opened, extending that part of the clubhouse given over to alcoholic pleasures twenty feet westward. One week later, a new Ladies' Dining Room, west of the old one and about three feet higher, opened for business. On June 14, the House Committee let it be known that a new employees' cafeteria would soon be completed in the basement of what had been 33 West 44th Street, with a lavatory and a rest room for women on the clerical staff. Incidentally, the management of 35 West 44th Street had filed damage claims against the Club because of cracks that had appeared in the building's east wall resulting, allegedly, from the Club's recent construction. Auditing Chairman Despard reassured his colleagues, however: the problem was not theirs to worry about, he told them; it was the contractors'.

Meanwhile, at Library Chairman Delafield's request, former President Welldon had been considering how to reallocate most equitably the second-floor space occupied by the Ladies' Dining Room kitchen, a facility no longer needed. Welldon concluded that that part of the space which had previously served as a reference room should be returned to the Library and the rest to the ladies. Chairmen Delafield and Thompson and finally the Board would all agree to this division.

In June, Treasurer MacFadden estimated losses from the strike during

May at $12,573, noting that, paradoxically, the Club had then been running at peak usage. The Board approved having John Lavalle paint President Whitney's portrait, and Secretary Righter announced that a large-screen television set would shortly be installed in Harvard Hall, in time for the major political parties' quadrennial conventions. Later that month, with Club members looking on from afar, the Republicans, in Philadelphia, again nominated Governor Dewey for President, and in mid-July the Democrats, also in the City of Brotherly Love, would nominate President Truman.

That summer, workmen installed new telephone booths off the entrance hall.

Week after week, meanwhile, Manager Howes stayed in contact with representatives of Local 6, and some time in August—the record doesn't say just when—the opposing sides arrived at terms acceptable to both, and after five months the strike was called off. The settlement would increase the Club's payroll by about $26,000 a year. Chairman Thompson summoned the House Committee into special session to congratulate Howes on the successful outcome of his efforts.

Around then, as noted in a House Committee report dated September 10, the Club took an important step, perhaps part of or related to the strike settlement, by subscribing to a plan of group hospitalization and surgical benefits offered by Metropolitan Life at an annual cost of $4,300. The committee recommended raising restaurant charges by 10 percent. Five days later the Board approved this increase after learning from Treasurer MacFadden that in the first eight months of 1948 the Club had lost $79,000, almost half of it from the strike.

In other business, Activities Chairman Livingston noted for the record a dinner honoring Harvard's new football coach, Arthur L. Valpey. Robert P. Patterson, sounding not at all like a recent secretary of war, reported that complaints of lukewarm or cold food in the Ladies' Dining Rooms had been stilled by the installation of a steam table in the second-floor pantry. On October 15 the House Committee recommended that the late Thomas W. Lamont's legacy of $5,000 be applied to restoring the Library's old reference room, a project his son, Thomas S. Lamont, had endorsed.

On November 4, to the astonishment of a nation led to expect a Dewey victory, President Truman won election to a full term. Two weeks later the Board named Carleton Sprague Smith '27 AM'28, a noted musicologist, chorister in place of Richard H. Dana, who resigned. At that meeting, President Whitney made a historic move: declaring himself fully in accord with the University's expressed wish to recruit boys who displayed leadership qualities as well as scholastic ability, he recommended that the Board create a schools committee to seek out well-rounded candidates and name Frederick R. Moseley, Jr., its chairman. Both suggestions were approved.

On the ground floor westward expansion had opened up new offices, not only for the Club manager, but also for the secretary, treasurer, and chairman of the House Committee. What was to be done, then, with the third-floor chamber (now the Weld Room) that had long been used as an office by successive holders of these posts? At the suggestion of Games Committee Chairman Henry Schniewind '31 it was provisionally slated for conversion into a resort for poker players.

The *Bulletin* for January 1949 contained, under the heading "Frank J. A. Melia," the text of a letter to Secretary Righter that must have pleased readers who had known the longtime former Club manager. This last public echo of the controversy, which six years before had aroused strong passions and threatened to divide the membership, was the joint creation of former President Langdon P. Marvin and former Secretary William G. Wendell.

> In the November issue of the *Club Bulletin* there appeared a notice concerning the death of Frank Melia which seems to us to need some supplementation. Both of us were officers of the Club and deeply interested in its welfare during a good many of the years when Mr. Melia was Manager. In several of these years the Club had had exceedingly hard going. However, the storm was weathered, due to careful attention to details on the part of those charged with the management, and to the fact that Mr. Melia put in habitually a sixteen-hour day in trying to make things go. His loyalty and devotion to the Club and to all of its members were selfless and without measure. He was known to a vast majority of the members and took such personal interest in giving them individual service that he may, at times, have neglected matters of larger import. Yet it is fair to say that Mr. Melia's kindly attentions to the welfare of hundreds of individuals served to maintain their loyalty to the Club and to prevent a considerable number of resignations which might otherwise have been tendered.

In deference to his memory and to the splendid work he did for the Club in time of stress, and in better times too, we hope that you will bring this letter to the attention of the members. Times change and memories fade, but Mr. Melia's devotion to duty will not be forgotten by those who were most closely connected with him.

Now in its third year, the Harry Cowles Invitational Singles Tournament was widely recognized as the country's premier squash racquets contest. The House Committee permitted one of the networks to televise the action over the January 22–23 weekend on condition that the Club not be named more than once. In the event, national champion Stanley Pearson, Jr., of Philadelphia defeated the Club's Germain G. Glidden.

On January 17, the House Committee, now headed by Philip B. Kunhardt '23 B'25, decided to convert the former secretary's and treasurer's office not into a poker room but another private dining room. Three days later the Board elected Coach Valpey a special member. Secretary Righter read aloud a letter from A. A. Berle '91. It was dated four days into the future, January 24, 1949, but this anomaly was soon explained: having been born the year the Club was organized, 1865, Berle wanted to present the gift accompanying his letter, a check for $500, on his eighty-fourth birthday. He asked that his gift be kept confidential, and that after his death the income from it be spent exclusively on books for the library in the fields of philosophy and American history, together with works of reference. "I have greatly appreciated my stay in the Club," he wrote, "and wish while I am still alive to know that this plan is acceptable." Without hesitation, the Board found it so.

The Berle '91 Fund thereupon became the eleventh of the Club's permanent designated endowment funds, joining the F. R. Appleton Fund, the C. S. and H. L. Fairchild Fund, the Nelson Fairchild Library Fund, the Lawrence E. Sexton Library Fund, the Edwin Wetmore Library Fund, the Grace A. Taylor Scholarship Fund, the A. C. Jackson Fund, the Plattsburgh Scholarship Fund, the James Byrne Fund and the Henry Renwick Sedgwick Fund.

One last item of business remained: noting that there was no room left in Harvard Hall for portraits, Art Chairman Robinson suggested, according to the minutes, "that future Presidents be hung in the Dining Room." Aware, as literate Harvard men, that human beings—even, conceivably, presidents of the Harvard Club—could be hanged, but their images only hung, Robinson's hearers did not take alarm.

At the annual meeting the next evening, Arthur W. Page was elected president, Devereux C. Josephs '15 vice-president and Edward M. Douglas '25 treasurer, while Volney Righter was reelected secretary. Of the 427 members partaking of the dinner that followed, the oldest was the celebrated lawyer C. C. Burlingham, ninety.

The February *Bulletin* noted the publication of *The History of Football at Harvard*, calculated to delight John G. Stewart '40 and the Club's many other supporters of successive Crimson elevens. Much research for the book and even some of the writing had been done in the Library by its three authors: Harry von Kersburg '06 and Hamilton Fish, all-Americans both, and William J. Chipman, Michigan '19, of the New York *Daily News*.

On February 19 the House Committee announced the imminent removal of four roomettes on the sixth floor to open up a lounge for squash players, and on the twenty-fourth Treasurer Douglas set aside $5,000 which, with the Lamont bequest, would presumably pay for restoring the Library's reference room. That month, Games Chairman and bridge team captain William A. Robertson '31 won the annual backgammon tournament; in March, the Art Committee loaned New England scenes by artist Barry Faulkner that had adorned the Ladies' Dining Room to the Downtown Harvard Club, now at 16 Liberty Street; in April, the House Committee urged the Board to set up a retirement plan for the employees. And in May, a list in the *Bulletin* of additions to the library's collection showed that the Club's authors had not been idle. It included *Father of the Bride* by Edward Streeter; *The Great Pierpont Morgan* by Frederick Lewis Allen; *Humanism as a Philosophy* by Corliss Lamont '24; *Cutlass Empire* by F. Van Wyck Mason; *Versus* by Ogden Nash; *The Dictionary of Sports*, edited by Parke Cummings '25; and *The Theory of American Literature* by Howard Mumford Jones, Faculty.

By August, a combination reading and reference room had come into being immediately west of the Library proper, its shelves, lining all four walls from carpeted floor to ceiling, filled with some 6,000 books. Soon thereafter, Library Committee Chairman R. McAllister Lloyd '19 took a step that should have won him the thanks not only of alumni but of biographers, historians, and other researchers. Aware that even with library personnel keeping watch, class reports, difficult and in certain cases impossible to replace, had been disappearing, Lloyd saw to it that most of the unspent portion of his committee's appropriation went to constructing, on all four sides of the main stairway landing between the Library and the Ladies' Club Rooms, glassed-in bookcases that would contain the bulk of the Club's precious collection of printed Harvardiana, the largest outside Cambridge, cases which were kept locked and to which only the librarian had keys.

At the Board's October meeting, Chairman Lloyd reported that poet member Percy Mackaye wanted to give the library an outsize, handsomely printed work he considered his masterpiece, *The Mystery of Hamlet, Prince of Denmark, or, What We Will: Tetralogy with Prelude and Postlude*, but could not afford the $100 price. At this, Athletics Chairman Beekman Pool spoke up: he and his brother, James L. Pool '28, he said, were planning to make a gift to the Club in memory of their late father, former President Eugene H. Pool, and he felt that Mackaye's book would do admirably.

On November 1, an Eastern Airlines plane crashed over Washington; among the passengers killed was former President Francis M. Weld. As Langdon P. Marvin noted in a memorial minute, Weld, a senior partner in the banking firm of White, Weld, was the sole chief executive in the Club's history whose father had previously held the top post.

Later that month, House Committee Chairman Kunhardt came up with a fresh solution to the familiar problem of overcrowding at lunchtime: setting up tables and chairs on the east balcony to accommodate lunchers when the Main Dining Room below was full. And as the year and the decade drew to their common close, Art Chairman Robinson noted some recent gifts: from the elder John Elliott, two framed group photographs, one destined to hang conspicuously for many years next to the ground-floor coatroom, of members in Army uniform at the Mexican border in 1916; an indoor-outdoor thermometer from Edmund Kerper; and, from Francis de L. Cunningham '15, three stuffed and mounted caribou heads and one moose head.

On January 19, 1950, the Board voted to name the new library extension, converted to that use largely with funds he had left the Club, for the late Thomas W. Lamont. And President Page said the time had come to drop wartime expedients—the 10 percent surcharge on house charges and the annual requests for voluntary contributions—in favor of confronting, openly, the need to raise the dues. On a lighter note, he announced that almost a third of the 123 members who had belonged since before the turn of the century would be attending the annual dinner, and indeed, the following night, after Henry Schniewind had been elected secretary and the other officers reelected, forty ancients were successively hailed by name and awarded certificates.

Again that year the Cowles tournament was won by a Philadelphian, G. Diehl Mateer, Jr.

That winter was unusually dry and pleasant. In April, for the first time since early in the war, members of the Harvard Glee Club raised their young voices in song in Harvard Hall, evoking an ovation, while members of the Board quietly voted to raise the dues, doubling the annual fee for the newest and youngest members to $20 and increasing that of members in the highest bracket from $60 to $85. The new schedule was to become effective the following January, but for the present it would not be made public.

By May, the city was experiencing a water shortage. The Club erected a cooling tower to ensure that the air-conditioning in the Bar continued to function.

On the night of Thursday, June 15, revelers in one of the private dining rooms damaged several of Art Chairman Robinson's prized naval battle prints. The occasion was a bachelor party given by Massachusetts Congressman (and former naval officer and hero) John F. Kennedy '40 for his brother Robert F. Kennedy '48. The host was not a member of the Club, but he had been sponsored for a guest card by an elderly nonresident member, Judge Daniel T. O'Connell '05 of Boston.

Next morning, the Kennedy family moved fast to set matters to rights: well before Robert married Ethel Skakel on Saturday in Greenwich, Connecticut, with Jack his best man, top-notch restorers were at work repairing the damaged prints. Their efforts would succeed. But the House

Committee could hardly overlook such a flagrant breach of decorum: it adopted new rules providing that no entertainment requiring private facilities could thereafter be given in the clubhouse unless the member host were present—as Judge O'Connell had not been—and that all bills for such an entertainment were to be sent to the said member host. (Since it reveals no new information about either of the star-crossed Kennedy brothers, this incident adds nothing important to the sum of American history, but because it prompted the House Committee to take significant action it is integral to the history of the Club.)

Sunday, June 25, brought disturbing news from the other side of the globe: North Korean troops had invaded South Korea. Two days later, President Truman pledged to support the Republic of Korea with arms. America was thus at war again, though a subsequent U.N. Security Council resolution backing Truman's stand would make the effort to stop North Korea's aggression a multinational one under U.N. command, with America contributing far more fighting men and material than any other country except the Republic of Korea itself. Given that hostilities would most likely be confined to the Korean peninsula, however, and given the enemy's presumably limited capacity to make war, these events had nothing like the impact on the citizenry that the Japanese attack on Pearl Harbor had had. Within the Club they affected relatively few members directly: those enrolled in reserve units of the armed forces and those with sons in their late teens and early twenties.

One likely consequence of the country's going on a war footing would be the rationing of food, especially meat: Manager Howes felt the Club should have its own freezer, and on September 18 the House Committee set aside funds to acquire one. A week or ten days later President Page finally notified the members of the impending dues increase; no firestorm of protest erupted, and in mid-October Secretary Schniewind reported no more resignations than usual at that juncture. Bayard F. Pope communicated to the Board an offer by Mrs. E. M. Statler to lend the Club another tapestry; the Board accepted, leaving the placing of the tapestry to Art Chairman Robinson, who in turn reported the gift, by Charles E. Nixdorff '00 L'04, of a bronze bas-relief portrait of Professor George H. Palmer '64 AM'67 LLD'06 by the sculptor Anne Whitney

(1821–1915), remembered in Cambridge for her statue of Charles Sumner in Cambridge Common.

By November, a walk-in freezer was installed in the basement; hunter members could rent game lockers in it for one dollar a month. And at 6 P.M. on Thursday, November 16, in the presence of two dozen relatives and friends of the late Thomas W. Lamont, President Page formally dedicated the Library's new Lamont Room.

Commenting, in December, on an upsurge of resignations, Secretary Schniewind acknowledged that the pending dues increase had taken a toll after all: 205 members had resigned, compared to 102 by the same date in 1949. Meanwhile, the Korean War (or "police action," as it was officially termed) had caused a drop-off of applications from young men subject to the draft. As 1950 ended, the Club had 6,308 members, down 87 in the first annual decrease since the war.

At the 1951 annual meeting Devereux C. Josephs was elected president and Edward Streeter vice-president, while Secretary Schniewind and Treasurer Douglas were confirmed in their posts. Once again, participants at the annual dinner saluted longtime members, but this year, as would be routine thereafter, the men so honored were limited to those who had completed a half century of membership during the previous twelve months.

In March, House Committee Chairman Kunhardt warned that the Club's elephant head, showing breaks in the skin, needed pachydermatological attention, and Library Chairman Lloyd, remarking on the comforts of the enlarged Library, suggested, deadpan, installing parking meters next to the armchairs. On April 3 the Club gave a lunch for the Cambridge University crew, which sixteen days later, on the Charles, outrowed the Crimson eight. Just hours after this, in New York, Athletics Chairman Daniel Ladd '41 informed the Board of another disheartening development regarding sports: there was, he reported, little interest at the Yale Club in continuing the two clubs' annual outing, and he recommended, reluctantly, discontinuing the fixture.

The next month, the Board members pondered ways to increase usage of the Club. They appointed Daniel Ladd head of a junior committee. They adopted a suggestion from George Brownell '19 AM '20 L'22 that over the coming summer the ground floor of the clubhouse be opened to wives and lady guests most weekday evenings, adding a caution that "This move is, of course, in the nature of an experiment."

In June, the minutes of a Board meeting on the fourteenth noted that the "Weld Room" was about to be converted to a private dining room. So it now had a name. That summer, workmen also redecorated twenty bedrooms, while experts rehabilitated the elephant head in situ. And on September 20, Chairman Kunhardt pronounced the "experiment" of welcoming ladies on summer evenings a resounding success, "both financially and in the members' acceptance" of it.

The next day, Art Chairman Robinson died, and on November 14 his successor, Hardinge Scholle '18, announced the acquisition of two paintings—*Fishermen's Wives* by Winslow Homer, and a dazzling oil sketch by John Singer Sargent titled *The Chess Game*—which instantly ranked among the most important in the Club's collection. They were the gift of former President Weld's widow, who, with other members of the family, was on hand, late in the afternoon of Thursday, January 3, 1952, for the

*Fishermen's Wives*, by Winslow Homer

*The Chess Game*, by John Singer Sargent

formal dedication of the Weld Room. Containing not only the Homer and Sargent canvases but fine portraits of Francis M. Weld '60 and Francis M. Weld '97, with a plaque memorializing these men on one wall, the room was, everyone agreed, perhaps the most attractive in the entire clubhouse.

By then the Club had also acquired a likeness of former President

Page, the joint gift of the sitter and his depicter, Elihu Root, Jr. The library collection numbered 21,142 books. Sixty-seven members (just over 1 percent) were in uniform. And a start had been made toward systematizing the payment of pensions with the establishment of a special Employees' Fund.

On January 18, 1952, Morgan D. Wheelock was elected treasurer, and ten days later G. Diehl Mateer, Jr., won the Cowles invitational for a third straight year. In February Albert Tilt, Jr., '26 took command of the House Committee and John B. Coffinberry '22 of the Library Committee. That winter, the Municipal Art Society, headed by member William H. Russell, launched a campaign to preserve buildings of historic or architectural interest in the city, and if the clubhouse was in no danger of being demolished, it was, according to the *Bulletin*, widely admired by architects and other citizens of taste and discrimination.

On March 20 Chairman Tilt outlined for his colleagues the ground-breaking labor contract signed just hours before. It abolished the six-day, forty-eight-hour work week in favor of a five-day, forty-hour week at the same pay. And it bound the Club to contribute half the cost of the union's health insurance plan and the whole cost of the Club's hospitalization plan. Finally, at Tilt's urging, the Board discontinued at last the 10 percent usage charge on food, beverages and rooms, simultaneously raising prices by 10 percent.

Two months later President Josephs relayed the cheering news that Bayard F. Pope and his fellow directors of Hotels Statler, Inc., had voted to give the Club the sixteenth-century Flemish tapestry Mrs. Statler had loaned it in 1946. The tapestry, showing Cadmus, with five men sprung from dragons' teeth, in the act of founding Thebes, hung—as it still does—above the elephant head.

In June, Junior Committee Chairman Ladd reported that a certain Admissions Committeeman had recently interviewed seniors in Cambridge, several of whom had expressed an interest in joining the Club. He recommended that next year a representative go up earlier, around the Christmas and Easter breaks, to recruit prospective members. And on the twenty-fourth Professor Copeland—Copey—died in Cambridge. He had, it would turn out, left the Club library a prized possession, a first edition copy of Dr. Johnson's dictionary.

One torrid Saturday in July Assistant Manager Alfred Martinez and John Pappas, an octogenarian baker reputed to have overseen the creation of five million popovers, were each handed a $100 check, in a ceremony that had become routine since the war, to mark their completion of twenty-five years with the Club. (Before 1952 was out, popular doorman Patrick Cronin would join their company.)

That summer, in unusually hot and muggy weather, bedroom occupancy fell to about 65 percent and the clubhouse emptied out over weekends. In addition to customary off-season maintenance, workmen carried out two special assignments. In front of the war memorial a sturdy table was set up, and two thick volumes of photographs and text recording the life stories of the honored dead bolted (of necessity, alas) to it. Meanwhile, in the Library, other workmen removed the three windows from the east wall and filled in the empty spaces, brick outside and plaster inside. The shelves placed where the windows had been could hold, in all, some 2,000 books.

In September, House Committeeman Ernest F. Gamache '27 B'29 reported that the Club's losses that summer had been the biggest since the war. Could the low level of use by the members be ascribed to competition from air-conditioned restaurants and hotels?

On October 25 Manager Howes dropped dead of a heart attack; Assistant Manager Martinez took over provisionally. And nine days later, to the satisfaction of most members, Republican presidential candidate Dwight D. Eisenhower, wartime supreme commander in Europe and until recently president of Columbia University, scored a sweeping electoral victory over former Illinois Governor Adlai Stevenson.

On November 20 Chairman Tilt made explicit what some Board members had seen for themselves: that the clubhouse was being air-conditioned. Sites where equipment had been installed, or soon would be, included the banquet rooms, the Ladies' Dining Rooms, the fourth- and fifth-floor bedrooms, the barber shop and the Library. Later in that meeting an old idea resurfaced: that the Club be reconstituted as a Harvard Club of New York Foundation to receive contributions for scholarships and bequests for charitable or educational purposes.

The following month, the Board authorized the officers to proceed with the incorporation of a Harvard Club Foundation.

Days after the start of 1953 President Conant let it be known that he was leaving Cambridge to become the high commissioner to Germany. On January 26, in Harvard Hall, the members present, a good-sized turnout, elected Edward Streeter president, George Brownell vice-president and Frank Streeter '40 secretary, and reelected Treasurer Wheelock. After dinner, guest-of-honor Conant delivered his last address as president of Harvard to a large audience of alumni. Also present was America's next ambassador to the Court of St. James's, Winthrop W. Aldrich '07 L'10, who would succeed his fellow Club member Walter S. Gifford '05. And although our new envoy to France, member C. Douglas Dillon, could not be present, his appointment was duly noted and applauded.

The Grill Room

$\boxed{15}$

# THE EISENHOWER
# YEARS
# (1953–1961)

After two years as high commissioner to the Federal Republic of Germany, former President Conant would stay on in Bonn as ambassador until 1957. In that year, Ambassador Aldrich would leave London and Ambassador Dillon would turn over the Paris embassy to his fellow Club member Amory Houghton '21, becoming in 1958 undersecretary of state for economic affairs. From 1955 to 1961, former Connecticut Governor John Davis Lodge '25 L'29 would serve as ambassador to Spain. The Eisenhower administration would tap other Club members for important jobs at home, among them Marion B. Folsom, B'14, secretary of health, education and welfare; Sinclair Weeks '14, secretary of commerce; former Governor of Massachusetts Christian Herter '15, undersecretary and secretary of state; Robert Cutler '16 L'22, special assistant to the president; and Elliot L. Richardson '41 L'44 and Roswell B. Perkins '47 L'49—both, at different times, assistant secretaries of health, education and welfare. Former members, too, would fill key positions: Charles "Chip" Bohlen '27 would be America's man in Moscow (1953–57) and Manila (1957–59) before returning to Washington as special assistant for Soviet affairs (1959–61), while former Massachusetts Senator Henry Cabot Lodge, Jr. '24, who had managed President Eisenhower's electoral campaign, would represent this country at the United Nations from 1953 to 1960.

In far-off Alaska, longtime member Ernest Gruening, its governor from 1939 to 1953, would play a central role in bringing that vast and beautiful land into the Union, as provisional senator from the territory (1955) and senator from the state after 1958. And the same Grenville Clark who had launched the Plattsburgh movement with General Wood would work tirelessly to advance the cause of world federalism.

As men like these helped to make current history, other members analyzed it, most notably Walter Lippmann in his New York *Herald Tribune* column. In *The Waist-High Culture* (1958), Thomas H. Griffith, Jr., Nieman Fellow '43 would deplore the mediocrity he saw pervading the nation's soul and psyche. Theodore H. White '38 would document *The Making of the President 1960* (Pulitzer Prize, 1961). Meanwhile, two historian members would review, on a heroic scale, grand and shaping events of the recent past: Arthur M. Schlesinger, Jr. '38 would chronicle the New Deal era in the three-volume *Age of Roosevelt* (1957–60), while Samuel Eliot Morison, having retired from the Navy as a rear admiral in 1951, would continue thereafter to oversee the publication of a monumental work that President Roosevelt himself had commissioned him to write, the fifteen-volume *History of United States Naval Operations in World War II* (1947–62). This series, incidentally, won the Bancroft Prize, named for George Bancroft, AB 1817, historian, diplomat, public servant, founder of the Naval Academy—and charter member of the Club.

Apropos of history, members James Parton '34 and Joseph J. Thorndike, Jr. '34, veteran writers and editors for *Time* and *Life*, would in 1954, with their colleague Oliver O. Jensen, launch *American Heritage*; four years later the same trio would begin publishing as well the quarterly *Horizon*. Gerard Piel '37 would continue, as he had since 1947, to put out the country's foremost science magazine for laymen, *Scientific American*. Gardner Cowles '25 would oversee the operations of Cowles Publications, including *Look* and the Des Moines (Iowa) *Register and Tribune*. And in tiny Dublin, New Hampshire, Robb Sagendorph '22 would produce, month after month, the popular regional magazine *Yankee*, together with its even more popular companion annual, *The Old Farmer's Almanac*.

Of the Club's book publishers in the 1950s Thomas J. Wilson III, University of North Carolina '21, should perhaps be mentioned first, as director of the Harvard University Press 1947–65, but as propagators of good books, Chairman Cass Canfield of Harper and Brothers and his colleague Simon Michael Bessie (who in 1959 would cofound Atheneum Publishing) hardly lagged behind him. Nor did steel company heir James Laughlin '36, founder and proprietor of New Directions, who would, as he does to this day, print works by unknown, avant-garde writers his competitors could never afford to publish.

The most controversial of the many professional writers who belonged to the Club at that time was surely Corliss Lamont, who, though a son of Morgan partner and Club president Thomas W. Lamont, was, as he remains today, implacably opposed to capitalism; during the Eisenhower years he was to lecture at Columbia, and in 1956 he would publish *Freedom Is as Freedom Does: Civil Liberties in America*, and see his indictment for contempt of Congress, brought years earlier by Senator Joseph McCarthy, dismissed. Writer Bernard De Voto '18 (*Across the Wide Missouri*, 1947, Pulitzer Prize) would conduct the "Easy Chair" column in *Harper's,* producing for it a little book, *The Hour* (1951), that would at once become the bible of martini drinkers, while longtime drama critic John Mason Brown would cover the theater and theatrical matters for the *Saturday Review*. Some critics would focus on letters, notably Malcolm Cowley '19 in *The Literary Situation* (1954), Mark Schorer AM'30 in *Sinclair Lewis: An American Life* (1961) and Harvard professor Harry Levin '33 in studies of Christopher Marlowe (1952) and of Hawthorne, Poe and Melville (1958). Witty and insightful commentary on the changing social scene would flow from the pen of Cleveland Amory '39 (*The Last Resorts*, 1952, and *Who Killed Society?*, 1960), while Ogden Nash would continue to turn out wry and totally original comments on the human condition in irresistibly droll verse.

Peter Viereck '37 AM'39 PhD'42 had won the Pulitzer Prize for poetry in 1948, and during the 1950s he would bring out two more collections. Robert Hillyer '17, who had long taught at Harvard, was to publish his *Collected Poems* in 1961, shortly before his death. And Robert Fitzgerald '33, having published *In the Rose of Time* in 1956, would in 1961 bring out a magnificent translation of *The Odyssey* in collaboration with Dudley Fitts '25.

The most prolific of the Club's fiction writers was probably Bermuda-based F. Van Wyck Mason, still turning out highly readable novels at the rate of two a year. The least prolific was, almost certainly, William Gaddis '45, whose huge satirical novel *The Recognitions* (1955), seven years in the writing, would puzzle reviewers and sell no more than a few hundred copies, but at last, after two decades as the object of an underground cult, win its own recognition as a modern classic. With *The Man in the Gray Flannel Suit* (1954), Sloan Wilson '42 would score a resounding success—and see his title freely appropriated to describe a representative figure of the time. And in *By Love Possessed* (1957), James Gould Cozzens '26, the author of *Guard of Honor* (1948), would produce a controversial bestseller, extravagantly praised by some critics and pronounced a disappointment by others.

If, a generation earlier, theater people had abounded in the Club, only producer George Abbott and set designer Donald Oenslager '23 remained from that time, while the one playwright member who might be thought of as belonging in the same company with O'Neill, Sherwood and Howard was Robert W. Anderson '39 AM'40, whose first Broadway play, *Tea and Sympathy* (1953), would earn him critical and popular acclaim. On the other hand, television, that relatively new entertainment medium, was widely represented in the membership in the person, notably, of the president of the Columbia Broadcasting System, Frank Stanton Vis. Familiar by sight to fellow members was Robert Saudek '32, the producer and host of the Sunday evening talk show *Omnibus*, which, as the one television program that dealt in depth with current events and issues, was must viewing for thoughtful New Yorkers. And few members owning television sets (by then, surely, a majority) can have forgotten the documentary series *Victory at Sea*, recounting the Navy's operations during World War II, which aired nationally at weekly intervals between the fall of 1952 and the spring of 1953.

*Victory at Sea* was conceived by one member of the Club, Henry "Peter" Salomon, Jr. '39, who had served under Admiral Morison with the Naval History Unit and brought three others into the project. When the idea for the series came to him, Salomon talked it over with his best friend and Harvard roommate, Robert W. Sarnoff '39; then the pair approached Sarnoff's father, Brigadier General David Sarnoff, the head of RCA. General Sarnoff felt the series could be an outstanding presentation for his National Broadcasting Company television network, with Salomon as producer and his own son shepherding the project along as an NBC vice-president. After months of negotiations, the Navy agreed to cooperate, whereupon the navies of America's wartime allies also made their film records available. Salomon chose his production staff, including two former naval officers (and Club members) he had come to know during the war, Daniel W. Jones, Jr. '42 and Douglas F. Wood '45, and engaged Richard Rodgers to compose a musical score.

Apart from Barry Faulkner and from Waldo Peirce, with his exuberant, Renoiresque depictions of rural life in Maine, the Club's better known painters were portraitists: John Lavalle, Gardner Cox '28 and William F. Draper '35. Its most eminent composer was Aaron Copland Spec., who in 1955 would compose his *Canticle for Freedom* for chorus and orchestra. And its composers of "frozen music" included two highly influential architects from Central Europe who had taught or were teaching at Harvard, Walter Gropius and Marcel Breuer; Spaniard Jose Luis Sert AM (hon.) '53; and a young immigrant from China who had both studied and taught in Cambridge and would, in 1955, set up his own architectural firm: I. M. Pei, M. Arch.'46.

Like these architects—and like some historians and others mentioned earlier—professor members in several disciplines would, during the 1950s, shed luster on the College and University with their publications, while occasionally enlivening their New York home-away-from-home by their presence. Astronomer Harlow Shapley would cap a distinguished career with *The Inner Metagalaxy* (1957) and *Of Stars and Men* (1958), and Paul J. Sachs '00 ArtD (hon.) '42 of the Fogg Museum would in 1954 issue his last major work, *Modern Prints and Drawings*. Psychologist Gordon W. Allport '19 AM'21 PhD'22 would deal with profound matters in *The Nature of Personality* (1950), *The Nature of Prejudice* (1954) and *Pattern and Growth in Personality* (1960). Anthropologist Clyde Kluckhohn PhD'36 would publish groundbreaking studies of cultural value systems and patterns. Finally, John Kenneth Galbraith AM (hon.) '50 would turn out books that would influence ordinary citizens in large numbers, as much as or more than they would his fellow economists, in particular *The Affluent Society* (1958).

One member a product of whose genius was to be found in millions of American homes was Edwin H. Land '30, inventor of the instant developer/printer camera that bore his name. Although Land had dropped out of the College to pursue his ideas and carry out experiments, Harvard would award him an honorary doctorate of science in 1957, twenty years after he had founded the Polaroid Corporation in Cambridge.

As well as Land (and cousins Amory and Arthur Houghton of Corning Glass), the Club contained a number of leading industrialists, men like George Merck '15 of Merck, Sharp and Dohme; Walter Mack '17 of Pepsi-Cola; and Lammot duPont Copeland '27 of DuPont. And besides such titans of finance as George Whitney and Thomas S. Lamont of Morgan, it included in its ranks John L. Loeb '24 of Loeb, Rhoades; Alexander M. White '25 of White, Weld; and David Rockefeller '36, soon to become (in 1961) president of Chase Manhattan. Meanwhile, its roster of lawyers still included both the venerable C. C. Burlingham and Judge Learned Hand, together with Harrison Tweed '07 L'10 LLD'58, president of the American Law Institute, as well as senior partners of many of the country's foremost law firms.

But if the Club's achievers of the 1950s could match those of the 1920s in some respects and outdo them in others, both they and their successors would conspicuously fail to come up to their predecessors' standards in the realm of sport. Where now were the Club's champions in squash racquets, squash tennis and court tennis, its world-class polo players, its victorious defenders of the America's Cup? But this falling off wasn't limited to the Club: the greater community of Harvard men, though far more numerous than they had been a generation before and constantly increasing in numbers, was never again to produce a Bobby Jones or a Barry Wood.

For some years, the Class of 1947 had held a New York dinner in the Biddle Room in late February, typically with a visiting dignitary from Cambridge who would talk about prospects for the coming football season. In the fall of 1952, member Donald E. Cummings '47 was asked to organize that winter's dinner; he invited President Roosevelt's widow,

Eleanor, to speak, and, somewhat to his surprise, she accepted. Her efforts, as a delegate since 1946 to the United Nations Human Rights Commission, to secure social and economic justice for disadvantaged peoples had earned Mrs. Roosevelt the gratitude and affection of multitudes around the globe, and while most of Cummings's classmates regretted her close association with the Democratic Party, they applauded her inspiring work overseas. Many signed up to come. Cummings suggested that they bring guests, and arranged to expand the affair into the North Room.

As the date of the dinner drew near, Cummings pleaded with the Club's governors to make an exception for his guest regarding the rule barring women from using the main entrance—in vain. On the appointed night, accompanied by his mother (he was then still unmarried), Cummings picked up Mrs. Roosevelt at her hotel and brought her in a taxi to 27 West 44th Street, where the former first lady of the land and now, perhaps, first citizen of the world, swept serenely through the door to the Ladies' Club Rooms. Their host then led his two guests along a circuitous route calculated to shield them as much as possible from members, and vice versa: up the stairs, west across the Ladies' Lounge to the lower Ladies' Dining Room, north to the Lamont Room, east to the Library, north again, then west again to the elevators, up one flight and north, finally, to the Biddle Room.

After dinner, Mrs. Roosevelt worked her customary magic, winning the admiration—and the hearts—of all present. And as Cummings recalls, the privilege of escorting her back to her hotel was claimed by J. William Middendorf '47, a future ambassador to the Netherlands (under President Nixon) and secretary of the Navy.

In April, Acting Manager Martinez was promoted to manager, and on May 21 the Board authorized the transfer of the Club's scholarship funds to the Harvard Club of New York City Foundation, now incorporated under the laws of New York State. Games Chairman Howard A. Reiling '10 expressed satisfaction with the new Card Room, formerly bedroom 412. And House Committee Chairman Tilt reported yet another timely act of generosity by Edmund Kerper. In those days, the Bar was often crowded, especially before lunch, and loud with animated talk and laughter as well as with the percussive sounds of ice cubes crashing about in

**Nathan M. Pusey**

shakers and dice rattling in leather cups or clattering onto the bar as tipplers called on the gods of chance to tell them who was to pay for that round. The House Committee had long wanted to sound-proof the place, but funds had been lacking, until Kerper, a faithful patron of the Bar on his visits to New York, gave the Club $500 for that purpose, stipulating that his gift be anonymous.

Early in June came word that Harvard's governing bodies had picked Nathan Marsh Pusey '28 AM'32 PhD'37, since 1944 the president of little Lawrence College in Appleton, Wisconsin, to head the University. Pusey's fellow Appletonian, Red-baiting Senator Joseph McCarthy, commented, "I do not think that Dr. Pusey is or has been a member of the Communist Party." And President Streeter, meeting the president-designate in Cambridge, where Pusey was attending his class's twenty-fifth reunion, reminded him that by custom the president of Harvard was the Club's guest every January at its annual meeting and dinner.

On July 27 an armistice was signed at Panmunjon in Korea, ending the three-year-long war there.

In September, the Board agreed to pay artist Raymond P. R. Neilson $1,500 to copy an existing portrait of former President Josephs. And a Library Committee spokesman revealed that the subscriptions to some of the twenty-five foreign publications the library received had been donated, including, he said, "somewhat to the Committee's embarrassment," one to *La Vie Parisienne*.

The following month, President Streeter confirmed that President Pusey would be the Board's guest in November—not in the Mahogany Room, where his hearers were sitting, but in the newest private dining room. Much thought, Streeter said, had gone into deciding on a name for that chamber, formerly the South Room or the Card Room, and at last someone had suggested calling it the Presidents' Room, apropos of the presidential portraits it would contain. The apostrophe, Streeter added with a smile, would definitely come *after* the word, guaranteeing that the place would never be identified with any particular person. The Board approved the name.

To help it welcome Harvard's new chief to its banquet in his honor, the Board coopted four members who were Overseers (Harrison Tweed, Roy E. Larsen, Jack I. Straus '21 and John Mason Brown) and one who was a member of the Corporation (Thomas S. Lamont). Two months later, on January 15, 1954, President Pusey made his first appearance at an annual dinner; 484 dinner-jacketed members showed up to greet him. Meanwhile, the space south of the newly air-conditioned Slocum Room had been redecorated and christened the East Room, the Club's seventh—and, it would turn out, last—private dining area. The air-conditioning of bedrooms and other spaces, begun in the fall of 1952, would continue into that winter and spring of 1954.

For eight weeks that spring, from April 22 to June 17, millions of Americans stayed close to their television sets watching a plotless, unscripted show consisting largely of middle-aged men talking and arguing around a long table in a crowded Senate caucus room. Among these millions were hundreds of Club members, and of these all but a few, chances are, were unaware that the young draftee whose treatment by the military had given rise to these so-called Army-McCarthy hearings was a fellow member.

Two years before, with Republican Senator Joseph McCarthy of Wisconsin repeatedly accusing the Truman administration of harboring Communists, young G. David Schine '49 had written a "Definition of Communism." His father had had it printed up in a booklet, copies of which had then been distributed throughout several hotels he owned. Coming upon a copy, McCarthy's young counsel, Roy Cohn, had recruited its author to the senator's staff as an expert on Communism.

After the 1952 elections had given his party control of both the White House and the Senate, McCarthy, as chairman of an investigative subcommittee, had stepped up his accusations that executive departments were coddling subversives. In March 1953 McCarthy had sent Cohn and Schine to Europe to check on the political orthodoxy of American personnel there; they had exposed the United States to ridicule by such antics as decrying the presence in a U.S.I.A. library of books by "seditious" authors like Mark Twain and Jack London. In July, Schine had been notified of his imminent induction, whereupon Cohn had sought to wangle a commission for him; Army Secretary Robert Stevens would have accommodated him had senior officers not found Schine unqualified for command. Following a stint of "basic training" with weekends off, Schine had been posted to a base in Georgia, and Cohn had pressed McCarthy to demand that the Army detach Schine to resume his vital work of ferreting out subversives in the government. When the senator did so, the Army had accused him of improperly seeking preferential treatment for Private Schine, whereupon McCarthy had countercharged that the Army brass were trying to impede his ongoing investigation of their department, using Schine as a "hostage." At last the other senators on McCarthy's subcommittee had set out to weigh, in a televised inquest, the validity of the Army's charges against their chairman.

These hearings provided an opportunity to observe in action a freewheeling bully who, preying on ordinary citizens' anxieties arising out of international Cold War tensions in a nuclear age, had, with his wholesale charges of treason, sown fear in government bureaucracies, the professions, academia and the press. Most Club members hoped to see McCarthy humbled, as did the Harvard administrators and professors who were frequent targets of his smears. Private Schine only testified early and briefly, but by degrees another, much older member of the Club increasingly made his presence at the long table felt. He was sixty-three-year-old Joseph N. Welch L'17 of Boston, a special counsel to the Army.

The defining confrontation between the antagonists came on June 9, when, for no apparent reason, McCarthy remarked that a young lawyer in Welch's firm, whom he named, had, while at Harvard Law School, belonged to an organization that had since been placed on the government's proscribed list. Welch's reply would long resonate in the memories of many of the men and women across America who saw and heard him make it:

> Until this moment, Senator, I think I never really gauged your cruelty or your recklessness. . . . Little did I dream that you could be so reckless and so cruel as to do injury to that lad. . . . I fear he shall always bear a scar needlessly inflicted by you. If it were in my power to forgive you for your reckless cruelty I would do so. I like to think that I am a gentle man, but your forgiveness will have to come from someone other than me.

Unabashed, McCarthy returned to the subject of Welch's young associate, but the other cut him short.

> Let us not assassinate this lad further, Senator. You have done enough. Have you no sense of decency, sir? At long last? Have you no sense of decency?

In the end, the subcommittee would assign blame on both sides. It would soon be apparent, however, that, thanks in no small measure to a diminutive bow-tied attorney who looked like a white-haired leprechaun, McCarthy had somehow lost his formidable power to intimidate. Before long his fellow senators would formally censure him for his conduct, and in 1957 he would die of various causes, including alcoholism, at forty-eight.

In November (when Germain G. Glidden delivered a promised portrait of Thomas Slocum he had done from a photograph), the Club held a dinner honoring the Graduate School of Education. With President Pusey in the chair, Dean Francis Keppel '38 and two professors addressed 50 guests involved in public education and some 125 members about efforts to improve tax-supported schooling for America's poorest children and about how the University could reinforce these efforts. That evening would be the first of several dedicated to Harvard graduate schools and departments.

On January 21, 1955, George Brownell was elected president and Cornelius C. Felton '16 vice-president, while Secretary Streeter and Treasurer Wheelock were reelected. A month later, the Board created a University Relations Committee charged with bringing alumni closer to the University than regular Club activities alone would do (an end much favored by President Pusey) and named R. McAllister Lloyd to head it. Then President Brownell took note of Edmund Kerper's latest gifts, including $1,000 in cash for replacing the soft-wood herringbone floors of the Grill Room and adjacent areas, which, from being continually walked on, looked, not for the first time or the last, worn and scruffy.

In May, House Committee Chairman Tilt announced the introduction of a practice that has been followed ever since at the Club, of listing the names of fifty-year members alphabetically on two sheets, framed and hung at either end of the mirror above the fireplace in the entrance hall.

That summer, a crew of workmen laid new floors of oak in the Grill Room, while other men atop tall ladders in the Main Dining Room went over that hall's vast ceiling, some filling undecorated panels with acoustical tiles and others painting. One of the painters had been there forty years before, having worked on the ceiling as a boy when it was constructed. (As a finishing touch, ten wall-bracket lights were set in place around the walls; they had been called for in the original plans, but not acquired in 1915 for want of sufficient funds.)

On September 24, President Eisenhower, on a golfing vacation in Colorado, suffered a "mild coronary thrombosis." Next day, Dr. Paul Dudley White '08 MD'11 SD (hon.) '50 of Boston arrived to treat the chief executive and head a team of cardiologists who would monitor his progress back to health. According to White's Harvard classmate S. E. Morison, the physician's treatments "probably saved President Eisenhower's life." (*The Oxford History of the United States,* page 915). Thus, for a second time in less than two years, a Bostonian member of the Club, a professional man whose monosyllabic five-letter name began with "W," saw the country safely through a crisis.

Eagerly awaited that fall was a concert on the eve of the Columbia game by a large contingent of the Harvard Band. On the Friday afternoon before it, however, the weather turned foul: high winds careered down city streets, driving sheets of rain before them. Even so, after dark some 425 members and guests battled their way to 27 West 44th Street, only to learn that the bandsmen were stranded at the Boston airport. Luckily, a skilled crowd-pleaser was on hand in the person of Francis Hatch '19, whose nimble-fingered pianistics had enlivened countless parties in and around Boston. Instead of simply providing a quarter hour of background music between sets of the band, Hatch gamely constituted the entire show for well over an hour. At last, around 9:45, the young bandsmen arrived and began to play.

The next afternoon, in weather as bad or worse, the Harvard eleven beat Columbia at Baker Field, 21–7.

On Hallowe'en—on the eve, appropriately, of All Saints' Day—the Club honored the Divinity School, also honoring, incidentally, its new dean, Douglas Horton AM (hon.) '55 DD'59, and his wife, Mildred H. McAfee, the president of Wellesley.

When the Board next met, on November 17, it had a guest, Edmund Kerper; this time, he had volunteered to pay for steam-cleaning the facade of the clubhouse. The Managers thanked him, then approved a proposal that members' widows be allowed to apply directly for signing privileges instead of having to enlist a sponsor. And Games Chairman Reiling reported a moment of detente in the war between the sexes. The previous week, he related, eleven couples had dined together at the Club and repaired afterward to the Card Room to play, for the first time ever, several rubbers of *mixed bridge*. The evening had, Reiling assured his colleagues, gone off smoothly.

Although the Ivy League colleges were, at that time, trying to deemphasize varsity football, enthusiasm for the sport remained high at the Club, and on December 3 the Athletics Committee gave a football dinner. Coach Lloyd Jordan spoke, and movies of selected plays were shown; almost every member of the team was there, as were nineteen holders and former holders of Club scholarships. And although the Cantabs had, unhappily, bowed 7–21 to the Elis, a great time was had by all, and it was clear that the football dinner would become a yearly fixture.

Before 1955 was out the Board committed the Club to spend a large sum, more than $70,000, for a central air-conditioning system capable of cooling Harvard Hall, the Main Dining Room and the Grill Room.

The Club ushered in (or almost ushered in) the year 1956 on January 2, with a fathers-and-sons dinner. This buffet event, in the Main Dining Room, attracted 287 members and guests, the latter group aged seven and up, and was followed by a skiing film. The first event of its kind in the Club's annals, it would also be the last, so insistent would be the pressure from many fathers to let their daughters, too, share in the fun.

On February 19 the Blue Hill Troupe presented selections from Gilbert and Sullivan operettas, apparently helping to set a new record for attendance: the audience was reported to have filled Harvard Hall and its balcony, while other devotees, settling for hearing the performers even if they could not see them, apparently made do in the Main Dining Room, the Grill Room, the Library and even the Slocum Room. These talented singers, so well drilled they hardly seemed like amateurs, would most certainly be asked back!

On March 15 the Board approved for accession a portrait by William F. Draper of former President Streeter. And five nights later a dinner for the Fine Arts department honoring Director John Coolidge '35 of the Fogg Museum drew 221 members and guests.

Throughout that spring and into the summer the installing of the central air-conditioning continued, but as nearly all the work was done from outside the clubhouse, inconvenience to the members was minimal. In April, Treasurer Wheelock resigned, and was replaced by S. Whitney Satterlee '30. Next, the Club's altered-state wildlife claimed the Board's attention: learning in May that some members of the Columbia Club were under the impression that Leo, the lion's head the Club had loaned it many years before, was theirs, the Board reasserted the Club's title to it. (This object, donated in 1909, with the elephant head, by the slayer of both animals, William G. Sewall, had long stared out menacingly from its glass box in the third-floor north-south corridor, the sight of it sometimes serving to calm the nerves of young applicants to the College and candidates for scholarships anxiously waiting to be interviewed in an adjacent private dining room.)

Later that month, before having the Grill Room's oak panels cleaned, the House Committee's Lawrence G. White had the staff take down every animal head in the place. Several were in "very decrepit condition." Then, in June, President Brownell spoke for the first time about an undertaking that would figure prominently in, and at times dominate, the Club's agenda for the rest of the decade: a major fund drive for the College, with particular objectives.

In this connection, President Brownell proffered a suggestion. Harvard's band and glee club both wanted to give concerts at the Club in 1956–57; instead, he said, why not have them put on a joint concert as a benefit? Harvard Hall would not be roomy enough, but Carnegie Hall would be about the right size—and it had an open date next March, a Friday. The Board adopted the plan by acclamation.

On July 20 the new central air-conditioning system began operating. That summer saw the introduction of a feature in the Main Dining Room that has persisted to this day: a long table for the use of members lunching or dining alone but wanting company. Meanwhile, the cleaning of the Grill Room was completed; it was the last service of many rendered to the Club by Lawrence White, who died on September 8.

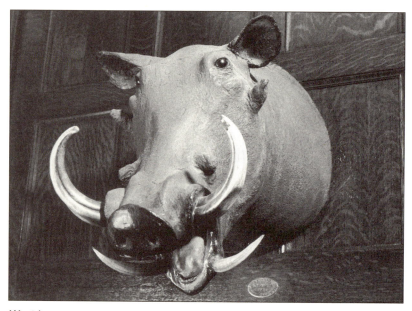

Wart hog

Members returning from the country or abroad found the Grill Room lighter than it had been and innocent of animal heads. John W. Norton '99, codonor of the heads with the late William G. Sewall, was understandably upset by their absence, but the only written protest to the House Committee came from members styling themselves the Committee for the Preservation of the Wart Hog. So eloquent was the C.P.W.H.'s appeal that the wart hog's head, with its spectacularly curling tusks, was rehung in a choice spot overlooking the backgammon tables.

On October 30 the Club feted the Department of Social Relations. By then, member Alexander M. White had agreed to chair the College's fund drive. And President Brownell, learning that Massachusetts Governor

Christian A. Herter would not be free to speak at the next annual dinner, had invited Massachusetts Senator John F. Kennedy.

Most Club members were undoubtedly pleased when, on Tuesday, November 6, President Eisenhower again defeated Governor Stevenson at the polls. That Friday, the Harvard Band gave a concert, a prelude to the Princeton game (which Princeton won, 35–20). And the following Thursday evening, as they filed into the Mahogany Room for their monthly meeting, the Club's governors, in black tie, espied the Club's familiar old upright piano (soon to be replaced by a new grand) and the equally familiar faces of Alexander M. White and Francis Hatch.

After dinner, the men present learned from their president that a description of the clubhouse, with illustrations, had appeared in a new publication of the Municipal Art Society titled *Index of Architecturally Historic Structures in New York City*. They listened to the reading of an auditor's report comparing the financial states of forty-five city clubs that ranked the Club just under the top. And they heard from Alexander White anent the fund drive.

Finally, the minutes related, Francis Hatch rose; he barely began to speak when, amid laughter, he was "forced to shut up and play."

On December 15 the Club's chess players welcomed sometime American champion Samuel Reshevsky; he played nineteen games simultaneously against members, winning all nineteen, then took on Club champion John L. Foster '38 blindfolded and defeated him. Five days later Secretary Streeter announced that Volney Righter would head the fund drive's New York committee. And President Brownell, asked about prospects for the Club's addition of new bedrooms, reminded the Board that when the western extension of the clubhouse had gone up in 1915, enough steel had been used in it to support several more stories.

The second so-called fathers-and-sons dinner, on January 2, 1957, included numerous daughters, but a good many women, wives of members and mothers of their guests, were there, too. The scene epitomized, in effect, that popular 1950s ideal, "togetherness."

On the eighteenth Cornelius C. Felton became president, Philip B. Kunhardt vice-president and Frederick Holdsworth, Jr. '40 secretary, while Treasurer Satterlee was reelected. (Felton's great-grandfather and namesake, of the Class of 1827, had been Harvard's seventeenth president, 1860–62.)

Around then, the Library Committee did something unheard of: it returned $1,290 in unspent funds to the House Committee and asked that its monthly subvention be reduced from $290 to $225! Reporting this to the Board in the absence of Chairman Coffinberry, House Committee Chairman Ernest F. Gamache could not account for it, and Library Committeeman Alan T. Wenzell '45 L'49 hardly clarified matters by saying he hoped the Board would treat his committee generously should the need arise.

The long-awaited evening of March 15 began with a buffet supper for 450 at the Club; then everyone headed uptown for a "Harvard Family Party." Partygoers in Carnegie Hall numbered 2,200, almost filling the house, while the stage easily accommodated the entire glee club, conducted by G. Wallace Woodworth '24 AM'26, and, alternately, the entire band, in uniform, conducted by C. Wright Briggs, Jr. '31 AM'35. Two compositions by Leonard Bernstein '39, one a choral number with words by Alan Jay Lerner '40, were performed in public for the first time. And for at least some people present, Alexander White's remarks likewise contained novelties: he called the campaign he headed by a name not often heard before, A Program for Harvard College, and gave as its goal a precise—if, for that time, awesomely large—figure, to wit, $82.5 million.

Six days after this, Chairman Gamache declared that, as the owners of the Gould-Mersereau building, at 35 West 44th Street, were not interested in selling, he would look into the feasibility of constructing three stories atop the portion of the clubhouse added in 1915, known as the annex. Board member Robert P. MacFadden reminded him, however, that a study had found the annex to be too narrow to justify the cost of such construction. And Library Chairman Coffinberry explained—after a fashion—his committee's baffling behavior. Because, he said, fewer books of interest to its patrons were being published, the library could get by very well on a smaller budget.

In May, the University Relations Committee gave yet another dinner in its series, centered on "Harvard and the Middle East," with the noted Orientalist Sir Hamilton Gibb presiding. No doubt as a result of pressure on the alumni to give to A Program for Harvard College, donations to the scholarships fund were down sharply. That summer, the Club's service elevator was converted to self-service. On September 18 the University Relations Committee presented a dinner honoring the Athletics Department, which, needless to say, attracted far more members than had any previous dinner honoring an academic department; the guests included "living legend" crew mentor Tom Bolles and the new head coach of football, John Yovicsin. (Poor Yovicsin: in his first season, Harvard would lose to Cornell, Dartmouth, Princeton, Brown and, finally, Yale—by the unprecedentedly ignominious score of 0–56.)

On the morning of October 5, Americans awoke to learn that the Soviet Union had lofted into space a 184-pound satellite that was orbiting the earth at 18,000 miles per hour. Spectacularly inaugurating the space age, Sputnik's advent triggered a rush to catch up with the Soviets in science and technology, with far-reaching consequences for education, not least at Harvard.

On October 14 Langdon P. Marvin died. "Never in the bright history of the University have the Alumni called upon one man to serve them and Harvard in more capacities," wrote former President Brownell. "It was not surprising," Brownell concluded, "that in his later years he was sometimes introduced as Langdon P. Harvard of the Marvin Club."

The Club greeted the arrival of 1958 with the usual open house, at which eggnog was ladled out of huge punch bowls into cut-glass cups. Next evening, the radically altered fathers-and-sons evening took place on schedule, under the descriptive, if rather bumpy-sounding, new name of Father, Son, Mother, Daughter Night.

That year, the University Relations Committee stopped giving dinners, in deference, Chairman Frederick A. O. Schwarz '24 L'27 would explain, to the many meetings being held in behalf of A Program for Harvard College. On the other hand, many members, having already contributed to that campaign, apparently resumed giving to the scholarships fund, Chairman Francis A. Goodhue, Jr. '37 L'40 reporting a twofold increase in receipts (to $23,214) from nearly four times as many contributors (1,153). Meanwhile, rising costs forced the Club to increase the prices of meals and bedrooms, and in June, by which time the Ladies' Dining

Rooms had been soundproofed and the last of the banquet rooms air-conditioned, the Board reluctantly raised the dues, for the first time since 1951 (to a minimum of $25 and a maximum of $115).

On October 1 Edmund Kerper died at seventy-one, mourned by, among others, a band of his cronies who went by the name of The Beavers. On the sixteenth Chairman Gamache called Kerper "a generous and good friend of the Club." And when Activities Chairman Peter H. Nicholas '39 announced plans to schedule more events on weekday evenings, he did not have to explain why: the Sunday afternoon events were plainly a holdover from a time when most resident members lived in the city, whereas now a majority were commuters.

The Board's December meeting was marked by a memorable exchange. Addressing Admissions Chairman Donald E. McNicol '43 L'48, Frederick M. Warburg '19 asked a question that had long puzzled many: Why, he inquired, shouldn't any Harvard graduate who wanted to join the Club be automatically admitted? McNicol, Volney Righter and Henry Schniewind did their best to reply, each in turn stressing the independence of the Club from the College and the University and the desirability of maintaining strict admissions standards to attract a good quality of applicant.

Under Alexander White, the fund that would finance A Program for Harvard College had grown to $45 million. And now that his term was expiring, his place was taken—almost as a matter of course—by another member of the Club, H. Irving Pratt '26 B'29.

On the evening after New Year's Day 1959, there was no sign at the Club of a Father, Son, Mother, Daughter Night—or of any regret over its absence. Did all that togetherness get to be just too much?

Two weeks later, members at the annual meeting elected Philip B. Kunhardt president, Frederick A. O. Schwarz vice-president and Charles F. Bound '32 treasurer, while reelecting Secretary Holdsworth. After dinner, President Pusey paid tribute to former President Lowell, but for many men present the evening's most memorable utterances were the brief and witty remarks, amplified by a microphone, of a small, bowed ancient who had been a sophomore during Lowell's senior year and had recently foiled an attempt to fete his centenary at the Club by threatening to boycott the party: Charles C. Burlingham, aged 100.

In February, the Board learned that a portrait of President Eliot at age ninety by the late Boardman Robinson would soon be given to the Club by the painter's widow and Mr. and Mrs. Alexander Campbell AM'28 of Geneva, New York. And in April, something curious happened. Admissions Chairman J. David Lannon '39 submitted to the Board the nomination of a certain Mrs. John R. McGinley, Jr., to chair a new sub-committee charged with deciding which Radcliffe graduates and women with Harvard degrees were to hold signing privileges. The Board prompt-ly approved her nomination, thereby endorsing quite casually the princi-ple that a woman could participate in the Club's affairs and even hold a position in its hierarchy fourteen years before women would be admitted to the Club as members!

On the last evening of that month, the University Relations Committee presented a symposium, following a dinner, on the creative arts at Harvard. Archibald MacLeish L'19 LittD'55, Boylston professor of rhetoric and oratory, moderated, and other participants included Dean Sert of the School of Design (a member), Randall Thompson '20 AM'22 of the Music Department and Arthur Kopit '59 of the Harvard Dramatic Club. (Kopit, unknown outside undergraduate theatrical circles in Cambridge, would become famous in 1962 with the production on Broadway of his absurdist play *Oh Dad, Poor Dad, Mamma's Hung You in the Closet & I'm Feelin' So Sad.*)

Since the fall of 1956, reciprocal guest privileges with the Harvard Club of Boston had been in effect, on a trial basis, but in May the Board voted not to renew them, mainly because the arrangement benefited members of the Boston Club far more than it did the Club's own mem-bers. As well as six holders of regular freshman scholarships, the Club was supporting two Slocum scholars, who were, as Chairman William J. Shallow '40 said, unlike most boys his committee ordinarily considered: one, a student at The Gunnery, in Connecticut, was blind, and also the stroke of his school's victorious crew; while the other, a senior at a parochial high school in the city, was "a colored boy of great promise."

For some years, Clement L. Despard, Jr. '52, a son and namesake of the Club's first insurance committee chairman, now deceased, had been a notably energetic chairman of the Schools Committee, but now, entering

Charles C. Burlingham

the export-import business and obliged to go overseas, he yielded the post to Robert B. Ross '46 L'50 B'52. Called on to speak by President Kunhardt, Despard stated that the committee was made up of forty to fifty volunteers interviewing seniors from forty-seven public high schools and several private schools in the city; that the current freshman class (of 1962) included seventy New York boys it had recommended; and that the College admissions people acknowledged that its appraisals of candidates were reliable and eminently helpful.

President Kunhardt called for a rising toast to young Despard.

On June 8, C. C. Burlingham died in his 101st year. He had been a member, active to the last, for seventy-four years.

Ten days after this, with certain activities of the fund drive about to be discontinued, President Kunhardt sought to gauge the campaign's progress locally. Metropolitan New York Chairman Righter said his office had exceeded its goal of $2 million. George G. Walker '24 reported that whereas his assigned goal as area chairman had been to raise $600,000 from 4,700 people, he had so far taken in $700,000; he also noted that gifts collected around New York averaged $240, compared to an average of $190 for those collected (from about twice as many individuals) in the Boston area. And Special Gifts Chairman William E. Hutton '30 declared that his department was over its quota by $700,000.

From time to time that summer, House Committee Chairman Oliver Iselin, Jr. '39 met with the owners of 35 West 44th Street to discuss terms for acquiring that property. But these talks proved fruitless. And at the end of August, Miss Alice Cassin, who, over forty-five years of producing exemplary secretarial work for successive Admissions Committees, officers and committee chairmen, had seen the Club grow from 3,831 members to 6,647, retired.

In October, Chairman Iselin announced that three London plane trees would soon be planted in front of the clubhouse, and that the Club had been offered, for $284,000, the building and a 21-by-100-foot lot at 24 West 45th Street, next to the clubhouse on the east. Citing timely actions taken in the past to snap up property for the Club, former President Brownell urged his colleagues to seize the opportunity. But it was not be be: over the next days, Iselin, real estate man Morgan D. Wheelock and architect William Potter '27 MA'33 inspected Number 24 throughout, and concluded, finally, that it did not meet the Club's needs.

On November 19 House Committeeman Dudley P. K. Wood '29 announced that new front doors would be installed "at a time when the revolving door is not revolving." Though scheduled to cease operations at the end of the year, A Program for Harvard College was short of its goal; Volney Righter reported, however, that while New York City's quota had been raised to $2,340,000, his committee's collections now topped $2,800,000 and were still growing. On December 17, in the Mahogany Room, President Kunhardt unveiled a portrait by Gardner Cox of former President Felton that won everyone's approval, including the sitter's.

While the Club's plane trees were in place for the start of the 1960s, its new front doors were not. As he had since 1957, Boston's Henri Salaun won the Cowles. At the annual meeting William Stackpole '49 became secretary, replacing Frederick Holdsworth, Jr., who resigned; the other officers were reelected. After dinner, Ambassador Henry Cabot Lodge told of accompanying Soviet Premier Nikita Khrushchev on a tour of the United States filled with unexpected and sometimes comic turns, and President Pusey reviewed the history of the just-concluded fund drive, to which the Club's David Rockefeller had been the largest individual donor. In its final, hectic weeks, certain Club members had played decisive roles. Walter W. Naumburg '89 had given $2 million and Lammot duPont Copeland an additional $1 million. To his earlier gift of $1 million for a drama center John L. Loeb had added $800,000. By December 31, $80 million had been collected; then Harold Vanderbilt had given $2.5 million, assuring the drive's success.

In March, the House Committee introduced the method for signing chits in use today, with an assigned audit number following a member's signature instead of, as previously, his (or her) College class or advanced degree and year of receipt thereof. And in the Bar, the Beavers got their wish when a metal plaque was affixed to the top of the counter at the corner spot habitually frequented by the man it memorialized. It read (and reads),

In Memory of
EDMUND KERPER '11
"C.D.B."
A generous benefactor to the
Harvard Club of New York City

"C.D.B." stands for "Chief Dam Builder." (Or "Damn Builder"?)

At the Board's June meeting, President Kunhardt spoke of a letter Chairman Iselin had received from member Rawson L. Wood '30, a Long Island businessman who, out of deep moral and religious conviction, had been striving for years to promote better understanding between whites and blacks. Wood asked that the Club's facilities be made available to fifteen officials from newly independent African countries who would be in New York throughout the coming fall and winter participating in a U.N. training program. The House Committee had recommended agreeing to Wood's request, but instead the Board "passed the buck," simply directing the House Committee to be guided by the rules for the admission of guests and visitors to Club privileges.

Admissions Committee Robert R. Barker '36 noted the curious fact that only three women in the world held honorary signing privileges at the Club: Eleanor Roosevelt, Mrs. James Bryant Conant and President Mary Bunting of Radcliffe. He proposed that the Board confer the same privileges on Mrs. Pusey, and it promptly did so.

In July, two Harvard graduates from Massachusetts were nominated for the nation's highest offices: in Los Angeles, the Democrats chose Senator Kennedy for president, and in Chicago, the Republican nominee, Vice-President Richard M. Nixon, picked Ambassador Lodge to be his running mate.

Were the members—some younger ones, at any rate—becoming more fitness conscious? Two developments suggested they might be. As Athletics Chairman Philemon E. Truesdale '44 reported in September, the newly reequipped seventh-floor gym was in constant use. Then there was the intriguing statistical finding of a long-range survey conducted by the Club's accountants into patterns of eating and drinking at various city clubs: that whereas the consumption of liquor had declined elsewhere since 1958 by an average of 1 percent, it had fallen at the Club by 4.4 percent.

On September 29 the Africa Service Institute, recently founded by Rawson Wood, gave a reception and dinner in the Biddle and North Rooms for African officials, all of whom now held guest privileges. Present as well were American Ambassador to the U.N. Joseph Wadsworth, the Club's officers and Rawson Wood. Chairman Iselin would recall the occasion a month later as a very pleasant one, but note that the African officials had since made little use of their guest cards.

On November 8 the American people went to the polls to elect a president. The vote was extremely close, and not until the tenth was it finally known that the victor, by an exceedingly narrow margin, was Democrat Kennedy. On the seventeenth President Kunhardt, responding to a suggestion, frequently advanced, that the Club sponsor educational tours, created a provisional travel committee to be headed by Ernest F. Gamache. And on the nineteenth Dr. Adolf A. Berle died at ninety-five, freeing the Board to reveal the existence of the Berle '91 Fund.

On December 22 Board member Taggart Whipple '34 spoke about the Club's approaching centennial: he proposed expanding the one official history of it he had uncovered, a few scant pages in the Club Book for 1928. But the Board tabled his proposal.

January 12, 1961, produced a new president and vice-president in the persons of F. A. O. Schwarz and H. Irving Pratt, respectively. Meanwhile, the *Harvard Alumni Bulletin* recorded the fact that John F. Kennedy '40 LLD'56 had resigned his Senate seat. "On January 20," the report went on, a bit coyly, "he will move with his family into a house in Washington occupied for many years by the late Franklin D. Roosevelt '04 LLD'29."

# 16

# THE
# SIXTIES
# (1961–1969)

To some citizens watching television at midday on Friday, January 20, 1961 (probably including some gathered around the big new color TV in Harvard Hall), the ritual being acted out in Washington, against a backdrop of the Capitol, suggested its remote classical antecedents. In freakish weather of a kind associated in the ancient world with momentous shifts of fate and fortune, gusts of snow alternating with brilliant sunlight, the oldest chief of state since the founding of the Republic ceded authority to the youngest ever chosen by the electors. Erect and bareheaded, the new chief looked suitably heroic, while the young woman at his side outshone any goddess. Finally, the transfer of executive power completed, an elderly bard started to declaim a celebratory ode from a text, only to be defeated by the furies of wind and glare.

The bard was, of course, America's unofficial poet laureate, Robert Frost '01 (hon.) '37. Frost had dropped out of the College in 1899, but decades later had returned to Cambridge to teach and ultimately to be awarded an honorary Litt.D. and even elected an Overseer. At eighty-six, he was hardly in line for a position in the new government, but a good many younger Harvard men were. From a list of twenty-two Harvard-connected appointees in that morning's *New York Times,* it was apparent, moreover, that these men were in the main a different breed from the Harvardians who had served in prior administrations: of the twenty-two, only eight held degrees from the College, while fourteen held advanced

University degrees. Eight had also taught at Harvard, primarily at the graduate level, and only two belonged to the Club: C. Douglas Dillon, secretary of the Treasury, and former dean of the Law School James M. Landis L'24, special assistant to the president.

That January, for a change, the Cowles tournament was won by a member, Charles W. Ufford, Jr. '53 L'59. And on February 3 came a rare treat, a production in Harvard Hall of *Romeo and Juliet* directed by an energetic young man named Joseph Papp.

April (dubbed "the cruelest month" by T. S. Eliot '10 AM'11 LittD'47, never a member) dealt American self-esteem a double body blow: on the twelfth the Soviet Union lofted Major Yuri Gagarin into orbit and recovered him, thereby winning the superpowers' race to put a man in space, and on the seventeenth, at the Bay of Pigs on Cuba's south coast, Soviet ally Fidel Castro routed an invading force of exiles armed, trained and fed by the United States. On the twentieth the Board demonstrated its confidence in President Kennedy by electing him an honorary member.

On May 3 the University Relations Committee finally gave a dinner honoring the Medical School. Hundreds of members listened in fascination as surgeons discussed experimental transplants of kidneys. And the next day (as he would relate in the *Bulletin*), Secretary Stackpole detected clear signs of unease around him in the Main Dining Room as lunchers discovered that the chef's daily special was . . . kidneys.

A week after this, word reached the Club that the Overseers had approved a controversial proposal by President Pusey to substitute English for the long-traditional Latin on Harvard diplomas. Members reacted, predictably, according to their years, elders tending to regret the change and juniors to welcome it, but there was plenty of indifference, too (Harvard indifference, of course), among members of all ages. Even some of these men, however, were curious to know where the most famous Overseer of all stood on the issue, and before long a diligent *New York Times* reporter came up with the answer. Aware that President Kennedy would be too busy to attend their meeting, several Overseers had sought his opinion, in case the vote was close; at first, he had opposed the change, but then McGeorge Bundy AM (hon.) '51 had convinced him it would be beneficial, since all students understood English. The word was passed to his fellow Overseers that the President favored the change, which won out, when put to a vote, by a margin, reportedly, of about two to one.

At its May meeting, the Board learned that the House Committee was trying to locate the optimal spot in the clubhouse for a fallout shelter in case of a nuclear attack on New York, that various designs for a club tie were under consideration and that one of the Club's plane trees had inexplicably expired, but that the Parks Department was obliged to replace it. (The tree's death would turn out to have been caused by a leak in a Con Edison main allowing gas to seep into the soil around its roots.)

Three days after this, on May 21, a Lufthansa Star Constellation, a DC-7 propeller plane, took off from Idlewild Airport for Paris with eighty-two passengers, who would return via a similar flight from London on June 14. With this first charter flight, arranged by the long-established travel agents Raymond & Whitcomb, the new Travel Committee inaugurated a service that for more than two decades thereafter was to offer members voyages to far-off places in congenial company.

Next month, Chairman Iselin revealed that a location for a fallout shelter had been tentatively decided on, but he did not disclose it. At the urging of Art Committee Chairman William P. D. Bailey '46, the Board accepted, from Henry M. Channing '02 L'04, a bronze bas-relief portrait of the late Louis Brandeis Wehle '02, who had for many years escorted C. C. Burlingham to annual dinners.

Around August 1, a new portrait of former President Kunhardt by William F. Draper went on display in the entrance hall, and early in September a party for matriculating freshmen (bidding fair, by now, to become a standard fixture) was adjudged a success—not least by a certain older member who was relieved to note only one beard among the 150-odd guests. And a week or so after this, the Club's first-ever club ties went on sale at the cigar stand. Both the four-in-hand and the bow tie featured narrow diagonal black stripes on a crimson field.

Although both room usage and food covers were down some 8 percent from the previous year, the enterprising spirit survived undiminished, and on November 2 the Activities Committee put on a new kind of entertainment in the Biddle and North Rooms: a wine-tasting. It proved a hit, attracting 375 people. And President Kennedy, some months after being notified of the fact, accepted his election to honorary membership.

In mid-November House Committeeman Eustis Dearborn '32 GSD'38, an architect, came up with a provisional estimate of $20,000 for constructing a fallout shelter.

One evening around then, after a Club member had made the necessary arrangements, the national governing council of the far-right John Birch Society met in one of the private dining rooms. When word of this meeting got out, many members were upset, and a few demanded that such groups be forbidden access to the clubhouse. President Schwarz conferred with his fellow officers and Chairman Iselin, and at the Board's last meeting of the year he quietly affirmed that attempts by members to bar the use of the Club's facilities to organizations they opposed would not be allowed to succeed.

In January 1962, at the annual meeting, Shelby H. Page '43 replaced Charles F. Bound, who had resigned, as treasurer.

On April 11 the newspapers reported a development that seemed sure to affect the Club profoundly sooner or later: in Cambridge, the faculty had voted to award Harvard degrees (the diplomas in English, of course) to graduates of Radcliffe. After 326 years Harvard was going coeducational: how much longer, then, members wondered, could the Club remain an all-male organization?

A few days earlier Robert R. Barker, now chairman of the House Committee, had attended a hearing before the Board of Standards and Appeals regarding the Club's bid for permission to construct more squash courts, and on the nineteenth he announced that his committee had appointed a Wine Committee charged with reorganizing the Club's cellar and improving the quality of the wines therein. It consisted of Taggart Whipple, Frank Streeter and, not least, oenophile Creighton Churchill '36, the author of *A Notebook on the Wines of France* (1961).

One happy committee chairman at that meeting was Stuart Scott, Jr. '33 of Scholarships, who reported contributions to the Club foundation's fund at the highest level ever. But this big increase in giving came none too soon: the cost of a Harvard education was soaring, undergraduate tuition alone now amounting to $1,520 a year.

In June, President Schwarz reported that the Club's membership had passed 7,000, standing at 7,002. But as Treasurer Page pointed out, members were still staying away in record numbers, leaving the Club operating at a loss. Why? To help him find out, Schwarz called on the expertise of McKinsey & Company, management consultants, several officers and employees of which, who were members of the Club, agreed to study the question without compensation. They drew up a questionnaire covering various aspects of club life and mailed copies to all members, with reply envelopes enclosed. The volume of the response (eventually, 40 percent of members would be heard from) surprised the McKinsey people and cheered the Club's governors, who saw in it heartening evidence that the members cared about their club's well-being.

As one might have expected, the respondents were mainly concerned about the food: most objected to the fare in general and the service in the Main Dining Room in particular. These complaints would bring about important changes over time, but in the meantime the McKinsey experts, guided by the returned questionnaires, set about formulating suggested courses of action. In the course of that summer they put together a document that would inevitably be dubbed, inevitably eliciting sly grins and mildly ribald comments, the McKinsey Report.

In line with a key recommendation of the report, President Schwarz set up six "task forces" to deal with specific problems and picked men to head them: Food and Dining Rooms (Barker), Bedrooms and Dormitory (Gamache), Communications (Schniewind), Athletics (Frank Streeter), Membership (Larsen) and Activities (Philip Boyer '33). Barker hired a professional food operations consultant, Arthur Dana '25, and weighed, with his task force, the possibility of contracting out the operation of the Main Dining Room as a concession. The situation Gamache faced was even more daunting, for although the Club's room rates were lower than those of the University Club and the Yale Club and well below those of Midtown hotels, fewer than two-thirds of its bedrooms had been occupied on a typical night during the summer just past. The McKinsey Report recommended hiring an interior decorator (preferably male) to suggest improvements, redoubling efforts to interest College classes in sponsoring bedrooms, installing showers in the common bathrooms and the 24 private ones containing bathtubs and raising the rates moderately; Gamache endorsed these suggestions, but remained convinced that a new sixth-floor dormitory would bring in more income, sooner and at less expense, than would any of the proposed amenities. (He and his task force incidentally also favored a McKinsey recommendation that 60 percent of the respondents to the questionnaire had opposed: modifying the bedrooms to provide weekend accommodations for members' wives.)

In October, Gamache persuaded the Board to adopt the dormitory concept over that of a restored swimming pool, one championed by a few older men. And Frank Streeter declared that although the Athletics task force wanted more squash courts it would, in view of the prohibitive cost of building even one, settle for expanding the available locker space and perhaps installing a sauna. The Board duly set priorities for spending: first, food facilities; second, dormitory; and third, locker area. And from the Advisory Committee, former presidents called for audacious action to dispel the enveloping malaise. "Make no small plans," advised George A. Brownell; "they do not stir men's souls," while Edward Streeter urged his juniors to "plan boldly."

On October 22, President Kennedy informed the nation of a menacing Soviet military buildup in Cuba that included a base capable of launching missiles with nuclear warheads and a range of 2,000 miles. He imposed an air-sea blockade on the island. For the next six days, until Kennedy and Premier Khrushchev agreed on a formula to end the crisis, many residents of East Coast cities, particularly Washington and New York, half-expected annihilation to rain down at any moment, and at the Club those members who scoffed at the notion of a fallout shelter were temporarily silenced.

In mid-November, the Board amended the Club's bylaws to make the Membership Committee a standing committee, reduce a basic requirement for membership from two years with a department of the University to one and raise the dues. Over the next couple of weeks member John F. Ducey, Jr. '36 assumed responsibility for redecorating the bedrooms, and interior decorator Theodor Muller (not a Harvard man) was retained to advise him.

On January 17, 1963, the members present in Harvard Hall elected three new officers. H. Irving Pratt became president, Roy E. Larsen vice-president and Samuel C. Butler '51 L'54 secretary, while Shelby H. Page stayed on as treasurer. A few days earlier, the Cowles fixture had been won, for the first time, by a Harvard undergraduate, Victor Niederhoffer '64, who also happened to be a Club scholar. And a few days later, on February 1, Harvard Hall was the setting of another first, a dinner dance with supremely danceable music supplied by the Meyer Davis orchestra. (By the standards of that day 1963 would be a big year for entertainments, though not of the innovative kind: among them would be sports films by three dependable regulars—John Biddle on sailing, John Jay on skiing and Stanton Waterman on skin-diving—whom Activities Chairman William W. Myrick '39 would wittily lump together, in his year-end committee report, as "the $H_2O$ group.")

In March, after announcing the hiring of expert John M. Gerecter to help Arthur Dana direct food operations, President Pratt unveiled a plan to simplify the day-to-day functioning of the Club through two "super-committees." A seven-man Executive Committee (the officers and three Board members) would oversee management of the Club, while an eight-man Programs Committee (the chairmen of committees that dealt with continuing pursuits: Activities, Art, Athletics, Communications, Games, Library, Pensions and Travel) would coordinate these committees' activities and policies. Between them, Pratt said, the Executive and Programs Committees would free the House Committee of various extra burdens, enabling it to concentrate on maintaining the clubhouse.

The Board readily agreed to the president's plan.

In its first meeting, the Executive Committee decided that since President Pratt and Vice-President Larsen were both, as Overseers, in frequent contact with the administration and faculty in Cambridge, the Club no longer needed a University Relations Committee, and so discontinued it. And at the Programs Committee's initial meeting, the committee chairman approved a suggestion by Games Chairman John L. Prescott '27 that ladies' bridge afternoons be encouraged to occur regularly and often.

But if this modest move toward diversifying the human mix within the clubhouse succeeded, another did not, as the Board members learned in April when Morgan D. Wheelock, for the Membership Committee, reported on preparations by the Admissions Committee to recruit members for the Club in Cambridge the following month. The usual letter had been drafted, he said, to the presidents of the undergraduates' final clubs, the Hasty Pudding and the publications, and to key people in the graduate schools, but this year, apparently for the first time, the Admissions Committee was actively seeking to bring in members from among the majority of graduating seniors who did not belong to an undergraduate social group. To reach these students, the logical intermediaries would be the masters of the houses in which they lived, but the house masters, to a man, declined to cooperate.

At that same April meeting, the Board moved to improve communications, as recommended in the McKinsey Report. The *Bulletin*, now edited by Irene Van Fossen, would start appearing regularly at the beginning of each month, and the Communications Committee would compile a pamphlet or brochure describing the Club's facilities.

On Monday, May 13, for the first and last time, the Harvard Corporation and the Board of Overseers held their annual joint meeting in the White House in Washington, guests of a certain Overseer completing his term. That day or soon afterward Miss Van Fossen, in New York, composed a paragraph for the June *Bulletin* that would strike readers as harmless fun, but in November would suddenly take on, in retrospect, a tragic significance.

### GOOD SHOOTING

Frank Carceres [*sic*], the banquet manager, telephonically orders "Shoot the Weld" or "Shoot the Slocum" to get food sent to banquet rooms. This system works well and has been a time saver, but one day this past week an especially large group, equipped with cocktails and awaiting the arrival of food, was startled into silence, save for the shaking of their glasses, by an unmistakable command from Frank in the telephone booth: "Shoot the President!" Terrifying as these words were momentarily, all recovered in time for an enjoyable luncheon in the Presidents' Room.

Toward the close of the squash season, Charlton MacVeagh, Jr. '57 won both the Paine memorial tournament and the Club championship. At the tournament dinner, Dr. Lawrence Pool '28 accepted, for the College, a portrait of the late Harry Cowles commissioned by the tournament committee and W. Palmer Dixon, and executed by Germain G. Glidden. Pool, Dixon and Glidden, all three former national squash racquets champions, had each learned their winning ways on the court from Harvard's legendary mentor, whose likeness would thenceforth hang in the Palmer Dixon Galleries in the Hemenway Gymnasium in Cambridge.

In a parallel development, Waldo Peirce gave the Club his colorful canvas *Harvard Tercentenary*, which had long hung in the clubhouse on loan.

In June, work began on the most ambitious program of reconstruction the Club had undertaken in many a year, to be funded largely by increasing the Club's mortgage. With workmen busy on every floor except the second and third, the clubhouse would have been a place to avoid, at least by day. The single biggest undertaking was the reorganizing of the kitchens and pantries, which were torn apart and reassembled according to plan. The object was to shift a major portion of the cooking from the basement to a space adjoining the Main Dining Room that had functioned until then as a way station for food brought up from below: once its steam tables were replaced by modern stoves and ovens, meals could be cooked to order instead of having to be prepared in advance and kept warm until they could be consumed. Redesigning this space was accomplished by two architects on the House Committee, Eustis Dearborn and William B. Tabler '36 GSD'39. Other improvements effected that summer included, from the top of the clubhouse down to its subterranean bottom,

- installing, on the seventh floor, a new dormitory with fourteen sleeping compartments;
- constructing a more attractive lounge on the sixth floor while expanding dressing facilities in the process;
- installing showers in half of the private bathrooms on the fourth and fifth floors and completely refurnishing three bedrooms;
- installing a new air conditioner in the ground floor Bar;
- acquiring a brand-new dishwasher in the basement to replace an "antique" bought second-hand in the early 1930s; and
- retiling and reequipping the garbage room.

By the fall, the annual scholarships appeal had brought in about $35,000, and Chairman Scott, expressing his gratitude to the Board, cited a gift of twenty-two shares of General Motors common stock that Donald Barnes '27 had just remitted, in partial repayment, he wrote, for the scholarship the Club had granted him forty-one years before. Some time around then, head squash pro John Jacobs welcomed Milton Russ onto his staff. And on November 21, former President Schwarz read aloud to his colleagues a memorial he had composed to former President Whitney, who had died on September 1.

Next day, a Friday, late lunchers in the Main Dining Room and the Ladies' Dining Rooms learned, as the report flew among the tables, that President Kennedy had been shot, perhaps fatally, in Dallas. The December *Bulletin* takes up the story:

> The Club, as the largest gathering place for Harvard men outside of Cambridge, was visibly and deeply saddened by the events of the past weekend.
>
> In the hours immediately following President Kennedy's assassination, the Club was deluged with inquiries by telephone and in person from all quarters. Those concerned with the scheduled appearance of the Harvard Band that evening at once began preparations for its postponement. At the moment the members of the Band, en route to New York by bus, were wholly unaware of the intervening events. Unable to make contact with the group, the Athletic and Band offices in Cambridge called here repeatedly for help. Upon arrival the Band members were advised of the tragedy and the postponement of the concert. They sat around forlornly in their red blazers and eventually bedded down for the night. The New Haven Railroad cancelled arrangements for the train to New Haven on Saturday and appropriate notices were immediately posted in the Club House. Also cancelled was a dinner, scheduled for that night, of the Committee on University Resources, whose chairman is the Club's Vice-President, Roy E. Larsen '21.
>
> Among the Manager's many problems were the food prepared for the buffet at which several hundred members and their guests were expected, and Harvard Hall all set up in readiness for the annual concert of the Band, which had to be dismantled as quickly as possible and returned to its normal and customary appearance.
>
> Monday brought a continued heightening of tempo as members free from their various office responsibilities came home to the Club for news and exchange of thoughts and opinions concerning swiftly moving events. Both radio and television were provided in several places in the building. Meanwhile, President Pratt had been in constant touch with affairs involving the Club and directed that a notice be posted requesting members, their guests and those of the staff who could be freed from their duties to assemble in Harvard Hall during the final interment and taps.
>
> To the minds of many sprang the poignant words from "Sacrifice" by Ralph Waldo Emerson, Class of 1821, inscribed long ago on a monument at the entrance to Soldiers Field and thus familiar to generations of Harvard men:

> *Though love repine and reason chafe,*
> *There came a voice without reply,—*
> *" 'Tis man's perdition to be safe*
> *When for the truth he ought to die."*

At its last meeting of 1963, the Board noted the imminent retirement, after ten years in his position and thirty-five with the Club, of Manager Alfred Martinez, and met his designated successor, John Paul Stack. President Pratt thanked House Committee Chairman Barker for overseeing the veritable transformation of much of the clubhouse. And Travel

Chairman Gamache donated to the Club foundation, for scholarships, a check for $4,000, representing profits from the year's tours and cruises.

Since the members had first faulted the Club's fare and the serving of it, Arthur Dana and, after March 1963, John M. Gerecter had reorganized the procuring, preparing and presenting of food. A new kitchen had been built next to the Main Dining Room, and Manager Martinez and others had begun to retrain the waiters. By the time Manager Stack took over, both the meals set before members and the manner in which they were set there had improved considerably. They would continue to improve, as would staff morale, but it would take time for the good news to get around.

In January 1964, the Programs Committee approved admitting ladies (as women were still called in and by the Club, and would be for at least another decade) to the squash galleries on Saturday afternoons; in February, the Executive Committee sanctioned, as an experiment, making six bedrooms with baths on the fourth floor available to members and their wives on summer weekends; and in March, Chairman Barker report-ed that so many members and wives or women friends were playing mixed pair duplicate bridge that the Ladies' Dining Rooms could no longer hold them all, with the result that some couples regularly invaded the Presidents' Room. Women (that is, ladies) were becoming familiar figures in the Club.

But not yet in the Bar. That chamber, its walls a rich crimson since its creation in 1948, had in February, on orders of the House Committee, been painted white, robbing it instantly of its uniquely warm, welcoming atmosphere. (Some patrons had likened the place, appreciatively, to a gigantic womb.) Indignant habitués signed in large numbers a petition demanding that the Bar be restored to its pristine state, and a struggle began that would finally end, long afterward, in a total victory of the romantic reactionaries.

Like the Bar, the Club *Bulletin* was undergoing major changes. From its first appearance three decades before, the publication had consisted of a strip of ivory or off-white paper six inches wide bearing on both sides parallel columns of type three inches wide; it was folded along the spaces between these columns, and could be opened out, fanwise, and then folded back together on itself to form a trim 6-by-3 $1/2$-inch packet that slipped easily into an envelope or a pocket. Whereas the *Bulletin* had formerly run to six or eight columns, it now extended to twelve or even fourteen. This increase in size reflected a shift in editorial policy. The Club secretaries who had edited the publication in the past had printed little more than news of Club elections, athletic events and games tournaments, but the new editor, Miss Van Fossen, saw her mission as not simply to inform her readers but to entertain them. Following a snippet of poetry keyed to the season, a typical latter-day issue might contain a historical note or two (nearly always drawn from English history, Miss Van Fossen being a confirmed anglophile as well as ailurophile), a chatty piece on some topic of current interest and excerpts from letters commending the Club for its food and service, its decor or whatever. Thus in March members learned, inter alia, that the Club had acquired "an attractive black cat with four white mittens and vest" named Bootsie Mitten, and in April that an English cat named Peter had just died after several years' duty as the Home Office's official mouser, its upkeep paid for by Her Majesty's Government.

The same issue noted the installation above the clubhouse entrance (there being, as yet, no canopy there) of a "call light" for summoning taxis and of two aluminum flagpoles replacing the old wooden ones. April saw the introduction of two rather more important innovations. On the second, Chairman Barker proposed to the Executive Committee that the Club operate thereafter on the basis of a fiscal year ending June 30, running concurrently with the College (or University) year, and two weeks later Treasurer Page told the Board that he was thinking of recommending the introduction of a service charge system, or waiters' incentive system, like the one that had enabled the Yale Club to reduce its restaurant staff while increasing the wages each waiter received. (The Princeton Club, too, had introduced this system in its new clubhouse one block south, with excellent results.) Observing, not for the first time, that labor costs were at the heart of the Club's financial problems, Page explained that the system encouraged waiters to work harder and more efficiently in the knowledge that by serving more customers they could make more money.

Regarding use of the clubhouse, the treasurer reported that for the first time in eighteen months the receipts for March had exceeded those for the same month last year, a hopeful sign. Frank Streeter cited evidence of gustatory trends in the popularity of two new restaurant items: a low-calorie lunch and small, modestly priced carafes of wine. And Schools Chairman Ross noted that one current recipient of a Club scholarship was an all-city football player who stood first academically in a class of 1,600.

Before the dinner preceding the Board meeting on May 21, the members, sipping cocktails, inspected a new portrait of former President Schwarz by George Augusta and voted to accept it. After dinner, Admissions Chairman Ralph G. Coburn, Jr. '33 L'36 expressed concern about the disproportionate number of former graduate students being admitted: two-thirds of the men admitted that month held no Harvard degree but an advanced one. With the escalation of American involvement in Vietnam, compulsory registration of young men had been reinstated, and Coburn theorized that many graduates of the College were avoiding military service by enrolling in some graduate school. Incidentally, the Harvard Business School Club wanted to know whether graduates of the "Busy" School's advanced management programs, lasting for weeks or at most months, could join the Club. Under the regulations they would not be eligible, having attended the University for less than a year, and the consensus of the Board was not to alter the relevant bylaw.

Treasurer Page, addressing Chairman Barker's proposal about the fiscal year, reminded the Board that the Club had never yet prepared an annual budget in advance, but said it should start doing so without delay. Projecting a budget on the basis of a calendar year, however, would not be acceptable, as the Club officers, elected in January, would have to operate for almost twelve months on a budget put together by others. Besides, Page added, the Club actually did operate synchronously with the College, its use peaking between September and June and with many events, such as visits by the Harvard band and glee club, the football team and the cast of the Hasty Pudding show, keyed to the participants' academic schedules. Speaking for the three other officers as well as himself, Treasurer Page recommended that the Club adopt a fiscal year running from July 1 to June 30, and his colleagues, after deliberating, voted to endorse his recommendation.

By late May, the last of ten showers had been installed in bathrooms that adjoined bedrooms, and the House Committee had extended the experiment of accommodating married couples throughout the week. Both of these moves were no doubt prompted, to some extent, by awareness that New York was, that summer, putting on a world's fair that was certain to attract hundreds of thousands of visitors to the city, among them, conceivably, nonresident members and their wives.

On June 18, Treasurer Page notified the Board that the Club would embark on a new fiscal year in just thirteen days. For a third month, bar, restaurant and bedroom receipts topped the previous year's, indicating that members were returning to the clubhouse in force. Page praised Manager Stack and Food Director Gerecter for effecting this turnaround. For his part, Chairman Barker proposed moving the banquet manager's office up to the third floor, near the banquet rooms. He also obtained his colleagues' approval for a service pantry on that floor, to replace facilities installed "on a temporary basis" in 1946.

Saturday, July 4, Independence Day, marked the fiftieth anniversary of an epochal event in the annals of international rowing, when, at Henley in England, the Harvard second crew had swept the Thames to win the Grand Challenge Cup. Half a century later less one day, the same nine men—all, remarkably, still alive and all still relatively fit—came together at the Henley regatta to commemorate that victory, and early in the morning of Friday the third, in New York, Secretary Butler, on behalf of the Club, sent a cablegram congratulating them on their triumph to one of their number, Club member David P. Morgan '16, who in 1914 had rowed Number 6 in the winning boat. Morgan read the cablegram while watching a race in progress, and that evening, at a dinner tendered the nine by the Harvard Club of London, the Club's congratulatory message was read aloud.

A few days later this information reached the Club in a letter from Morgan, who closed by saying, "Who knows, it may have been your encouraging words that gave us the heart to go through with the program and row (slowly) down (a part of) the Henley Course on Saturday (the actual anniversary)." The *Bulletin* was to print the whole text of Morgan's letter, along with a note from the crew's captain:

> May I thank you on behalf of the Harvard Henley Crew of 1914 for your thoughtfulness in sending us a telegram of good wishes. We had a splendid, successful trip. The English are generous in their hospitality and courtesy, and made our time so happy that it will be a memory that will always remain with us. Many thanks for your greeting.
>
> Leverett Saltonstall '14
> U.S. Senator

Thanks largely to the world's fair, most of the bedrooms were occupied most nights that summer. And politics were much on members' minds. In mid-July, the Republican convention in San Francisco turned into an ugly confrontation between Arizona's archconservative Senator Barry Goldwater and New York's moderate Governor Rockefeller, whose views on most issues were widely shared at 27 West 44th Street. Goldwater emerged the nominee, with his "Eastern Establishment" rival humiliated. Although in August President Johnson significantly increased the American military presence in Vietnam in response to alleged North Vietnamese attacks on our destroyers in the Gulf of Tonkin, the Democrats would succeed in portraying Goldwater as an irresponsible and dangerous warmonger.

On September 25, a year to the day after Chief Engineer Ebeling's resignation, Banquet Manager Frank Caceres resigned, having been with the Club nineteen years. For no discernible reason, the last twelve months had seen the departure, after extensive careers with the Club, not only of Ebeling and Caceres, but also of Manager Martinez, Chef Charles Rollet and Comptroller Herbert M. Miller.

Recently, Miss Van Fossen had written a facetious piece in the *Bulletin* about members of the Board's Inspection Committee touring the little-known but presumably dusty recesses of the clubhouse in quest of irregularities, and in October she gamely printed a bluntly disparaging comment:

> Time was then the Club *Bulletin* just gave us the essential news. Now it's a vehicle for trite comments, amateurish advertising copy, and endless articles about pussy cats and Club officials coyly described as chimney sweeps and vigilantes.

No self-respecting instructor in Freshman English would pass such drivel.
I vote we get back to the facts—and save some paper and printing costs to boot.
Walter E. Albrecht '49

Next month came a gallant rejoinder:

I have been reading the *Bulletin* regularly since—and only since—it has become "a vehicle for trite comments, amateurish advertising copy, and endless articles about pussy cats and Club officials coyly described as chimney sweeps and vigilantes."
If you want to retain one reader, keep up this new development.
J. Harry Wood '26

On Election Day, President Johnson trounced Republican Goldwater, and for a change comparatively few members seemed to mind. Two days later President Pratt formally thanked E. Thayer Drake '44 L'49 for having brought contract talks with Local 6 to a successful conclusion, in part by helping to hammer out a mutually acceptable version of the service charge system for compensating waiters, which both parties agreed to call "the commission system." Programs Chairman Wheelock told the Executive Committee that William F. Draper had completed his portrait of the late President Kennedy (actually, a copy of one he had done earlier, from life, for

**President John F. Kennedy**

Kennedy's preparatory school, Choate). Finally, the committee members talked about compiling a history of the Club, to be published in 1965 in connection with its centenary.

Shortly before Christmas, House Committee Chairman Barker declared that with the centennial year about to begin, cleaning Harvard Hall was a top priority, especially since the Club would, in May, be hosting the annual meeting of the Associated Harvard Clubs. Art Chairman Bailey added that the vast chamber had probably never been cleaned since it was constructed. Both Bailey and, later, former President Schwarz spoke of that event as having occurred in 1913 rather than 1905, without any of their hearers setting them straight. A club history of some sort might have proved useful!

Although the banquet rooms were closed as usual on New Year's Day 1965, the commission system became effective on that date throughout the Banquet Department: Thereafter, a charge of 15 percent would be added to all bills for banquet food and beverages, the money to be distributed among the service people: waiters, headwaiters, captains and bartenders. One week after this, Vice-President Larsen told the Executive Committee that Edward Streeter would be the ideal person to write a centennial history of the Club. And on January 21, 1965, what were billed as the centennial meeting and dinner finally came around. At the former, John F. Harvey '43 B'47 was elected treasurer, replacing Shelby Page, and after the latter came a trio of Harvard College "insider" speakers: President Pusey, retiring Treasurer Paul Codman Cabot '21 B'23 and Senior Fellow Charles Allerton Coolidge '17 L'22. Rounding out the program was a droll, low-key and delightfully nostalgic account of life at the Club over five decades by former President Streeter, who, by composing and delivering it, had surely absolved himself of any further obligation (not that he was under one) to produce a detailed, and necessarily less amusing, club history. (The text follows page 315.)

That evening, there opened in the Ladies' Lounge an exhibition, to run through February, titled Great Treasures from Private Collections of the Harvard Family. In assembling them, Chairman Bailey had had the help of certain staffers at the Fogg and of Theodore Rousseau '34 AM'40, curator of European paintings at the Metropolitan Museum of Art in New York. A principal lender was David Rockefeller.

Starting February 1, visitors to the clubhouse basement were surprised not to encounter the short, squat bootblack, Nicholas ("Nick") Gallucci, in or around the Barber Shop, and saddened to learn that after forty years at the Club he had retired. Nick's English was somewhat rudimentary, but that did not prevent him from sounding off on many topics, and his personality was so forceful that he would long be remembered.

On or about February 10, workmen commenced the formidable task of restoring Harvard Hall to its state of almost sixty years before. Their first objective was to remove the deposit of dirt that had collected on virtually all surfaces. The oak paneling would be washed down to the original dark stain and then given a coat of shellac followed by a varnish: in contrast to the light-colored paneling in the Grill Room, the woodwork would glow with a dark brown, reddish color. The wooden ceiling beams would be treated in the same manner, and the plaster between them painted the original off-white. The imitation stonework forming the walls above the wainscotting would be washed and painted a warm grayish tan approximating the original tone. Finally, the two great fireplaces would be scoured to their original limestone surfaces.

The next month, Secretary Butler, perhaps reflecting an awareness on the officers' part of what a glorious spectacle the hall would be after its facelift and how tempting to photographers, proposed an addition to the House Rules:

VII

4. No photographs, whether still, moving or candid, shall be taken in any part of the Club, for any purpose whatsoever, and no photographic equipment shall be brought into the Club for use, without the approval of the House Committee.

The Board would adopt this new rule in June, whereupon the new House Committee Chairman, Maurice F. Healy, Jr. '41, revealed that a certain member wanted to take color photographs in the Main Dining Room. The committee's E. Thayer Drake had drafted an agreement to be signed by that photographer (and, presumably, any and all others with the same purpose in mind) pledging that his or her pictures would be kept confidential, and not sold or otherwise distributed.

Finally, Secretary Butler suggested that the Centennial Committee consider issuing an updated Club book containing a brief history of the Club. (The 1965 Club book, subtitled "Centennial Edition," would include a two-page list of "Highlights of the First Hundred Years"). And Chairman Healy reported that the union had agreed to the extension of the commission system into all of the Club's dining areas. This would mean, Healy and Treasurer Harvey explained, that the cost to the Club of restaurant operations would go down while the cost to members would go up; also,

# HARVARD CLUB CENTENNIAL SPEECH AT ANNUAL DINNER
### Thursday, January 21, 1965
### by Edward Streeter '14
### (President 1953–55)

A number of years ago I gave a talk before the Harvard Fund Council. During the course of it I distressed a number of class agents by saying that in my opinion the average alumnus gave to Harvard because of his nostalgic memories of what it had been like when he was there as an undergraduate rather than because it had become a world center of scholarship since World War II.

The same might be said perhaps of our attitude toward all institutions, whether educational, social, or even commercial, and would most certainly apply to the Harvard Club of New York. The various worlds in which we live from our first to our second childhood are in truth the only worlds which we really know. When we step into a new world in which we have never participated, we are like an untraveled man who suddenly finds himself in the streets of Bangkok. He looks about him with interest, perhaps, but certainly not with understanding.

My role tonight is to discuss briefly the Harvard Club of New York, but although I have worn the black tie of the Board of Managers for many years, have been a member of its super-efficient House Committee, and have carried the baton of the Treasurer, Vice-President, and finally the President, the changes have been so great since I retired from the last office in 1955 that I find myself totally unable to handle my subject past the point where I was an intimate part of the life of the Club. And let me say that there are few members who have a less intimate part in the daily life of the Club than past presidents.

This is neither a complaint nor a lament, but the way things should be, for past presidents belong to past worlds and institutions must constantly move to new worlds or wither.

I joined the Harvard Club shortly after World War I. At that time its total membership was approximately 5,000. Resident membership dues for those in the oldest and most expensive bracket were $40 a year. According to a menu of 1920, the price of entrées ranged from soft shell crabs at $.40 to guinea chicken at $1.40, and I suspect the latter item was merely window dressing.

These few figures, however, symbolize the change which has taken place in the Club during the intervening period. Anyone could have run the Club during those early halcyon days with both hands behind his back. The dinner meetings of the Board of Managers were hilarious banquets unburdened with knotty financial problems. There were always two or three carefully seeded members on the Board like my dear old abrasive friend, George Martin, who could be depended upon to object violently to the mildest and most harmless proposal, and to do so with such barbed and scathing wit that the lights from the candles dwindled to points of sulphurous yellow.

No one paid much attention to the Treasurer's report at those meetings. He was always in trouble, but it was the trouble of a squirrel that tucks so many nuts away for future contingencies that he is always on the verge of starvation. We knew that before the end of the year he would present us with the problem of whether to anticipate our annual mortgage payments for the next three or four years or bury our gains in the reserve for refurbishing and repairs.

Our more impassioned debates concerned themselves with such matters as the fate of the animal heads which covered the walls of the Grill Room and the Bar. The nature school, influenced perhaps by Oriental culture, were bare wall addicts and wished to retain nothing larger than a dik-dik. The fight finally boiled down to the matter of preserving the wart hog and the elephant head in spite of the fact that the latter was in such an advanced stage of senility that it had threatened for years to disintegrate on some sleeping member. I am proud to say that both the head and the member are still there.

There were so many characters to give color to the scene in those ancient days both among the staff and the members. There was always faithful Dan peering with gargoylish face over the front desk—Dan, whose pride it was to haul members off to bed when in his sole opinion they had arrived at a critical state of bewilderment and without regard to what other plans they might have made.

Or there was the gentleman whose permanent home was a cubicle which at that time abutted the squash courts. It contained besides its occupant a shiny tuxedo, a white suit, a dark suit, a battered Panama hat and suitcase, and several hundred copies of the *N.Y. Times* stamped "Harvard Club."

Each evening he left the Club at exactly six o'clock. Each morning he returned at precisely seven and went to bed. At three in the afternoon he was awakened with a double whiskey sour which he drank, lit a cigarette, and immediately went back to sleep. From time to time as was to be expected he set fire to the cubicle. This was inconvenient, but he was such an amiable character that he was forgiven, until we were obliged to seek the cooperation of the N.Y. Fire Department. Then he disappeared, probably to become a Buddhist monk, in which role he has undoubtedly cremated himself long since in the streets of Saigon.

Then there was Mr. X, who arrived at the Club each morning around nine with a paper bag. He spent his time until noon reading the papers. At noon he would rise from his chair and enter the old bar through the South Door peering near-sightedly about for a friend who wasn't there and finally passing out the North Door. On his way out he would stop at the cheese table and fix himself a fistful of cheese and crackers. These he would place carefully in his paper bag and return to the bar. When he had accumulated a nourishing lunch, he took the paper bag into the darkest corner of the big room, spread out the cheese and crackers on the *Illustrated London News,* extracted a pint of milk and a paper cup from the bag and proceeded to eat.

They are gone, the characters, gone like colorful leaves which have been swept away by the strong winds which now blow daily through these erstwhile windless chambers. The growth in membership plus the rising costs of goods and labor have made increased operational efficiency necessary to survival, and increased operational efficiency is an enemy to deviations, colorful though they may be.

If we sometimes wish that we might swap a bit of the new efficiency for a bit of the old elbow room, a bit more of the composure of former days, it must be remembered that the Harvard Club of New York is only a small cross section of the world at large. As the University grows with a growing world, so does the Harvard Club of New York, and we are proud of the ever-strengthening relationship which makes this so.

I have allowed an old member's mind to wander too long through the fields of the past. We should concentrate on what we are rather than what we were. This year the Harvard Club of New York is 100 years old and 100 years young. Through the tireless and devoted efforts of a handful of unselfish men these familiar and beautiful rooms remain unchanged in a world of bewildering changes—only the decibels have changed. This is no Bangkok, but rather a familiar and beloved sanctuary which attracts its members from all parts of the world to renew their fealty to Harvard and to be glad and proud that they are its sons.

A happy birthday to you, 27 West 44th Street, and may you be as lithe and lissome at the end of another hundred years as you are tonight.

that the Club's income would be reduced, since the commission charges obviously would not count as income. Meanwhile, both the employees and the Club would have to take risks, the former of lower salaries against the possibility of increased earnings from their commission and the latter of the possibility that the increase of costs to members could cause a drop in patronage. The House Committee would carefully monitor the working of the commission system.

Late in March, Athletics Chairman Ufford announced that squash pro John Jacobs would be retiring in September after forty-six outstanding years. Ufford recommended that Milton Russ be appointed to Jacobs's position. Chairman Bailey reported that a second centennial show, of twentieth-century art, would go up in May, and that an exhibition of Harvard memorabilia would be on view, in Harvard Hall, during meetings of the A.H.C.

Although the Harvard Corporation appeared to be unwilling to part temporarily with the last remaining book in John Harvard's library and the charter of the College, Bailey reported that a blowup of the latter would be available for display behind such cherished relics as the President's chair, the President's seal, the Great Salt (a large silver salt-cellar given the College in 1644), the Stoughton Cup and George Washington's honorary degree.

By May, after the great cleanup, Harvard Hall looked as grand as it ever had, even the elephant head having, the *Bulletin* reported, "received a quick wonder-working beauty treatment via a long-handled brush."

Around 6 P.M. on Wednesday, May 12, the Grill Room and Harvard Hall began to fill up with alumni and their wives and other guests, almost 700 in all, getting acquainted and reacquainted over cocktails. After dinner, these visitors boarded waiting buses, and by 7:30 the fourteenth and last bus, loaded, was heading uptown to Lincoln Center, where 600 more alumni and guests, a third of whom had dined at Lincoln Plaza, were taking their seats in the New York State Theater, which the Club had reserved for the evening. Following a superb performance by the New York City Ballet, one choreographed and directed by George Balanchine, the audience repaired to the first-ring promenade for a reception, a champagne supper and dancing both square and conventional.

The next day, Thursday, was officially designated Harvard Day at the world's fair, which had recently reopened for a second and final season, and around midday some 800 visiting Harvardians and guests came together at the New England States pavilion. The Krokodiloes, an under-graduate singing group too new to be familiar to most of its auditors, pro-vided a close-harmony accompaniment to lunch; they were followed by Club member Paul Killiam, Jr. '37 L'41, well known for his re-produc-tions of old silent films, who put on three or four "interludes" or skits, one featuring his classmate, actor Daniel Keyes '37. Finally, the redoubtable Robert Moses (Yale '09), president of the fair, welcomed the visiting Harvards, claiming kinship with them by virtue of his own Harvard degree (LLD [hon.] '53).

Friday was the longest day of Harvard Comes to New York and was confined to the Hotel Waldorf-Astoria. There, in the morning, Dean Franklin L. Ford AM'48 PhD'50 of the Faculty of Arts and Sciences presided over a panel discussion on "Teaching in the College." The University luncheon in the Grand Ballroom was attended by about 750 persons, who heard Jose Luis Sert speak on "The Urban Crisis." And in the afternoon, in a Waldorf-Astoria reception room which, though uncon-nected with the last speaker, was called the Sert Room, after the artist who painted the murals in it, the alumni and their guests looked on and listened as President Pusey moderated a discussion among three faculty members on "Harvard and the Problems of Society."

That evening came the climax to the three-day meeting when, once again in the Grand Ballroom, 1,500 Harvard men and their female con-sorts sat down to a dinner honoring President and Mrs. Pusey. As had almost always been the case at nineteenth-century Club dinners, a band was present, on this occasion the Harvard Band, and it was while these crimson-jacketed youths were setting up that Harvard Comes to New York encountered its first and only snag with the discovery that the bass drum, of all things, had vanished. According to the *Bulletin*, the band's leader appealed to the hotel's kitchen staff, who shortly produced a huge and shiny cauldron, but before this object's percussive properties could be test-ed, the missing bass drum mysteriously reappeared. Composer Leroy Anderson '29 AM'30 then conducted the band in some of his own popular works, including a medley familiar to generations of Harvard people incorporating the theme of "Wintergreen for President," to prolonged applause.

Introduced by dinner chairman David Rockefeller, the retiring president of the Associated Harvard Clubs, Thomas F. Mason '30, tore up his prepared speech and tossed the pieces in the air. This extravagant gesture was entirely in order, for at a meeting of the A.H.C. the day before, it had been decided, following conversations spanning several years, that that organization would merge with the Harvard Alumni Association, effective July 1, in a new and stronger body to be known as the Associated Harvard Alumni (A.H.A.). Even though, technically, the A.H.A. didn't yet quite exist, Chairman Rockefeller expressed its appreciation of Mr. and Mrs. Pusey, owners of a twenty-three-foot sailboat, by presenting them with a chronometer and a barometer, whereupon President Pusey spoke sympathetically about the undergraduates' impatience concerning pressing problems of the time. And the sixty-eighth and last annual gathering of the Associated Harvard Clubs, the third ever held in New York, ended with, inevitably, the singing of the opening stanza of "Fair Harvard."

At the Board's next meeting, President Pratt praised member Laurence Johnson '39 (who had modestly absented himself) for his masterly planning of Harvard Comes to New York. Treasurer Harvey announced that first, thanks to the commission system, outlays on wages and salaries were sharply down, and that second, the federal excise tax on club dues would probably be lifted on January 1, 1966. In June, with a new fiscal year impending, year-end committee reports revealed more cheering facts. Having earned the Club a tidy profit from the consumption of food and drinks by 5,000-plus attendees at some fifteen entertainments, Activities planned to put on nineteen entertainments next year. Heightened interest in squash had reduced the Athletics Department's annual loss from $8,000 to $2,000. And Chairman Gamache, retiring at last from that post, revealed that the Travel Committee was turning over $5,000 from its reserves to the Club foundation, $1,000 of it for scholarships and $4,000, the committee was hoping, toward the preparation of a Club history.

Asked by President Pratt about his inquiry into problems the Club might encounter in admitting women members, Vice-President Larsen likened it to opening "a veritable Pandora's box." Much more information was needed. Even so, he and Pratt believed that the Club's future would depend largely on women participating in it, adding that if the present clubhouse could not accommodate them all, efforts should be pressed to acquire 35 West 44th Street. Meanwhile, it should still be possible, Larsen felt, to retain a portion of the clubhouse as a male hideaway in which Club traditions could be maintained.

On July 1, a new automatic telephone switchboard went on-line. And over the summer the House Committee approved two actions whose consequences remain with us: erecting a sidewalk canopy at the clubhouse entrance and renaming the Ladies' Club Rooms the Cambridge Rooms.

In mid-September, the Board elected squash pro John Jacobs a special member for life. Two weeks later, 130 members and male guests assembled in the Biddle and North Rooms for a gala dinner honoring Jacobs, who had been to the Club what Harry Cowles had been to Harvard.

On November 1, the inexpensive balcony lunch, long talked about and even tried out experimentally, became at last a regular amenity. The lunch consisted of soup, a sandwich and coffee, tea or milk, for $1.60 plus tax and a 10 percent service charge. As well as providing a much-needed economical midday meal practically all members could afford, it would surely tempt some lunchers up from the Main Dining Room below, relieving overcrowding there.

Two days later, something curious happened at the clubhouse. While a few members, perhaps checking the commemorative tablet to confirm it, may have realized that the Club had been founded exactly 100 years before, the Club's governors, whether deliberately or by inadvertence, seem to have ignored the fact, and the day passed without any official acknowledgment of it. Nor was the matter mentioned, apparently, the next day, when the Executive Committee met. All in all, the contrast with what had happened on November 3, 1915, could hardly have been starker.

Late in the afternoon of Tuesday, November 5, the Grill Room and Bar were beginning to fill up when, at 5:28, every light in the building went out. So began, at the clubhouse, the great blackout of 1965, triggered by a power failure in an Ontario power plant. Manager Stack and Resident Manager Franklin S. Reynolds sprang into action, and in minutes the ground-floor public rooms, the Cambridge Rooms and the Library were bathed in candlelight. Minutes after this, an employee returned from a nearby hardware store with enough flashlights to bring the Club's supply to twenty; they were used to guide members down from the squash courts and the bedrooms, where candles were strictly forbidden.

Over the next hour or so, members despairing of getting home by their usual means of public transport kept arriving at the Club. Many headed for the Bar. In the candlelit kitchen, Chef Ken Sune Borgedahl saw to the preparation of enough chicken à la king to feed everyone who wanted a hot meal. His crew also made 150 sandwiches, which the barflies happily devoured. That night, all of the sleeping accommodations were, of course, booked, but many guests cheerfully let cots be set up in their bedrooms. Elsewhere, other temporarily homeless men (and women, five of whom were stranded in the Cambridge Rooms) bedded down wherever they could, on sofas, in armchairs, even on stretches of carpet. At 4:27 A.M., lights suddenly went on throughout the clubhouse, but few sleepers stirred; hours later, on arising, they would find improvised shaving kits awaiting them in the ground-floor and basement washrooms.

The 500-plus survivors of that night were unanimous in praising the two managers and the staff for their swift response to the emergency and their unflagging concern thereafter for the members' well-being. In the *Bulletin*, Miss Van Fossen would call attention as well to the contribution of Bootsie Mitten, patrolling "the entire Club, her eyes beaming like headlights and not missing a trick."

One day that fall, former Treasurer Sheridan A. ("Sherry") Logan, long a familiar figure in the clubhouse, was missing from his accustomed place at the head of the Club table in the Main Dining Room. Embedded in the seat of the chair he had vacated, moreover, were two shiny new metal plaques. Having retired from banking, he had returned to his native St. Joseph, Missouri, to pursue various projects, among them a biography of his former employer, longtime member of the Club George F. Baker, Jr. '99. The explanation of the plaques went back more than four decades, to when young Logan, newly arrived in New York, began taking breakfast at the long table. Then and for many years thereafter, the table talk was dominated by the learned Congregationalist minister Adolf A. Berle, but when, nearing ninety, Berle ceased coming to the table, Logan's fellow regulars, prizing his lightly worn erudition, prevailed on him to take their mentor's place. And when, about ten years later, Logan announced his imminent departure, his friends had a plaque inscribed with his name and class and "Treasurer 1936–45" affixed to the seat of his chair, later adding below it another plaque bearing the legend *Hic sedit et auditores instruxit* ("Here he sat and instructed his hearers.") Incidentally, Logan, now in his midnineties, still visits the Club regularly twice a year.

The death on November 8, in a plane crash, of a younger member, Steven Robert Easton '55, prompted some of his friends to establish a Club scholarship in his memory, and by December 16 a fund bearing his name amounted to $6,091. On that date, President Pratt told the Board he was inviting the masters of the College houses to next month's annual dinner, travel and other expenses paid, in the hope of interesting them in the Club and persuading them to let its representatives distribute literature to resident seniors. Meanwhile, the alertness of member Walter J. Salmon, Jr. '30 had effected a tiny but not trifling alteration in the frontal appearance of the clubhouse. Noticing one day that the taxi-summoning light at the apex of the Club's new canopy blinked blue whereas the Princeton Club's flashed red, Salmon suggested that the two clubs switch bulbs, and they very soon did.

The previous June, Board members had hailed the anticipated rescission of the federal tax on club dues as offering a godsent opportunity to raise the dues without inflicting pain. And in November, they imposed a 10 percent increase on all members' dues, effective midnight, December 31. That moment found New York with a new mayor, liberal Republican John V. Lindsay, Yale '44, and a strike of transit workers that shut down all of the municipal subways and bus routes. The first two days of 1966 fell on a weekend, but on the morning of January 3, the influx of innumerable cars into Manhattan resulted in the worst traffic tie-ups the city had ever known, with motorists in, say, Midtown barely able to proceed as much as a single block between red lights.

As had happened during the blackout, not a few Club members found a cozy and convenient refuge at 27 West 44th Street. Every bedroom and cubicle was occupied, while sales of meals and drinks soared. For most employees, however, living far from the clubhouse, the strike constituted a hardship: those residing in a particular neighborhood would assemble as instructed around daybreak to be picked up and transported to work by a hired driver in a trip that might take three hours, while others would arrive—very slowly—in taxis, paid for, of course, by the Club. At the end of their workday, some staffers, unwilling to make the long trip home, opted to sleep on cots in a private dining room, or to stay, two or three to a room, at a nearby hotel.

This routine took a toll. On the sixth, Manager Stack reported that Club staffers were exhausted and their morale at low ebb: Could the dining and bar facilities be closed down over the January 8–9 weekend to give them a rest? The Executive Committee decided that they could be and would be, then heard a suggestion from Programs Chairman Wheelock that the football dinner, attendance at which had slackened in recent years, be replaced by a dinner honoring all of the undergraduate sports and teams.

On January 14, the city government and the union reached an accord, whereupon both transit and traffic returned to normal. Six nights later, members gathered for the Club's 100th annual dinner elected Roy E. Larsen president, Morgan D. Wheelock vice-president and Peter S. Heller '48 L'52 secretary, while retaining John F. Harvey as treasurer. Present, in addition to President Pusey and assorted deans and fellows, were the masters of six upperclassmen's houses and Dudley Hall, the day students' center: all looked pleased to be there, a good augury, surely, for their future cooperation. Before the annual meeting was adjourned, a deputation of three employees, including newly retired headwaiter Herbert Barreau, presented retiring President Pratt with a color print of the College and a leatherbound album containing the signatures of every one of the Club's employees, under a statement that one of the presenters read aloud:

> We shall miss your steady hand at the helm, Commodore. We have all received profound inspiration from your leadership during the past three years.

While the minutes do not record "Commodore" Pratt's response, it is safe to assume that he was touched by this remarkable tribute.

In February, the Club's squash racquets A team defeated the Racquet Club's formidable first team to capture the league title, 38–7. Two other noteworthy developments were, of all things, gustatory. At their annual conference, the Club Managers of America, some 1,200 strong, judged the Club's soup-and-sandwich bar one of the five best new ideas presented. And on the twenty-fourth, the Club put on its first-ever gourmet dinner, with musical accompaniment by classical guitarist Reyes de la Torre. Although it was a success even before it occurred (500 members applied, but only 250 could be accommodated), the event set the Club back financially: not even in 1966, it seems, did eleven dollars a head quite cover the cost of a truly Lucullan repast.

On March 17, two Board members came up with ideas for boosting the Club's income. Admissions Chairman George W. Gibson '31 pointed out that the Club could instantly acquire hundreds of new resident members, paying top dues, simply by limiting nonresident members to those with homes and offices fifty miles or more from the clubhouse. And Harvey L. Thomas, Jr. '44 B'49 proposed renting cubicles to undergraduates. Vice-President Wheelock suggested making such cubicles available only on the recommendation of a house master, which suggestion former President Pratt endorsed as calculated to strengthen the Club's bonds with the house masters. Finally, at President Larsen's urging, the Board approved authorizing the house masters to recommend juniors and seniors to use the Club's unoccupied cubicles at any time.

Though no one could have foreseen it, the Club would soon be the focus of unwanted publicity. On March 21, the Supreme Court upheld, 5–4, a five-year prison sentence and a $28,000 fine imposed by a lower court on Ralph Ginzburg, publisher of *Eros* and other erotic publications, for sending obscene matter through the mail; forty leading media figures, among them playwright Arthur Miller, film producer Otto Preminger and Hugh Hefner, the publisher of *Playboy*, formed a Committee to Protest Absurd Censorship, naming as their chairman novelist—and Club member—Sloan Wilson. Wilson called a press conference, and at the appointed hour on Saturday, April 2, in the Slocum Room, he and three members of his committee received reporters, who before long were drinking coffee out of the enormous cups that had long been a Club fixture. (According to unverifiable Club tradition, the first such cup had been made for Theodore Roosevelt, who loved coffee and had been heard to remark that the first cup always seemed to taste better than the second.)

Next morning, newspaper reports uniformly gave the venue of Wilson's press conference as the Club. *New York Times* reporter Franklin Whitehouse wrote that while the author of *The Man in the Gray Flannel Suit* had expressed "the highest respect" for the Court, he had then characterized the justices' action in the Ginzburg case as "the last vestige of Victorianism." "They're old men," Wilson had continued. "They've been brought up to be afraid of sex. They're afraid the beast will be let out. . . . I'm not, frankly, worried about sex in print. I'm worried about violence on television."

At the end of his article, reporter Whitehouse rather mischievously quoted a remark let drop by *Library Journal* editor Eric Moon, a member of Wilson's committee, after retrieving his overcoat downstairs: "'It's ironic,' he said, crossing the crimson carpet strewn with leather chairs, 'but the coat-check clerk was reading *Playboy*.'"

Sloan Wilson's unauthorized press conference occasioned much subsequent hand-wringing, one Board member declaring that the newspaper stories it generated could leave readers with the impression that the Club favored pornography. But in spite of the Club's aversion to publicity it soon again figured in the columns of the *Times*, twice: on April 27 in a report that the Radcliffe Club would be moving into the clubhouse and a day later in an article about the Landmarks Preservation Commission's plans to designate 31 city buildings as landmarks. Other listed buildings included St. Thomas Church, St. Patrick's Cathedral, the Central Synagogue, the University Club, the Racquet and Tennis Club and three hotels: the Gotham, the St. Regis and the Plaza. If the Club's governors were gratified to find the clubhouse in such distinguished company, however, they were not at all pleased about the restriction a landmark designation would impose on their freedom to expand or alter it, and in late May President Larsen would send the commission a letter drafted by the Club's legal counselor, Francis Goodhue, formally objecting to the proposed designation.

Meanwhile, on May 19, Admissions Chairman Gibson informed the Board that, whereas the Club defined resident members as those "having a residence or a principal place of business in any of the five boroughs of the City of New York," practically all other city clubs defined them as members living and/or working within a given radius of the clubhouse, ranging from 25 miles (the Yale Club) to 100 (the Union League Club).

What a year was 1966 for unwanted media attention! On August 27, the *Times*'s second section led off with a story that must have amused some members, but just as surely irritated others:

### And Now the Harvard Club Lets
### Radcliffe Alumnae Club Move In

There was a time when the Harvard Club meant strictly the company of good fellows—and absolutely no women allowed. But as George Bernard Shaw observed, "Women upset everything." And so, next Wednesday, the old stone building* with the crimson door at 27 West 44th Street, occupied by the Harvard Club since 1894, will also become the headquarters of the Radcliffe Club of New York.

Barbara Norton, alumnae secretary of Radcliffe College, confirmed yesterday from Cambridge, Massachusetts, that the Radcliffe Club of New York would move from the Berkshire Hotel, Madison Avenue and 52nd Street, and set up its main office and hold its regular meetings in the Harvard Club building. . . .

But a spokesman for the Radcliffe Club in New York insisted that Radcliffe alumnae had no intention of invading the 100-year-old club's sanctuaries.

"We shall simply enter the building by the women's entrance and go to the meeting rooms we will be permitted to use, or to our office," she said.

"They've invaded the college, it's just a matter of time until they invade the club," said one club member gruffly. "I guess it's been coming since the day they stopped binding women's feet," growled another.

Of seven members who wrote President Larsen about the Radcliffe Club's moving into the Cambridge Rooms, five strongly opposed it, but Larsen told the Executive Committee that these objectors didn't realize how little difference the presence of a few score Radcliffe graduates without signing privileges would make in a club in which nearly 1,600 women already held these privileges. Before long, incidentally, Vice-President Wheelock would consult with Mrs. Harriet C. Barry R'54, president of the Radcliffe Club, about an awkward problem: some men who were eligible for membership were not joining and some members were actually

*In fact, the clubhouse was, in 1966, as it had been in 1894 and remains today, not stone, but brick

resigning as their wives or daughters received signing privileges, confident that they could avail themselves of these privileges and avoid having to pay dues. When the Radcliffe Club, planning a cocktail party, requested the names and addresses of young, unmarried Club members, however, Wheelock turned them down, saying that at this initial stage of their relationship the two clubs should remain scrupulously separate.

In September, the Board voted to substitute an all-sports dinner for the traditional football dinner and to open the annual dinner to women guests, but in November the Executive Committee refused to allow the Library to serve as the setting of a television interview of longtime member John Rock '14 MD'18, the principal developer of the first effective oral contraceptive ("the Pill"), in order not to establish a precedent that could one day prove inconvenient. And on December 9, with George A. Plimpton '48, author of the hilarious bestseller *Paper Lion*, as master of ceremonies, the Club's first all-sports dinner was judged by everyone who came to it a thumping success.

With all four officers being returned for another year, the 1967 annual meeting was even more routine than usual. This business concluded, however, the doors at the south end of Harvard Hall swung open, and for the first time at this event, women in evening gowns streamed in, wives and guests of members, together with a few ladies holding signing privileges. There followed a reception honoring both President Pusey and President Mary Bunting AM (hon.) '60 of Radcliffe, then dinner.

On February 1, the House Committee decided to end the practice of paging members wanted on the telephone, for decades a nuisance that had occasioned endless complaints. Later that month, Club Foundation President David W. Devens '42 reported the curious fact that numerous people without any Harvard connection had contributed to the Steven Easton '55 Fund—now, in line with a suggestion from Easton's widow, providing a single four-year scholarship instead of a few of briefer duration. And on March 1, Daniel P. Moynihan AM (hon.) '66, director of Harvard's and M.I.T.'s Joint Center for Urban Studies, delivered the fourth of six lectures by professors at Cambridge's two great institutions of higher learning on "The Future of Education." His topic was "The Evolution of the Urban Poor," and in a surprising show of social consciousness and perhaps, too, of social conscience, 650 members and guests turned up for this talk, which hardly promised an hour or so of light entertainment.

Early in April, President Larsen brought up a possibility that previous Boards had considered and future Boards would consider: that the Club lease or purchase the next-door Hotel Webster. And Larsen hailed the forging of closer ties with the University, as manifested in the house masters' cooperation with the Club's recruiting efforts and the outstanding success of the Harvard-M.I.T. lectures.

On May 3, the House Committee voted to admit ladies to the Main Dining Room for breakfast on Saturdays, and the next day, after approving this recommendation, the Executive Committee heard a report from William B. Tabler on a tour of the Hotel Webster he had undertaken with his fellow architect Eustis H. Dearborn. The Webster, as Tabler described it, was a typical old loft hotel, with narrow, dormitory-like rooms. Its bathrooms were antiquated, with exposed pipes. And it was listed in municipal records as being fireproof.

The hotel's floors were not situated at the same levels as the Club's were, but Tabler and Dearborn believed that the two buildings could be joined at their respective fourth floors. But should they be? Having concluded that converting the Webster to the Club's use would require its being substantially remodeled, at great expense, the architects advised against acquiring it, recommending instead acquiring the building and property adjoining the clubhouse on 44th Street, at Number 35 West. With that lot in its possession, the Club could, Tabler said, raise an addition ten or twelve stories tall.

Next, Tabler reported on another tour he and Dearborn had made for the Board, of the clubhouse itself, in an attempt to arrive at the probable cost of effecting certain capital improvements President Larsen and his associates had in mind. These projects, from automating the passenger elevator to constructing new squash courts, were not exactly minor undertakings, and the architects' estimated price tags were commensurately high. But the Club's most pressing structural need might, with luck, be met relatively cheaply: the problem of where to put the Radcliffe Club office, temporarily and all-too-publicly occupying the second-floor landing between the Library and the Cambridge Lounge. Before long, a solution would be found: dismantling the washroom off the mezzanine leading to the Cambridge Lounge and converting it into an office.

In June, two employees retired who, exchanging pleasantries with members entering and leaving the Club over the years, had won a special place in their affections: cigar stand operator Joseph Samuels and ladies' coatroom attendant Mae Winters, with her bangs and her ready smile, still fondly remembered today by most members over fifty. And on the seventh, the House Committee set priorities for the execution of the capital improvements, already presented to the Executive Committee and the Board, based on the assumption that their cost would be spread out over three years:

Priority I
1. Renovation of the entrance hall "lounge," combining cigar stand, front office and theater desk.
2. Relocation of the Radcliffe Club office.
3. Immediate repairs to the squash courts.

Estimated cost: $75,000.

Priority II
1. Air-conditioning the third-floor banquet rooms.
2. Improving the lighting on the third floor.
3. Converting both elevators to automatic control.
4. Renovating the sixth and seventh floors, including enlarging two squash courts to standard size.

Estimated cost: $190,000.

Priority III
1. Air-conditioning the Cambridge Rooms.
2. Constructing a doubles court and two singles courts.
3. Improving the lighting generally and converting all electricity to alternating current.

Estimated cost: $220,000.

Next day, after approving these priorities, the Executive Committee decided to reclassify as nonresident members only those living and working more than fifty miles from the clubhouse, thereby acquiring at a stroke some 550 new resident members. At the next Board meeting, someone suggested assessing the members to pay for the capital improvements instead of raising their dues, but Programs Chairman Frank Streeter came up with a persuasive argument for the latter course: when the 20 percent federal tax on club dues had been rescinded as of January 1966, he pointed out, the Club had raised the dues only 10 percent, so that another 10 percent increase would merely bring the dues up to a slightly higher level than those of 1965. Treasurer Harvey concurred, citing another alternative to an assessment in the fact that the Club possessed substantial borrowing power, and in the end the Board approved a 10 percent dues increase, the extension of resident membership to fifty miles from the clubhouse and, for good measure, a proposal that Radcliffe Club members be permitted to dine in the Cambridge Dining Rooms on payment of a fee.

At an Executive Committee meeting in July, Chairman Streeter talked enthusiastically about an idea someone had for a series of "conversations" with eminent and interesting people, spontaneous dialogues between guests and audiences. What sort of guests? Well, McGeorge Bundy, say, or Richard Nixon. . . . And indeed, on Wednesday, September 13, the former vice president and presidential candidate starred in a memorable evening of give-and-take in Harvard Hall during which no fewer than 2,025 people were counted entering the clubhouse.

The first program of the new season presented by the University Relations Committee was a talk in early October by Dr. Graham B. Blaine, Jr. '40, the University Health Service's chief of psychiatry, on "The Alienated Student: Villain or Victim?" It would be followed in November by two evenings of discussion on another subject of growing public concern, "Crisis of the Cities." (In July, a race riot had erupted in Detroit that left forty-three dead; similar outbreaks occurred in Rochester, New York; Birmingham, Alabama; and New York's Spanish Harlem, less than four miles from the clubhouse.) Meanwhile, the Travel Committee announced a planned trip, not just to Europe, but to India and Nepal, and the next month—not entirely by coincidence, one suspects—the Activities Committee put on a "Festival of India" featuring the celebrated sitarist Ravi Shankar.

For November 15, the Activities Committee scheduled China Night, the centerpiece of which was to be *China: Roots of Madness*, a film, written by member Theodore H. White, about the Cultural Revolution raging throughout Mao Tse-tung's domain. After the signal success of Festival of India, Chairman Rupert Hitzig '60 was expecting a good reception for its successor, but nothing like what happened: so many people came that hundreds, literally, had to be turned away. The event was, quite simply, *too* successful.

On January 18, 1968, Secretary Heller was reelected and three new officers were chosen, presumably with a mandate to press on with a capital improvements program destined to cost, by William Tabler's latest estimate, $520,000. They were President Morgan D. Wheelock, Vice-President Albert H. Gordon '23 B'25 and Treasurer John J. Dorgan, Jr. '45 B'48.

As Club members were of course aware, the flight of comparatively well-off white New Yorkers to the suburbs and beyond that had been going on since World War II was continuing, accompanied by an influx into New York (and other major cities) of poor and mostly unskilled blacks. Since August 1965, when the Los Angeles ghetto of Watts had exploded in six days of rioting, black discontent had boiled over in violence elsewhere, so it was hardly surprising that when the University Relations Committee announced a symposium on "The City," hundreds of members signed up to attend.

That spring, growing opposition in the country to the Vietnam War sparked dramatic developments in the contest for the Democratic presidential nomination, causing much lively speculation at the Club. Antiwar Senator Eugene McCarthy almost defeated Johnson in the New Hampshire primary, liberal Senator Robert F. Kennedy '48 entered the race and, on March 31, President Johnson dropped out of it. Then on April 4, in Memphis, a sniper killed America's foremost champion of civil rights, the Rev. Martin Luther King, Jr. Blacks rioted in Washington and violence flared briefly in Harlem, but before long another kind of disturbance erupted next door in Morningside Heights, where mostly white Columbia undergraduates, many belonging to Students for a Democratic Society (SDS), seized five campus buildings and occupied them for six days. They were protesting the university's conducting research for the Defense Department and constructing a gymnasium on land they felt should be reserved for the use of the Harlem community.

Could such a thing happen at Harvard? Some Club members wondered. But President Wheelock and his colleagues were eager, at a time of rising prices, to get on with the capital improvements. Incidentally, Treasurer Dorgan revived the long-disused practice of posting the names of members whose house accounts were overdue for payment with, it appears, salutary results.

On June 4, in Los Angeles, Robert Kennedy had just won the California primary when he was shot and killed.

At the Club, meanwhile, all was serene. William A. Robertson, individual bridge champion in 1951 and 1959, won the title a third time to retire the Crichton Cup, donated by Oliver C. Wagstaff '07. During the summer, with the Cambridge Rooms (and banquet rooms) closed down, the Algonquin Hotel welcomed ladies with signing privileges to lunch in its restaurant on credit. Early in August, Republicans convened in Miami nominated former Vice President Nixon for President, and at the end of the month, amid scenes televised nationwide of Chicago policemen clubbing young people demonstrating against the Vietnam War outside the convention hall, the Democrats nominated Vice President Humphrey.

On September 19, the Board members, before getting down to business, viewed a new portrait of former President Larsen by William F. Draper and approved it for accession. Meanwhile, the many friends of lawyer Gavin P. Murphy L'54 in the Club had started to consult the sports pages daily for news of him in Mexico City, where the summer Olympics were still in progress. Months before, reading that Mexico had, as host country, added to the scheduled events the sport of fronton, a form of jai alai played with a heavy racquet that was virtually unknown north of the Rio Grande, Murphy, for eight years squash tennis champion of the Club, had set out to master the sport and organize an eight-man team, which included several Harvard graduates. After weeks of practice at the Racquet Club, the octet, duly certified as the first and only Olympic athletes ever to represent the United States at fronton, had flown to Mexico. Murphy's team would stay in competition into October, finishing about halfway between the strongest and weakest of its largely Basque and Hispanic opponents.

Though far less well known than the late Dr. King, another civil rights leader, a member of the Club, had long pursued similar goals. He was Whitney M. Young, Jr. AM'61 LLD (hon.) '68, executive director since 1961 of the National Urban League. Young advocated a "domestic Marshall Plan" to raise black people's educational and economic levels. On October 2, in "A Conversation with Whitney M. Young, Jr." in Harvard Hall, he urged the Club to award more scholarships to black youths in the city and to help black graduates coming to the city to adjust to life here.

Eight days later, the University Relations Committee focused on another volatile segment of the population in a panel discussion. Titled "The New Student and the Old University," it featured two deans, Franklin L. Ford and Fred L. Glimp '50, and Professor Erik H. Erikson PhD'36. Months afterward, attending members would recall in wonder what Erikson had then stated flatly: that a head-on collision between enraged students and their sclerotic institutions of learning was not simply likely but inevitable.

On October 14, the Executive Committeemen voted Whitney Young a special honorarium and referred his proposal regarding scholarships to the Scholarships Committee. While they concluded that helping black graduates adjust to the city was not a proper function of the Club, they called on individual members to lend these newcomers a helping hand. Days later, Schools Chairman Ross told the Board his committee would redouble efforts to find worthy candidates in ghetto areas, and Scholarships Chairman Scott said he would explore with Dean Chase Peterson the possibility of increasing financial aid for black students.

On November 5, to the satisfaction, surely, of most members of the Club, Republican Richard M. Nixon was elected President, albeit by a slender margin. And on the twenty-first, the Board agreed to, among other requests, one from Programs Chairman Streeter for $3,150 with which to provide closed circuit television coverage, two days later, of the Harvard-Yale gridiron classic, to be played that year at the Stadium between two previously undefeated teams. Streeter's timing was uncanny, for that contest turned out to be "The Game," in which, during the last incredible 42 seconds of play, the Harvard team, sixteen points behind, miraculously put across a pair of touchdowns and another pair of two-point conversions to even the score, 29–29, depriving the Elis of what had been a solid, well-earned win to achieve a "victory" sweeter, perhaps, than any actual one.

In New York, the Columbia campus was again in turmoil, and Harvard Law's Archibald Cox '34 L'37 launched a private investigation from afar into the causes of the previous April's insurrection. On January 16, 1969, after the four officers' reelection and the dinner that followed, the professor reported his findings, and while he could not guarantee that a similar upheaval would not occur in Cambridge, he left the impression that he would be surprised if it did.

On March 1 Rufus Osgood, who had run the library for a quarter of a century, retired; he would be replaced, in time, by Lounsbury D. ("Biff") Bates L'28, a retired lawyer who loved books—and cigars. And on the twelfth, an innovative program titled "Crime: The Police versus the Courts," starring Harvard professors of history, government and law, filled New York's 1,500-seat Town Hall to capacity, with members and guests and other invited Harvard alumni.

No one at Harvard, not even the ultimate perpetrators, could have predicted the tumultuous events of Wednesday, April 9, for as longtime member E. J. Kahn, Jr. '37 would point out in *Harvard: Through Change and Through Storm* (1969), the College's SDS chapter had, the night before, thrice voted *not* to occupy University Hall. The group's leaders had then, however, called a meeting for noon the next day to reconsider, and by that hour hotheaded militants were already storming Harvard's main administration center, evicting deans, secretaries and everyone else. From their new stronghold, the revolutionaries issued "non-negotiable" demands, the chief one being the abolition of the College's R.O.T.C. units.

Some 200 miles west southwest, horrified Club members watched these events, filmed, on the evening television news, and the next morning learned, by radio and television, of the aftermath. At 5 A.M. on the tenth, on orders from President Pusey, concurred in by the senior deans but not the faculty, which had not been consulted, state and local policemen forced their way into University Hall to rout the occupiers. The Cambridge policemen wielded their billies with a will, and of the 186 young men and women taken into custody, 40 were injured. Within hours, however, most of the arrested students were released, and before long radical elements, seizing the initiative anew, proclaimed a College-wide strike.

At 27 West 44th Street, reaction to these events ranged from shock to dismay to near-apoplectic outrage.

The centennial year annual dinner, January 21, 1965

# 17

# WOMEN COME ON BOARD (1969–1976)

Never in Harvard's long history, now spanning a third of a millennium, had an event in the Yard sent a shock wave of like magnitude through the ranks of her far-flung alumni. At 27 West 44th Street members debated what the student strike—backed, it appeared, by a number of professors—might portend, at least one of them solemnly asserting that the College would never recover, and was doomed, before long, to disappear. The Club's official stance was more positive: twice, in the days following the police "bust," President Wheelock dispatched telegrams to President Pusey expressing, on behalf of the Executive Committee and the Board, their unqualified support and unreserved endorsement of his action.

The following month, with men from the Admissions and Membership Committees ready to head northeast to interview prospective members, the Board suggested that they inquire into the applicants' views regarding the University Hall riot, taking pains, in particular, to pin down the attitudes of faculty members who were applying. President Wheelock revealed that the University Relations Committee would bring professors to New York to discuss the riot and strike, and in June he reported that a group of Overseers chaired by member Henry J. Friendly '23 L'27 was trying to gauge alumni response to these events through the presidents of all of the Harvard clubs.

At the close of fiscal 1969 the Club had 7,653 members, 115 more than on July 1, 1968. Construction was under way on the sixth and seventh floors and on the roof. And late in the evening of Sunday, July 20, as hundreds of millions of people around the globe looked on via television, astronaut Neil Armstrong opened the hatch of a lunar module landing craft, descended a short ladder and stepped onto the moon's surface to plant the first human footprint there.

Early in September, President Wheelock appointed a five-man committee headed by Alexander Aldrich '50 L'53 to find out how Club members felt about the upheaval of the previous April and to report its findings to Cambridge. Meanwhile, for all the outpourings of disgust and disaffection those events had provoked, proofs were not lacking of continuing loyalty to Harvard. Contributions by members to the Club foundation, for example, had held up well since April, so well, indeed, that the Club was able to provide $50,000 in scholarships, the largest sum the College had ever received for this purpose from any Harvard club. Nor were aspiring Harvardians put off: of 1,401 applicants admitted days before the University Hall riot, 1,170 turned up in Cambridge in September. (Acceptances were, to be sure, down 1.7 percent from 1968, but Schools Chairman Ross attributed this decrease largely to Yale's having gone coeducational.)

In late January 1970, the Club presented a stimulating conversation with Henry Kissinger '50 AM'52 PhD'54, national security adviser to President Nixon. On February 1, Clyde J. Harris, long associated with the senior management of the Ritz-Carlton, Plaza and Waldorf-Astoria Hotels, became manager, replacing John Paul Stack, who had resigned the previous fall; meanwhile, with Treasurer Dorgan's employer transferring him to London, Wheelock, with the Board's assent, named banker Bruce M. Merchant '56 to the post. And on February 17 a front-page article in the *New York Times* revealed that President Pusey would be stepping down in June 1971, two years earlier than planned. Meanwhile, stacks of returned questionnaires from the April 9 Ad Hoc Committee's mailing had been duly collated, and on March 19 President Wheelock, proclaiming this sounding of alumni sentiment one of the most important activities the Club had ever undertaken, introduced Chairman Aldrich, who presented his committee's findings:

Of 1,731 alumni who had filled out and returned their questionnaires,

• 51 percent believed that the University had not responded properly during the 1969 spring demonstrations;

• 42 percent believed the University had responded properly;

• 7  percent gave no opinion or did not respond to the question.

Regarding contributions to the University,

• 19 percent said they had contributed less money as a result of the disorders;

• 5 percent said they had contributed more;

• 73 percent said they had contributed about the same as before.

Among alumni who had graduated since 1960, 91 percent said they would send their children to the University, and 70 percent said that they felt students should have a greater role in running the University; by contrast, only 67 percent of alumni fifteen or more years out would send children to the University, and only 63 percent believed that students should have more say in administration. The older alumni were almost equally divided on the question of whether the board of the Associated Harvard Alumni should include younger members, whereas 77 percent of younger alumni believed it should. On the other hand, almost 82 percent of alumni of all ages felt that students should not have a voice in faculty promotions and tenure decisions.

The Aldrich Committee's report would be circulated widely—to President Pusey, the Dunlop Committee (the University's Committee on Governance, chaired by Club member John T. Dunlop AM [hon.] '46, Fac), the Corporation, the Board of Overseers and, of course, to members of the Club. In April, it would be released to the press.

On April 9, a year to the day after the University Hall occupation and bust, the University Relations Committee, eager to foster alumni understanding of those mysterious creatures, the students, put on "An Evening with Some Undergraduates," among them young James M. Fallows '70, former president of the *Crimson*, who was destined to become a well-known journalist. On the sixteenth, Chairman Aldrich, while requesting that the April 9 Ad Hoc Committee be disbanded, pointed out that only hours earlier rebellious students had invaded the Center for International Education in Cambridge and that two members of a visiting committee had been trapped in a cab, while on April 15 a serious riot had rocked

Harvard Square. The moral: such incidents were by no means a thing of the past. Acknowledging the truth of this, President Wheelock thanked Chairman Aldrich warmly for a job well done.

Student disaffection apparently extended beyond the College to include alumni organizations: on May 1, seven Admissions Committeemen arrived in Cambridge and managed to flush out only fifty-four applicants, a mere twenty-five of them graduating seniors. In contrast, however, a determined phalanx of thirteen Radcliffe students descended on the interviewing site to demand full membership in the Club. Three weeks later, Membership Chairman George W. Gibson '31 proposed to the Board that in the future representatives of the Ladies' Committee attend these sessions to interview applicants for ladies' signing privileges.

Chairman Gibson noted, furthermore, that President Wheelock was doing his best to cope with a veritable torrent of appeals for full membership for women, mostly from female Business School graduates who confessed, candidly enough, that they would rather take business contacts to lunch in the impressive Main Dining Room than in the simpler, more homelike Cambridge Dining Rooms. At Wheelock's suggestion, the Board appointed a committee consisting of himself (while president), Vice-President Gordon, Chairman Gibson and Admissions Chairman Raymond C. Guth '43 L'48 to consider instituting full membership for women.

Although increased bar and restaurant prices went into effect on December 1, no complaints reached the ears of Treasurer Merchant during the two weeks thereafter. Meanwhile, the Club agreed to a three-year labor contract with Local 6, and the treasurer observed that the November financial results reflected the retroactive effect of wage increases. On the plus side, the Club, with six courts now for squash racquets and two for squash tennis, all air-conditioned, plus seven new showers, could boast the finest squash facilities of any university club in the city.

As 1970 ended, the clubhouse and its various amenities were all in good condition, but for reasons no doubt rooted in the Zeitgeist fewer members, particularly younger ones, were using it and them. And more were resigning or being dropped for nonpayment than were joining or being reinstated.

On January 9, 1971, word came that the Harvard Corporation had picked Law School Dean Derek C. Bok L'54 as president of the University, and three days later that the Overseers had approved its choice. On the twenty-first, Harvard Hall throbbed to an ear-splitting "rock festival." The next evening, at the 1971 annual meeting, Albert H. Gordon was elected president and Roswell B. Perkins vice-president, while Secretary Heller and Treasurer Merchant were reelected. That

Derek C. Bok

evening marked honorary member Nathan Pusey's last appearance at the Club as president of Harvard, and from the size of the crowd and the warmth of its reception it would have been hard for an onlooker to imagine that anyone there could ever have criticized his handling of the student uprising almost two years before.

The Board's March meeting was interrupted, agreeably, by a visit from President-designate Bok; after a few minutes of introductions, congratulations and expressions of goodwill, Bok left and deliberations resumed. Membership Chairman Gibson asked whether, in view of the awkward situation his colleagues and the Admissions Committeemen had found themselves in the previous May regarding the admission of women to the Club, it might not be the better part of valor to skip the visit to Cambridge this year. The Board agreed that it would.

In mid-April, after the Easter spectacular, with its hunt for 1,500 colored eggs, the Club put on two memorable evenings. On the fourteenth no fewer than 600 people swarmed into Harvard Hall to audit and take part in a free-form "conversation" with Governor Nelson Rockefeller and his wife, "Happy." And on the seventeenth the Hasty Pudding Club-Institute of 1770 sponsored a gala dinner to celebrate its bicentenary. About 250 members (members as well, presumably, of the Pudding) came. In that month, too, a friendly and unmistakably Irish face appeared behind the cigar stand counter: that of Niall McGovern.

On April 15, Archer W. Trench '37 proposed the creation of a permanent committee to inspect the clubhouse at regular intervals and visit other clubs, then to make recommendations to the House Committee, the manager and the Board: at President Gordon's suggestion, the Board thereupon called into existence a standing Inspection Committee, with John P. Horgan, Jr. B'49 as chairman and Trench vice-chairman. Gordon then revealed that at his request retired banker Donald F. Bush, his classmate and friend of half a century, had undertaken a survey of members' attitudes toward admitting women to the Club. He also noted the discrepancy between the costs of Radcliffe Club membership and ladies' signing privileges, saying he hoped this inequality could and would be corrected.

Meanwhile, sweeping changes were occurring in that sanctum, the Library, which a certain portion of the membership, probably remaining much the same over the decades, continued to regard as the heart and center of the Club, if not its very reason for being. The culling of duplicate books and outdated material begun in 1970 had since proceeded apace, with the discards being sold to dealers or donated to various institutions, and the collection now numbered about 17,000 volumes. For the first time since the 1880s, when Evert Wendell assembled the Club's earliest collection of books, moreover, a procedure had been set up enabling members to take out certain titles for specified periods, and Library Chairman G. Barry McMennamin '45 reported that between 75 and 100 members were borrowing books each month.

When, after the summer lull, the Board reconvened on September 19, President Gordon revealed that he had met with some women graduates of the Business School to discuss making membership sex-neutral, and would be meeting with them again. That evening, a dinner for President-elect Bok drew more than 500 members and guests, eager to see and hear the first head of Harvard since the seventeenth century who had not graduated from the College. He made an excellent impression with a frank and clear exposition of the College's and the University's main concerns.

The Club's main concerns around then certainly included the precipitous drop in applications. Like their counterparts in similar all-male social organizations, the Club's governors were aware that to many well-educated young Americans—"turned off," in the parlance of the time, by the Vietnam War, by the supposedly corrupting values of Wall Street, and by the racism and sexism that men's clubs were presumed to exemplify—the Club was just another temple of the despised Establishment. How to soften this harsh judgment? Letting in women should help, but much would depend, too, on the actions of the United States government with regard to Southeast Asia.

Meanwhile, declining membership caused rising losses. That fall, the Board approved a 15 percent increase in the dues and Treasurer Merchant's proposal to extend the Club's mortgage and increase it to $900,000. And House Committee Chairman Donald F. Bush launched an effort to reduce the staff, largely through attrition, by as many as eighteen persons over the next few months.

In December, the Board debated, hotly and at length, extending full membership to women; at last Vice-President Perkins offered a resolution, which was unanimously adopted, calling on the Board to consider at its February 1972 meeting "such changes in the bylaws as may be necessary or desirable to permit women to become members of the Club." President Gordon then announced that Stuart Scott, Jr., was resigning as chairman of the Scholarships Committee. In eleven years heading this body Scott had raised well over a third of a million dollars, helping to send hundreds of promising young scholars to Harvard.

Since President Bok's visit the Activities Committee and the University Relations Committee had produced some notable evenings, including talks by Professor David Riesman '31 L'34 of *Lonely Crowd* fame and Professor Clifford Charles Lamberg-Karlovsky, archaeologist, on diggings in Iran, as well as "conversations" with Ambassador to the United Nations George H. W. Bush and New York Senator James L. Buckley.

On January 7, 1972, in line with the resolution adopted three weeks earlier, Vice-President Perkins wrote all resident and life members outlining the Board's plan to hold an open meeting in Harvard Hall on the twenty-seventh for the purpose of hearing their views about admitting qualified women. Two nights prior to that date, women were present, for the first time, at the annual meeting, which saw the reelection of all the officers except Secretary Heller, whose place was taken by fellow lawyer George P. Kramer.

Although thousands of people had been notified of the open meeting, only about fifty showed up in Harvard Hall at the appointed hour, including the Club officers and members of the Board as well as regular members, holders of signing privileges and even a few nonmembers. Polled, this minuscule sample voted 2–1 in favor of admitting women. Some no-show members complained of not having had sufficient notice of the meeting, but they and quite a few others committed their thoughts and feelings to paper: of 225 communications on this matter received at the Club by February 17, when the Board next met, 162 favored admitting women, 61 were opposed and 2 reflected indecision. Reading portions of these letters out loud, President Gordon observed that two potential consequences of letting in women seemed to cause widespread discomfiture: the prospects of overcrowding in the Main Dining Room at lunchtime and of women turning up in what had always been exclusively a men's bar. Numerous letter writers urged that the decision on the vitally important matter of admitting women be made by the full membership.

The ensuing discussion suggested, in its scattershot character, that the issue of admitting women to the Club, seemingly so simple, was in reality hedged about by complications.

• President Gordon believed that prevailing sentiment within the Club favored keeping women out of the Bar and the athletic facilities. He predicted (quite accurately, as it would turn out) that no more than fifteen or twenty women would apply for membership in the first year they were eligible for it.

• Treasurer Merchant felt that no restrictions on membership, as exemplified by signing privileges, were possible, and that the call now was for full equality in membership.

• Board member Nicholas Benton '51 favored polling the members on the issue, adding that any covering letter should be strictly impartial, containing no hint of the Board's sentiments.

• Archer Trench felt that, on the contrary, written communications to the members should include all significant details, such as what the prevailing attitude was to be with regard to signing privileges.

• Peter Heller applauded the idea of a letter to the members but asserted that the Board should first decide what it really wanted and then exercise leadership by informing the members.

After more discussion, it was

> RESOLVED, that the Board of Managers authorizes the Executive Committee to obtain an expression of opinion from the membership concerning a change in rules so as to admit women to full membership,

whereupon a show of hands on changing "man" to "person" throughout the bylaws revealed a majority in favor.

The Board then decided that the Executive Committee would, under Thayer Drake's direction, prepare another letter to the members, soliciting either their presence at a new special meeting or their proxy votes on the question of admitting women to membership. This done, Drake, on behalf of the House Committee, brought up another matter involving the opposite sex: upon a motion having been made and seconded, it was unanimously

> RESOLVED, that members and spouses may utilize bedrooms at any time during the year, with present restrictions as to usage hereby terminated.

After further discussion it was decided that the letter to voting (resident and life) members would state that the Board believed that "membership should be available to all eligible persons regardless of sex."

At about this time, Irene Van Fossen retired as a full-time employee. She would continue, however, to edit the *Bulletin*, holding the honorific title of Club historian and archivist.

Reporting in April that the Admissions Committee had interviewed only 244 candidates over the past twelve months, the worst showing in years, Chairman Wellington A. Newcomb '46 L'53 was eager to resume recruiting in Cambridge, with other recruiters, on May 19. But he wanted guidance: assuming the vote at the special meeting on May 4 opened the Club to women, what should he tell women applicants about the facilities to which they would and would not have access? The minutes record no answer to Newcomb's question, but President Gordon noted, apropos of the upcoming vote, that a preliminary count of proxies indicated that members favored admitting women by almost exactly two to one.

On April 23 the Club's first fully automatic elevator began operating. Ten days later, on the eve of the long-awaited special meeting, four women graduates of the University lodged a complaint against the Club in the District Court for the Southern District of New York. Their suit was in the nature of a class action, each of the plaintiffs representing a class allegedly aggrieved by the Club's denial of full membership to women. Cited as defendants were the Club itself, President Gordon, the Board of Managers and various liquor companies, the suit maintaining in essence that women, through being denied full membership, were thereby being denied the right to equal protection of the laws, and that the state, by granting the Club a license to serve liquor, was abetting this discrimination.

To most of the members who came to it, the special meeting in Harvard Hall late the next afternoon was a frustrating experience, not because of the lawsuit, of which many were as yet unaware, but because the wishes of the majority of them were denied, and by a tantalizingly small margin, the resolution to admit women failing by a mere 18 votes to obtain the required two-thirds of the approximately 2,500 cast. Some newspapers ignored the landslide endorsement of female equality by Harvard alumni to feature the old guard's success in blocking change, portraying the members as stick-in-the-mud fuddy-duddies bent on preserving the status quo. While this characterization was clearly unfair, the result of the vote was the same as if it had not been, and reaction was

*The New York Times*, May 5, 1972. Copyright © 1972 by The New York Times Company. Reproduced by permission.

swift. Three members resigned, and three more threatened to. The Associated Harvard Alumni decried the Club's vote, as did a number of Harvard deans. And Eleanor Holmes Norton, executive assistant to the mayor and chairman of the city's Human Relations Commission, sent the Club a frosty letter warning of a possible lawsuit for discrimination.

Asked to comment, the Club's counsel, Francis Goodhue, advised first answering Mrs. Norton's letter, whereupon the Board authorized him to assure her that it would resubmit to the members "at an appropriate time" the amendment providing for the admission of women, together with the Board's strong recommendation that they approve it. The Board then granted President Gordon discretionary power to take whatever steps might be required between meetings to further this policy. As to the four women graduates' lawsuit, Goodhue deemed it advisable to seek an accommodation with the plaintiffs rather than enter into litigation that could prove both extensive and expensive.

President Gordon suggested that during the coming summer the House, Library and Athletics Committees conduct a feasibility study of practical problems the Club would face with the admission of women. And he asked Treasurer Merchant to look into, first, the costs involved and the projected gains and losses that would result from admitting women, and, second, possible changes in the existing system of signing privileges.

On the eve of the recruiters' trip to Cambridge, the Board advised the new Admissions chairman, Kelso F. Sutton '61, to have his colleagues hand young women who wanted to join the Club applications for signing privileges, telling them that these forms would be treated as applications for full membership if and when the relevant amendment to the bylaws was adopted. Membership Chairman Gibson declared that his committee would recommend that graduates of the Business School's Advanced Management Program and Program for Management Development be considered eligible for membership. The ensuing discussion brought to the surface profound misgivings about possibly weakening the Club's ties of loyalty to Harvard by admitting men who had spent only a few months in Cambridge (or Boston) improving their business skills. And yet the Club did badly need new members. . . .

In Cambridge, to their surprise, Chairmen Sutton and Gibson encountered no backlash whatever from the recent—and well-publicized—vote at the Club denying women full membership. The recruiters signed up 97 new members. But at the end of fiscal 1972, the Club had 7,234 members, 214 fewer than on June 30, 1971.

Like other Club presidents, Gordon used the Board's annual reports as a medium through which to set forth and explain policies to members. In the 1972 report he listed three aims the Board was pursuing: one, stringently controlling costs without unduly sacrificing services and amenities; two, broadening the membership base, with emphasis on full membership for women in the near future; and three, refinancing the mortgage to meet the Club's cash needs. Then he came to the subject that would constitute the central theme of his remarkable presidency:

> Since 1962 the mortgage debt of the Club has increased from $350,000 to $825,000 and annual interest charges from $19,250 to $57,000. It is imperative that the debt be reduced.

On the burning issue of the moment, the president stated that

> We have been moving toward full women's membership for the last three years. Women now have access to all but a few of the facilities of the Club, notably the steam bath and the men's bar. This evolution, too fast for some, has not been fast enough for others.

In the course of that summer, President Gordon met with two of the plaintiffs in the pending lawsuit, and in September he proposed going back to the members early next year for another vote on admitting women. The Board agreed. Gordon pronounced the experiment of letting women lunch in the Main Dining Room a great success, whereupon Chairman Bush, for the House Committee, recommended that women continue to lunch there and on the balcony, but not in the Grill Room. Treasurer Merchant reported that the Club now had just 192 employees, 18 fewer than at the start of the calendar year, but added that contractual arrangements were nevertheless expected to raise the Club's labor costs by 8 percent. And Chairman Bush announced that a dinner one week thereafter to Professor John Kenneth Galbraith was fully subscribed. (The witty, crowd-pleasing economist was to speak on the economic policies espoused by Senator George McGovern of South Dakota, the Democratic candidate for president.)

In October, to Chairman Bush's satisfaction, the second automatic passenger elevator went on line.

For weeks now, Bush, on his own initiative but with the knowledge and approval of President Gordon, had, as the head of an informal committee, sought out certain affluent members to enlist their help in reducing the Club's swollen mortgage debt. On October 19, the president informed the Board that Bush had already raised $30,000 in capital funds, adding that he, Bush, and Treasurer Merchant would be conferring on ways to increase the Club's revenues through smaller but more numerous voluntary contributions.

The Board finally agreed to make graduates of the Business School's advanced management and management development programs eligible for membership, and to enlarge the Admissions Committee from twenty-one members to twenty-four, thereby enabling it to include three nonresident Cambridge members who could facilitate the admission to the Club of faculty members and of students graduating from the College or graduate schools.

On October 31, Republican Senator Jacob Javits of New York visited the Club to make "The Case for the Republicans," and just a week later, to the satisfaction of the Club's largely Republican membership, President Nixon was reelected by a landslide over Senator McGovern.

With the provisions of a new labor contract adding $7,000 a month to the Club's operating costs, Treasurer Merchant felt another dues increase would have to be expected soon, but on November 16 he said he would seek a voluntary contribution. In an explanatory letter he would mail out to members with their statements, he would stress that every penny thus collected would go to retiring the mortgage.

In December, Merchant revealed that the staff was now down to 189, and that overtime pay had been drastically curtailed. Chairman Bush reported that his committee had obtained $32,000 in cash and $15,000 in pledges toward reducing the debt, inspiring spontaneous applause. As for the proxy voting on admitting women, President Gordon said it was proceeding satisfactorily, and that he was looking forward to a positive decision on the matter in three weeks.

While the president's easy confidence would prove to be well placed, the special meeting on January 11, 1973, was not without a modicum of drama. Motions were made to change "man" to "person" throughout the bylaws and to affirm that masculine pronouns therein, and in the various rules, were to be construed as including their feminine equivalents; but then member Edmund F. Stefanson B'39 proposed tabling both resolutions until feasibility studies could determine the costs involved in admitting women. Stefanson's motion was duly seconded, but in the dry language of the minutes it "did not carry." Finally, the original motions were put to a vote, whereupon the Harvard Club of New York City, the last remaining all-male bastion among the city's university clubs, opted to admit women by a lopsided majority of 2,067 to 695—not just two to one but very nearly three to one.

That same day and four days later, in Washington, five of seven men who were being tried for breaking into the Democratic National Committee's headquarters in the Watergate office complex the previous June, a crime a Nixon administration spokesman dismissed as a "third-rate burglary" and disclaimed all knowledge of, pleaded guilty. The other two would be convicted January 30. So began the extraordinary national drama and trauma called Watergate, which would preoccupy the country, and occasion endless talk at the Club, over the next two years.

At the annual meeting on January 19, 1973, the Club's four officers were continued in office for another year.

A week after this, Harvard Hall was once again transformed into a theater for the presentation of *Nash at Nine*, a revue based on humorous verses by the late Ogden Nash (who had died in 1971), probably America's best-loved twentieth-century poet and long a member of the Club. This production, scheduled to open soon on Broadway, where it would enjoy a respectable run, proved a smash hit, drawing a capacity crowd of around 600 and helping to bolster the Club's finances.

On January 27, in Paris, a cease-fire agreement was at long last signed by representatives of the belligerents in Vietnam, officially ending the longest and most divisive foreign war in America's history. In Washington, Secretary of Defense Melvin Laird announced the end of the military draft. As it was Saturday, few members were at the clubhouse, but wherever they were, they shared with practically all other Americans feelings of profound relief.

When, around 5 P.M. on February 13, a Tuesday, seventeen members of the Admissions Committee filed into the Mahogany Room, they were, of course, perfectly aware that the acts they were about to carry out were, in terms of the Club's history, momentous. Considering, in turn, the cases of thirty-seven candidates, they held over fourteen of them (mainly so that these individuals could meet more committee members) and elected seventeen to resident membership plus six to nonresident. Five of the former group were women.

The first woman elected to the Club was Heidi Nitze Dv'62, a daughter of Paul H. Nitze '28, a longtime policy adviser to American presidents. The next four were all, as it happened, recent MBAs: Ellen R. Marram and Mary C. Metzger (Class of 1970) and Patricia C. Barron and Beverly Brandt (Class of 1972).

But the committeemen had not yet completed their historic labors: before adjourning, they voted to recommend for election by the Board three graduates of the Business School's advanced management program: Kenneth H. Straus AMP '57, Richard S. Creedon AMP '70 K'74 and Jack Sacks AMP '72.

Two nights later, the Board duly acknowledged the admission of the Club's first women members and duly elected its first AMP graduate members. It also admitted President Jerome Wiesner of M.I.T. as a special member.

At the Board's March meeting, Treasurer Merchant revealed that the Club would accept ITT's bid of $69,500 to revamp its telephone service and that the mortgage had been reduced by $82,500 in large and small contributions. Chairman Bush announced that the Club would shortly welcome a new barber who for ten years had enjoyed an excellent reputation at the Columbia Club, which was about to close, its governors having put their clubhouse up for sale.

At its April meeting, the Board clarified By-Law XV (Dues) in such a way that all dues categories were clearly understood to be based on the number of years a member had been out of the college from which he or she had received an undergraduate degree, not the number of years out of Harvard University. And President Gordon, with evident relish, announced that the last remaining lawsuit over the status of women in the

Club had been terminated. Before they withdrew their action, he said, the plaintiffs had been assured that women requesting drinks at the bar would be served.

Once in a great while, the ever-active Activities Committee miscalculated: thus on April 16, it carefully limited an "oyster festival" (thirty dollars a head, plus service charge and tax) to just sixty participants . . . and forty came. Six days later, however, the Easter spectacular (a buffet, egg hunt, and chimpanzee-and-puppets show) drew a squealing, shrieking mass of happy celebrants. And on April 25, the opportunity to converse on lunar matters with astronaut Harrison Schmitt PhD '64, the first civilian, scientist and Harvard man to walk on the moon, attracted hundreds of enthusiastic earthlings to his illustrated talk.

Five days later, top Nixon aides H. R. Haldeman, John D. Ehrlichman and Attorney General Richard Kleindienst resigned amid charges of White House efforts to obstruct justice in the Watergate case. The President requested and received the resignation of counsel John Dean. To replace Richard Kleindienst as attorney general and to head the Watergate investigation, President Nixon named a member of the Club, Secretary of Defense Elliot Richardson.

In May, President Gordon informed the Board that Manager Clyde Harris was retiring, and that Frederick Shaner, Cornell University School of Hotel Administration '50, would take over from Harris July 1. And Treasurer Merchant expressed concern about a sudden rash of resignations, some unquestionably prompted by the admission of women.

Finally, Art Chairman Bailey, reporting the receipt from the University of a portrait photograph of President Bok, asserted that in his opinion the Club's appearance would benefit from the presence of contemporary artworks on its walls. From the resounding silence that greeted this remark and others he had made earlier to the same effect, it would seem that Bailey was alone, or nearly so, in his opinion.

When, on September 26, the Board reconvened, Chairman Bush had much to report. The new ITT telephone equipment was in operation. Through the generosity of George A. von Peterffy B'57, chrysanthemums had been planted in the 44th Street window boxes. And complaints were continuing to be heard about members who turned up at the Club sans jacket, tie or even shoes. (The impeccably turned out Counsel Goodhue offered to donate a pair of socks "as an alleviative measure.")

The most disturbing news the chairman had to impart in the September 26 Board meeting was that the Naval Academy had finally claimed a collection of naval prints bequeathed to it many years before by the late Beverley R. Robinson, prints that since well before their donor's death had decorated various corridors, public rooms and other spaces throughout the clubhouse. Parting with them would be bad enough, but a check of the collection uncovered the embarrassing fact that 15 of the 113 prints were missing. In the course of the following weeks two of these were located, but the search for the rest would go on.

The following month, the arrival of which Miss Van Fossen hailed in the *Bulletin* with a prose poem titled "October Harmonies," the world suddenly seemed to go haywire. On the sixth—Yom Kippur, the Jewish high holy Day of Atonement—Syria, Egypt and Jordan attacked Israel as they had in 1967; and while Israeli forces soon sent the attackers reeling back, the Arab states, seeking to weaken American support of their common enemy, would embargo oil shipments to the United States, effectively assuring this country growing shortages of that indispensable commodity, accompanied by skyrocketing prices and lengthening lines at the gas pump. On the tenth, with Arab-Israeli hostilities in full cry, Vice President Spiro T. Agnew resigned, pleading no contest to charges of tax evasion, and on the twelfth, Michigan Congressman Gerald R. Ford was sworn in as his successor. And on the twentieth, finally, members of the Club who might understandably have thought they had seen everything by now, were stunned, on returning home from a dinner party or a show and switching on the television news, to learn of the latest twist in the Watergate saga: President Nixon had summarily fired Archibald Cox, the special prosecutor investigating the scandal, and his deputy, William D. Ruckelshaus, because Cox had threatened to secure a judicial ruling that the President was violating a court order to turn over crucial evidence—tapes—to Judge John J. Sirica. Cox's former law student and present superior, Attorney General Richardson, had then resigned. This "Saturday Night Massacre" had implications for the Club, not simply because Richardson was a Club member, but, more significantly, because

Cox, as a longtime professor at the Law School, had taught scores, possibly hundreds, of the Club's very many lawyer members.

Two days before all this Chairman Bush had informed the Board that in order to replace on clubhouse walls at least some of the prints that would be going to Annapolis, he had arranged to borrow thirty-five prints on naval themes from the New-York Historical Society. Then he ventured a bold suggestion: why not sell a few of the Club's better paintings and apply the proceeds to reducing the mortgage? This time, it seemed, the House Committee's universally liked and respected chairman had gone too far. Without debate, his colleagues unanimously voted down his proposal.

Secretary Kramer proposed Mrs. Matina Horner, president of Radcliffe, for honorary membership, and the Board forthwith elected her.

Although no president of the Club since Langdon P. Marvin (1932–36) had served longer than three years, the previous fall's nominating committee had not hesitated to offer Albert Gordon a fourth year in office. Nor had Gordon hesitated to accept the burden. As it had during the Great Depression, the Club found itself led, during a trying time, by an able and resourceful leader, and gladly followed his lead. Thus on January 31, 1974, Gordon was reelected, along with his three fellow officers.

Two weeks later, the Admissions Committee welcomed two women to its ranks, Margaret Heimann R'52 and Heidi Nitze. And just days after the Blue Hill Troupe presented *Trial by Jury* in Harvard Hall, an eight-column headline in the *New York Times* proclaimed that a federal grand jury in Washington had indicted seven Nixon aides, including H. R. Haldeman, John Ehrlichman and former Attorney General John Mitchell, on charges of covering up the Watergate scandal.

In the March *Bulletin*, an aggrieved member accused certain parties in the Club of another crime.

> I will come right out with it. There is something wrong with the Club's martinis—always has been. Even with the most mediocre ingredients, it is almost impossible to make a bad martini at any ratio of gin to vermouth of 6-to-1 or upwards—unless the gin is of a highly aromatic variety and the vermouth is poured from an old tennis shoe—but the Club succeeds. Please ask the Martini Committee to study this matter.
>
> E.C.K. Read '40

Having, in recent years, greatly expanded the range of the diversions available to members, Activities Chairman John H. Limpert '55 this season introduced yet another innovation, the post-dinner cultural foray by bus. The first such foray the previous fall, attracting 300, had been "an evening at the Brooklyn Museum with Akhenaton and Nefertiti," and at 7:30 P.M. on March 12, almost as many members and guests, having dined at the Club, headed uptown in buses to the Metropolitan Museum to feast their eyes on "Masterpieces of Tapestry," billed as "the most important show of medieval tapestries ever assembled."

At the Board's March meeting, Treasurer Merchant announced the revival of an old tradition: each chair in the Mahogany Room, he pointed out, now bore a plaque with the name of a Board member, who could purchase the chair at the close of his (or her) term. Vice-President Perkins reported telling Radcliffe Club President Eleanor L. Zuckerman '53 MAT'55 that the Club's governors increasingly felt that her group should only be allowed to use the Club on payment of comparable dues. And President Gordon revealed that the mortgage was down to $560,000.

Following "A Conversation with [novelist] John Updike '54" in April, Chairman Bush proposed setting up a reciprocal arrangement with the New Club of Edinburgh. (The Club already had such an arrangement in force with the Oxford and Cambridge Club in London.) But the matter of the missing naval prints remained, in Bush's word, "vexatious": it now appeared that the Robinson collection had numbered 119 prints, of which 19 could not be found, and that the Naval Academy wanted $7,250 in compensation.

Early in May, the annual recruiting trip to Cambridge proved successful, with committeemen interviewing 186 students and faculty members. This turnabout no doubt reflected a lessening of young people's hostility toward their elders occasioned by the country's withdrawal from the conflict in Southeast Asia and by the ending of the military draft. But President Richard Nixon, the chief executive who brought about these welcome changes—finally—derived little political benefit from them: on May 9, indeed, the House Judiciary Committee opened impeachment hearings against him.

On Saturday, May 25, the *Times* carried a depressing news story about a longtime neighbor: the Columbia Club, facing an operating loss of $10,000 a month and with liabilities exceeding $800,000, had asked a New York State Supreme Court justice to dissolve its operation. (One year later, the Reverend Sun Myung Moon's Unification Church would purchase the former Columbia Club building, at 4 West 43rd Street, as its national headquarters.)

If the Club's racquet wielders had again triumphed with a consistency become almost boring (its Team A dominant citywide, Victor Niederhoffer once more national champion and Charles W. Ufford, Jr., national veterans titleholder), they could still surprise: that year, for the first time in years, the squash department operated at a profit. Meanwhile, the Club's chess team, sparked by its best player, writer Cleveland Amory, enjoyed a memorable season, defeating all local metropolitan area comers only to succumb to a team representing the United Nations.

At the Board's June meeting, Secretary Kramer moved that life membership be conferred on President Gordon, and the motion was approved by acclamation. Treasurer Merchant reported that the staff was down to 176. Then the president called on Osgood Nichols '32 to summarize certain conversations the two men had had. Nichols suggested that his hearers consider, over the summer, establishing a committee on long-range planning goals for the Club. Serious thought should be given, he said, to what form the Club should take in coming decades. The new committee ought, he felt, to include a goodly representation of younger members.

Admissions Chairman Tweed Roosevelt '64 was understandably pleased to report that his committee had, just hours earlier, elected 221 new members, including 24 women. Yet membership was still declining, and the slow rate at which women were applying was, to many, a disappointing surprise. (Sixteen months after the first women were admitted, the Club's female membership, including Radcliffe President Horner, was only sixty. About ten times that many spouses of members held signing privileges—including, now, two husbands.) All the same, there was, as President Gordon pointed out, cause for satisfaction in the Club's greatly improved financial health. For a second year, it had operated at a profit—a minuscule one, to be sure, of just $16,700 on revenues of $1,830,000—but infinitely preferable to 1972's deficit.

Whether or not the Club's governors pondered the Club's future that summer, there can be little doubt that many, if not most, members spent much of that season avidly following developments in Washington culminating in President Nixon's resignation, and, in September, President Ford's blanket pardoning of him.

At summer's end, Chairman Bush announced that a reciprocal arrangement had been arrived at with a third foreign club, the University Club of Montreal, which would, like the New Club of Edinburgh and the Oxford and Cambridge Club of London, guarantee its members' accounts here. Discussions were still going on with federal officials about the missing naval prints. And the employee roster stood at 165.

In November, Treasurer Merchant told the Board that another dues increase was needed to keep the Club solvent, to maintain its physical plant and to finance its labor costs. Before long, his hearers agreed on a dues schedule ranging from $70 for a recently graduated resident member to $285 for a resident member nine years out of the College (or a college).

That fall, Jack Limpert, impresario, was active, as ever. On October 17, said the *Bulletin*, he "may have struck a new height" with an evening of wine and cheese tasting presided over by Alexis Bespaloff B'57, author of *The Signet Book of Wine* and *Guide to Inexpensive Wines*. The event, titled "Value and Variety," focused on low- and moderately-priced wines, which may help explain why it drew 325 participants.

But it was on November 20 that Chairman Limpert and his committee truly outdid themselves by presenting, for the first time ever at the Club, an evening of dinner-theater, a form of entertainment dating back to the last century that, having long since fallen into disuse, had lately been revived by certain theater groups and was enjoying a modest vogue. Limpert's choice for a fully costumed production in the Main Dining Room was inspired: it was Victor Herbert's *The Red Mill* (1906), which, with such hit numbers as "In Old New York," "Every Day Is Ladies' Day With Me" and "Because You're You," could probably not have failed to enchant its large and appreciative audience.

In December, Osgood Nichols, recalling the useful precedent of the McKinsey Report of a dozen years before, again urged the formation of a group that could undertake periodic analyses of what and how the Club was doing and, taking the long view, make recommendations to ensure its survival. The Board duly established a long-range planning committee "to study such facets of the Harvard Club operations as may be necessary to develop a five-year plan for the Club." Then, necessarily taking a very short view, Chairman Bush reported startling news: termites had attacked in force in the basement, and strong countermeasures were called for, costing about $8,400. His hearers quickly voted to launch a counteroffensive.

Next, Chairman Bush read a tribute to President Gordon, who was "handing to his successor a vigorous and vastly strengthened institution." The Board members drank to the health of their departing chief and cheered him; then, without dissent, they agreed to honor his wish by changing the name of the annual appeal "To Reduce the Mortgage" to "A Program to Extinguish the Mortgage by 1980."

On New Year's Day, 1975, a few hours before members started arriving in the Grill Room to sample the festive eggnog, former Nixon aides Haldeman and Ehrlichman and former Attorney General John Mitchell were found guilty in Washington of the Watergate cover-up, thus somehow writing finis to that national nightmare.

Three weeks later, Roswell B. Perkins was elected president and Walter N. Rothschild, Jr. '42 vice-president, while Secretary Kramer and Treasurer Merchant were reelected. During and after the ensuing dinner, two old customs were revived. The banquet was accompanied by music— not, as of yore, popular airs and football songs pumped out *con brio* by a brass band, but a selection of chamber music pieces played by young musicians. And at the conclusion of the evening, the members and guests present found themselves, no doubt to their surprise, singing (from a printed program) two full verses of "Fair Harvard"—not all four, to be sure, but twice as many as had been sung on this occasion as far back as any but the oldest among them could remember.

At the sports dinner on February 14, a dramatic moment came when former Congressman Hamilton Fish, at eighty-six the last survivor of Walter Camp's all-time all-American eleven, rose to his imposing height of six-five to compliment Coach Joe Restic and the Crimson team on the latter's recent thrill-packed 21–16 victory over Yale.

President Perkins used his first Board meeting as chief executive, on February 20, to outline three goals he intended to pursue: one, a substantial increase in the membership, looking ultimately to 8,000 members; two, improved communication with the members through the establishment of a committee working solely toward that end; and three, the enhancement of the Club's programs of continuing education. Next, he proposed creating a finance committee, charged with overseeing and periodically reviewing the Club's finances, and a communications committee, which would, as a first step, study the pertinent McKinsey Report recommendations. The Board approved both proposals.

On March 3, the Communications Committee met for the first time. The members, professionals drawn from the fields of publishing, advertising and public relations, talked about needed changes in the *Bulletin*'s content.

As it happened, the current *Bulletin*, for March, carried a notice of a forthcoming one-day symposium, sponsored by the Radcliffe Club, on "Women, Men and Power." For some elderly Club members, some of the listed lectures and workshops ("Sexuality and Power") and speakers' bona fides ("Phyllis Chesler, author of *Women and Madness*") must have made for unnerving reading, but on the ninth the seminar went off without incident, leaving the clubhouse still standing. And four nights later, the Main Dining Room reverberated to the strains of Johann Strauss's *Die Fledermaus*, sung by a costumed cast of eleven, the second half of the Activities Committee's latest felicitous venture, dinner-theater.

If, as the figures indicated, the Club's operating costs had risen steeply in February, they had done so, Treasurer Merchant told the Board on March 20, largely because of two effects of the continuing energy crisis: a doubling of the cost of steam and a 22 percent increase in the cost of electricity. But there was another cause, he said: a big drop in the demand for alcoholic drinks, resulting in a substantial decrease in profits from that source.

While solid-citizen New Yorkers were, presumably for health reasons, reducing their liquor intake or swearing off the stuff altogether, they can hardly have overlooked the temples of carnal pleasure euphemistically known as massage parlors and typically located one flight up from the street that were proliferating throughout the city's business districts. Several such establishments had recently opened for business near the Club—one unacceptably close by at 7 West 44th Street—and Chairman Bush was determined to banish them. As he told the Board, he had sought help toward this end from various good neighbors: the Bank of New York, the Morgan Guaranty Trust Company, the Algonquin Hotel, the City Bar Association and the New York Yacht Club.

Aware that former students at the University's graduate schools, excluding those who had previously attended the College or Radcliffe, now made up 61 percent of living Harvard alumni and alumnae, President Perkins sought to woo these men and women for the Club. He had already sent letters to all nonmember graduates of the Law School, and similar missives would go out shortly to graduates of the Business School and the Graduate School of Education. Nearer home, he had communicated to the Radcliffe Club a plan for a five-year transition, in the course of which, with the gradual elimination of signing privileges, its members would become full members of the Club. As he told the Board, Radcliffe Club members wanted to work with the Schools Committee and the Activities Committee.

Meanwhile, a crisis had erupted in a normally tranquil corner of the clubhouse. On Saturday, April 26, the *New York Times* reported that as of the previous Thursday, "The Harvard Club's eight-to-one martini, a concoction that has befuddled some of the finest minds in the country," had "become a casualty of red ink," with "the bartenders at the U-shaped bar . . . under instruction to rely on jigger glasses instead of their sense of gentlemanly hospitality. The result has been a martini of two parts gin or vodka and one part vermouth," a change that had understandably "caused something of a tempest in a martini glass."

Could a deed of such colossal folly actually have been perpetrated? The "newspaper of record," whose reporter had gathered his facts at the Club bar itself from patrons and bartenders, did not doubt it, and on May 2 it reported that

> Spirits have been restored . . . at the Harvard Club. The 8-to-1 martinis are back. After a flood of protests by Club members and reports that martini sales were at a record low, the Club reversed a policy that sought to weaken martinis in the name of a stronger economy. The bartenders are back to making the drinks with a free hand yesterday.

An article in the June *Bulletin* titled "On Vini (Two-to-One) No Veritas" would call the newspaper's account of the Club's temporary lowering of the ratio of martini ingredients "a tale" based on an "unfounded rumor started from the substitution of a two-ounce jigger for the one-and-a-half ounce jigger previously in use," and would go on to quote some freshly penned lines dropped off at the Club by one Holger Lundbergh of the Century Association:

> How can one act gay and alive
> With smaller quantum of gin than five?
> Much better six, or even seven,
> Or maybe eight (that would be heaven).
> What is this old world coming to
> When Harvard orders one to two
> While Yale and Princeton gaily pour
> Their fine libations one to four?
> Oh, I beseech you, friend of mine,
> Bring on martinis one to nine.

The *Times* gleefully reprinted these lines on June 16, pointing out an incontestable fact: that far from contradicting its earlier account, they confirmed it. Final score: *Times* 1, *Bulletin* 0.

In May, the Board had approved a proposal by President Perkins to create a standing Investment Committee, responsible for the investment and reinvestment of the Club's various funds, and in June, former President Gordon, the chairman and (as yet) only member of the Finance Committee, revealed with evident pleasure that the Club's once-threatening mortgage debt now stood at $360,000, more than 80 percent of the members having responded to the voluntary appeal that year. Chairman Bush, too, had succeeded in collecting funds, those earmarked for refurbishing, exclusive of the income from endowment funds, now totaling $17,000. He asked the Board's approval (which was quickly granted) to install television sets in the bedrooms, the cost to be amortized by raising the nightly rates for the rooms by a dollar. And he reported that a copy of the portrait of President Bok by George Augusta now hanging in the Harvard Club of Boston would cost the Club $6,000. The Board balked at approving this expenditure.

Introduced by President Perkins as chairman of the Communications Committee, Kelso F. Sutton of Time, Inc., reported that his committee was hard at work redesigning the *Bulletin* and mapping out broad changes in its content while preserving the historical flavor with which Miss Van Fossen had imbued it. He recommended that the Board authorize hiring Edward E. White, Jr. '50, a professional editor employed by the New York Public Library, to oversee the preparation of the *Bulletin*, and the Board did so. President Perkins then proposed that Miss Van Fossen be confirmed as the Club's archivist and historian and be asked to begin work, at her own pace, on a history of the Club.

Over the summer, workmen spruced up the third-floor banquet rooms. Around midday on Friday, August 1, however, the Club's peaceful hot-season routine was shattered when the dining room and bar personnel walked off their jobs. They were protesting the dismissal of Pedro Lopez, a head porter who had been with the Club fifteen years, but a *Times* reporter, questioning striking employees in the clubhouse, concluded that their action had deeper roots in grievances against General Manager Shaner, who had dismissed Lopez and who, one bartender complained, "tries to make us do three or four jobs at a time." When a man identifying himself as the manager, presumably Shaner, spotted the reporter, he escorted the latter firmly out onto 44th Street, where the newsman began buttonholing exiting members for comments. "Harvard men, by and large, are very conscious of working conditions and elements of fairness," one lawyer told him, adding that he had studied labor law with Archibald Cox. Another member blamed "hard-nosed" management for the disruption of service: "[Shaner is] trying to run a private club like a hotel, without a heart," he said. (He was also, it should in fairness be added, trying to run the Club with a work force, now numbering 159, that had been reduced by a full quarter.)

Although the *Times* would carry no more news of this strike, the newspaper's seeming preoccupation at this time with teasing the Club would result in one more such item, a brief report on August 16 to the effect that the distinguished economist and sociologist Gunnar Myrdal LLD (hon.) '38, a 1974 Nobel laureate in economics and President Bok's father-in-law, had been posted at the Club and his privileges suspended for nonpayment of charges totaling $163.50.

When, on September 18, the Board reassembled in the Mahogany

Room, former President Pratt unveiled an oil painting of former President Gordon. It was no ordinary likeness. Looking for something different from the competent but rather staid portraits in the Club's collection, Gordon had chosen, to memorialize him on canvas, Fairfield Porter '28, a critically acclaimed landscapist who had rarely attempted portraiture. In one sense, Gordon had chosen well, for as his colleagues agreed, the rather odd-looking individual shown seated in a library chair in no way resembled any of the earlier Club presidents whose images were on view. But neither, in the opinion, tactfully unspoken, of several of the picture's initial viewers, did it much resemble their friend, the sitter.

Gordon himself, however, pronounced himself pleased with Porter's handiwork—which indeed has since come, over time, to appear somewhat more appealing than it first did to certain beholders.

Announcing that the first issue of the new *Bulletin* would be out in October, editor Edward E. White, Jr., described the publication's new nine-by-six-inch format, designed by Don Page GSD'48. The *Bulletin* would continue to appear monthly except during the summer, White said, but would contain many more photographs, drawings and other design elements. Dropping Miss Van Fossen's practice of printing tags of verse and presenting all Club news as filtered through the sensibility of a single feminine observer, the new editor would seek the help of committee chairmen and others in promoting upcoming events and reporting past ones in a variety of voices. Most important of all, the *Bulletin* would, White hoped, function as a conduit by means of which the Club's governors and salaried managers could communicate with the members on important matters.

In October, the strike was amicably settled, and the union's business agent, the source of much friction in the past, was replaced. At the Board meeting on the sixteenth, Membership Chairman McMennamin praised the new *Bulletin*, saying copies of it would be sent to each of the more than 10,000 men and women in the metropolitan region who had received a membership solicitation letter from him during the previous year. And President Perkins broached a subject close to his heart. He called on his colleagues to think about setting up a continuing program of adult education, saying he hoped the Club might become "a cultural center of sorts."

In November, Treasurer Merchant reported an unexpected upturn in the Club's fortunes: for the first time in recent memory the Food and Beverage Department had, in October, shown a profit. This was largely due, it seemed, to a 60 percent jump in banquet business, which in turn was presumably not unconnected with the face-lifts given the banquet rooms the previous summer. Heartened, the Board decided to retain the present dues schedule unchanged through 1976.

Donald Bush was slated to retire in January from both the Board and the chairmanship of the House Committee, and at his colleagues' final meeting of 1975 they paid him due tribute and drank his health. As President Perkins had stated in the last annual report, Bush had "written a new record of distinguished and loyal service to the Club."

Although eggnog had been served as usual in the Grill Room on Christmas Day afternoon, there was none to be had there on January 1, 1976. By fiat, presumably, of the House Committee, the Club's long-standing custom of greeting the new year with an open house at which the traditional holiday libation was ladled out gratis to all comers was discontinued. Instead, members and guests could (for six dollars) partake of a brunch that included a Bloody Mary or a screwdriver.

If, in the spirit of the season, the Club's governors paused to take stock and look ahead, they must surely have felt encouraged. The punishing inflation of 1973–75 had abated somewhat, and their decision not to raise the dues—a gamble, considering that no one could know whether prices would hold—had unquestionably kept hundreds of members from resigning in the last weeks of 1975. Indeed, the Club's membership was, for the first time since 1971, growing. The clubhouse was in tolerably good shape, and while losses from food sales continued heavy and beverage sales were still declining, the demand for bedrooms was up. Levels of membership activity, interest and involvement likewise remained high: the Activities Committee, expanded to twelve members in various sub-committees (theater, music/concerts, films, Harvard football films, lectures/conversations, wine-tasting and publicity), would present no fewer than forty-five events during the September-to-June season, and even the Library Committee, never before known to venture outside its preserve, was, under Chairman A. Kip Livingston '37, planning to mount a series of cultural programs. The University Relations Committee, chaired by Gerard Weinstock '39 L'42, had sponsored or scheduled a dozen appearances by members of the faculty. Meanwhile, an impressively large portion of the members, about four-fifths, was continuing to support with their contributions "A Program to Extinguish the Mortgage by 1980."

A well-informed member assessing the situation at 27 West 44th Street might have concluded, altogether, that the lean years were over and the future bright. In fact, they were, and it was, the Club's fortunes being destined to improve steadily, with only occasional setbacks, throughout the remainder of the Seventies.

First woman member Heidi Nitze and first woman Manager Karen Loud

# 18

# OUT OF DEBT
# AND GROWING
# (1976–1980)

Following the reelection of all four officers on January 15, 1976, Ambassador to the United Nations and former professor at the John F. Kennedy School of Government Daniel Patrick Moynihan spoke about officially silenced political prisoners in Communist East Europe and Asia, saying that "We must learn to listen to whispers." Then President Perkins, citing a record "unparalleled in its dedication and effectiveness," hailed the Schools Committee's careful screening and evaluating, year after year, of several hundred applicants to Harvard and Radcliffe, and bestowed on Chairman Robert B. Ross an award for distinguished service to the Club.

During the dinner, pianist Richard Kogan '77 had entertained the company; on the twenty-first, the Blue Hill Troupers sang; on the twenty-seventh and twenty-ninth came the premieres of two series devoted to jazz and chamber music respectively; and on February 14, the Harvard-Radcliffe Collegium Musicum, about to tour England and France under the sponsorship of Presidents Bok and Horner, Leonard Bernstein '39, Nadia Boulanger and others, gave a concert of choral music. As usual, music flourished at the Club. Meanwhile, Travel Chairman Paul C. Sheeline '43 L'48 sought, in consultation with the Raymond & Whitcomb Agency, to put together inexpensive travel packages of relatively brief duration that younger members could afford. And Vice-President Rothschild continued, at President Perkins's request, to seek a replacement for General Manager Shaner, who had departed some weeks earlier, leaving Comptroller Robert FitzGibbon in charge.

Late in February, the Library Committee presented a program of poetry unlike any the Club had ever seen—or heard. It began at 5:30 in the Cambridge Lounge with a talk by poet Stratis Haviaras, curator of the Woodberry Poetry Room and the Farnsworth Collection in the Lamont Library, who described the 5,000-plus recordings of poems available to Harvard students and recounted the history of the Poetry Room and its collections. After a break for cocktails and dinner, Professor Haviaras spoke in Harvard Hall about various devices used to record speech, beginning with Thomas Edison's cylindrical phonograph, and then played some recordings. Not without awe, his audience heard Alfred, Lord Tennyson, recorded in 1888, read an excerpt from his "Charge of the Light Brigade," Ezra Pound recite a dramatic sestina to a kettledrum accompaniment and T. S. Eliot intone "Gerontion" in a sepulchral voice, in a recording he made on a visit to his alma mater in 1930. Among other poets heard were Robert Frost, William Carlos Williams, Dylan Thomas and Marianne Moore.

Poetry not being everyone's cup of tea, the professor's audience of 130 was relatively small, but it was highly enthusiastic. And Chairman Livingston was well content. That "round table," he said, was the first of several with a two-session format that would bring key members of the Harvard Library community to the Club.

On March 9, some fifteen months after the Board summoned it into being, the Long-Range Planning Committee met for the first time. Chairman Alonzo L. McDonald, Jr. B'56, managing director of McKinsey & Company, led his colleagues (who included one woman, Karen A. G. Loud R'57) in exploring such questions as where the Club would fit into the city's demographic and social structure fifteen years from then, whether it depended overmuch on members' dues to make up the deficit in food service and what its principal attractions were to its members. In effect, the discussants were formulating questions for a new questionnaire soon to be compiled and sent out to the membership.

One week later, to mark the bicentennial of American independence, the University Relations Committee welcomed Professor of American

Literature and master of Eliot House Alan E. Heimert '49 PhD'60 to talk about Harvard's role in the American Revolution. On March 22 the Library Committee presented a second round table, on the theater, involving representatives of Broadway, Off Broadway and Off Off Broadway. Days after this, the Pudding's 128th annual production, *Tots in Tinseltown*, came to New York. And on April 1 Steuben Glass presented in its showroom, a dozen blocks uptown on Fifth Avenue, a preview for Club members only of Harvard's celebrated glass flowers.

Opening a Board meeting on April 15, President Perkins paid tribute to former President Edward Streeter, who had died on the fifth; then Chairman McDonald delivered the Long-Range Planning Committee's first interim report. His group's primary goals, he said, were to reduce the operating deficit through vigorous financial management and to increase the membership while matching up new members with activities of particular interest to them. Speaking for the search committee he headed, Vice-President Rothschild reported the selection of a new general manager. His name was John Charles Kekllas, and his qualifications seemed impressive: a past president of the Food and Beverage Managers of New York, he had been general manager and food and beverage manager for the city's Holiday Inn Coliseum, and had had experience with the Hotel Manhattan, the Sheraton Motor Inn and the Park Sheraton Hotel.

Finally, former President Gordon spoke briefly, mentioning in passing the construction of new athletic facilities on Soldiers Field, including the field house that would bear his name.

Further to Travel Chairman Sheeline's efforts, the May *Bulletin* announced an upcoming ten-day cruise in the Bahamas, in thirty-foot sloops, for would-be and novice sailors and their spouses, at the relatively affordable all-in price of $540 a head. Another article reported that all six winners of the recently announced National Book Awards, the country's most prestigious annual literary prizes, were Harvard graduates: in poetry, John Ashbery '49 for *Self-Portrait in a Convex Mirror*; in history and biography, David Brion Davis AM'53 PhD'56 for *The Problem of Slavery in the Age of Revolution: 1770–1823*; in fiction, William Gaddis for his novel *JR*; in children's literature, Walter D. Edmonds '26 LTD (hon.) '52 for *Bert Breen's Barn*; in the arts and letters category, Paul

Fussell, Jr. AM'49 PhD'52 for *The Great War and Modern Memory*; and in contemporary affairs, Club member Michael J. Arlen '52 for *Passage to Ararat.*

In May, President Perkins reported that the questionnaire about members' attitudes and interests had elicited a better-than-expected response, and noted the appointment of a subcommittee to inspect the Hotel Webster, upon which, over the years, a number of past presidents had cast curious and occasionally covetous eyes. Secretary Kramer would report simply that the hotel contained 110 rooms, was for sale or long-term lease and carried a mortgage of $400,000.

Prior to its and the Admissions Committee's recent Cambridge trip, the Membership Committee had written some 3,300 students graduating from the College, from graduate schools and from those special postgraduate courses graduates of which who were eligible for membership; this assiduity paid off, and in June Admissions Chairman Paul E. Konney '66 announced the election of a record-breaking 266 new members. The Club would end the fiscal year with 7,138 members, for an annual gain, the first since 1971, of 151.

Contributions to eliminating the Club's debt had exceeded $107,000, and the mortgage now stood at $245,000. President Perkins called the difference between that figure and the $825,000 of 1972 "a monument to the wisdom of my predecessor, Al Gordon, in setting us on a course of mortgage reduction." Another annual appeal, moreover, had achieved a remarkable turnaround: the Scholarships Committee (D. Broward Craig '50 L'53, chairman) had raised $40,892 from 732 givers, compared to $23,674 from 405 in fiscal 1975.

Just as the Club had ignored its own centennial on November 3, 1965, its governors chose not to observe the nation's bicentennial with ceremony, but many resident members who were not out of town (the Fourth of July fell on a Sunday) were surely among the millions of New Yorkers and visitors who by day watched tall ships from the seven seas proceed in stately file up the Hudson and after dark thrilled to a dazzling display of fireworks over the Upper Bay. Eight days later Democratic delegates from across the country converged on New York, for the first time since 1924, to choose a candidate for President; again they convened in

**Murals by Christian White: The Yard, looking east . . .**

Madison Square Garden, but it was a different hall, in a different location, from the one in which the Club's Franklin D. Roosevelt had put Governor Alfred E. Smith's name in nomination. And on the fourteenth, the delegates, by acclamation, picked Georgia Governor Jimmy Carter as their standard bearer.

That summer, the three Cambridge Rooms were closed for redecorating, but Art and Architecture Chairman Harold E. Buttrick '52 GSD'59 stopped by almost daily to check on how the work was progressing. For months, Buttrick, an architect, had been after the Board to let him brighten up the pallid, all too "ladylike" Cambridge Rooms. The Board was willing to pay for the purchase and installation of wallpaper, leaving the choice of pattern to him and his committee. But Buttrick had a bolder idea. He summoned a recent graduate of the Rhode Island School of Design to the Cambridge Rooms; this young painter, Christian White, was a son of Buttrick's friend, sculptor Robert White, a grandson of the Lawrence G. White who had for many years headed the Club's Art Committee and a great-grandson of Stanford White. Buttrick proposed that the youth paint, on the west wall of the lower Cambridge Dining Room, from photographs he himself would supply, scenes of the College and vicinity—for a fee amounting to precisely what the Club would have paid to have the same square footage covered with first-class wallpaper. Young White accepted, and a few weeks later the dining room glowed with three large, colorful murals showing a view of downtown Boston, the Johnston Gate to Harvard Yard as seen from Church Street, and riverfront Harvard houses seen from the Business School across the Charles.

... and Harvard houses, seen from across the Charles

In July or August, the Club's first mascot, Bootsie Mitten, died, aged fourteen. Irene Van Fossen wrote an affectionate obituary for the September *Bulletin*, which contained as well another depressing item: more than 100 books, it seemed, were missing from the library, having been abstracted without anyone filling out a borrower's slip.

On September 16, President Perkins, whose vision of the Club's potential had always included adult education at its core, took particular pleasure in announcing that its first Program for Continuing Education, an inquiry into the likely state of the world in 2000 A.D., would begin on April 20, 1977.

When the Cambridge Rooms reopened on October 4, most members were delighted with their fresh, inviting appearance. Christian White's bright renderings of scenes long imprinted in members' memories were, for most, a complete surprise, and a thoroughly welcome one.

On October 20, the Club's dinner-jacketed officers and managers, in the Mahogany Room, sat down to a dinner honoring retired lawyer Goldthwaite Higginson Dorr '97 L'00 one night before he turned 100. Secretary Kramer read aloud excerpts from the front page of the *New York Times* of Dorr's birthdate, October 21, 1876, and briefly retraced the life history of the Club's oldest member; then President Perkins read Dorr's Fiftieth Reunion report, crammed with fascinating incidents. When an oversized birthday cake bearing 100 candles appeared, former President Brownell offered a toast to the guest of honor, and as his hosts drank his health, the latter, with a little help from Presidents Perkins and Brownell, blew out all 100 candles, for which he received a standing ovation.

Minutes later, the near-centenarian addressed his fellow diners, and for the next half hour kept them spellbound with his reminiscences of a long and varied career in the military (three wars), the law (founding partner of a prestigious firm) and public service. Recalling a student riot in Cambridge in 1894 that had landed him in jail, he observed that "to look through bars is educative" and declared that "No gentleman should get through Harvard without one run-in with the police." Of his first visit to the Club, in the late 1890s, he remembered that "it seemed to me a palace. For dinner they served steak and potatoes." Dorr had joined the Club in 1909, at which time his name was duly entered into the record in the hand of a younger man, a fellow lawyer who happened to be secretary of the Admissions Committee: Franklin D. Roosevelt.

When Dorr, properly escorted, left the Mahogany Room, House Committee Chairman Tabler reported that the massage parlor at 7 West 44th Street had been closed down. And President Perkins persuaded the Board to allow the soliciting of funds for the Club barber, Mario Campo, who was seriously ill.

On Election Day, Democrat Jimmy Carter narrowly defeated President Ford for the nation's highest office. Most Club members were probably disappointed, but as New York City Republicans still tended to be more liberal than Republicans elsewhere, some, not having quite forgiven Ford for pardoning President Nixon for his Watergate crimes, may not have greatly minded their man's losing.

At the Board's last meeting of 1976, on December 16, two ideas were put forward, for the first time in a Club-wide forum, that presaged important changes. Richard W. Kimball '50, the chairman of an ad hoc committee studying all aspects of the dues, said that in recognition of the recent emergence of certain metropolitan suburbs as work centers, with concentrations of offices, his group was considering introducing a new class of membership, suburban, between the resident and nonresident classes. And Club Foundation President Goodhue reported that he was looking into the possibility of creating another foundation that could channel tax-deductible gifts to support the operations of the Club library.

On January 25, 1977, Walter N. Rothschild, Jr., was elected president and Frederick R. Moseley, Jr., vice-president, with Secretary Kramer and

Treasurer Merchant being retained in their posts. After the ensuing dinner retiring President Perkins hailed the Club as "a center for intellectual stimulus, artistic appreciation . . . and a continuing source of strength for Harvard and fun for ourselves." And he conferred a Distinguished Service Award on E. Thayer Drake for his "wise and patient" counsel in dealing with "that enormously complex, sensitive and human subject, employee relations."

That winter, exceptionally cold weather forced the Club to exceed its budget to heat the clubhouse. Meanwhile, extensive renovations to the kitchen curtailed service in the Main Dining Room, where, for the time being, only lunch was served on weekdays and there was no service whatever on weekends. And while members were pleased to see Mario the barber back on the job after a long illness, hundreds of them, perhaps thousands, were saddened by the departure of genial Pat Cronin, the doorman, after forty-nine years with the Club.

Early in February, for the first time, the annual sports dinner honored not only those young men who had participated in intercollegiate sports for Harvard but the College's young women athletes as well. And three weeks later the Activities Committee sponsored another first, a bourbon tasting in which blindfolded participants rated four different brands of Kentucky bourbon whiskey for bouquet, body, mellowness and flavor. (Old Forester won out over Wild Turkey, Old Granddad and I. W. Harper.)

While the Club had often hosted talks by and conversations with politicians, including some running for office, its symposium of March 24, presenting a small army of declared and undeclared contestants for the mayoralty, was without precedent in its annals. Panelists who agreed to participate included former Congresswoman Bella Abzug; Congressmen Herman Badillo, Mario Biaggi and Edward I. Koch; New York State Senator Roy Goodman '51 B'53, a member; Manhattan Borough President Percy Sutton; New York State Assemblyman Andrew Stein; broadcaster Barry Farber; former City Club Chairman Joel Harnett; and former Democratic County Chairman Edward Costikyan. The moderators were two political journalists: Ken Auletta of the *Daily News* and *The New Yorker* and Steven Weisman of the *New York Times*.

That evening generated much excitement. So did another six nights later. The Italian Night, as it was billed, also represented a new departure: instead of sitting down to dinner after cocktails, participants were encouraged to wander around the Main Dining Room, sampling characteristic dishes and wines of five different regions of Italy before repairing to the café in Harvard Hall. More than 700 members and guests came! With such a mob, and given the ambulatory nature of the event, traffic jams inevitably occurred, causing delays but, luckily, little bad feeling. The Activities Committee, while satisfied that the evening had been a success, was to apologize in the *Bulletin* for the "logistic confusion."

That winter and spring the Club's chess players had once again defeated all of their opponents before a combined Harvard–Yale–New York Athletic Club team lost to the United Nations. Incidentally, the Club had a new champion in Gisela K. Gresser R'27, wife of member William Gresser '17 AM'18 L'25. Nine times the national women's champion, Mrs. Gresser had seven times represented this country in women's world championship play, and was, as of 1977, the only American woman chess player ever to have been ranked a master. As longtime chess chairman Murray M. Stern B'35 would write in the annual report, the chess team was "very proud" of her.

April's most significant development was surely the delivery at last of the opening lectures in the long-awaited series on prospects for the coming turn of the millennium by two distinguished Harvard professors: historian John King Fairbank '29 on "China and America in 2000 A.D." and law professor Abram Chayes '43 L'49 on "The Prospects for International Order in 2000 A.D." The following month, the series would conclude, with professor (of technology and public policy) Harvey Brooks PhD'40 SD'63 speaking on "Natural Resources, Environment and the Quality of Life: 2000 A.D.," divinity professor Harvey G. Cox, PhD'63 on "The Age of the Spirit? Religious Dimensions in the Third Millennium" and Professor (of business administration) George Cabot Lodge '50 on "The Future of Free Enterprise."

At its May meeting, on the twenty-sixth, the Board, informed that Treasurer Merchant would soon be moving to London, appointed Michael A. Taylor '59 acting treasurer. President Rothschild thanked Merchant for his service, and then, "with the able assistance of R. B.

Perkins '47 and accompanied by enthusiastic applause," as the minutes put it, he unveiled a new portrait of former President Perkins by George Augusta, who had previously painted likenesses of former Presidents Schwarz and Pratt.

Concerning next year's freshman class, Schools Chairman Ross revealed in June that one in five of the young men and women admitted belonged to a minority, and that scholarship assistance to each of some 620 recipients would average $3,552. While the Club was still a long way from providing $50,000 a year in scholarships (an increasingly modest goal, with the cost of education constantly rising), Scholarships Chairman Craig took comfort in the fact that collections were up 10 percent from 1976. He noted that the Club foundation was again soliciting funds for scholarships. As its president, Francis A. Goodhue, Jr., had recently announced, the foundation was this year, for the first time, awarding scholarships to two graduate students: first-year Business School students Bruce B. Batkin and Stephen B. Silk. This new policy reflected, President Goodhue explained, the fact that growing numbers of former graduate students had joined the Club and given generously to the foundation.

Apropos of the Club foundation and the Business School, Assistant Secretary J. Dinsmore Adams, Jr. '66 was looking into setting up another foundation to operate the library, while Vice-President Moseley was negotiating with the Harvard Business School Club, which wanted to move its office into the clubhouse.

That summer saw the installation of the first of many through-the-wall air-conditioner/heater bedroom units. Late in August Christian White returned to the Cambridge Rooms to paint a fourth mural, this one looking east into the Yard, with Harvard and Massachusetts Halls at left and right and, just visible through trees, University Hall. On September 1 Viktor Korchnoi, the world's Number 2 chess player after Anatoly Karpov, spoke at the Club about his defecting from the U.S.S.R. and his hope of playing Bobby Fisher; then he played nineteen members on nineteen chessboards—and won all nineteen games.

In September, the Admissions Committee considered some controversial proposals: Chairman Christopher A. Smith '55 revealed the decisions of that traditionally autonomous body in the *Bulletin,* noting that in addition to graduates of the Business School's Advanced Management Program (AMP) and Program for Management Development (PMD), applicants would thenceforth be eligible for membership who had successfully completed courses in the Senior Management Program (SMP), the Smaller Company Management Program (SCMP) and the Institute for Educational Management (IEM). The *Bulletin* carried another interesting notice: with special trains to football games a thing of the past, the Activities Committee was chartering a bus to New Haven for the Yale game. Within a couple of days, all forty-seven seats would be taken.

Meanwhile, General Manager Kekllas had hired a new food and beverage manager, Tasso Leon, the Harvard Business School Club had occupied its new office in the basement, next to the Club's financial offices and across the corridor from the Barber Shop, and a plan had gone into effect stationing an assistant manager at a desk in the entrance hall.

On October 20 Activities Chairman Don B. Elliott '58 called his colleagues' attention to two upcoming events: lunches in Harvard Hall honoring Ambassador to the United Nations Andrew Young and C.I.A. Director Admiral Stansfield Turner AMP'66. Membership Chairman David M. Kirby B'68 displayed a new club scarf, a twenty-seven-inch silk square, white, with borders of parallel crimson lines and a design at each corner based on what the manufacturers called the Club crest: a capital H imposed on a capital C on a shield flanked by upright scrolls. The new club tie, crimson, featured the same device in white.

On Election Day, November 8, Democrat Edward I. Koch was elected mayor. On a Friday evening later that month the Harvard Band did its joyous and noisy thing in Harvard Hall, and the next morning, at 10 A.M., forty-seven members climbed into a bus for New Haven. Many more followed by car and train, but despite their ardent support the Yale team triumphed.

At the Board's December meeting, the main item of business was the formation of a tax-exempt organization to conduct the affairs of the Club library. This would require the approval of the Board of Regents of New York State and a ruling from the Internal Revenue Service confirming that the organization was in fact a public foundation. The Club would

**The Library**

have to transfer its books irrevocably to the library, which in turn would have to make itself available to nonmembers engaged in legitimate research. The Board approved creating the foundation, subject to the approvals of the I.R.S. and the Board of Regents.

A few days into 1978 the *Times* ran an article reviewing New York

City's clubs. Noting that "all over town men's clubs have been closing their separate ladies' entrances" (as President Gordon had done nearly five years before), the author ascribed women's success in storming bastions of maledom less to expanding social consciousness than to the bastions' need to admit new members in order to survive.

For years now clubs had seen their memberships dwindle as a consequence of various developments: the flight from the metropolis of corporate headquarters, the exodus of middle-class couples with children to the suburbs, the tendency of couples who stayed in the city to socialize in public places less than they once had and the preferences of many young couples who did go out at night for the faster pace, greater diversity and, often, better food that restaurants afforded. While club use declined, moreover, the cost of everything from labor to fuel oil kept mounting.

As for the university clubs—nearly all, by now, open to both sexes—some smaller ones had escaped the financial squeeze by selling their costly-to-maintain clubhouses, while larger ones had countered their own falling memberships by renting space to newly homeless clubs and opening up their facilities to the latters' members. Thus the Yale Club had taken in the Dartmouth Club, the Princeton Club the Columbia Club, and the Cornell Club the Fordham Club, while the Brown Club now shared the facilities of the Women's Republican Club, and the Williams Club offered affiliated membership to graduates of no fewer than ten colleges.

Although the *Times* article did not mention the fact, the Harvard Club was, as of 1978, the last single-university club left in New York. And the reporter's generalizations, while applicable to most city clubs, emphatically did not apply to the Club, which had already gone through years of declining membership even while welcoming its first women members, but was now, once again, confidently growing.

Members attending the annual meeting on January 19, 1978, reelected the president, vice-president and secretary and elected Michael A. Taylor treasurer. The five members they raised to the Board of Managers included, for the first time, a woman: Karen A. G. Loud.

On February 12 the media noted the death, the day before, of James Bryant Conant, for many years an honorary member of the Club. At 27

West 44th Street his death without doubt most affected those members, between their midforties and around seventy, who had been students during Conant's presidency of the University (1933–53). As his obituaries made clear, however, the world would remember him no less for his achievements as a research chemist, a key government official in wartime, a postwar diplomat and, especially, an elder statesman and philosopher of American higher education.

One day in February—for some reason, the record does not say which—the Club paid off the last penny still owing on the mortgage, and on the twenty-seventh the Board tentatively decided to invite certain past presidents to a meeting to express the Club's gratitude to them for their efforts toward this end. On March 10 the Activities Committee put on, in Harvard Hall, what it innocently mislabeled "the first annual Harvard Hall formal dance" (actual year: 1968). President Rothschild was to pronounce it a "spectacular success." And six days later the Board approved a new suburban category for dues, suburban members to be defined, in the amended bylaws, as "regular members of the Club having a residence or a principal place of business within a radius of fifty miles of the Club House but neither a residence nor a principal place of business within New York City."

The Club, founded largely by young men in their twenties, had always sought to attract young members, and the entertainments it offered in the first half of 1978 showed that youth was still being served 113 years later. "Golden oldie" movies, long a staple, were no longer being shown, and in addition to other all-ages activities—chamber music recitals, Library Committee round tables (on publishing and antiques), gala nights with a romantic foreign theme and the annual Easter spectacular—the calendar featured half a dozen parties of the very active Recent Graduates' Committee (founded late 1976), including a Valentine's Day dance that drew 500 and eight tastings and seminars centered on that current obsession of young people, wine. Among the speakers, meanwhile, were three young men with obvious appeal to young people: one who worked as a commercial fisherman, another who had sailed alone around the world and a former C.I.A. agent who had, in defiance of the agency, published a first-person exposé of it.

On the other hand, the activity that overshadowed all others, the second annual continuing education program, may well have appealed more to members long enough removed from classrooms to recall them with nostalgia than to those who had recently quit them. The program's six lectures, delivered on consecutive Wednesday evenings in April and May, consisted of two series, "The Middle East: Oil, Culture and Conflict" and "Japan: Artistic Expression, Business Success and World Role." In the *Bulletin*, Dean of Continuing Education Michael Shinagel AM'59, PhD'64, hoped that "We can look forward to a tradition at the Club in continuing education: an educational rite of spring each year."

During the academic year of 1977–78, Harvard's varsity swimmers had racked up an extraordinary record of eight wins to no losses, and on May 23, in Harvard Hall, an enthusiastic crowd of members watched videotapes of the undefeated team in action. They cheered its star, freshman Bobby Hackett '81, the winner, in the 1976 Olympics, of a silver medal. And they heard swimming coach Joe Bernal and diving coach John Walker speculate about the swimmers' chances of participating in the 1980 Olympics. (The United States would boycott the 1980 Moscow Olympics, rendering the question moot.)

Of 221 new members elected on June 19 by the Admissions Committee, 40—33 men and 7 women—were of the brand-new suburban variety. Four days later, the Club having received assurances of approval from the I.R.S. and the Board of Regents, the Harvard Library in New York was incorporated under the Not-for-Profit Corporation Law of New York State for the purpose of, among other things, establishing and maintaining a library "for the use of members of the Club, alumni of Harvard University, visiting scholars, accredited members of historical, literary or comparable organizations, and other interested members of the public, whether or not alumni of Harvard University."

At the close of fiscal 1978 the Club had 7,524 members, including 327 women (4.35 percent of the total). It was the highest year-end tally ever recorded since 1970's all-time peak figure of 7,761.

On July 10, the Club library was closed down for inventory, and when it reopened on the fourteenth, the Club formally transferred its entire collection of books to the newly created Harvard Library in New York.

Three days later, Mario Campo, the popular barber, died. And on August 16, after duly notifying the members, the Club changed its telephone number from MU 2-4600 to 840-6600.

Although the sixth-floor remodeling was supposed to be completed by October, it dragged on. This did not keep the squash players from playing, however, and in mid-October Nancy Havens B'71 arranged a round-robin of female players to mark the opening of the women's locker room and to establish a women's ladder. Janet Stott '70 won the tournament. Meanwhile, Activities Chairman Elliott had reported that every one of 1,400 available tickets to a special showing next March of the "Treasures of Tutankhamen" exhibit at the Metropolitan Museum had been sold, at $25 apiece (of which $13.50 would go to the scholarships fund), with 60 percent of the subscribers opting for a "package" that included lectures at the Club.

On November 15, club bow ties in two different shapes, butterfly and bat wing (both $10), went on sale at the cigar stand, together with a crimson scarf ($15), joining a white club scarf ($15) and a four-in-hand tie ($13). All items were of silk, and all displayed the Club crest. Five days later, an exhibit marking the centenary of Radcliffe College opened in the Cambridge Rooms: a pictorial history of Radcliffe's first 100 years, it would remain on view for two weeks before returning to Cambridge for display in the Lamont and Hilles Libraries. And on the following Thursday, the Club served up its customary Thanksgiving Day feast. At least some of the regulars must have noticed that while the menu was unchanged from last year's, the price of the meal had increased by almost one-third. (The ever-rising price of a Thanksgiving—or Christmas—dinner at the Club during the second half of the Seventies provides a useful, if not perfectly accurate, measure of the relentless upward surge of living costs in the city: 1975, $10; 1976, $10.50; 1977, $11.75; 1978, $15.50; 1979, $17.)

Although the Club was growing at a healthy rate, not all recruiting ploys proved efficacious. Membership Chairman Kirby told of one total failure. Invitations to a solicitation party at the Club were sent to 1,400 AMP and PMD graduates in the city. Sixty-five replied. Twenty-five accepted. And six came!

The following month, Kirby reported signing up thirty-four AMP and PMD applicants on a visit to the Business School. Numerous and welcome though they were, however, the younger members were a long way from dominating the Club's affairs: thus Daulton J. Lewis, Jr. B'73 L'74 of the Activities Committee noted that the most popular recent events had been two old favorites, John Jay, with his ski films, and the Blue Hill Troupe.

But what of the Hotel Webster? Vice-President Moseley said its owners wanted $2.2 million for it, which seemed high, even with real estate values in the area appreciating considerably. The Club's advisers, J. P. Morgan Interfunding, had suggested that $1.5 million would be a more reasonable price.

President Rothschild felt the acquisition deserved support if the projected income from the new facility sufficed to amortize the necessary debt obligation, but stressed that he was not asking the Board to authorize any purchase. After lengthy discussion, the Board decided that Moseley should continue talking with the hotel people, looking to a purchase price of around $1.5 million.

At midnight, December 31, Recent Graduates thronging Harvard Hall saw the New Year in with noisemakers and song; thirty-one days later, older members calling themselves Not-So-Recent Graduates would see January out with a mixer in the Cambridge Rooms. Throughout 1979 these two groups would remain highly visible, the juniors typically hosting youthful entertainments and their elders socializing over cocktails.

Once again, wine tastings and seminars on wine (ten of them!) would draw the biggest crowds, oenophilia having become so entrenched at the Club that a report from the House Committee's Wine Subcommittee (Robert B. Glynn '51 L'56, chairman) would, for a third year running, appear alongside those of the standing committees in the Board's annual report. In addition to nine evenings of instrumental and chamber music and a choral concert by the Collegium Musicum, members would take part in colorful galas celebrating the music, dance, costumes and cuisines of Greece, Egypt, Poland and Hawaii, as well as a country-and-western evening and an in-house Oktoberfest. The year would bring innovations: an initial appearance at the Club of a Radcliffe singing group, the

Pitches; a first-ever cabaret night, produced and presented by the Recent Graduates; and "Crimsongs: Music and Lyrics by Harvard," an evening of musical comedy conceived and performed by undergraduates.

Meanwhile, thanks to the efforts of the Activities Committee, the University Relations Committee and the Harvard Library in New York (replacing the Library Committee), speakers and lectures would span a wide spectrum. Members focused on their own financial and physical well-being could hear journalist Ken Auletta discuss the city's financial crisis and future, or Professor Otto Eckstein AM'52 PhD'55 the national economy, or Professor James Wilson and former New York City medical examiner Dr. Michael M. Baden crime and the city. Those interested in cultural matters could ponder reflections on architecture by Professor Louis Bakanowsky MAR'61, artist-poet Charles Patrick's views on current art movements, remarks by playwright/Professor William Alfred AM'49 PhD'54 tracing the evolution of drama from Aeschylus or a panel discussion on illuminated manuscripts, while supporters of local cultural institutions could listen to reports on the New York Public Library by its director, Richard Couper G'48 (a member), and on the New York City Opera by its longtime director and principal conductor, Julius Rudel. Adventure lovers could watch a film, narrated by explorer Norman Baker, of a trip by reed boat down the Tigris to the Persian Gulf; the health-conscious could learn about diets and dieting from Columbia Medical Professor (and Club member) Theodore B. Van Itallie '41; and individuals looking for literary and dramatic diversion could hear actress Shirley Romaine recite prose and poetry by women writers. Finally, serious seekers of enlightenment might profit from the insights and speculations of Astronomy Professor Eric J. Chaisson AM '69 PhD'72 on "The Destiny of Our Civilization," of Government Professor Michael L. Walzer PhD'62 on "War and Morality," and of two celebrated authors, Professor Stephen Jay Gould AM (hon.) '73 and Kettering Institute president Lewis Thomas MD'37, on "The Meaning of Darwin's Revolution."

All this was in addition to the year's principal cultural offerings: special showings at the Metropolitan Museum of "The Treasures of Tutankhamen" on three different Mondays, following lectures the previous Sundays by noted Egyptologists, and the third annual program of continuing education, comprising six lectures. Not to mention a multitude of other, routine events that would give pleasure to countless members: the invitational squash tournaments and attendant festivities; successive matches in Metropolitan League play; tournaments in bridge, backgammon and chess; visits from Cambridge by the Krokodiloes, the Hasty Pudding show cast, and the Harvard Band; football films; a John Jay ski film; children's parties on Easter and Hallowe'en; Easter brunch; banquets on Thanksgiving and Christmas Day ...

Was 1979 to be, then, an exceptionally busy year for activities? Not really: no more than 1978 had been, and slightly less, perhaps, than 1980 would be, with sixty-eight events. Had they thought about it, the many members of the Club who frequented other clubs would surely have agreed that the nourishment afforded their minds and hearts, eyes and ears, palates, muscles and funny bones at 27 West 44th Street outmatched, in abundance and variety, that offered up by any other social organization.

On the evening of January 18, 1979, Frederick R. Moseley, Jr., was elected president and Robert R. Barker vice-president, while Secretary Kramer and Treasurer Taylor were reelected. After dinner, Dean of the Faculty of Arts and Sciences Henry Rosovsky '53 PhD'59 gave the main address, but before he spoke retiring President Rothschild conferred a Distinguished Service Award on House Committee Chairman Tabler and distributed certificates to the fifty-year members present.

The high point of the proceedings came when Rothschild, standing at his place flanked by former Presidents Gordon and Perkins and former Treasurer Merchant, held the Club's paid-up mortgage out at arm's length, applied a lighted match, and dropped the flaming document into a big silver bowl. In accordance with an old Nantucket custom the ashes would be deposited in a hole drilled in the newel post at the first landing of the main staircase, which would then be plugged with a button made of whalebone. A metal plaque noting the ceremony and the date would be affixed to the side of the newel post.

The results of the squash weekend later that month suggested that Philadelphia had regained its erstwhile supremacy at squash racquets, with University of Pennsylvania undergraduates winning both the Cowles

The Main Staircase

and Jacobs tournaments. Meanwhile, William F. Draper was completing a portrait of former President Rothschild, which on February 7, in a brief ceremony, would be unveiled and hung in the entrance hall.

At its February meeting, the Board demonstrated that the anglophilia so deeply ingrained in Harvard Club hierarchs retained its force by agreeing at once to a House Committee recommendation that a certain young aide at the British consulate general be elected a temporary member. Of late the authority of Bootsie Mitten's successor as Club cat, striped and short-haired Carey, had been rudely challenged by a stray feline that had moved in, wherefor the managers were pleased to learn that House Committeeman Richard M. Chapman L'49 was prepared to relocate the interloper to his Connecticut farm. And Activities Chairman Elliott reminded his colleagues that the Club's "second annual formal dinner dance" was scheduled for March 30.

Anent the Webster, President Moseley reviewed the background to the Club's present bid for $1.4 million and the owners' asking price of $2.3 million. Board member Peter L. Malkin '55 L'58 suggested that the Club rent office space in the Berkeley Building next door and convert its present offices into banquet rooms, and Moseley noted that certain younger members were seeking an appropriate space for a bar in which they could relax in informal clothes. Finally, Chairman Stig Host '51 presented the Long-Range Planning Committee's recommendation that the Club aggressively pursue acquiring the Webster.

The following month, President Moseley informed the Board that the Hotel Webster had changed hands, but that the new owners wanted to continue negotiations with the Club. Crocker Luther B'62, assuming the chairmanship of the House Committee, said he sensed that the Club's "ambiance" had slipped somewhat. And Activities Chairman Elliott revealed, a bit anxiously, that there were plenty of reservations still available for the dinner dance coming up in just fifteen days.

At 10 A.M. on March 25 there commenced, in Harvard Hall, the first of three Sunday seminars on funerary objects, mostly of gold, found in the tomb of the pharaoh Tutankhamen; this "cram course" continued, with time out for lunch, until 4 P.M., preparing participants for their visit the next day to the exhibition at the Metropolitan Museum. But if the "King

Tut" lectures and showings were fully booked, the dinner dance was not: well short of its goal of 225 warm bodies, the Activities Committee reluctantly canceled the event, dooming, thereby, a promising Club "tradition."

There was another impending event, however, that, having scored successes two years running, seemed destined to claim a permanent and honored place on the Club calendar. Writing in the March *Bulletin*, Dean Shinagel said as much, asserting that the Club had "already established a strong tradition in continuing education" and adjuring his readers to "begin to think about Act IV, which we will present in the spring of 1980." Since the topics of the two series of lectures making up this spring's program, Russia and the fine arts, had been the top choices of last year's participants, the dean had ample reason to believe that the upcoming program would be well attended. But unfortunately it would not be: while the 1977 talks had attracted, on average, more than 200 members and guests and the 1978 program around 150, attendance in 1979 would average 100, not enough to meet expenses. The Club would abandon for the nonce its bold experiment in continuing education, dashing hopes for yet another "tradition."

Meanwhile, double-digit inflation, reaching an annual rate of 14 percent in April, forced the Club to raise prices—7 percent on meat and fish dishes, a dime on cocktails and highballs, a nickel on a glass of beer. Board member John F. Tulenko '54 M'58 wanted to know why the cost of employees' meals had shot up 25 percent while the work force was being reduced, and what explained recent huge expenditures for utensils; Treasurer Taylor's replies would convey what he was told, but the true answers would have to await the airing of certain practices as yet unrevealed to the Club's governors. On the plus side, Chairman Luther reported that the kitchen staff had begun to steam vegetables instead of boiling them, thereby retaining both their flavor and certain nutritional values, but on the minus side Luther, Chairman Host and Secretary Kramer agreed that, even taking inflation into account, the Club's food costs seemed remarkably high. Saying that his primary concerns were food costs and inflation, President Moseley reported that the Club's accountants, Harris, Kerr, Forster & Company, would analyze how the Club's operating expenses compared with other clubs'. At his suggestion, then, the Board adopted a dues increase of 8 percent to take effect July 1.

President Moseley now turned again to the tantalizing subject of the hotel next door, and before long the Board heard, for the first time in open meeting, strong arguments advanced for not purchasing the Webster. Vice-President Barker cited three principal reservations: first, the coming into being in recent years, by construction or conversion, of many—perhaps too many—hotel rooms in the city; second, the risks posed by unknowable future occupancy trends; and third, the Club's probable inability to renovate what some had called a third-rate hotel. But Barker seems to have made few converts, if any. Secretary Kramer pointed out that over decades innumerable nonresident members had resigned because the clubhouse lacked enough bedrooms to assure them of accommodation when they came to New York. Both former President Rothschild and Board member Christopher A. Smith spoke of the desirability of the Club's having plenty of rooms available. And Chairman Luther asserted that if the hotel were purchased the Club's present employees would be quite capable of running it.

Over the next weeks, negotiations with the hotel's owners became stalled. At the Board's June meeting Secretary Kramer read aloud a letter from Chairman Alfred G. Parmelee '52 of the Continuing Education Committee expressing the writer's appreciation of the help provided him, in his efforts to produce and publicize the recent program, by Evelyn McQuade of the manager's office. Parmelee's words struck a chord, triggering an outpouring of similar sentiments from people present, including the secretary. Their praise and gratitude were heaped, not only on Miss McQuade (who bore on the Club roster the not-very-descriptive title of administrative assistant), but also on Thelma Leventhal, secretary to the Admissions Committee, who over many years had compiled, with never a complaint and almost never a typing error, lists of names that grew ever more numerous and ever more orthographically challenging.

Impressed by these spontaneous tributes, President Moseley said he interpreted the sense of the Board to be that these loyal, cheerful and singularly helpful women should be accorded financial recognition. "Further discussion," the minutes would relate, "confirmed the president's interpretation."

Though rarely seen by most resident members, the old photographs, prints and pictures lining the fourth- and fifth-floor corridors and adorning the walls of bedrooms constituted a vital element of the Club's decor, contributing powerfully to an ambiance that visitors from across the country and around the world found captivating and unique. That summer, as during several summers past, Olga vom Hofe R'46 of the Art and Architecture Committee put in long hours voluntarily cleaning and reframing these pictorial reminders of Harvard's past. Her work epitomized Chairman Buttrick's often-stated aim of achieving "improvement without change."

When the Board reconvened in September, Activities Chairman Elliott reported what he called "the last word ever on 'King Tut,'" to wit, that his committee had turned over some $25,000 in proceeds of those museum showings to the scholarship fund. And Admissions Chairman Laurence B. Rossbach, Jr. '50 L'53 related a curious tale of how, all inadvertently, his committee had elected to membership a woman who had been asked to withdraw her application. The Board then asked Peter Malkin and Chairman Buttrick to prepare a report on the Hotel Webster. Again Vice-President Barker expressed doubt that the hotel could be successfully renovated and managed by the Club, or any club, and after further heated discussion—and a wholly unscheduled visit by President Bok—Peter Malkin spoke up. He endorsed the idea of acquiring the Webster, with reasonable financing and limited liability for the Club. And he opined that in order to produce a detailed and comprehensive report he might need the help of an engineer, another architect and a specialist in hotel management, whereupon the Board authorized him to hire these experts.

Around October 1, Edward E. White, Jr., moving to Florida, ceded the editorship of the *Bulletin* to John G. Stewart, a writer and editor with many years' experience on the staffs of New York daily newspapers and national magazines.

As Peter Malkin was unable to attend the Board meeting on October 18, Secretary Kramer read his report out loud. It was surprisingly brief. Having inspected the Webster with three experts, Malkin had found it in very poor condition, with defects in the layout, the plumbing, the wiring and the elevators that would cost a great deal to correct. The group's unanimous recommendation was that the Club not proceed with plans to purchase the hotel.

In unaccustomed silence, the Board voted to accept this recommendation. Expansion of bedroom facilities, so urgently needed, would have to take place elsewhere.

Crocker Luther then reported that he and President Moseley had met with Joseph Baum, a former president of Restaurant Associates and the man responsible for setting up food operations at the spectacular downtown restaurant Windows on the World, atop one of the World Trade Center towers. Luther proposed a two-phase program, by which the accountants Harris, Kerr, Forster would prepare a report covering all aspects of the Club's actual food operations, including purchasing, menus, preparation and serving, whereupon Baum would review the report and make suggestions for improving operations. The Board agreed to finance the first phase, the accountants' report. Finally, President Moseley read aloud a gracious letter from that overworked but ever-cheerful pair, Evelyn McQuade and Thelma Leventhal, thanking the Board for their bonuses.

In November, Chairman Luther proposed that the Club offer a fixed price soup-and-sandwich lunch on the Main Dining Room balcony for about five dollars. The Board approved. Next, Roseanne F. Gaulkin R'55, now co-chairman of the Activities Committee, described some events planned for 1980: they included innovations that would call on members' creative skills (a photography workshop, a songwriters' festival) and one, a gourmet dinner for $100, aimed, without apology, at members' cravings for gustatory gratification. The Not-So-Recent Graduates' get-togethers had become so popular, she said, that they were being held every month. Karen Loud presented further details: the brilliant young cellist Yo-Yo Ma '76 would give a concert at the Club, and a new play would be performed there to benefit Harvard-Radcliffe scholarships.

While January 1980 ushered in a new decade, it left the Club's officers in place. The annual squash weekend, in contrast, expanded into a three-day affair marked by the inauguration of a new tournament for players thirty-five and older named after nonresident member John M. Barnaby '32, mentor of numerous championship teams and honorary chairman for the weekend. On Friday the twenty-fifth, Philadelphian Barbara Maltby, top-rated nationally for the last four years, took on Boston's Henri Salaun, fifty-two, who had been national singles champion the year of Mrs. Maltby's birth, but since theirs was purely an exhibition match the outcome was not recorded. The Saturday night dinner saw the unveiling of a portrait of Honorary Chairman Barnaby by Germain G. Glidden. And on Sunday Harvard senior Michael Desaulniers '80 won the Cowles.

Around then, a group of investors from the Philippines bought the Hotel Webster for $2 million, eliminating for the time being any further possibility of the Club's acquiring it.

In February, Board member Diana T. Butterworth R'60 inquired about the eligibility for membership of those men who, during World War II, had attended a Navy Supply School at the College for periods of three months to a year. Secretary Kramer declared that the bylaws covered the matter by providing that anyone who had been enrolled in the University and had been recommended by the Admissions Committee could be elected by the Board on an individual basis. Theory apart, however, Ms. Butterworth would soon have an answer of a practical kind.

On February 25 the Activities Committee hosted, through its wine tasting subcommittee (Aldo F. Tenaglia '79, chairman), its very first beer tasting, and on Sunday, March 9, it staged another, quite spectacular, innovation: an exhibition, in Harvard Hall, of gymnastics by members of the brand-new Harvard/Radcliffe Gymnastics Club. Meanwhile, the *Bulletin* ran an article titled "A Harvard Woman Looks at the Harvard Club," which delighted readers of both sexes. In it, Linda K. Rawson '76 candidly and wittily reviewed the strides toward full acceptance she and her sisters had made in the seven years since they had been admitted into the Club and the four since she herself had joined. "All indications are," she concluded, "that this progress will continue as more of the male members discover with George Bernard Shaw that 'Woman is the female of the human species, and not a different kind of animal.'" (Although three women—Charlotte P. Armstrong R'49 L'53, Diana T. Butterworth and Karen A. G. Loud—served on the Board, constituting one-fifth of that body, the Club's female membership still amounted to only 406, about 5 percent of the total. Fourteen years later, in January 1994, the percentage would be just under 15 percent.)

On April 17 Admissions Chairman William S. Kelly '70 moved that Malcolm Klein, who had received a certificate from the Naval Supply School at Harvard in 1942, be admitted to membership; duly seconded, the motion was unanimously approved. With that matter thus settled, some questions remained as to the eligibility of cross-registrants, students at other institutions who had taken at least one course at the University, but that question, too, would soon be answered. Meanwhile, Chairman David A. Goldberg '54 L'57 of the University Relations Committee announced happily that 330 members had signed up for an evening devoted to psychohistory featuring Harvard's Professor Robert Coles and New York's feisty Norman Mailer '43, whose latest best seller, *The Executioner's Song*, was, in Dr. Coles's view, an excellent example of the genre.

On April 21 the Club's top bridge players competed for the title of best individual player. For the first time a woman member, science professor Edith J. Woodward PhD'36, participated. She won! (When, the following month, Genuine Risk would win the Kentucky Derby, the first filly to do so in sixty-five years, the Games Committee's Shepherd I. Raimi L'55 would hail her and Dr. Woodward's parallel feminine victories in the *Bulletin*, but not all women readers would be amused.)

Six days later the Activities Committee came up with still another intriguing novelty: an extraordinary feature-length motion picture titled *John Harvard: Movie Star*. Composed of footage culled from half a century of Hollywood movies with Harvard/Radcliffe story lines and stars like Bob Hope, Mary Astor, Buster Crabbe, Hedy Lamarr, Buster Keaton and Rudolph Valentino, it was narrated in person by its creator, old movie buff, historian and repackager Paul Killiam, Jr. '37, a longtime member.

In mid-May, the Board unanimously approved a motion to admit to the Club Eduardo Helguera, an Argentine lawyer who had been cross-registered at Harvard while attending Tufts University as a Fulbright scholar. President Moseley reported that several recommendations in the accountants' food study had been put into effect, imposing stricter controls on receiving supplies and on payroll. And Co-Chairman Gaulkin announced three forthcoming events entirely without precedent: a New York street fair in Harvard Hall, a Father's Day champagne brunch and a family outing—by bus to Essex, Connecticut, by old-fashioned steam train north to actor William Gillette's fantastic "castle" and finally, after a picnic lunch, by paddle boat around the lower reaches of the Connecticut River.

At a Board meeting on June 26, President Moseley expressed regret at being forced by mounting costs to ask for the new dues increase it had just approved. Then, in a quiet voice, he reported that the House Committee wanted General Manager John Kekllas's resignation at once. And he asked Richard Chapman of the House Committee to fill in the background.

Chapman began by citing certain deficiencies in the Club's food operations noted in the auditors' study, adding that his committee was determined that the study's recommendations for correcting these deficiencies be implemented without delay. But could the existing management do this? Obviously not.

Chairman Luther now reported that he and President Moseley had discussed with member Max Pine B'58, president of Restaurant Associates, the possibility of that firm's taking on the Club's day-to-day operations, and been assured that it could provide on short notice all of the personnel needed to keep things running smoothly. At Luther's request, Restaurant Associates had submitted a letter of intent outlining conditions and terms for such an arrangement. If the Board agreed to ask for Kekllas's resignation, the chairman concluded, the House Committee recommended that Restaurant Associates be retained to manage the Club's food, beverage and bedroom operations.

After discussion, the Board unanimously authorized the Club's officers to obtain the resignations of the general manager and of other employees whose departure would, in their judgment, be in the Club's best interest, and to negotiate an agreement with Restaurant Associates in line with that firm's letter of intent.

The next morning, a Friday, Chairman Luther, accompanied by President Moseley and E. Thayer Drake, stopped by Kekllas's office. After salutations, Luther said he wanted to talk about certain "irregularities." Without uttering a word, Kekllas drew forth a sheet of paper, picked up a pen and wrote out a one-sentence resignation. Further resignations were received from Food and Beverage Director Tasso Leon, Chef Carl Osbourne and Steward Gus Constantine. And by July 1, a handful of Restaurant Associates people, headed by the new general manager, Gunther Wirth, were firmly in charge of Club operations.

# 19

# THE EARLY
# REAGAN YEARS
# (1980–1985)

As of July 1, 1980, the Club had 8,083 members. Although the latest dues increase had been sprung on them without warning, few protested, if only because frequent jumps in the cost of just about everything had become routine. Thereafter, the Admissions Committee would regularly take in more candidates at each meeting than it had during the same month of the preceding year, while resignations would remain, as a rule, at a moderate level; this process would persist throughout the decade, ultimately expanding the membership to five figures.

In the meantime, a member sampling the talk going on around him would have heard much grumbling about persistent high inflation and interest rates, and much indignation expressed over the plight of fifty-odd Americans being held as hostages in the American embassy in Teheran by militant followers of a charismatic Islamic fundamentalist, the Ayatollah Khomeini. Aware that millions of his fellow citizens shared these members' feeling of frustration, the eavesdropper would probably have predicted defeat for President Carter in the coming elections. He would have been right, of course, and when, in January 1981, former California Governor Ronald Reagan became president (with the Iranians obligingly freeing their American captives at almost the same moment), the national ship of state would execute its widest turn, resulting in its biggest course change, since March 1933. Reducing taxes, curtailing or eliminating government regulations, increasing outlays for defense while cutting spending on social programs, the new administration would create an economic climate singularly favorable to business, and after a severe but brief recession in 1982, with inflation levels coming down at last, the economy would surge forward on its longest peacetime boom ever.

Many—indeed, most—Club members would benefit materially from these developments, as would the Club itself, through the appreciation of its investments. But the consequence of the new prosperity most conspicuous at 27 West 44th Street would be the rather sudden appearance there of young men and women, typically just out or recently out of the Business School or Law School, commanding starting salaries that only a year or so before would have seemed ludicrously inflated. These young people, derisively dubbed "yuppies" by the media, would sometimes treat the Club as an extension of their workplaces, a pleasant location in which to continue to talk business, strike deals or "network"; predictably, this behavior would annoy and occasionally infuriate older members accustomed to thinking of the Club, or any club, as precisely the opposite of an office: a refuge or retreat from workday cares and concerns.

On July 13, gamesman Howard Reiling died at age ninety-two, having left the Club, it would later be revealed, a legacy of $25,000. "May he find some backgammon players where he is now," Walter J. Salmon, Jr., of the Games Committee would write in the annual report.

In August, Admissions Chairman Kelly reported a startling statistic: of the record 751 new members taken in during fiscal 1980, 270, more than one in three, were women! He also reported that a silver bowl had been bought for Thelma Leventhal to mark her quarter of a century with the Club, out of contributions from past and present members of his committee. It was presented to her, with due ceremony, on September 25.

On the night of Tuesday, November 4, in Harvard Hall, some 200 members and guests joined Lieutenant Governor Mario Cuomo, State Comptroller Edward Regan, City Comptroller Harrison J. Goldin and Manhattan Borough President Andrew Stein in an "election night watch." For all these men except Republican Regan it proved to be something of a wake as their fellow Democrat, President Carter, was buried under an avalanche of votes for G.O.P. standard bearer Ronald Reagan.

Two weeks after this, Treasurer Taylor informed the Board that since the budget for fiscal 1981 projected a surplus of $200,000, there would be no need to raise prices. This projection reflected, he said, benefits the Club derived from Restaurant Associates' bulk purchasing and its improved management. House Committee Chairman Luther agreed that the Club was functioning smoothly under the new regime, but added that Restaurant Associates wanted to assign Gunther Wirth to other responsibilities, whereupon Vice-President Barker declared that a search for his successor would begin at once.

In December, Chairman Luther submitted to the Board, for its consideration, the name of Paul C. Buck, Jr., the unanimous choice of the vice-president's search committee. Long Gunther Wirth's chief assistant, Buck had worked at the Ford Foundation, Lincoln Center and the Kennedy Center, and at the Club he had won high praise for his ability to get on well with both members and employees. Without dissent, then, the Board approved naming him general manager.

At the 1981 annual meeting on January 12, Robert R. Barker was elected president and Richard W. Kimball vice-president; George P. Kramer was reelected secretary for another year and Newton P. S. Merrill '61, concluding a prolonged apprenticeship as assistant and acting treasurer, became treasurer *tout court*. That month saw the disappearance of two high-profile figures at the Club: greatly liked Librarian Lounsbury ("Biff") Bates, who collapsed one day at his desk, never to regain consciousness, and Board member Gerard Weinstock, a moving force behind the creation of the Harvard Center for Jewish Studies and a staunch supporter of the Club. Both men, exceptionally, would be memorialized, in separate ceremonies, in Harvard Hall.

Entertainments that winter would follow each other in such quick succession that the staff, undergoing reorganization, would be unable to cope with the volume of activity, obliging President Barker to ask the Activities Committee to slow down. Most programs that season would be repeats of past successes, but Activities would introduce innovations, too, in addition to the Club's first election night watch the previous November. One was a forum in which three of America's leading architects—Edward Larrabee Barnes '38 Ds'42, John Burgee and Der Scutt—would talk about corporate headquarters skyscrapers they had designed that would soon rise in Midtown—respectively, the IBM building, AT&T headquarters (with Philip Johnson '27 BAR'43) and Trump Tower. Another was a four-evening series of talks on nutrition and fitness, concerns of increasing interest to members of all ages. And in May, the Club would hold its first formal dance in a few years, styled "Swing into Spring" and billed, inevitably, as the "first annual" event of its kind.

Convening the Board on February 18, Secretary Kramer, beaming yet solemn, announced the arrival on planet Earth, on February 3, of Diana Townsend-Butterworth, Jr., the first child ever born to a member of the Club's Board of Managers. Her mother graciously accepted compliments all around. Next, President Barker introduced another relative newcomer, General Manager Buck, who spoke about two challenges facing the Club: to rebuild the quality and morale of the staff and to retain or hire first-class department heads. In the two months since he had taken command, Buck had impressed the Club's governors by his dedication, and would continue to do so, President Barker having stated in the 1981 annual report that Buck had worked seventy- and eighty-hour weeks during this period.

After announcing that the Club had concluded a three-year pact with the union, President Barker touched on the possibility of leasing the Gould-Mersereau building next door, at 35 West 44th Street. The following month, he proposed combining the functions of the Scholarships and Schools Committees in a single body, the Harvard/Radcliffe Schools Committee, to be chaired by Richard Rodwin '52 L'55. The Board endorsed his proposal.

With membership now well over 8,000, instances of overcrowding were increasing. Admissions Chairman Cyrus W. Brown II '60 reported a general tightening-up of requirements for admission. And for the Harvard Library in New York, President Livingston announced that Adrienne Fischier, long associated with the Mechanics and Tradesmen Library across 44th Street, had been hired as our new librarian.

At about 11:25 P.M. on Saturday, April 18, with the clubhouse almost deserted, a well-dressed man entered by the front door and, producing a pistol, held up the clerk at the front desk and made off with about $1,600. The Club's insurance covered the loss, but the incident would prompt the Board to adopt a new regulation limiting the cash kept in the office in the evening to $200, and generally to enhance security.

When the Board met again the following Thursday, Treasurer Merrill triumphantly reported that during the first nine months of fiscal 1981 the Club had realized a net profit of $238,000, as compared to about $6,000 at the same point in fiscal 1980. Admissions Chairman Brown noted a new rule his committee had adopted requiring that candidates must have been known for at least two years by their sponsors and at least one by their seconders; this rule would not apply, however, to candidates interviewed in Cambridge, who were assumed not to know any members. Finally, House Committee Chairman Richard M. Chapman L'49 suggested, in view of the large number of employees staffing the Cambridge Rooms and the Main Dining Room balcony—thirteen and three respectively—that service be eliminated in these spaces in favor of self-service, while the last vestiges of self-service be simultaneously banished from the Main Dining Room. This would, he claimed, improve service in the latter hall, while a modestly priced buffet in the Cambridge Rooms might well lure more lunchers and diners to that attractive but underused facility.

By May 21, the Club's profit for the fiscal year to date exceeded a quarter of a million dollars, but since the Club's governors had some major capital outlays in mind, President Barker proposed, even so, an across-the-board 10 percent increase in the dues. The House Committee and Executive Committee having previously approved this hike, the Board now followed suit. It also approved a move by Barker to abolish the Finance Committee and establish an Investment Committee in its place.

During the season now ending, the Club's bridge and chess teams had fared moderately well in competition, but the backgammon team (Joseph P. Smyth B'67 captain, E. J. Kahn, Jr., champion) had covered itself with glory by winning the first annual championship of the newly formed New York Backgammon League, a body comprising, in addition to the Club, the University, Yale and Princeton Clubs, the New York and Downtown Athletic Clubs and the Union League Club, with the Union Club and perhaps the Metropolitan Club about to enter the fold.

In June, the Board's Senator Goodman reported that a handful of the 6,000 members of the basement tenant, the Harvard Business School Club, had, of late, taken to using the Harvard Club as if it were their own.

The MBAs' president would soon, Goodman said, remind his members in a circular not to use the Club's facilities—and suggest that they apply to join the Club. For the newly consolidated Schools Committee, Chairman Rodwin provided key facts about the Class of 1985, among them that 483 of the 2,115 applicants admitted were from minority groups of the population, and that the annual cost of attending Harvard in 1981–82, excluding travel expenses, would be $11,450. Finally, Chairmen Buttrick and Chapman described possible ways to improve and enlarge the Club's plant, two of which would involve expanding into the adjacent site of the Gould-Mersereau building:

(1) Renovating the existing clubhouse, including installing bathrooms to adjoin all bedrooms, a new steam boiler and other improvements. Estimated cost: $3 million.

(2) Constructing a nine-story building, perhaps with a store at street level and with restaurant facilities on the second floor, banquet rooms on the third floor and bedrooms, forty to forty-five in number, on the fourth through ninth floors. Estimated cost: $4.2 million.

(3) Constructing a twelve-story building with nine floors of bedrooms, seventy-two to eighty-one in all. Estimated cost: $8.6 million.

The owner of the Gould-Mersereau building had, Chairman Chapman reported at last, offered to lease it to the Club for $120,000 a year and other considerations. And as the fiscal year ended, on June 30, the Club had admitted a record 879 members, including 204 women, during the previous twelve months. Membership now stood at 8,554.

Over the summer, negotiations continued with the owner of the building next door, looking toward the Club's entering into an option to lease and then acquire it and the twenty-five-by-one-hundred-foot lot on which it stood. At a Board meeting convened, most unusually, in August, Chairman Chapman revealed that the option as envisaged would last through January 1 or January 31, 1982, and would cost the Club nothing. If it were exercised, the Club would possess a twenty-year leasehold, and be obliged to pay rent of $120,000 for each of the first five years, $130,000 for each of the next five years, then $144,000 each for five more years and $160,000 each for the remaining five. At the end of twenty years the Club would have the option of buying the property at eleven times the then rent, i.e., $1,760,000.

President Barker cautioned his colleagues that the Club still had at least a million dollars' worth of work to be done refurbishing its public and private rooms and repairing its heating plant, and could not commit itself to the proposed option until it was assured of a prudent course of financing. Even so, they authorized him to negotiate and execute an agreement on the lines of the option Chapman had outlined. As for the Club's other negotiations—with Restaurant Associates, over the existing five-year contract—the president reported that a proposed draft had been presented to the House Committee that day and to Max Pine of Restaurant Associates that afternoon. Following a wide-ranging discussion, the Board empowered Barker to negotiate and sign a new contract with the firm.

In the fall, self-service was discontinued in the Main Dining Room and introduced in the Cambridge Dining Rooms. The Board's October meeting evolved into a lively discussion of overcrowding and what to do about it. Louis J. Appell, Jr. '47 rejected such proposed countermeasures as erecting barriers to admission and raising prices faster than inflation dictated, saying that further analysis of the overcrowding was needed, particularly with regard to the availability of the bedrooms. The Club's governors should, he thought, be focusing on the following questions: Did they want the Club to keep growing? Would the construction of more dining space and many more bedrooms on the Gould-Mersereau property turn the Club into a kind of business? Should certificate holders enjoy all the rights other members enjoyed?

Secretary Kramer observed that the Club was growing at the rate of about 600 members a year, and Alfred G. Parmelee suggested that it might not be charging enough for some services. Anthony B. Barton '69 felt that the Club should discontinue its recruiting drives to slow down growth and restrict membership to a size consistent with the dimensions of the clubhouse. Finally, President Barker suggested that either the Long-Range Planning Committee or an ad hoc committee look into the pros and cons of limiting the membership and raising prices at the Club.

The discussion ended there, but it would resume at the November meeting when Admissions Chairman Brown stated that 7.8 percent of the new members admitted in fiscal 1981 had been certificate holders. Mrs.

Townsend-Butterworth said she opposed barring applicants who qualified as certificate holders but favored discontinuing the recruiting trips to Cambridge, whereupon President Barker called for restricting eligibility but not halting recruiting. Chairman Brown put in that the April Cambridge trip ordinarily accounted for about half the new members each year. The president declared that if the membership was to be reduced the Membership Committee should have a say in determining how it was to be done. And Louis Appell wondered how the Club decided, among the various certificate programs that were offered, which conferred eligibility on their graduates and which did not.

Meanwhile, on the eve of Hallowe'en, 279 members and guests took part in a "Sleuth Night." After dining on fried oysters and grouse as Sherlock Holmes and Dr. Watson had done while solving the mystery recounted in *The Sign of the Four*, they watched, in Harvard Hall, a "spellbinding drama about a pleasure cruise aboard a millionaire's yacht that ends in foul play, complete with chilling visual and sound effects." They then had to solve the mystery posed by this foul play—and, with some difficulty, did.

Another novelty, a permanent one, now occupied a counter at the south end of the Main Dining Room, next to the counter at which for decades members had stopped by, on their way to a table, to pick up a plate of oysters. On November 2, the *New York Times* took note of its existence in a short essay by Jacob (Jack) Rosenthal '56 INS'76. "The presence of a sushi bar at the Harvard Club," he wrote, "suggests something more than tolerating Japanese manufactures; it suggests a genuine curiosity and welcome for aspects of Japanese culture. In a small way, it signals a new cultural convergence."

Over the weekend of November 7, the mounted head of a waterbuck disappeared from its spot near the northwest corner of the Grill Room, between the two elevators, but on the nineteenth, by coincidence, Chairman Buttrick was able to report that the Club had been given a moose head, together with—rarest and most appreciated of gifts—a fund for its maintenance. That evening, honoring Virgil Thomson '22 on his eighty-fifth birthday, four distinguished singers and instrumentalists sang and played selections from his works in Harvard Hall. The concert, attended by a large and enthusiastic audience, was followed by a champagne reception.

At the Board's December meeting, President Bush of the Club foundation reported that he had raised $46,000 so far for scholarships and hoped to raise $50,000—that sum targeted for so many years but only once attained, in 1969—by the end of the year. (He would do it.) President Barker revealed that former President Gordon was looking into ways to finance major undertakings like buying 35 West 44th Street. And Crocker Luther suddenly and spontaneously praised Harry Buttrick for doing so much to restore the Club's glorious interior.

By then, the missing waterbuck head had mysteriously reappeared. After a quick touch-up at the taxidermist's it would be back in place.

Although all four of the Club's officers were returned to office on January 21, 1982, change was in the air. Within days came the first of three panel discussions about change to come: this one, on communication, would be followed by panels on "Science: Fact and Fiction," with Isaac Asimov, and on future architecture and design, featuring Buckminster Fuller. In February, Membership Chairman Jacqueline E. Jeffrey B'72 suggested to the Board several ways to slow the Club's growth, including creating a waiting list for resident members by only admitting a limited number each year, perhaps 200. And March brought changes in the committee structure: the establishment of an Audit Committee, the reestablishment, at Treasurer Merrill's initiative, of a Finance Committee and the reinstatement of an Inspection Committee charged with regularly inspecting the entire clubhouse.

At that meeting, the Board adopted one of the Jeffrey proposals: to discontinue summer and December visits to the Business School in quest of certificate holders. And President Barker reported having signed an option to lease the Gould-Mersereau building and land, an option he had been given 120 days to exercise. Chairman Buttrick described for his colleagues the hoped-for end product: a structure thirteen stories tall with two elevators, banquet rooms and forty-five to eighty-one bedrooms, to cost in all between $6 and $8 million.

In April, the Club received two Cold War communiqués: talks by Chief of Naval Operations Admiral Thomas B. Hayward on the Navy's global mission and by former ambassador to Poland William Schaufel, Jr., on the crisis in that country, now under martial law. On a lighter note, the Recent Graduates offered lessons in ballroom dancing, on which they themselves, raised in the rock era, had largely missed out. (The series, interestingly, would sell out quickly.) In response to appeals from the House Committee, Robert Metzger B'63 and his brother Ronald gave the Club a Steinway baby grand; it had belonged to their mother, and it would, fittingly, debut at the Club on Mother's Day, May 9, following a champagne brunch, when a young Juilliard pianist, Kristina Suto, would play pieces by Chopin, Beethoven, Debussy and Haydn.

The following month, the Board balked at yet another 8 percent dues increase to counteract inflation, but then agreed to it. Reminding his hearers that they would have to decide next month whether the Club was to exercise its option, House Committee Chairman Chapman read aloud a message from the absent Senator Goodman urging them to "seize the flood at full tide" and do it. Finally, Activities Co-Chairman Ann L. Maitland R'51 summarized the events, an amazing eighty-three in number, which were making the current season the Club's busiest ever for entertainment and instruction. They would continue into the summer: coed softball games with the Yale Club in Central Park, a visit to a flight simulator to "fly" a jumbo jet, even a dance.

In June, it was duly

> RESOLVED, that the Board authorize the President to acquire the Gould-Mersereau premises at 35 West 44th Street.

The die was cast, and most Board members surely felt relieved, but then came a melancholy reminder of how things can go wrong as Treasurer Merrill reported filing a claim with the Club's insurance carrier involving former General Manager Kekllas and former Food and Beverage Director Tasso Leon. Losses in goods and cash blamed on the pair, incurred between July 1978 and June 1980, had been discovered and reported to the bonding company in December 1981: they amounted to $114,493, but the maximum coverage under the Club's policy was $35,000 per employee.

Even though the economy was in recession, the Club was still growing, and at the start of fiscal 1983 membership stood at 8,924, a net gain for the year of 370—almost exactly a member a day.

By September, the Club had received insurance compensation of $70,000 (offset, unfortunately, by $15,000 in collection costs) for its loss from the depredations of Kekllas and Leon. Chairman Chapman informed the Board that the Club would be taking possession of 35 West 44th Street in December, that the House Committee had appointed a Development Committee headed by himself and that this new group was hoping to rent out space in the new premises for as much as $200,000 a year, considerably more than the anticipated annual carrying cost of $135,000. The meeting ended with a report that may be unique of its kind in the Club's annals: Co-Chairmen Stephen L. Wald '57 B'59 and Oscar Schafer '61 B'64 of the Travel Committee had resigned from their posts with a recommendation that their committee be disbanded for want of interest on the part of members. The Board accepted their resignations, but tabled their proposal.

On October 21, Secretary Kramer reminded the Board that the year 1990 would mark the 125th anniversary of the Club's founding, and suggested that a history of the Club be prepared for that occasion. After much discussion it was decided to ask the Communications Committee to begin research and make recommendations as to the format and authorship of a Club history.

Inspired by the eager response of their contemporaries the previous spring to the offer of ballroom dancing lessons, the Recent Graduates offered more lessons that fall in the fox trot, the rhumba and the waltz; again, the series would soon be sold out, and at least a few of its faster learners presumably joined their elders and their guests in Harvard Hall on November 12 to glide gracefully through an evening of Viennese waltzes. Meanwhile, a panel discussion sponsored by the Radcliffe Club drew attention to the fact that among recently admitted new members Business School graduates far outnumbered graduates of the Law School or any other branch of the University except the College. Its title asked the question "The MBA: Gilt or Gold?" (Most holders of the degree, of either sex, would presumably have opted for the latter alternative—at least until a certain day in October five years in the future.)

On December 2, a unique event in the history of the Club occurred when its first woman member, soprano Heidi Nitze, presented a recital of songs by Scarlatti, Berlioz and others. Happily, the evening was a resounding success.

Eleven days later, the Board learned that a $300,000 central air-conditioning system would be installed on the fourth and fifth floors, replacing the bedroom units, and former President Moseley paid tribute to Secretary Kramer for the "superb job" he had done throughout eleven years, one of the longest tenures on record, in an ever more demanding post. He pronounced himself delighted that his old friend and classmate Bob Barker had agreed to stay on as president for another year.

At midnight on December 31, 1982, as, in Harvard Hall, Recent Graduates and their guests welcomed the New Year with horns, noisemakers, funny hats, paper streamers and champagne, responsibility for overseeing day-to-day operations at 27 West 44th Street passed from Restaurant Associates to House Committee Chairman Chapman.

Beginning the previous September, the *Bulletin* had run a series of articles on aspects of the Club's past under the heading "Copperplate and Clippings." Written by Daniel A. Shepard '43, soon to succeed James O. Wade '62 as chairman of the Communications Committee, these pieces would continue to appear through the coming year.

On January 20, participants at the annual meeting reelected the president and vice-president, then elected a new secretary, J. Dinsmore Adams, Jr., and a new treasurer, John L. Casey, Jr. '45 L'48. President Bok spoke after the dinner, and his portrait, long on view in the entrance hall, was at last officially unveiled; it was the sixth by William F. Draper to hang in the clubhouse, after likenesses of President Kennedy and of former Club Presidents Streeter, Kunhardt, Larsen and Rothschild.

That January saw the first expansion of the Club's athletic facilities in several years with the opening, in renovated space on the eighth floor, of a gym equipped with Nautilus, Universal and other exercise machines. The Cowles tournament ended in an all-Harvard finale, with sophomore David Boyum '85 besting freshman Kenton Jernigan '86. And in March, at a well-attended reception in the Cambridge Lounge, the Club's racquet wielders bade farewell to Coach Frank Iannicelli, retiring after thirteen years of imparting the fine points of the game in words bright with his own brand of wit. It was an emotional occasion. Happily, the Club was able to procure the services, as assistant to Milt Russ, of John Greco, for eighteen years squash pro at the University Club.

In April, with John R. White '42 and his Development Committee pondering ways to finance the 35 West 44th Street project (now estimated to cost $10 million), the Board adopted a budget for 1984 including still another 8 percent dues increase. President Barker noted that Restaurant Associates, acting this year as a consultant, was conducting its first internal audit of the Club's operations. And Vice-President Kimball brought the meeting to a rousing close by recounting how the redoubtable Albert H. Gordon had recently, sixty years after last running for Harvard, competed in a marathon footrace in London, finishing the standard course of 26 miles and 385 yards in six hours.

On May 3, in the Biddle Room, Lieutenant General Robert C. Kingston delivered a Cold War briefing on the Rapid Deployment Task Force, which he commanded; then, after an oboe-and-harpsichord concert, a Mother's Day champagne brunch, a German wine seminar, a talk about ocean liners, and a gourmet dinner awesomely priced at $125, the Club witnessed, on the afternoon of Saturday, May 14, a romantic event: the wedding, in the Cambridge Lounge, of Executive Secretary Nancy Eikey and General Manager Buck. In the June *Bulletin,* Editor Stewart ran a reproduction of a *New Yorker* cartoon by Gardner Rea, the framed original of which had long been on display in the clubhouse, showing newlyweds leaving a church, with the bride anxiously asking the groom, "Does that 'forsaking all others' include the Harvard Club?"

In May the Board, at President Barker's request, disbanded the Travel Committee. And Membership Chairman Diane K. Schulz B'63 reported recruiting, with her colleagues, 350 applicants in Cambridge and Boston at a cost to the Club of $3,500, or ten dollars apiece. At fiscal year's end, the Club had 9,220 members, up 296 in a year. The library, too, had grown, notably through donations by two members. Kenneth J. Stuart, Jr. '63 gave 100-plus new books, while E. Kennedy Langstaff '44 B'49 contributed a collection of Harvardiana comprised of more than 200 items, some virtually impossible to duplicate, belonging to his late father, B. Meredith Langstaff '08, a member of the Club for over fifty years.

By then the entire fourth floor was off limits as a two-year renovation

*"Does that 'forsaking all others' include the Harvard Club?"*

**Drawing by Gardner Rea; © 1959 The New Yorker Magazine, Inc.**

of the bedrooms got under way, the most ambitious program of its kind the Club had undertaken since 1947. That summer, members basked gratefully in the coolness produced by the powerful new 140-ton air conditioner, and on July 21 a Western barbecue drew a good-sized crowd. September saw the arrival in the executive office of Carol Ann Danko, who, in the many-faceted post of assistant to the general manager, would soon be playing an increasingly active and central role in the life of the Club. By mid-October the reconstruction of the fourth floor was complete: four private bathrooms had been added, as well as new double hung windows, new wiring, thermostatic controls in each room and a central smoke detection and fire alarm system.

In November, University Relations Committee Chairman Goldberg reported that 200 members had reserved seats for the upcoming University-sponsored "Harvard Comes to New York." As chairman of an ad hoc Committee on Committees set up in February to review the functions of the various committees in the management of the Club, Vice-President Kimball revealed its conclusions: that there were too many committees; that the committee structure should be simplified and improved in line with the Club's improved management; that the Executive Committee should have certain oversight responsibilities; that the reporting arrangements of all committees should be clearer; and that the budgets for which the various committees were responsible should be better coordinated.

As December began, the Club hosted "Harvard Comes to New York," a weekend program of continuing education featuring eminent scholars down from Cambridge. On Friday the second, President Bok spoke of Harvard's growing concern for and involvement with the Third World. He stated that each year about 900 students from developing countries were enrolled in the University, adding that five of South Africa's eight leading black newspapers were headed by former Harvard students. On Saturday, overflow audiences attended seminars ranging from the ancient Greeks to preventing nuclear war.

Twelve days later the Board approved the findings of the Committee on Committees and voted to dissolve that body. President Barker reported on the status of a computer system, designed and programmed by Winthrop Brown & Company to speed up the Club's accounting, that was being installed under the supervision of Carol Brown, wife of former Admissions Chairman Cyrus W. Brown II. It was, Barker declared, almost completely in place. But computer systems, according to a tradition of no great antiquity, were supposed to have names. What to call the Club's? In delighted unanimity, the Board seized on a suggestion from Treasurer Casey that it be named after that lonely freshman of yore and lore, Rinehart.

As his final act of both the year 1983 and his presidency, Barker asked his colleagues to approve the expenditure of $970,000 in the coming year for renovating the fifth floor. The Board obliged.

The arrival of the year in which the late George Orwell had set his bleak novel of the future, *1984*, found the Club's prospects anything but bleak. Membership was increasing, day-to-day operations were proceeding smoothly under the direction of General Manager Buck and his able lieutenants and hopes were high that before long a lofty addition to the clubhouse would rise alongside it. Indeed, 1984 would bring positive developments, most conspicuously the renovation of the fifth-floor bedrooms, the debut of Rinehart and, not least, a wholesale simplification of the Club's table of organization.

Elected president and vice-president, respectively, at the 1984 annual meeting, were Richard W. Kimball and D. Broward Craig. Secretary Adams and Treasurer Casey were reelected. And before January was out, a start was made toward rationalizing the Club's complex organizational structure. The Employee Welfare Committee (formerly Pension & Retirement) took over the functions of the Investment Committee, in particular managing the retirement fund, and welcomed Chairman Stephen L. Wald (former co-chairman of the now-defunct Travel Committee) to its ranks. Similarly, the Admissions Committee took in Membership Chairman Schulz while absorbing her committee.

The next month, Rinehart went on-line. Its usefulness would grow, for in addition to speeding up accounting, it could gather and report information on the uses members were making of the Club, data of considerable value to officers, Board members and others trying to frame programs and lay plans for the Club's future. On February 16, the Board agreed to the creation of an Executive Committee, composed of the four officers and, initially, Messrs. Chapman, Kramer and V. Lee Archer, Jr. '65, to oversee the Club's operations. In late March, the Board granted the Executive Committee all of its own powers between its meetings.

Meanwhile, the Club's dozens of dedicated bridge players were elated by their team's triumph in the College Club Bridge League's annual tournament. "Rarely," the *Bulletin* commented, "does a club win every match in the League, one of America's oldest bridge organizations. *But Harvard did not lose a match!*"

In line with the trend toward consolidation, the Activities Committee, having earlier taken over the functions of the Recent Graduates, joined forces with the men and women sponsoring appearances by Harvard professors in the name of University Relations to form a Program Committee. President Kimball announced the signing of a union contract to run for thirty-nine months. Late in May, the Board agreed to a 9.5 percent dues increase recommended by the Executive Committee, and a few days later members could read in the June *Bulletin* about an honor being conferred on one of their fellows:

> Albert H. Gordon, President of the Harvard Club from 1971 to 1975, is to receive the Harvard Medal on Commencement Day. The medal is the only award honoring extraordinary service to the University.
>
> After College and Harvard Business School, Mr. Gordon rose to his present post as Chairman and Director of Kidder, Peabody, Inc. A former Overseer of the University, he is currently Co-Chairman of the Harvard campaign. He has always been a generous benefactor and a tireless fund-raiser for Harvard. And he is a great believer in keeping fit. To symbolize his enjoyment of competitive running, the Albert H. Gordon Track and Tennis Center was named in 1981, and the road between the Business School and the playing fields was dedicated as the Albert H. Gordon Road in 1973.

On June 21, Development Chairman White, updating the Board on the status of that perennial target of takeover hopes, the Webster, confirmed reports that representatives of the Cornell Club were talking with the holder of the hotel's second mortgage about the possibility of acquiring it. White was told to stay on the case and keep the Board informed, but when, on July 17, he reported back, the Club's governors realized that, with the hotel's first and second mortgages both in default, numerous holdover tenants still occupying rooms and a partial renovation of a building in shambles, acquiring and remodeling the property would be an exceedingly dubious undertaking should the Cornell Club withdraw from negotiations—as it very soon did.

That summer saw an expansion of "year-round programming," with the now-traditional late June clambake followed by a "Western Night" in July and a "Caribbean Night" in August. And later that month the Executive Committee decided that Communications Chairman Shepard should act as senior editor of a history of the Club to appear in 1987, marking the centennial of the Club's incorporation.

At the end of October, Club Auditor Kenneth D. Weiser B'49 informed the Board that by the end of fiscal 1985 nine more computer terminals would be in place. The next month, a default judgment was handed down in New York State Supreme Court, New York County, against John Kekllas and Tasso Leon; the Executive Committee resolved to see to it that this judgment was recorded as well in Nassau, Suffolk and Westchester. Meanwhile, Chairman (and editor-designate) Shepard had left the Club.

With membership hovering around 9,500 and growing, the Club had long since stopped needing to make concessions to gain members, and on November 28, the Board at last adopted a recommendation by the Admissions Committee that holders of certificates of graduation from nondegree courses no longer be eligible for membership. Then, in mid-December, the Executive Committee's V. Lee Archer told the Board about his search for a new Communications chairman and senior editor of a Club history—to appear, he specified, in 1990, for the 125th anniversary of the founding of the Club in 1865. Archer neither accounted for nor even mentioned the postponement by three years of the potential book's publication, but common sense suggests a likely explanation: on realistically appraising what would be involved in preparing such a history, Archer and company may have perceived that the task could take considerably longer to complete than they had first thought.

The year 1985 was just sixteen days old when General Manager Buck called for the hiring of a catering director, a repair and maintenance secretary, a banquet headwaiter, a dining room manager and a housekeeper. The Executive Committee accepted this rather tall order without demur. President Kimball then announced that Linda Rawson had agreed to serve as chairman of the Communications Committee.

At the annual meeting, the incumbent officers were reelected. The following week, the yearly squash "weekend," now four days long, began, as usual, with Jack Barnaby conducting a "clinic" in which he demonstrated various fiendish tricks for winning. Last year's Cowles runner-up, sophomore Kenton Jernigan, triumphed this year, while the Barnaby Cup went to Kevin Pickens, editor and publisher of *Racquet Quarterly.*

On February 21, President Kimball discharged the Development Committee, with thanks to Chairman White and his associates, and at a

Board meeting one month later he congratulated Donald Bush on the Club's foundation's having raised more than twice as much in donations for scholarships as had any other Harvard club in the country. Program Committee Co-Chairman Nehama Jacobs '73 then told about an informal survey she and her colleagues had conducted among new and young members to determine why so few attended black-tie events: perhaps surprisingly, in that supposed heyday of the pushy, overpaid yuppie, it turned out that the main deterrents were diffidence and lack of the wherewithal.

In mid-May, Chairman Chapman informed the Executive Committee that the lease of Electrical Enterprises, Inc. of the ground-floor premises at No. 35 was running out, and because that tenant had often been behind with the rent, would not be renewed. Around then, scaffolding appeared high on the clubhouse's rear facade as workmen began replacing the copper plates, worn thin by time and weather, that formed a kind of skin on the mansard roof above the fifth floor. Their task would be completed by mid-June, as would the installation of a new and more flexible telephone system. And on May 22, after approving operating and capital budgets for fiscal 1986, the Board learned about an interesting new development. Whereas teams representing the Club had for decades competed with teams from other university clubs in squash, in tennis and golf, in baseball and softball—and at bridge, chess and backgammon—its members had never joined with those of other clubs in purely pleasurable activities. Now, Nehama Jacobs announced that, on an evening in late July, members would have the option of cruising around Manhattan in a chartered Circle Line boat with male and female graduates of Yale and Princeton. That cruise (which would actually take place in the fall) would prove to be the first of countless events of various kinds at which young Club members have ever since mingled happily with alumni and alumnae of other, mostly Ivy League, institutions.

Before the meeting adjourned, former President Gordon, recalling an even bigger break with precedent, "regaled the company with tales of the tumultuous sexual revolution of the early '70s at the Club."

The Club's principal tenant, Electrical Enterprises, did not decamp on schedule, so in June the store was emptied of its contents and its sales force evicted. On June 10, the Board appointed a preliminary building committee (Edward L. Saxe '37, chairman, Michael Yamin '53 L'58 and, ex officio, President Kimball) charged with interviewing at least five architectural firms as a first step toward picking the one that would design the new addition. And as of July 1, the Club, its managerial staff strengthened by the addition of a new executive housekeeper, Eithne Doniguian, numbered 9,822 men and women.

On the evening of August 12, Donald Bush, eighty-four, was walking home from the Club when he was felled by a fatal heart attack. As President Kimball's tribute in the September *Bulletin* would make clear, Bush had been one of that small band of individual members, beginning with Evert Wendell, who gave of themselves no less unstintingly than most presidents in the service of the Club.

On October 16, George Kramer told the Executive Committee about conversations he had recently held with a certain member who, joined by a few others, had for many years privately sponsored the annual football dinner (renamed the sports dinner) and now wanted the Club to take on this responsibility. The men hoped that the dinner's traditions could be continued, in particular the presentation to a deserving lineman on the football team of a trophy named for the late Charles A. ("Tubby") Clark, Jr. '19, a guard on Harvard's 1919 eleven and afterward a much-liked member of the Club; the award had been given every year since Clark's death in 1960. The matter was referred to the Program Committee, which would agree that the Club should indeed sponsor the event, traditions and all.

At the next Board meeting, Chairman Saxe of the Building Committee recounted how he and his colleagues had gone about interviewing architectural firms. After seeking advice from various sources, including the dean and chairman of the Department of Architecture at the Harvard Graduate School of Design, they had met with eight highly qualified candidates, interviewing six of them twice. In the end, his committee recommended that Edward Larrabee Barnes be retained as architect for the initial phase of the expansion project.

As always, the activities available to members that fall were extraordinarily varied. Some were cultural (biographers Justin Kaplan '45 and Burke Wilkinson '35 discussing, respectively, Mark Twain and Augustus

Saint-Gaudens; Professor David G. Mitten AM'58 PhD'62 on ancient Lydia; architect Moshe Safdie on his new Columbus Circle building project; screenwriter-lawyer Alan Trustman '52 L'55 and novelist-play-wright-psychiatrist Stephen Bergman '66 MD'73 on themselves). Others were musical (jazz, Mozart, the Harvard Band, a choral concert), theatrical (*As Is, Two's a Crowd*), and sybaritic (champagne brunches, food and wine tastings and seminars, Thanksgiving and Christmas dinners). Thursday lunchtime football films enabled members to follow the fortunes of the Crimson eleven without stirring from the clubhouse; cinema nights brought back great foreign films that could be seen nowhere else; and on November 15 Harvard Hall and the Main Dining Room once again became the setting of a formal dinner dance, with a good many waltzes: "A Night in Old Vienna."

That gala event was already in its fourth year, while the Club's other regularly scheduled dances—the one on New Year's Eve and May's "Swing Into Spring"—had been fixtures even longer. But some events seemed linked to current trends: thus an illustrated lecture on the Victorian photographer Alice Austen and a panel discussion among women mystery writers, both sponsored by the Radcliffe Club, could be seen as feminist affirmations. And two other events, a once-postponed "midnight cruise" around Manhattan, with dancing, and an evening of mixed doubles tennis in the huge facility called Tennisport, ushered in the latest thing in Club distractions, events shared with members of other university clubs.

In November, the House Committee decided to rent the ground-floor space at 35 West 44th Street to the Barson Hardware Company. And on the twenty-first, the Board reached two decisions concerning the supposedly forthcoming Club book: first, that, preparatory to the bylaws being published in it, Secretary Adams would incorporate in them those recommendations of the Committee on Committees that the Board had approved on December 15, 1983, and second, that the book, similar in format to the last one, which had been published in 1980, should appear every two years.

Late in the afternoon of Friday, December 20, an era quietly ended as Thelma Leventhal cleaned out her executive office desk and left the clubhouse, no longer an employee. She had been with the Club since 1955, and since 1965 had, as admissions secretary, carefully gone through the dossiers of uncounted thousands of applicants, in the process breaking in more than a score of novice admissions chairmen and hundreds of their volunteer committee members. She may well have been the Club's foremost expert on the bylaws, the membership matrix and the procedures leading to election.

Two days before Christmas, the Club was again in the news, in a *New York Times* report by Susan Heller Anderson and David W. Dunlap:

### THE HARVARD CLUB
### WEIGHS EXPANSION

Another McKim, Mead & White building, the Harvard Club at 27 West 44th Street, may be getting a new look that is meant to respect the old.

The club is now taking "steps toward a possible expansion of the clubhouse on the site occupied by a small building at 35 West 44th Street and the two-story portion of the present building," Richard W. Kimball, president of the club, wrote in a December 10 letter to fellow members.

An architectural challenge is posed by the fact that the site lies between Charles McKim's restrained Georgian clubhouse and the exuberant Beaux-Arts New York Yacht Club at No. 37.

"We have not specified the number of floors to be built on the site," Mr. Kimball wrote. "We have only specified that the expansion should be a responsible contribution to the urban landscape, respectful of its landmark neighbors and of a scale which will not harm the club's traditional character.

"If, as a result, the club finds itself with excess development rights [air rights], we may have an opportunity to sell them to someone who plans to develop a nearby property."

Edward Larrabee Barnes, class of 1938, has been chosen as the architect. Design plans and a proposed financing program will be ready for review by late spring, Mr. Kimball wrote, "before a decision is made whether and when to proceed."

Alumni who hope to get a swimming pool may be discouraged to learn that it has been overruled by the Board of Managers as a "staggering cost."

Traditionalists will likely be cheered by the board's conclusion that "Harvard Hall and the main dining room are sacrosanct, and that the grill room, the main staircase and the Cambridge lounge all have a special character which should not be affronted."

Squash pro Milt Russ at work—or is it play?

# 20

# TO BUILD OR
# NOT TO BUILD?
# (1986–1989)

When General Manager Buck told the Club's leaders he wanted to become an independent consultant to clubs, hotels and restaurants, a search began for someone to replace him. By the start of 1986, two candidates were still being considered, and on January 15, the Executive Committee decided to offer the job to Robert Arnold, a graduate of the Cornell School of Hotel Administration who, after Army service, had spent five years in managerial positions with Restaurant Associates and three supervising food service operations at museums and performing arts centers as well as restaurants. The following evening, D. Broward Craig was elected president and Edward L. Saxe vice-president, while Secretary Adams and Treasurer Casey were reelected. Some time around then, too, Richard Chapman yielded the chairmanship of the House Committee to Ames Brown, Jr. B'61.

During the squash weekend, Kenton Jernigan again won the Cowles, Joseph Dowling '87 the Jacobs, and member John G. Nelson '62 B'69 the Barnaby. "So far as anyone can remember," Athletics Chairman Philip H. Horwitz L'63 would assert in the *Bulletin,* "this was the first time that all three tournaments were won by Harvard." (No reader would challenge this statement, though in fact Harvardians had swept the annual tournaments as recently as 1981.)

In mid-February, the Board learned that Robert Arnold had accepted the Board's offer, and that Patricia Kaye would be taking on Thelma

Leventhal's job. On March 2, Arnold began work at the Club, operating in tandem with Paul Buck until the end of the month. And at a Board meeting on March 20, Program Co-Chairman Winthrop D. Perkins '74, citing the success of the first football dinner his group had organized, reported that he and Co-Chairman Jacobs were studying data generated by Rinehart to find out which programs rated highest with the membership. Meanwhile, the smorgasbord of events offered that winter and spring suggested that the tastes and concerns of that particular era were being abundantly catered to: in addition to concerts and recitals, brunches and wine tastings, films, illustrated talks and lectures by Harvard professors, members could learn from and perhaps benefit from programs devoted to "Greed and Glory on Wall Street," speculative investing, collecting art for profit, second marriages and personal computers. (Incidentally, the Employee Welfare Committee took steps around then to transfer the bulk of its retirement fund investments from fixed income instruments to equity stocks.)

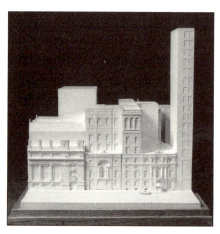

The following month, Barson Hardware balked at paying the Club $120,000 a year; negotiations would continue until September, when a mutually acceptable rental would be arrived at and a new lease signed. Then, on April 30, the Board members, convened in

The proposed Barnes addition (center)

special session, looked and listened intently as Edward Larrabee Barnes showed them drawings of the proposed eight-story addition, describing the building's internal features floor by floor and commenting on its unconventional facade. His presentation over, the architect invited questions on all aspects of the project except its cost.

That matter was dealt with at another special meeting one month later, when Barnes again reviewed the plans. Chairman Saxe reported that a feasibility estimate had put the cost of raising the addition at about $20 million, and although this figure was much higher than any previous guess, a show of hands revealed a solid majority of the men and women present in favor of going ahead with the project.

Meanwhile, the Board had approved a 4 percent dues increase and a recommendation by the Executive Committee that the Long-Range Planning Committee be disbanded.

When the Executive Committee next met in mid-June, the emphasis was on improvements in the existing clubhouse. General Manager Arnold reported, in particular, an unusual project on the fifth floor, where a common door was going to be hung in the corridor outside Rooms 508 and 509 to create connecting rooms, the Club's first suite. And Treasurer Casey announced that the Club would cooperate with the city's Human Rights Commission to help enforce Local Law 63, affecting private clubs. (This was the law, framed by City Council President Carol Bellamy INS'76, that would lead the Century Association—but not the Union, Knickerbocker or Racquet and Tennis Clubs—to admit women members.)

As of July 1, the Club's roster included 9,936 members. The increased value of its portfolio, moreover, gave the retirement fund a surplus, precluding the need for any contribution to be made to it during fiscal 1987.

That summer, with renovation of the third floor proceeding, the Club seemed to be moving inexorably toward realizing what would soon come to be called the expansion project. President Craig, Vice-President (and Building Committee Chairman) Saxe and banker Donald L. Shapiro '57 B'61 engaged Ralph Howell, a retired principal of E. W. Howell, Inc., to fill the key role of owner's representative in dealing with architect Barnes, potential construction managers and a project cost estimator he would hire. With regard to financing the project, different individuals explored different avenues: former President Gordon made inquiries in Cambridge anent the possibility of the University's providing some money, Treasurer Casey consulted fund-raising organizations about strategies and Donald Shapiro spoke of the Club's perhaps issuing bonds.

Between the fourth and seventh of September, in Cambridge, the Tercentenary Theatre (that part of the Yard enclosed by Widener Library, Emerson and Sever Halls, Memorial Church and University Hall) was the scene by day of successive colorful ceremonies celebrating Harvard's

350th birthday. George Kramer, resplendent in top hat and morning coat, was on hand as the Club's representative on the board of the Harvard Alumni Association, and as such its envoy.

Back in New York, Chairman Saxe recommended, on September 16, that the Executive Committee accept Barnes's proposal of architectural services in connection with interim construction, and his colleagues did so.

On October 6, the *New York Times* ran a small paid notice of the death at ninety-three of Irene Van Fossen, editor and author of the *Bulletin* from 1962 to 1975, and since then titular historian and archivist of the Club. "There was an elfin quality about her," former President Edward Streeter had observed in print on her retirement, "that makes time inconsequential, and we cherished her as a part of the Harvard Club which was very precious to all who knew her."

Three days after this Chairman Saxe presented the Executive Committee with recommendations strongly suggesting a retreat, for reasons of financial prudence, from the goal of very soon erecting an addition next to the clubhouse. The Building Committee wanted to proceed with the expansion project on a strictly limited basis, beginning with the renovation of the basement and the entrance hall and the creation of a flight of fireproof egress stairs from the third floor down to the second. Capital funds for the first two of these projects had been budgeted over the next three years. To achieve these limited goals Edward Larrabee Barnes would be asked to quote fees covering planning for the entire project, but planned in stages so that the work could be stopped at any time.

As of mid-November, the Building Committee still doubted that the Club could afford an addition any time soon. Its members had, said Chairman Saxe, proposed, for the next five fiscal years, to spend about $4.4 million to renovate the basement and to consider, as well, rehabilitating the elevators, renovating the entrance hall and constructing those fireproof stairs. Even to achieve these modest goals, Saxe declared, the Club would have to borrow about $1.3 million and tap $500,000 in capital funds.

President Craig said he suspected that an answer to financing the expansion project would be forthcoming in two or three months, but in the meantime, the Executive Committee felt the Club should concentrate on needed projects realizable within the capital budget, as supported by operations. The consensus was that the elevator project should be undertaken first, and the others postponed. Accordingly, Chairman Saxe was directed to ask Barnes to stop work for the time being on the main project, postpone work on the egress stairs and entrance hall renovations but continue work on the elevator rehabilitation and on securing the approval of the city's Landmarks Preservation Commission for his construction plan.

Four evenings after this, on November 20, President Craig concluded a routine meeting of the Board by leading a discussion on a painful subject: the proliferating stories in the press linking Ivan F. Boesky, a Wall Street arbitrageur who days before had been fined a record-breaking $100 million for illegal insider trading, with the Club.

Although Boesky had never attended any branch of the University, he had, in fact, belonged to the Club since 1981. Reporters had quickly learned how, after lunching at the Club as a guest one day and finding the place to his liking, he had contrived to join it. He had donated a substantial sum, reportedly $25,000, to Harvard's School of Public Health, an institution with many fewer wealthy graduates than, say, the University's schools of law, business or medicine, and promised to donate the same amount each year thereafter; understandably grateful, the school's governors had named him to their visiting committee, charged with monitoring the school for the Board of Overseers. It was his membership of that visiting committee that had enabled him to join the Club.

Since then, Boesky had become a familiar figure in the Grill Room and Harvard Hall on weekday afternoons, often huddled with one or more guests. Some members, recalling seeing him there, must have cringed at the thought that he could have been carrying out his dubious business under their very noses. But certain other members had long resented Boesky's presence: they were squash players, who day after day had been reduced to sputtering frustration waiting for a court while the one the arbitrageur had reserved (for three or four hours at a stretch, in case the desire and the opportunity to play should coincide) remained vacant. These men must have been overjoyed to learn, as they soon would, that Boesky had resigned.

In December, Margie Mizrahi joined the executive office force as admissions administrator, replacing Patricia Kaye, who had resigned. And two days before Christmas, the Club finally filed plans for an addition with the municipal body that passed on proposed alterations to landmark buildings or their neighbors. The following day, in an article by David W. Dunlap illustrated with an architect's rendering of the proposed structure, the *New York Times* gave New Yorkers an inkling of what the Club's governors were thinking, somewhat tentatively, of putting up in Midtown:

### THE HARVARD CLUB
### TAKES OLD FOR NEW

To build for the 21st century, the Harvard Club has borrowed its architectural plans from the 19th.

Wishing to expand its overburdened landmark home at 27 West 44th Street, the club submitted plans yesterday to the New York City Landmarks Preservation Commission.

A two-story addition at the west of the clubhouse and an adjacent three-story structure at No. 35 would be razed and replaced by an eight-story brick building designed by Edward Larrabee Barnes Associates.

Its most arresting feature would be a neoclassical arched window, fully two stories high, complete with an enormous semicircular light and flanking limestone columns.

Both the great central window and the set-back facade are meant to reconcile the building with its two distinguished but very distinct neighbors: the original Harvard Club building by McKim, Mead & White, and the New York Yacht Club, another landmark.

"The idea was to deal with the area as a whole," said Edward L. Saxe, chairman of the club's building committee. The landmarks commissioners seem generally satisfied, although they postponed a vote and quarreled with some details.

The vice chairman of the panel, Elliot Wilensky [*sic*], said the columns looked like pipes. Commissioner Anthony M. Tung said he worried that the design was "too coarse a stroke."

"There *is* a lack of finesse," the commission chairman, Gene A. Norman, said about the plan. "But I find that fine, in keeping with today's building techniques. There is no confusion with what was the original landmark."

If the addition were built as planned, the whole Harvard Club would take up 120,000 square feet, leaving 160,000 square feet of unused development rights that could be sold to another builder.

With the landmarks arbiters poised to bestow their blessing on architect Barnes's plans (and with office towers going up all over midtown Manhattan), it was only a matter of time before the Club would oust its tenants and commence demolition. Or was it? Seven years later, both the three-story No. 35 and the clubhouse's two-story western extension still stand, and the Club, though bigger and busier than ever, remains confined within its historic walls.

Why, after such protracted and painstaking preparations, was the addition not erected after all? Two developments that would occur in the year 1987 suggest a provisional explanation. First, the Club's governors, already reluctant to incur massive debt and facing problems in the clubhouse that demanded their attention, would unexpectedly find themselves compelled to spend sizeable additional sums to comply with new laws. Second, the crash of stock prices in October would shake public confidence, effectively putting the Club's building plans, along with those of many other institutions, on hold.

The year 1987 opened with a flurry of victories for both Harvard and the Club. Following the reelection of the four officers, Darius Pandole '88 won the Cowles tournament, James Lubowitz '84 the Jacobs, and Anil Nayar '69 the Barnaby; member John Nelson, moreover, was to score a hat trick in Metropolitan Squash Racquets Association competition by capturing the titles for men's singles, for the over-thirty-fives and for the over-forty-fives. In February, the Club's four-person bridge team nailed down the 1986–87 College Clubs Bridge League championship with a 6–1 record, while its chess players defeated the Yale Club in what would turn out to be an undefeated season.

On February 11, Building Chairman Saxe informed the Executive Committee of the Club's immediate goals: to, one, renovate the basement, two, install a sprinkler system, three, rehabilitate the elevators and four, construct fire stairs. Projects two and four were mandated by Local Law 16, concerning fire prevention. The Club would, Saxe said, implement the first two projects, maintain the elevators and defer action on the stairs until a decision was reached regarding construction next door.

The next evening, some three dozen Club members attended a new play by Horton Foote, *The Widow Claire*, at a Greenwich Village theater, then met to discuss it. This was the first of three such theater parties, the other plays being *Death and the King's Horseman*, by Nigerian Nobel laureate Wole Soyinka, and John Pielmeier's *Sleight of Hand*. One week later, 250 members and guests braved freezing temperatures to take in a panel discussion sponsored by the library's program committee (Ann L. Maitland, chairman) and moderated by James O. Wade on "How to Get Your Book Published." Meanwhile, as during so many winters past, the Schools Committee's approximately 100 volunteers, some but not all members of the Club, interviewed about 800 applicants to the College, mostly on weekends and mostly in the third-floor banquet rooms. Around fifty young men and women would receive a portion of their College expenses out of funds provided by the Club foundation, which that year would total $110,000, a record.

The performing arts were certainly not scanted that season, and various musical programs were appreciably enhanced by the participation in them of a Steinway grand piano, the extraordinary gift to the Club of John S. Rodgers '51 L'54 and his wife, Janet. On March 17, climaxing several evenings devoted to screening and discussing films, screenwriter and director Oliver Stone talked about his movie *Platoon*, based on his own military experience in Vietnam, and fielded questions. The event, in Harvard Hall, drew 600 people.

Later that month, General Manager Arnold presented an updated capital budget that included two major projects that the House Committee had passed on. The first, for which $45,000 had been allocated, was the relining of the entrance hall fireplace chimney, and the second, the removal of asbestos, in particular from the basement.

This last item was on the agenda because of recent legislation requiring building owners to root out the substance, long and widely used for fireproofing and for electrical insulation, that had lately been found to threaten health. As renovation of the basement could not begin until the asbestos was gone, $100,000 had been budgeted for its removal, but Chairman Saxe warned that the cost could well go higher, much higher. Incidentally, he reported that the Club's application for approval of the Barnes plan was moving through the Landmarks Preservation Commission more slowly than expected, chiefly owing, it appeared, to opposition to the large central window in the facade.

By mid-April, a House Committee study had computed the cost of removing asbestos throughout the clubhouse as "astronomical." Meeting in early May, the Executive Committee heard House Committee Chairman Brown call for "complete sprinklerization" instead of gradual installation of sprinklers to meet the law's minimum requirements, and on the twenty-first, the Board approved budgets for the coming fiscal year, including a 4 percent dues increase.

Hopes persisted of somehow obtaining funding for the "development project" next door. Early in June, a presidential trio—Messrs. Craig, Gordon and Barker—traveled to Cambridge for talks with University Treasurer Roderick MacDougall '51, but they failed to extract a commitment from the University. Meanwhile, Chairman Saxe was busy discussing the possible sale of air rights with potential buyers.

When fiscal 1988 arrived on July 1, the Club's membership came, for the first time, to five figures: 10,128. And also for the first time the library—the Harvard Library in New York, as it was now designated—possessed, thanks to a generous gift from Lester J. Tanner L'49, a capital endowment fund. This was, for the library, a true milestone. Other benefactors included Dr. Howard Schomer '37 G'40, who gave a set of the *Encyclopaedia Britannica*, and friends of Ronald S. Daniels '50, who purchased the multivolume *New Grove Dictionary of Music and Musicians*. Among books repaired and restored were first editions of poems and essays by T. S. Eliot and the first edition of Dr. Johnson's dictionary that "Copey" had left the Club.

One evening in July, a number of men and women came together in the Cambridge Lounge for drinks. Members all, they were all also unattached—unmarried, divorced or widowed—and aged thirty-five or older. They were endorsing, by their presence, an idea whose time had evidently come: to wit, that since they presumably had much in common, they should meet from time to time to share it. Before breaking up, in any case, they made plans to meet again in the fall.

On July 21, Building Manager Paul Hines presented the Executive Committee with certain major concerns. Although the fire code did not require it, he called for constructing an emergency egress stairway from the northwest corner of the Main Dining Room down to the 45th Street sidewalk, as recommended by the Barnes firm; the committee approved building it. Local Law 16 obliged the Club to keep an abundant water source on hand in case of fire; Hines suggested constructing a tank in the vault beneath 45th Street, and again the committee agreed. Citing studies, the building manager said that damage to the three main active chimneys, those rising from the entrance hall, the Grill Room and the Cambridge Lounge, was worse than thought, and that repairing them might cost $50,000 each; the committee decided that repair of the entrance hall chimney should proceed forthwith. Finally, the committee authorized constructing a doorway between the front desk and the cigar stand, which would make it possible to receive overnight guests in the entrance hall itself, with better security than at present.

Six weeks after this, President Craig informed the Executive Committee that painter Everett Raymond Kinstler had delivered his portrait of former President Barker. And the committee approved, inter alia, the purchase of four personal computers for the use of, respectively, Carol Danko, the Budget Department, Food and Beverage Controller Alan Dutton and Building Manager Hines's office.

The opening event of the Club's 1987–88 season happened to be a lecture, comparing Shakespeare's and Verdi's treatment of the Othello story, by Bridget Paolucci, a writer and broadcaster who had often in years past discussed operas before enthusiastic audiences. In the September *Bulletin*, informing members of her talk, there also appeared an announcement of a "Fall Singles Soiree" slated for late October; the notice called on unattached over-thirty-fives to join those who had convened in July at a special dinner table before the Paolucci lecture. This was the first mention in print of a new "club within the Club" whose members would soon be calling themselves Solos.

On September 14, the *New York Times* reported that former Harvard government professor Daniel Patrick Moynihan, already a member of what is sometimes called the world's most exclusive club, the United States Senate, was "applying for membership in the somewhat less exclusive Harvard Club of New York City." He was "taking no chances," the newspaper added, having picked to sponsor him no less exalted a personage than President Bok. Applicants were to be elected that night. Three days later, however, the *Times* claimed it had been informed by an anonymous caller that the senator had been rejected for not submitting to enough Admissions Committee interviews. Reached by telephone, the general manager's office had declined to comment, but before the month was out, the October *Bulletin* put the story to rest by listing Senator Moynihan among fifty-five new members elected on September 14.

Late in the afternoon of Monday, October 5, members arriving in the Grill Room for cocktails saw an unfamiliar ritual being performed at the far end of the chamber. While one waiter closed the folding doors to Harvard Hall, others set up, in front of them, a long, broad table on which they placed serving dishes heaped with colorful hors d'oeuvres. Had they asked, the newcomers would have learned that these tempting comestibles were traditional Spanish delicacies called tapas, described in the *Bulletin* as "bite-size snacks made of meat [or] fish, smoked, cured, baked, sauteed, raw or marinated." Before long, the tapas bar would become an established and popular accompaniment of the cocktail hour.

Earlier that year, the fifth in what was being hailed as the longest continuous bull market since the 1920s, the Dow Jones average of selected common stock prices had, for the first time, topped 2000, but on Friday, October 16, it dropped 50 points. On Monday, the dam broke: the Dow plunged 508 points, with stocks losing a fifth to a quarter of their value. In the Bar, the Grill Room, the Dining Room, the squash players' lounge, members asked each other whether the events of October 1929 could be recurring. Over the ensuing days stock prices would not rebound, but they would not keep falling, either, and feelings of panic would gradually subside. Still, confidence had been severely shaken. It dawned on Wall Streeters that the fat years were over. And with layoffs looming throughout the financial industry, much of yuppiedom was in crisis.

No visiting guru of finance, unfortunately, had tipped off members to the impending crash, but the Program Committee nonetheless strove as always to shed light on vital issues. Between Hallowe'en and Christmas, a member could take in a discussion of relations with Japan involving that country's envoy, the president and CEO of Mitsubishi, an assistant deputy secretary of state and the Kennedy School of Government's Robert Reich; another discussion on aid to the Third World featuring the head of the U.N.'s development program and the *New York Times*'s Leonard Silk; a talk by the Club's (and the Board's) Arthur L. Liman '54, former special counsel for the Senate select committee investigating military sales to Iran and military aid to the Nicaraguan contras; and an appearance by Dr. Ruth Westheimer, TV and radio's "Dr. Ruth," on matters of intense interest to everyone. Meanwhile, the Solos had signaled their arrival on the scene by holding their fall soiree, sponsoring a major event (Arthur Liman's "Irangate" talk) and seconding one of their number, Nathan Weston '47, to the Program Committee.

The Club's awesome Christmas tree was in place in Harvard Hall when the Executive Committee met again to consider capital projects. The general manager warned that displacements necessitated by upcoming work would force the Club to shut down two upstairs facilities: the masseur's quarters, needed for storing and issuing linen, and the dormitory, needed for use as a men's locker room. The masseur would be assigned other quarters, but there was no space anywhere in the clubhouse available for conversion into a dormitory. The committeemen were fully aware that the disappearance of the dormitory would represent a grievous loss to less affluent nonresident members who had long depended on its spare but affordable accommodations on visits to the extortionate metropolis, but they felt helpless to block it. As if to emphasize the finality of the move, Arnold said the relevant certificate of occupancy would probably be changed, eliminating the need to install sprinklers in the space. With, undoubtedly, considerable regret on the part of several men present, the committee voted to close down both facilities forever.

The Board's last meeting of 1987 was largely ceremonial. On behalf of the Board, writer and sometime backgammon champion E. J. Kahn, Jr., saluted President Craig for his leadership, whereupon Craig, after thanking the five retiring Board members for their service, announced that William R. Knapp '42, a senior editor at *The New Yorker*, would write and edit the Club history.

By January 13, 1988 (when Ambassador to the Soviet Union Arthur A. Hartman '47 L'50, back from Moscow, briefed the membership on that arresting figure Mikhail Gorbachev), General Manager Arnold and Chairman Brown had between them selected contractors to carry out the Club's impending projects. To the Executive Committee, they recommended that the Calcagno Construction Company renovate the basement and that AAA Sprinkler install sprinklers throughout the clubhouse.

The 1988 annual meeting brought the Club, unusually, four new officers: Edward L. Saxe became president and J. Dinsmore Adams vice-president, while George P. Kramer resumed the secretaryship he had held from 1972 to 1983 and Kenneth D. Brody B'71 took on the post of treasurer. Then came the squash weekend: if it produced no Harvard winners, it generated some excitement with the victory, in the Cowles, of that tournament's youngest-ever winner, seventeen-year-old Rodolfo Rodriguez, a Mexican boy attending a school in Pennsylvania.

In February, work began at last on renovating the basement, and although it went on out of their sight, it affected the members: the fact, in particular, that employees now had to ascend to the seventh floor to change into and out of work clothes increased congestion on the elevators, slowing up-and-down traffic in the building. With the laundry room out of commission, moreover, the Club had to send out its linens, tablecloths, towels and other fabrics to be laundered commercially, at considerable expense.

A paragraph in the March *Bulletin* noted a change in the tapas bar offerings, which now consisted of "tempting tastings with an international flair" prepared by Chef Arnold Fanger and defined as "Generous platters of Gravlax, Bunderfleisch and Escabache, [which] spill into abundant helpings of Calamari, Ceviche and Caponata."

On March 15, General Manager Arnold put the cost to date of asbestos removal at $190,000, and warned that, while those parts of the clubhouse covered by the original survey would ultimately be free of the material, there could be no guarantee that more of it might not appear when ceilings were opened up preparatory to installing pipes and sprinklers. Arnold also announced a development of interest to many members, especially squash players wanting to reserve a court: a new direct-in-dialing (DID) telephone service was in place, with separate numbers for each of eleven frequently called facilities in the clubhouse.

In April, William R. Reader began work as the Club's controller, and on the twelfth the Executive Committee discussed, without seriously considering it as an option, the practice then being followed by several New York clubs of assessing their members to finance major capital undertakings, notably those concerned with fire protection that Local Law 16 had made necessary. Reviewing the Club's ongoing projects, General Manager Arnold reported that work on the members' and staff's basement lavatories had slowed for the moment awaiting clarification of what was required by still another piece of municipal legislation, Local Law 58, governing access to such facilities by handicapped individuals. On the other hand, sprinklerization was proceeding apace on the bedroom floors, with no thought of the Club's forfeiting revenue by leaving bedrooms unoccupied, the *Bulletin* publicly promising that "Members and guests willing to rise a bit earlier and vacate their rooms so that work can begin will be rewarded with a complimentary Continental breakfast."

At the Board's April meeting, the revelation by Admissions Chairman John Katz '60 L'63 that his team had interviewed only 283 applicants in Cambridge caused little surprise, as the drop was obviously attributable to the reduction of job openings in the city. And President Saxe congratulated Frank Stanton LLD (hon.) '85 and his wife on their having endowed chairs at the graduate schools of design and government. Meanwhile, workmen carrying out their subterranean labors had made a startling discovery: that the upright timbers supporting the telephone room off the entrance hall were in an advanced state of decay, having been host to generations of termites. The telephones were hastily relocated for the nonce in the former ladies' entrance lobby, and the enfeebled wooden uprights replaced with steel ones.

Convening on May 19 at the special meeting called by President Saxe, the members of the Board reviewed questions set forth in a memorandum prepared earlier as a basis for discussion by Donald L. Shapiro, now chairman of the House Committee, and Communications Chairman Walter S. Isaacson '74. President Saxe sought comments from former Presidents Barker, Kimball and Craig on related matters they had dealt with when in office, notably the Barnes organization's feasibility study anent constructing an addition next door at a cost of—now—some $28 million. "A generalized discussion then ensued," the minutes relate, "as to what the Club is, what it should be, its proper constituency and its role in the local branch of the Harvard community." The meeting, unique in Club annals, quickly became a free-form soul-search. Subjects touched upon and questions raised included

• On the membership: The Club anticipated a net annual increase of about 300 members (about 200 in 1989). Was this acceptable? Should the membership be kept at its present level of about 10,000? What demands could be expected from an increased membership? Was it important to encourage younger graduates to join? One suggestion: that the demographics of the Club's current membership be analyzed.

• On operations: Should food services, athletic facilities and the like be subsidized? To what extent should facilities such as banquet rooms be used by nonmember groups, particularly commercial organizations having little or nothing to do with the Club? To what extent should the Club cater to the guests of members? What, in fact, *was* guest usage? Should guest charges for dining and for the use of other facilities be increased?

• On facilities: Should the membership be polled to determine what facilities they want? What should the Club's timetable be with regard to building the addition? Were there any guidelines as to what the Club could afford? Would it make sense to plan the building project in stages? What was the actual situation regarding the need for more bedrooms? What was the real cost of creating additional banquet facilities? Was there not a need for specialized facilities for programs, in particular a multipurpose auditorium equipped with state-of-the-art audio-visual systems? To what extent should athletic facilities be enlarged? Was a swimming pool desirable? And how much more office space was needed?

Summing up the discussion, President Saxe declared that the questions raised and tentative answers offered constituted an agenda for follow-up action.

The next night, Harvard Hall throbbed to the smoothly rhythmic beat of Stan Rubin's orchestra accompanying the Club's annual Swing Into Spring Ball, the multiclub second annual Rock & Roll Ball having filled the great hall less than a month before. And the scheduled events of the following weeks would show the Club, once again, in two seemingly contradictory but in fact complementary aspects: on the one hand, citizens concerned about vital issues of the day, and on the other, individuals belonging to one or more of the numerous groups into which so large and varied a membership as the Club's must inevitably divide. Thus on May 24 four panelists—an Israeli professor, an Arab professor, an American

Jewish think-tank member and Sir Brian Urquhart, lately of the United Nations—discussed what American policy should be with regard to the Arab-Israeli impasse. On the twenty-sixth, the Solos and singles of all ages, including Elis and Princetonians, gathered to compare group travel plans. On the thirty-first, the Radcliffe Club, marking the first anniversary of the establishment at Harvard of an honors-only concentration in women's studies, presented a talk by the head tutor in that field. And on June 15 James B. Stewart L'76 of the *Wall Street Journal* talked about the subject of a book he was writing that was destined to be a best seller: insider trading and the previous October's stock market crash.

At eight o'clock in the morning of Thursday, June 23, with a Board meeting scheduled for late afternoon, President Saxe called to order a special meeting of the Executive Committee, convened to follow up on the May 19 Board meeting. There were, he said, two fundamental questions requiring immediate attention: to wit, what facilities were needed and how soon, assuming annual membership growth of 300? And what could the Club afford to build, with or without help from Harvard—i.e., how much debt could the Club carry?

At the Board meeting, Treasurer Brody noted that the 1989 budget reflected a rise in labor costs, especially employee benefits, and included a 5 percent dues increase to keep pace with inflation. The Board approved it. President Saxe revealed that in view of the many doubts expressed at the May 19 meeting the Building Committee had been temporarily disbanded. And Chairman Isaacson announced that, as William Knapp had retired from *The New Yorker* and decided, on moving with his wife to the country, to withdraw from the project, he was recommending that Ormonde de Kay '45, a freelance writer and sometime magazine editor, write the Club history.

One week later, at the start of fiscal 1989, the Club's membership stood at 10,331.

Early in July Harvard Hall, the Main Dining Room, the Grill Room and the banquet rooms were all shut down for the installation of sprinklers and smoke alarms, and throughout the summer of 1988, while the Democrats nominated Massachusetts Governor Michael Dukakis L'60 for president and the Republicans Vice President George Bush, Yale '48, the

Club existed in a kind of half-life. But its governors stayed on the job. In August Controller Reader revealed to the Executive Committee plans to upgrade the Club's microcomputer system, expanded to include personal computers for each of eight operating departments, that would accelerate processing and permit the storage of much more data.

Thanks to concerted efforts by the staff, urged on by Executive Housekeeper Doniguian and Director of Facilities (formerly Building Manager) Hines, the banquet rooms, Grill Room, Main Dining Room and Harvard Hall were restored to the members on Monday, September 12. By then, President Saxe and his lieutenants had settled on the firm of Buttrick White & Burtis as consulting architects for capital projects, and on September 14 Treasurer Brody told the Executive Committee that an analysis of the Club's cash flow showed that funds were available to pay for a stepped-up capital program.

By September 20, when the Board met again for the first time since June, all asbestos had been removed from the clubhouse and renovations to the laundry, linen room and bake shop were complete, leaving all three operational. Secretary Kramer reported a curious development that, considering the bleak prospects confronting young job-seekers in finance, corporate law and other fields, was perhaps not so curious after all: that most of September's forty-eight new members had been out of the University ten years or more. And Chairman Shapiro praised the resilience of the members in coping with inconveniences the capital improvement programs were causing, such as the closing down of the basement ladies' room for installation of facilities for the handicapped and the consequent reassignment of the adjacent men's room, temporarily, to the exclusive use of women.

Should the Club's capital plans be reprogrammed? If so, how? From a discussion within the Executive Committee in mid-October it emerged

• that the Barnes plan for an addition remained the central document of record with respect to design goals;

• that plans to renovate the entrance hall would be reexamined after receipt from the consulting engineer of an elevator traffic survey, presumably including a sketch or rendering of a proposed lobby-to-third floor elevator rising from the present telephone room;

• that the conversion of squash courts one and two into a single regulation-size court would go forward; and

• that the consulting architects had suggested changes in the Library expansion plan (i.e., the plan to convert the Cambridge Lounge into a reading room) that called for a budget review.

Citing the critical shortage of office space, the general manager and the director of facilities said they would meet soon with the consulting architects to explore possible solutions, not excluding occupying the upper floors of 35 West 44th Street. And after discussion the committee rejected Chairman Shapiro's proposal to contract out the operation of the cigar stand.

On Election Day, to the satisfaction of most members, even the lawyers, Yale's Bush decisively outpolled Harvard Law's Dukakis for president. And on December 1, for the first time, the Club played host to the Christmas Revels, a program blending carol singing, a brass quintet, drama, dance and ritual performed by adult and child volunteers integrated with a troupe of professionals in medieval costume. First staged at New York's Town Hall in 1956 by folk singer John Langstaff (a brother of E. Kennedy Langstaff), the Revels had since been put on seasonally in Cambridge, Boston, New York and elsewhere. The production at the Club, featuring a mummers' play and morris dancing, was followed by a medieval dinner. Everyone—members, spouses, children—got into the spirit of the occasion to make it a joyous celebration—in short, a revel.

On December 7, by coincidence the anniversary of the Japanese raid on Pearl Harbor that plunged the country into the war he had vociferously opposed entering, former Congressman and Harvard football great Hamilton Fish turned 100. His family and friends feted him at the Club, and although the media were excluded, as required by the House Rules, reporters nonetheless managed to cover the story. "My mind is as good as it ever was," Fish told the *New York Times*'s Eric Pace in a telephone interview. Of his quondam upstate neighbor, fellow Club member and political archenemy Franklin D. Roosevelt, he said, "I know he hated me, but I really don't believe in hate. So now I don't hate Roosevelt—but frankly I despise him."

At the Board's last meeting of the year, Board member Frederic M.

Comins '37 noted that Evelyn McQuade—gentle, ever-cheerful Miss McQuade—would be retiring in January. He accordingly proposed, and his colleagues

> RESOLVED, that the Board of Managers of the Harvard Club of New York City express to Evelyn McQuade on behalf of the entire membership its deepest gratitude and appreciation for her many years of loyal, dedicated and tireless service.

As 1989 began, the Club's capital improvements program was entering its final phase, but a visitor would have been hard put to it to recognize the fact. On the sixth, seventh and eighth floors workmen were still installing sprinklers and fire alarms, to be activated that month, while others were constructing a new squash court. Elsewhere, painters and plasterers were restoring rooms and passageways to their pre-sprinkler condition. The addition of library shelving in the Cambridge Lounge had necessitated the closing of the Cambridge Dining Rooms, and the installation of facilities for the handicapped in the basement ladies' room kept that space off limits.

Needless to say, all this activity cost the Club more than mere inconvenience: On January 11 the Executive Committee approved a revised capital budget for the current year of $3,018,000. This figure included $225,000 for library expansion, more than double the original estimate, and an additional $65,000 for an extra glass wall at the seventh-floor exercise area, a new pro shop and office and a bridge connecting the gallery of the new court with courts seven and eight.

At the annual meeting a week later the incumbent officers were reelected. The after-dinner guest speaker was, for the first time, a woman: honorary member Matina S. Horner, who would be retiring in June from the presidency of Radcliffe.

Over the squash weekend the Cowles Committee awarded a trophy to pro Milt Russ, marking his first quarter of a century with the Club.

On February 7, the Club welcomed former West German Chancellor Helmut Schmidt LLD (hon.) '79; so enormous was the turnout for his lecture that closed-circuit television had to be employed. Schmidt's was the first of four talks delivered that year at the Club by four past and present leaders on four continents, the other three being former Nigerian head of

state General Olusegun Obasanjo, Japanese Ambassador Masamichi
Hanabusa and former Peruvian Prime Minister Manuel Ulloa. Later that
month President Saxe told the Board that he had had more mail about
Schmidt's appearance than about any other event. He had also received
numerous complaints of greatly increased third-floor traffic resulting
from the Harvard Business School Club's preemption of banquet rooms
for business meetings.

By March, all of the alterations and additions to the athletics floors,
including the new squash court, the expanded exercise area and the
bridge from the seventh-floor gallery to courts seven and eight, had been
completed. Just inside the clubhouse entrance, to one's right on entering,
rose a bulky and hideous "fire command station" mandated by Local Law
16: the hope was that future renovation around it might render it less conspicuous.

On March 16, House Committee Chairman Shapiro noted that an
entrance to the lower Cambridge Dining Room from the second landing
of the main staircase would be opened up that summer, adding that there
would be much less construction in 1989 than there had been in 1988.
Vice-President Adams declared, anent the expansion project, that implementing the Barnes plan would now cost $30 million. Finally, President
Saxe revealed that he, Treasurer Brody and member Samuel H.
Lindenbaum '56 L'59 were discussing with Rockrose Associates a proposal that the developer make use of the Club's air rights and a portion of
its prospective building site.

On the last day of March the Club bade farewell to retiring Main
Dining Room captain Jose Morales, affectionately known to members
and staffers for over thirty-seven years as Rocco. And on April 3 the
Cambridge Rooms, all three of them, reopened. Two weeks later the
Board, having studied proposed amendments to the House Rules,
approved ten, most notably one enjoining members from allowing anyone
to sign their names or use their audit numbers on chits.

Meanwhile, a bizarre incident had again thrust the Club into the news.
At about 6 P.M. on Saturday, April 15, a pair of policemen arrived at the
clubhouse and produced a warrant; they were shown upstairs to a bedroom where, in response to their knock, a middle-aged man opened the

door. Entering the room, the policemen started to search through its contents, and soon found what they were looking for, a cache of thirteen ancient coins; they arrested the occupant of the room and bore him off into the gathering dusk, to be booked on a charge of grand larceny.

The Club's overnight resident (a guest and not a member) was a California heart surgeon and coin collector, in New York to look over rare coins at the headquarters of the American Numismatic Society. Noticing after his visit that thirteen coins worth $70,000 were missing, an official of the society alerted the police, whose subsequent discovery of the coins in his Club room had made the surgeon a prime suspect in the disappearance from the same society's collection of additional coins worth some $250,000. But the plot kept on thickening: two days later the Californian, chastened and contrite, promised to return no less than $500,000 in coins he had purloined from the society, and was duly released on bail.

Early in May, with the handicapped-accessible facilities installed at last in the basement ladies' room, the men's room next to it reverted to its normal function. And before lunch on Friday, May 12, head bartender Alfredo Tamayo, erect and smiling behind the U-shaped bar, stirred and poured his last martini there; after twenty-two years at the Club he would soon enplane with his wife to retirement in his native Bilbao, in Spain. On the tenth, Treasurer Brody told the Board that employee wages and benefits were rising at a markedly faster rate than the cost of living. President Saxe called for a 6 percent increase in the dues, citing as a further argument heavy expenditures contemplated in the 1990 budget, including $700,000 to continue basement renovation. The Board complied.

Was Mayor Koch due for another term in City Hall? Aware that the winner of the Democratic primary in September would probably be elected their next mayor, many members were keen to know more about Koch's challengers. And although the Program Committee's "mayoral breakfasts" began at the early hour of 7:45 A.M., they would draw good-sized crowds. Four contenders appeared—Mayor Edward I. Koch, Richard Ravitch, Comptroller Harrison J. Goldin, and Manhattan Borough President David Dinkins. Both Republican hopefuls, former District Attorney Rudolph Giuliani and businessman Ronald Lauder, declined to participate, but the former would address a breakfast meeting in August.

On June 7 the Executive Committee agreed that talks with Rockrose Associates should continue, within certain guidelines: one, that no offer of less than $14 million for the Club's air rights and part of its site would be acceptable; two, that the developer should retain the Barnes organization in at least an advisory capacity and three, that the Board should be shown a model or rendering of the proposed structure. General Manager Arnold had both good and bad news to impart. Recalculation of the 1990 operating budget had resulted in a 15 percent reduction ($315,000) in the previously budgeted loss before membership income; that was encouraging, but the discovery that the basement still contained unknown quantities of asbestos was not. Removing it all, Arnold estimated, might cost as much as $100,000.

Renovation in the kitchen began on June 15, and that evening, when the Board met, President Saxe promised that the main tasks just ahead, rehabilitating the elevators and opening up a new door to the Cambridge Dining Rooms, would be carried out with minimal disruption. When fiscal 1989 expired fifteen days later, the Club's head count was 10,360; this represented a small gain for the year, but resignations had rocketed to 464, and when to this figure were added the 287 men and women who had been dropped, it turned out that 751 members had opted out of the Club in the last twelve months. Still, other New York clubs were also losing members, and in the Board's annual report, Saxe, referring to the Club's ambitious and costly capital projects, would assert, with pardonable pride, that "unlike other institutions faced with similar challenges, prudent planning made it possible to finance this $3,500,000 program without burdening the membership with assessments or debt."

As of mid-July, all summer construction projects were on track except in the basement, but then a licensed asbestos abatement firm was hired, and soon demolition commenced there. On the nineteenth, the Executive Committee increased the 1990 budget item for asbestos removal to $150,000.

That month, Loretta Brady resigned as manager of the front office, and David Goldstein, following five-year stints in the Accounting Department and as the Club's reservationist, took on the job of program coordinator. Meanwhile, certain suspicions regarding the facilities director were confirmed: confronted, one day, with evidence that he had removed valuable property from the clubhouse, Paul Hines abruptly resigned. An investigation was immediately launched, and in August the Executive Committee decided to retain a lawyer with criminal expertise. (By that time, incidentally, it had emerged that the Facilities Department had, of necessity, been exempted recently from strict controls because of the extraordinary volume of the construction materials continually being delivered.)

Early in September Fire Department inspectors found violations in the Club's fire alarm system. During the many months since the Club had filed a plan to comply with Local Law 16, that law had been amended, through Local Law 58, to require protection for deaf people, and it now appeared that smoke-activated strobe light alarms might have to be installed.

On the twenty-first Secretary Kramer presented the Board with a resolution to amend By-Law VII (Nominations for Office) by setting back the deadline for the Nominating Committee's submission to the secretary of a list of its nominees for the various offices, from "not later than December fifteenth" to the Board's November meeting. The resolution carried. Kramer then proposed that the Board elect the new president of Radcliffe, Dr. Linda S. Wilson, an honorary member, and it did so.

Carrying on a practice initiated a few years before, General Manager Arnold delivered his annual "State of the Club" report, noting, among much else, that the cost of employee benefits was rising rapidly and that the "Saxe Entrance" to the lower Cambridge Dining Room was in place. Chairman Shapiro reported that Chef Fanger had created a variegated menu of low-calorie dishes for the Cambridge Dining Rooms, scheduled to reopen in just six days. And President Saxe reported that he had sent President Bok a detailed proposal outlining how the University could help finance construction of the long-planned—and badly needed—addition.

In October, David A. Andelman '66 resigned as co-chairman of the Program Committee, but that month's scheduled events attested to the fact that he and Co-Chairman Judith Minton Ed'55 were effectively catering to the multifarious tastes of the Club's vast and diverse membership. In addition to the regular Thursday lunchtime filmed replays of the previous Saturday's Harvard football games and commentary thereon, sports enthusiasts could review, on film, in the company of former Olympics star and longtime Coach Bill Cleary '56, the Harvard hockey team's victory in the NCAA finals in St. Paul the previous spring. October's programs began with a recitation of poems by William Butler Yeats alternating with Irish ballads and ended with Indian poet Nissim Ezekiel reading from his own works, featuring, between these two events, concerts by a Chinese pianist and a Norwegian chamber music trio. But there was much, much more: for history buffs, a lecture on scientists and the French Revolution; for idealists, a talk by Father Bruce Ritter of Covenant House; for theatergoers, an evening capped by *Orpheus Descending*, starring Vanessa Redgrave; for oenophiles, a wine tasting; for the business-oriented, an evening about banking and finance with Martin Mayer '47 and another devoted to investing in motion pictures; and for terpsichoreans of all ages, a Hallowe'en Ball (at the Yale Club). All this in a single month!

With renovation of the basement all but complete, the Executive Committee was prepared, around Columbus Day, to concentrate thereafter on providing access to the clubhouse for the wheelchair-borne and on upgrading the athletics floors. Vice-President Adams revealed that the Club was planning to terminate masseur Nick Tsongas, absent since late June. And a week later attorney Henry Putzel III told the Board about talks he had held with Paul Hines's lawyer, recommending a course of action aimed at recovering as much as possible of the "misappropriated" funds and valuables. After amending the lawyer's recommended terms to make them tougher on Hines, the Board members directed him to proceed.

On November 7, Democrat David Dinkins defeated Republican Rudolph Giuliani by a small margin to become New York's first black mayor. Next morning onetime mayoral hopeful Richard Ravitch addressed a breakfast meeting in the North and Biddle Rooms on issues confronting the mayor-elect, who would take office in January. And some hours later the Executive Committee met in the Weld Room. Chairman Shapiro reported that Athletics Chairman E. William Judson '53 had presented to the House Committee a plan to renovate the sixth and seventh floors that bore a price tag of $750,000. Shapiro promised that a description of the plan, with drawings, would be posted on the sixth-floor bulletin board, for the attention and possible reaction of squash players and other users of the athletic facilities. And President Saxe spoke of two committees he felt would be useful: an ad hoc group to focus on the governance of the Club and another body, to be chaired by Dr. Frank Stanton, concerned with issues of marketing and communication.

Three days after this Americans watched on their television screens amazing scenes of jubilant young Berliners tearing down stretches of the wall that for twenty-eight years had divided their city as soldiers and policemen looked on impassively—images that brought home the stunning fact, still hard for people to credit, that after more than four decades the Cold War was ending.

At the Board's November meeting the Nominating Committee's report contained a surprise, recommending for the vice-presidency not one candidate but two, Charlotte P. Armstrong and Richard E. Gutman '66. Committee Chairman (and former Treasurer) John L. Casey explained that the two would have equal status, with neither possessing any claim on a future nomination to the presidency. He suggested, too, that the Nominating Committee remain in being all year round instead of only a few months, and that the secretary and treasurer serve, as a rule, for three years. It being the sense of the meeting that these recommendations were in order, Secretary Kramer said he would reword the bylaws to conform with the changes.

Chairman Shapiro announced that Secretary Kramer and member Malcolm M. Knapp B'63 would together review the perennial problem of members' publicly displaying business papers, adding that the House Committee was trying to decide how to deal with a related problem: the rather excessive use of the banquet rooms by the Harvard Business School Club, which during the last year had hosted no fewer than 124 events at the clubhouse, preempting space that would otherwise have been available for Club events and bookings by members. And President Saxe announced the creation of the two committees he had spoken of earlier: the first, headed by former President Barker, to explore ways of making the Club's system of voluntary self-management more efficient and more responsive to the members' wishes, and the second, to be chaired by Frank Stanton, a Marketing Resources Committee.

On December 12, with broad ribbons of bright red poinsettia flowing up both sides of the grand staircase and with a huge tree festooned with lights rising in Harvard Hall, the Board received a slightly premature but immensely welcome Christmas present in the form of a promise of solid assistance from Cambridge toward constructing an addition to the club-house. For months, as President Saxe related, Robert H. Scott AM'56 PhD'61, Harvard's financial vice-president, had been going over the Club's proposal with his colleagues, and only hours ago had finally com-municated the University's decision to certain unnamed members on the scene representing the Club. The Harvard administration, Scott had told them, agreed with the Club's objectives and was prepared to cooperate with it to make its expansion a reality.

There remained, to be sure, a few matters to be thrashed out with the University, but the news from Cambridge certainly made for a gratifying close to a year, a presidency and a decade.

Radcliffe Presidents Matina Horner (1972–89) and Linda Wilson (1989– )

# 21

# TO THE AGE THAT IS WAITING BEFORE (1990–1994)

Many members were undoubtedly relieved to see the last of the Eighties, though not a few had done very well by that "decade of greed." And now that the University was going to help fund its growth, the Club seemed destined to expand physically during the Nineties. Once again, however, such hopes would prove illusory. With the Club's governors forced to keep spending heavily to maintain the existing club-house, a less than robust economy would limit members' use of it, even as employees' wages and benefits, especially health benefits, were increasing at a rate twice that of inflation, consuming an ever greater share of the Club's revenues.

Like the student populations in Cambridge and Boston on which it drew, the Club was now more cosmopolitan in its makeup than ever before. Having begun early in the century to take in sons of new Americans from eastern and southern Europe, it had long since ceased to be composed almost exclusively of men of British or northern European descent. In the last couple of decades, moreover, it had, responding to demographic shifts within the College and graduate schools, admitted increasing numbers of minorities.

Keeping such a diversified membership entertained and involved was a challenge, but Judith Minton's Program Committee would meet it handily, in one season (1991–92) presenting twice as many events as its predecessor committee had done only five years before.

On January 24, 1990, in Harvard Hall, a good-sized crowd in evening dress elected an almost all-new slate of officers made up, for the first time, of five persons: President J. Dinsmore Adams, Jr., Vice-Presidents Charlotte P. Armstrong and Richard E. Gutman, Secretary Nehama Jacobs and (again) Treasurer Kenneth D. Brody. After the annual dinner that infrequent visitor to New York Derek Bok spoke about threats to the supposed supremacy of American higher education, in particular professors who shirked teaching to pursue research that was often of somewhat debatable utility.

That weekend, the yearly squash tournaments produced a record number of matches ending 18–17 in the fifth game. The surprise winner of the Cowles was freshman Mark Baker '93.

The following month, amid murmurs of relief, the Board accepted an offer of $110,000 from a lawyer representing former Building Manager Hines in settlement of all civil claims against him. But other financial developments were less rosy: returns from both banquet and à la carte service were down, and admissions were well below recent levels. In ongoing contract negotiations with Local 6, General Manager Arnold reported, contention focused on the skyrocketing cost of medical insurance. The Club wanted union members to pay a portion of this expense, but in the end it would drop this demand in order to obtain an agreement.

Meanwhile, the Board had approved the creation of a standing Nominating Committee, with seven to nine members instead of five, to be chaired by Frank Stanton.

In mid-April, Chairman Richard Rodwin revealed that nearly a quarter (23 percent) of all New York City applicants had been accepted into the Class of 1994 as compared to only 18 percent nationwide. (That spring, incidentally, in recognition of his many years of dedicated work with the Club's Schools and Scholarships Committees, Rodwin was picked to be one of the first eight recipients of a new Harvard Alumni Association Award.) Days later, a task force of present and past Admissions Committee members flew to Boston in quest of new Club members after having earlier bombarded prospective graduates of the College and the professional schools with letters and mounted a publicity barrage in the *Crimson, Harbus News* and other University publications. Thanks largely to this marketing blitz, they interviewed 513 applicants, 45 percent more than had been interviewed the year before, wiping out at a stroke fiscal 1990's cumulative admissions deficit.

On April 16, meanwhile, an unlikely but appealing entertainer had appeared in the Slocum Room: he was Stephen Powelson '38 G'40 L'41, a C.P.A. and resident of Paris, who had memorized all 15,693 lines of *The Iliad* and was prepared to recite virtually any of them on demand. Powelson's unique act was a hit, and in years to come he would be more than once asked back at his fans' insistence. Among events keyed to the contemporary world, a discussion the next evening between Israel's Abba Eban and Amre Moussa, Egypt's permanent delegate to the United Nations, rewarded attendees with insights they might never otherwise have received. Citing this evening and a subsequent talk by city Schools Chancellor Joseph Fernandez at the May Board meeting, Chairman Minton noted, too, the success of the dinner-theater evenings, routinely sold out, which had become even more popular since the introduction of a set pre-theater dinner costing under twenty dollars.

These dinners may well, as Dr. Minton claimed, have earned the Club an extra $10,000 per annum, but Treasurer Brody worried about employee wages and benefits ballooning by a full 10 percent in the previous twelve months, to the point where they accounted for 60 percent of the Club's expenditures. President Adams called for a 6 percent dues increase, and the Board obliged.

At the end of May the newspapers reported that President Bok would be stepping down next spring from what the *New York Times* called "the most prestigious post in American higher education." And one month later, on the final day of fiscal 1990, the Club's members numbered 10,542, a year-end head count never equaled before or since.

That summer, for the first off-season younger members could recall, no noisy, messy structural work whatever was carried out in the clubhouse. When, in August, Iraqi troops overran Kuwait and President Bush dispatched a huge land, sea and air military force to the Persian Gulf and Saudi Arabia in Operation Desert Shield, peace reigned at the Club, but in the fall rumblings of political warfare were heard from the Biddle Room, where breakfasts showcased in turn two rival candidates for governor of New York, Conservative Herbert London and Republican Pierre Rinfret. (Democratic Governor Mario Cuomo, the ultimate victor, would sidestep repeated efforts by the Program Committee to lure him to the breakfast table.)

On Sunday, October 7, three days after the official reunification of his homeland, former West German Chancellor Willy Brandt LLD (hon.) '63 spoke in Harvard Hall about a unified Germany's prospective role in world affairs. While members who attended were doubtless pleased that their Club had been deemed a worthy setting for such a historic address, they may have been less pleased to find themselves outnumbered, two to one, by guests from New York's German community and diplomats from many lands. Still, with President Bush lining up support from friendly governments for a concerted stand against Iraqi aggression, an international outlook prevailed at 27 West 44th Street; this was evident, in any case, from the events being offered members that month, including a talk by a Soviet economist about the impact of *perestroika* on the West, speculations by Harvard's Professor Samuel P. Huntington PhD'51 on the apparent worldwide trend toward democratization and a warning by Sir Brian Urquhart, a former undersecretary-general of the United Nations, of the urgent need for world leaders. (During the same month a member could also take in displays of Yugoslav folk dancing and Indonesian art, a lecture on the Jews of Yemen and such Middle European diversions as an Oktoberfest party and the traditional waltz evening known as "A Night in Old Vienna.")

More evidence of openness to things foreign was provided by the cordial reception accorded courses introduced that fall in conversational French and Russian. Both accompanied lunch in the Cambridge Rooms, but the Russian course, for beginners, was also taught over dinner.

By mid-November the Club had reached agreement with Local 30 on a four-year contract providing for modest wage increases and employee contributions toward medical coverage. This was, of course, gratifying, but it did nothing to ease the Club's cash shortage, resulting from a general economic downturn accompanied by a rash of resignations, particularly among resident members in their thirties who were just entering the age group paying the highest dues. Regarding the Club's weak financial position, House Committee Chairman Shapiro observed, astutely, that data for the years 1985–90 might well prove useless for predicting future membership gains and losses, revenue and economic activity, given the disappearance since then of two basic features of that period: "baby boom" demographics, which had exerted an abnormal impact, and a super-affluent revenue base provided back then by a booming financial services industry.

Concluding their meeting, the Board members congratulated publisher Robert Arnold, editor Carol Danko and their costaffers on the first issue of *FYI*, a newsletter about the Club that would appear from time to time promoting the various services and facilities available to members. And Secretary Jacobs announced that she was resigning to take on an executive position in Los Angeles with Price Waterhouse.

On Friday and Saturday, December 7 and 8, the Club was again host, for the first time since 1983, to "Harvard Comes to New York." Presidents Bok and Wilson headed a corps of professors who held forth all day Saturday, before an appreciative audience of around 400, on topics of general interest.

A week after this, Chairman Shapiro informed the Board that the House Committee had received a revised bid of $813,000 to renovate the athletics floors, an undertaking that could be accomplished between March and August 1991; the planned improvements would, he promised, appeal irresistibly to younger members of both sexes. His colleagues promptly authorized the expenditure. Next, the chairman proposed changing the House Rules to relax the dress code on weekends, arguing that members might otherwise opt not to take meals at the Club after a squash game or a workout, and to permit the display of business papers in certain public areas. The Board's initial reactions were cautious, agreeing that the dress code could be relaxed on weekends but not at other times, and that showing papers might just be allowed at mealtime, but only in designated and limited areas, with prescribed standards.

The Admissions Committee had already waived the dues of a serviceman member in Saudi Arabia, and now, at the request of Chairman Joseph J. Handlin '73, the Board excused members called into military service from having to pay the second half of their annual dues. Then

President Adams reported a development that had not occurred in the Admissions Committee since 1958: although Chairman Handlin's term was about to expire, his colleagues had appointed him to fill a vacancy and elected him chairman for another year.

Early in January 1991 the firm of Wildman and Bernhardt, contractors, signed on to translate the plans of architect member Carl R. Meinhardt Ds'64 into solid three-dimensional reality on the sixth and seventh floors. They would begin construction in a few weeks.

Meanwhile, members could have taken in a lecture on *The Magic Flute*, an author's reading, and, on the fifteenth, "Everest the Hard Way," an account by Dr. Mimi Zieman, with slides, of a death-defying climb she had made, as doctor and sole woman member of an expedition, up and across two miles of the sheer east face of the world's tallest mountain. Dr. Zieman's talk was in the grand tradition of narrations by mountaineers, balloonists, ocean sailors, cave explorers, deep-sea divers and other adventurous types, but programs had proliferated so greatly of late that instead of its being one of, say, fifty events that season it was one of over a hundred. More events than ever before, too, were being held now outside the clubhouse, in theaters, opera houses and museums, in historic neighborhoods, on board excursion vessels and in the clubhouses of other university clubs, and more of them than ever—mixers, dances, an ice-skating party and the like—were being produced in collaboration with these clubs. As always, musical offerings ranged from classical to avant-garde, from folk to jazz, played and sung, solo and in ensemble performances; as always, the entertainments varied in kind: films, dramatic readings, cabaret, recountings of adventures, shows of mystery and magic; as always, the speakers—on politics and government, crime and justice, morality and ethics, language and literature, history and biography, law, medicine, psychology, artificial intelligence, computers, public education, retailing, life under a Communist regime—were qualified experts. Some of the most informative talks were on topics taken straight from the daily news: AIDS, welfare, democracy in Poland, the plight of refugees from the world's trouble spots and, in particular, threats to the global environment, to which no fewer than five evenings would be devoted in fiscal 1991.

On January 16 President Bush won Congressional approval of an air assault on objectives in Iraq, and the next day the assault commenced. At the annual meeting the incumbent officers retained their posts, with two exceptions: Vice-President Gutman was replaced by Donald Shapiro, who nonetheless remained House Committee chairman, and Charles T. Lee replaced Nehama Jacobs as secretary. After dinner the guest speaker was Judith R. Hope L'64, the first woman to serve on the Harvard Corporation.

On the eighteenth Hamilton Fish, a member for three-quarters of a century, died, aged 102. For decades a familiar outsized figure at football dinners, he would be remembered thereafter by the award bearing his name, which since 1988 had been given out annually on that occasion, together with the "Tubby" Clark award.

One week later Jeremy Fraiberg '92, the College's foremost racqueteer, won the forty-fifth annual Cowles tournament.

In mid-February, as work began on the seventh floor, the Executive Committee endorsed a House Committee recommendation to reduce rates for bedrooms on weekends and hourly squash court fees at off-peak hours on weekdays. The House Committee, possessing the authority to do so on its own, promulgated revisions of two long-standing regulations. Thereafter, ties and jackets would no longer be required in the clubhouse on weekends, and displaying papers would be allowed in the Cambridge Rooms at lunchtime and on the Main Dining Room balcony, at the northwest corner, at other times.

On February 21 President Adams brought the Board up to date on the status of the expansion project. In view of the near-impossibility of raising five to ten million dollars from a few wealthy individuals, he said, the $30 million Barnes plan was clearly unrealistic. The Building Committee had asked Lee S. Jablin Ds'76, an architect member of the House Committee, to come up with a simpler, less expensive design. In Jablin's addition, the ground floor would contain an enlarged entrance hall, a ladies' room, an expanded cloakroom and another lounge on the 44th Street side. The second floor would feature a large, multipurpose assembly room beyond the upper Cambridge Dining Room, while on the third floor the Weld Room would be opened out westward and two more meeting rooms added on.

The fourth and fifth floors would each contain twelve bedrooms, some with balconies, and the addition would be served by two elevators.

How was all this to be paid for? It was the planners' intention—or hope—to erect the addition at a cost that could be borne by the Club's revenue stream, amounting, by Treasurer Brody's estimate, to around $12 million with conventional financing and around $15 million at the lower rate the University was offering to provide.

On February 24 President Bush ordered the ground war in Iraq to begin. In a lightning campaign, American and Allied forces smashed through Iraq's defenses, routing the armies of Saddam Hussein. After just 100 hours of fighting the president ordered a cease-fire, and the Gulf War ended.

Next month, on March 25, the Club and the world learned that Neil L. Rudenstine PhD'64, a Renaissance scholar and vice-president of the Andrew W.

Neil L. Rudenstine

Mellon Foundation, had accepted the presidency of Harvard. In late April Admissions Committee recruiters bagged 457 new members in Cambridge and Boston. In May the Board set a dues increase of $6^{1}/2$ percent for fiscal 1992. And in June the Executive Committee, mapping out a capital budget for the coming year, focused on three major projects:

• the first phase of a two-year project to replace windows throughout the clubhouse with better-fitting ones to save energy;

• the conversion of six bedrooms, four without baths, into five (later changed to four) with baths; and

• new equipment in the laundry.

Had the Soviet Union's recent transformation from formidable archenemy to impoverished, quasidependent client somehow robbed its speech of satanic appeal? On the evening of June 16, in any case, conversational Russian lessons were dropped in favor of lessons in conversational German, a language, perhaps, to do business in.

In his review of chess activity for the Board's annual report, Chairman Leonard Seglin G'39 chronicled a successful season culminating in a $3^1/2$–$^1/2$ defeat by the Russian delegation to the United Nations followed, miraculously, by the Club team's victory over the Russians in a series of five-minute games. But Chairman S. George Gianis '42 B'48 reported that backgammon activity had, by contrast, been "in the doldrums." One reason, he wrote, was the absence of two of the Club's best players: six-time champion Lewis M. Isaacs, Jr. '28, who had recently closed down forever the law firm his great-grandfather had founded in 1853, and two-time champion E. J. Kahn, Jr., the writer, who now lived on Cape Cod most of the year. But Gianis cited another reason:

> Secondly, the regular backgammon crowd has become infected with a yuppish [*sic*] style of play which places a premium on winning at any cost over the customary good fellowship and relaxation found at the Club's backgammon tables over the past 60 years. The frequent absence of common courtesy has driven some gentlemen away from the tables.

As fiscal 1992 began the Club had 10,434 members, 108 fewer than a year earlier, the first decline in membership since 1975.

That summer Harvard was technically without a head, President Bok having stepped down as of July 1 and his successor not scheduled to be sworn in until October 20. The Club welcomed members of the New York Yacht Club for meals and drinks from July 26 to September 8 when their handsome clubhouse almost next door was closed for renovation.

In his State of the Club report to the Board in September, General Manager Arnold announced that the staff would be reduced before July by ten employees. He called for renaming the Employee Welfare Committee the Human Resources Committee in recognition of its expanded responsibilities, and for changing requirements in order to permit the appointment to it of any members with experience in employment benefits, investment management and personnel management. The Board agreed to both suggestions.

By then the athletics floor renovations were complete or nearly so. On the sixth floor the men's and women's locker rooms boasted new saunas and steam rooms, as well as additional showers and changing booths, while the pro shop, relocated to that floor, occupied one end of a rectangular space, comfortably furnished and equipped with a television set, that invited passing squash players to tarry. One flight up a new masseur's room had been created, but the most impressive sight there by far was the new Fitness Center, extending south to 44th Street in the space once occupied by the plunge and the dormitory, with its awesome array of exercise machines.

As expected, young women and younger members generally flocked at once to the new facility, but the latter's various devices would soon be regularly put to use as well by older members, including seniors in their seventies.

With resignations—some, no doubt, recession-linked—running in the hundreds, mostly in the twenty-six-to-thirty-five age group, and monthly head counts dropping below five figures, Admissions Chairman Handlin took resolute action: compiling the names and addresses of all eligible individuals he could find in the metropolitan region, he mailed out 20,000 invitations to an open house. Some 500 people accepted.

That this would bring the Club important gains was not immediately apparent, and in November the Club's governors worried about their main tenant, Barson Hardware, being seriously in arrears and about the probable costly impact on the Club of the new Americans with Disabilities Act (ADA), due to become effective the following year. By the Board meeting on the twenty-first, however, a more confident spirit prevailed. Pointing out that the number of scheduled events was now double what it had been in fiscal 1987, Chairman Minton opined that the Program Committee was approaching the limits of the staff's and the clubhouse's capacity. Reporting a falling off in contributions to the scholarships fund, foundation President Craig suggested a voluntary checkoff for this purpose on members' bills. And Chairman Shapiro noted the completion of the four new bedrooms on the fourth floor, representing, the *Bulletin* commented, "the Club's initial venture into the 'de luxe' category."

But the most arresting developments, surely, had to do with the expansion project, which, now stripped down to its essentials, suddenly seemed, once again, tantalizingly realizable. The Building Committee had reduced its overall cost from $16 million to $13.5 million by eliminating two elements: a subcellar, saving $750,000 (but sacrificing extra office space) and the seventh and eighth floors, saving $1.7 million; then, too, construction costs had, thanks to the recession, declined by 15 percent, helping to save another $1.6 million. But some $1.5 million in necessary capital improvements had been added to the project, including a new water system, air-conditioning on the third floor and in the squash courts and the remodeling of bedrooms. The committee anticipated a cash flow of $1.1 million from the expanded clubhouse, and reckoned that the Club would face a debt service of $1 million, assuming a thirty-year amortization at 7 percent interest.

Were the impact on earnings during construction and the increased maintenance costs adequately reflected in these figures? A few Board members feared not. All the same, the Board was unanimous in urging President Adams to meet soon with University officials to talk about financing.

In December, Chairman Handlin informed the Board, with understandable pride, that his committee had elected 137 new members at its latest meeting and held over another 55 for consideration at its next. So far this fiscal year the Club had taken in 221 men and women, compared to 110 by December 1990. The Board congratulated Handlin and his committee on their extraordinary feat of recruiting so many new members in the midst of a recession. Finally, it approved an annual dues checkoff to support the Club foundation, of twenty-five dollars for R-1 members and commensurately less for others.

At the annual meeting on January 23, 1992, the Club's five officers were reelected for another year. More than 330 people partook of the ensuing banquet, many, no doubt, drawn there by the opportunity to see and hear Harvard's new president, Neil Rudenstine.

Three days later, senior Jeremy Fraiberg again won the Cowles. The upgrading of the sixth-floor facilities had increased the ranks of squash players, and numerous recent frequenters of health clubs now worked out regularly at the seventh-floor Fitness Center. On a typical weekday, indeed, more than 250 members took some kind of exercise at the Club.

Although 1992 would, to the relief of many members, bring a winding down of construction, the men and women responsible for the venerable (and vulnerable) clubhouse could hardly relax their vigilance. For the House Committee repairs, replacements and restorations were a constant preoccupation. But with receipts from operations continuing to fall short of expectations, such expenditures put the Club in the awkward position of running a cash flow deficit. Speaking for the absent Treasurer Brody, Michael C. Murr '73 B'75 told the Board on February 20 that the Club had already spent $1.4 million on capital improvements in fiscal 1992 and was committed to spend another $400,000. His advice to his colleagues: "Think poor."

Dr. Minton, presiding again over a season jam-packed with events, predicted that these would earn the Club $30,000 that year. And two ad hoc subcommittees of the Communications Committee submitted recommendations. One suggested that, instead of seeking to establish reciprocal arrangements with other clubs, the Club should explore setting up relationships with selected small hotels in the United States and abroad. The other called for revising the Club's "antiquated" facilities brochure before launching a direct mail campaign to recruit members.

In the next weeks Barson Hardware was served with a notice of default, and House Chairman Michael Yamin, reporting for a group appointed to study the probable impact on the Club of the ADA, recommended setting aside funds in fiscal 1993 to construct an entrance to the clubhouse negotiable by wheelchair.

March 18 marked the debut in Harvard Hall of an extraordinary event entitled "Death by Chocolate." Presented by Chef Fanger, whose Swiss homeland was and is the source of some of the finest chocolate products on earth, and by Pastry Chef Jurg Sporri, it featured mouth-watering cacao bean–based confections in awesome profusion, for consumption on the spot. Soft drinks for clearing palates were also available. The fulfillment of a chocolate addict's most far-out fantasy, the event attracted—and richly rewarded—250 chocoholics, guaranteeing that it would be put on again in seasons to come.

In mid-April Nathan Weston became co-chairman of the Program Committee. Treasurer Brody speculated glumly that the Club might finish the year negatively. A week later, Chairman Yamin reported receiving a proposal to create an accessible entrance to the clubhouse that included a wheelchair lift and other devices for about $150,000. Yamin's subcommittee was also having metal panels installed in the elevators next to the indicator buttons bearing the numbers of the floors in Braille for the blind, and elsewhere strobe light fire alarms for the deaf.

In May, Treasurer Brody informed the Board that although the Club now had ten fewer employees than in September 1991, its labor costs, what with successive hikes in the cost of health insurance, had gone up. The Board approved a dues increase of 5 percent, whereupon Chairman Shapiro called for raising various fees, including that for using the Fitness Center. Some of his hearers objected, however, asserting that the growing financial burden of membership was causing a spate of resignations. They stressed the necessity of keeping the Club accessible to all qualified men and women, including those in ill-paid occupations like teaching and writing.

President Adams, finally, brought up a long-term goal regarding the advisability of which there could be no disagreement: the purchase of 35 West 44th Street. Five years later, in 1997, the Club would need $1.6 million with which to exercise its option to buy that property; not to do this would be simply unthinkable, so the Club might well, the president said, want to make sure that a sufficient sum would be on hand in 1997. He suggested, for future discussion, establishing a sinking fund for this purpose.

One day in late May or early June, Secretary Lee and former President Kimball visited the City Midday Club atop the Marine Midland Bank building at 140 Broadway, where, amid dazzling views of Financial District skyscrapers and the harbor, they talked with the club's president and general manager about establishing signing privileges there for Club members. The meeting proved fruitful, and when the Board next met, in June, it authorized President Adams to enter into an agreement with the downtown eating club.

Treasurer Brody's report was less upbeat: with the fiscal year ending in a matter of days, the Club's annual income would be, as he had feared, after depreciation, below the line, a negative figure, for the first time since 1977. Donald Shapiro's last report as House Committee chairman was factual: work on the entrance for the handicapped would begin when the Landmarks Preservation Commission approved the plans, and lawyers had been retained to help evict Barson Hardware. For the Admissions Committee, Chairman Bahman Mossavar-Rahmani '73 B'79 announced that he would soon mail 5,000 letters to eligible exurbanites preparatory to his committee's conducting interviews in Hartford and New Haven in July.

Incidentally, the committee's Cambridge trip had netted almost exactly the same number of recruits as had the trip the previous April of the team headed by then-Chairman Handlin. Thanks to the latter's metropolitan recruitment drive in October 1991, however, Chairman Mossavar-Rahmani was able to report total admissions for fiscal 1992 of 959, compared to 659 for fiscal 1991. This unprecedented figure, added to the 202 previously resigned or dropped members who had rejoined during the year, brought the total increase in admissions to a staggering 1,161. But this increase, huge though it was, brought the Club a net gain of only 42 members, as the total *decrease* for the year came to an equally staggering 1,119, all but 70 of whom, deceased members, had resigned or been dropped.

During fiscal 1992 more than a tenth of the Club's members had opted out, while a like number of outsiders had chosen to join. Never had the Club been more volatile!

A House Committee decision to suspend balcony lunch service and to direct soup-and-sandwichers to the Cambridge Rooms caused mild grumbling, but the main topic of conversation that summer, at the Club as elsewhere, was the electoral race between President Bush, Democratic Governor Bill Clinton of Arkansas and—after a still not fully explained eleven-week withdrawal from the contest—billionaire populist H. Ross Perot. In July, disappointingly, the Admissions Committee recruited a total of only fifteen members in two of Connecticut's largest cities, and in August, the Club's governors worried about a bill Congress was ready to pass barring citizens from deducting dues paid to private clubs in computing their taxable incomes. Meanwhile, signaling a change of heart regarding Barson Hardware, Vice-President Shapiro started renegotiating that firm's lease.

In September Richard Rodwin stepped down after more than a quarter century of dedicated service with the Scholarships and Schools Committees, including several years as chairman of the latter. At President Adams's request, the Board asked the Club foundation to establish a scholarship for public and parochial school students in Rodwin's name. And Maryanne King '70 took over the chairmanship of Schools.

Auditor Weiser, presenting his annual financial statement for fiscal 1992, noted that revenues had kept on declining with fixed charges and real estate taxes rising, and that the I.R.S. had found discrepancies in the Club's tax returns for 1988 and 1989, obliging it to pay the Treasury $196,000. General Manager Arnold termed fiscal 1992's results the worst since the early Eighties except for a few bright spots, among them the performance, beyond all expectations, of the Fitness Center. In contrast Vice-President Shapiro's news was all good: Barson Hardware would pay the Club $60,000 in back rent and a monthly rental thereafter of $5,000. On his recommendation, moreover, the Board set aside a sum in the 1993 capital budget, ultimately fixed at $250,000, for a sinking fund, which, if paid into at the same rate in years to come, could guarantee the Club's being able to buy the property next door in 1997.

Around mid-September work began on transforming the former ladies' entrance on 44th Street, closed since the admission of women as members in 1973, into an entrance for the handicapped. And the House Committee, alerted by complaints of the havoc cellular telephones could cause, banned their use on the first and second floors.

On September 24 there opened, at the Museum of Modern Art, what promised to be one of the most important exhibitions of the decade, bringing together 400 paintings by the great French Impressionist Henri Matisse. Tickets to a group viewing by Club members sold out in three hours, whereupon the University Club invited disappointed members to a private viewing on the seventh. And on the twentieth, in Harvard Hall, MoMA curator and lecturer Gail Stavitsky guided still more members through a "tour" of the Matisse retrospective, using slides. Meanwhile, the Program Committee had presented lectures and discussions on dismantling apartheid, Reagan-Bush policies toward Iraq, violence in American schools, the state of the global economy and contemporary China.

With Election Day approaching, an apt choice for a dinner-theater production on October 19 in the Biddle Room was actor Jim Cooke's one-character *Calvin Coolidge: More Than Two Words*, about America's taciturn thirtieth president. Had the audience been polled about the coming elections, Coolidge's fellow Republican, George Bush, would surely have won, but on November 3 the winner nationwide was, of course, Governor Clinton. (The minutes of the next Executive Committee meeting would nevertheless note that President Bush had vetoed a tax package that, among other things, would have made it unlawful to deduct club dues for tax purposes.)

In November, after talks by a former tutor of the Dalai Lama on Tibet and by a British pundit on political changes sweeping the world, the legendary investor George Soros spoke about what to expect in the former Soviet Union and East European states in transition. More than 400 people attended this last event, on the eighteenth. By then, the entrance for the handicapped was almost complete, and the Landmarks Preservation Commission had approved the design of a canopy to extend out above it. House Committee Chairman Yamin warned the Board, however, that the water tower atop the clubhouse would have to be replaced.

Before the end of that meeting advance copies of a profusely illustrated new brochure highlighting the Club's facilities and services were handed out for inspection; they quickly elicited expressions of praise for the brochure's begetters: Joseph J. Handlin, J. Thomas Westring B'64, Don B. Elliott and Carol Danko. All members would be sent copies in December. Apropos of publications, the Board agreed that the Club book, last issued in 1980, should be updated and reissued soon, without waiting for the completion of the Club history, now more than three years overdue.

One day in December 1992 there suddenly appeared on the brick facade of the clubhouse, a few feet east of the canopy, a stubby crimson replica of the latter, sticking out above a doorway framed by ungainly-looking metal objects and a staring electronic eye. This doorway was commonly referred to—just how aptly few realized—as the "handicapped" entrance, or the "disabled" entrance. Members found it an eyesore, and said so. On January 8, 1993, the House Committee recommended removing the new canopy, together with the subjacent lights, heater and closed circuit

television camera, on aesthetic grounds, and a few days later the Executive Committee agreed.

On Saturday, January 16, the Club hosted another "Harvard Comes to New York" day. Between 8:30 A.M. and 5:30 P.M. half a dozen professors summarized what they were teaching in Cambridge about Islamic fundamentalism, the contemporary university literary canon, economic reform in China and Vietnam, the cosmos, advances in atomic physics and the post–Cold War outlook. If most of their auditors were no longer young, their enthusiasm hinted at the presence within the Club of a sizeable potential audience for programs of continuing education.

At the annual meeting the following Thursday, Donald L. Shapiro was elected president, Preston Townley '60 B'62 a vice-president and Deborah Waroff '70 treasurer, while Charlotte P. Armstrong and Charles T. Lee retained their posts as, respectively, vice-president and secretary. The featured speaker at the annual dinner was member Arthur A. Hartman, a former ambassador to France and the Soviet Union and currently president of the Board of Overseers.

In February matters took an unpleasant turn—two turns, actually—in connection with a speech in Harvard Hall by President Turgut Ozal of Turkey. First, 300 to 400 angry protestors—Greeks, Greek Cypriots and Greek Americans—massed outside the clubhouse, blocking 44th Street and chanting defiance of their hated enemies, the Turks. Second, President Ozal's sponsors invited so many people that a number of members who had made reservations could not be seated. The event's organizer would be asked to resign from the Program Committee, which in turn would be exhorted by the Board not to invite speakers whose mere presence could spark such disturbances.

At the same Board meeting, Deborah Waroff, the Club's first woman treasurer, executed a simple maneuver that would, for a time at least, bear important consequences. Presenting an unsigned banking resolution in which were typed, below the spaces for signatures, the putative signers' titles, Waroff moved to substitute for "chairman" in the document the gender-neutral "chair." Duly seconded, her motion carried, establishing a precedent that would soon be followed by other members and committees.

Admissions Chairman (as she was still styled) Katherine L. Harrington

AM'67 PhD'77 reported taking in only 198 new members to date in fiscal 1993 compared to 420 one year earlier, whereupon President Shapiro announced the appointment of an ad hoc committee chaired by Joseph Handlin to explore means of promoting the Club. Acceding to the importunings of early-rising exercisers, the House Committee agreed to open the Fitness Center at 6:30 on weekday mornings, though squash players would have to wait until 7 to play. It called for designating certain rooms as nonsmoking areas, and expressly prohibited smoking in the low-ceilinged and often crowded Grill Room.

Early in March (when members could hear thirty-four-year-old Dwight Collins relate how he had pedaled across the Atlantic in a custom-built "bicycle boat"), the new "handicapped" canopy in front of the clubhouse was at last taken down, and the apparatus below it, except for the wheelchair lift, removed. On the eighteenth Joseph Handlin told the Board about certain ideas his committee was pursuing, among them enhancing the value of Club membership by offering members discounts at small, centrally located hotels in various cities. And House Committee Chairman Yamin suggested that his colleagues familiarize themselves with an important aspect of the Club by staying overnight in a bedroom.

Secretary Lee opened the next Board meeting, in April, by handing out copies of the revised and updated bylaws. He explained that with a new Club book in the works it had become necessary to review the numerous amendments that had been adopted since the bylaws were last published in 1980, as well as others that had never been formally adopted. Just recently, he added, additional changes had been made to render the bylaws gender-neutral throughout.

Without ado the Board approved the amended bylaws.

A brief recess for the Club foundation's annual meeting enabled its president, D. Broward Craig, to report that his contribution checkoff idea was working well: contributors were up from 350–400 to more than 3,300, and contributions from $60,000–$70,000 to about $92,000. On the other hand, Craig said, donors would probably have been more numerous and generous if scholarship funds had not been earmarked for undergraduates only, given the fact that a good many members had not attended the College.

With memories of President Ozal's turbulent visit still fresh, some members feared that Pakistani demonstrators might disrupt a scheduled appearance by India's ambassador, but on May 18 all went well. Reporting this to the Board, Program Chairman Weston suggested that the Club celebrate in the coming year the centennial of the opening of the clubhouse, or, rather, the original part of it. His colleagues liked the idea.

Treasurer Waroff, presenting an operating budget for fiscal 1994, noted that for the first time since 1986 it did not include a dues increase. She cited compelling reasons for this: first, declines in both new members and member usage; second, the approach, for R-1 members, of the thousand-dollar mark, the breaching of which psychological barrier could conceivably trigger multiple resignations; and third, on the positive side, the availability of cost controls capable of improving operating results. In this last connection, Waroff pointed out that the proposed budget called for eliminating nine staff positions, saving $250,000.

The Board approved, and in June the treasurer presented a capital budget; its biggest item, $405,000, was to upgrade the Club's water system by eliminating the antiquated rooftop water tank and installing basement pumps to provide more cost-efficient and environmentally sound service. Of the quarter million dollars appropriated for the sinking fund, only $161,000 would actually go into it that year, the treasurer said, the balance being reserved for projects yielding short-term paybacks that would in successive years be paid into the sinking fund. The Board approved this, too.

Niall McGovern having retired in April, the cigar stand in the entrance hall now stood empty; it would soon be replaced by a new front desk half a foot higher than the one immediately west of it. Chair Harrington reported happily that two Cambridge trips in April had brought in 534 new members. President Shapiro announced that Catering Manager Michael Smith had resigned to become general manager of the Williams Club; this was, Shapiro said, another tribute to the leadership of Robert Arnold, three of whose senior-level managers had previously left to manage other clubs. And he reported that Vice-President Armstrong had injured herself in an accident while returning from England, but that her distress had presumably been assuaged somewhat by her having been elected an Overseer.

Another election loomed in the fall, that for mayor of New York, and in June the candidates again made their respective pitches at breakfast meetings: first, Republican Rudolph Giuliani, then longshots Andrew J. Stein and Roy Innis and finally Democratic Mayor Dinkins. Thereafter, the Program Committee, aware that younger members no longer left the city for long periods in the hot months, had scheduled more events than in any previous summer. Most were social (happy hours, a harbor cruise, a beer tasting) or sporting (a softball game with the M.I.T. Club), while the talks (on tropical fish and baseball cards) were hardly calculated to overtax their audiences' mental capacities.

The July 1 head count showed a small increase for the year, bringing membership to 10,522. That month, Cristina Gjomarkaj joined the staff as director of catering. And shortly after noon on the fifteenth Vice-President Armstrong, arriving at the Club in a taxi and being helped into a wheelchair, entered the clubhouse through the "handicapped" entrance. Arriving at the Weld Room, she informed her Executive Committee colleagues that her ride on the wheelchair lift had been "smooth and uneventful." At the meeting, Treasurer Waroff said she had received many favorable comments on the dues not being raised, and President Shapiro announced that Truda C. Jewett Ed'83 would oversee the events and festivities the following year celebrating the clubhouse's centenary.

In August, Chairman Yamin told the Executive Committee that work on the water system project could not begin until the Landmarks Preservation Commission was satisfied with the redone entrance for the handicapped. And President Shapiro announced that the Club would retain member Raymond G. McGuire L'64 as its principal labor counsel.

When the committee met again in September, President Shapiro reported that a search was on for portraits of eminent women graduates of Radcliffe and Harvard that could be borrowed and hung in the clubhouse. Chairman Yamin announced that classes in aerobic dancing would soon begin. The prospect of additional foot traffic to and from these classes and the reality of increasing dress code violations had, between them, prompted the House Committee to recommend that the Club's 45th Street rear entrance be made available to arriving members headed for the athletics floors.

Five months after approving Secretary Lee's revised and updated bylaws, the Board, on September 23, approved revised and updated house rules, as presented by Chairman Yamin. Then it appointed Maryanne King, Schools Committee chairman, to head the Scholarships Committee as well. (From the minutes of the Board and the Executive Committee it would appear that the use of "chair" as a gender-neutral noun, though now enshrined in the bylaws, was often being dropped in practice in favor of treating "chairman" as itself gender-neutral.) General Manager Arnold declared that, for the third year in a row, sales of food and drink were declining and that the percentages of sales income going to labor costs were rising, to an unacceptably high 73 percent. If lunchtime business did not improve, he said, either the Main Dining Room balcony or the Cambridge Rooms would have to close.

Chairman Yamin had much news. A work center was planned for the basement room recently vacated by the Harvard Business School Club in which members could use their laptop computers and have access to telephones, fax machines and copiers. The Landmarks Preservation Commission had approved a new plan for the handicapped-accessible entrance, and the water system was being upgraded. The cigar stand was being demolished and the Presidents' Room renovated, while soundproofing curtains were being hung between the North and Biddle Rooms.

In the wee hours of October 5, an incident occurred that illustrated the difficulty of securing the clubhouse completely against entry. Crossing the space between the buildings by a broad plank, high up, from the deserted Hotel Webster, then undergoing reconstruction, an intruder entered a fourth-floor bedroom, struck the awakening occupant on the head with a flashlight and made off the way he had come with several hundred dollars. His victim was rushed to a nearby hospital, where his injuries were attended to and where he was soon joined by General Manager Arnold, who, upon being informed by telephone of what had happened, had immediately driven in from the country. The unfortunate nonresident member did not blame the Club for his plight and expressed gratitude for Arnold's timely show of concern, but the Club's governors were deeply upset, and Chairman Yamin, in particular, sought expert advice on how to improve security.

Security would likewise be key to a procedure soon to be introduced on a trial basis by which members arriving at the clubhouse in casual or athletic attire would be admitted via the employees' 45th Street entrance, where, under the surveillant eye of a closed-circuit television camera, they would gain access by showing the duty security guard a photo identity card before taking the service elevator up to the sixth floor.

On October 21 the Board, accepting the recommendation of an ad hoc committee chaired by Richard M. Broad '75, voted to double the entrance fee, currently 35 percent of first-year dues, to 70 percent, and it enthusiastically extended its support to Crimson Impact, a volunteer service organization composed mostly of young Harvard and Radcliffe graduates. Founded a few years earlier by Harvard graduates on the model of Phillips Brooks House and organized as a not-for-profit corporation, Crimson Impact now tutored students at a school on the Lower East Side, helped to run a soup kitchen and took underprivileged children on outings throughout the year. Its officers wanted to affiliate with the Club and become a standing committee within it. The Board, for the most part, sympathized, more than one member commenting that projecting a community-oriented image would probably enhance the Club's appeal to younger graduates—and to members.

On Election Day, to the satisfaction of most resident members, Republican challenger Giuliani narrowly defeated Mayor Dinkins at the polls. He would take office on January 1, 1994. With the Club's labor contract due to expire one day before then, President Shapiro urged labor counsel McGuire, the latter's associate, Harlan J. Silverstein, and the Club management to begin educating the staff in advance of approaching negotiations as to the Club's actual financial situation.

On the night of Saturday, January 15, 1994, a guest in a bedroom smelled smoke and called the front desk; the alarm went out, and in minutes firemen burst into the smoke-filled entrance hall to put out a blaze in the chimney. Little damage had been done, but the Fire Department enjoined the Club from using either that fireplace or the one in the Grill Room until both stacks could be repaired and recertified.

No further talks with Local 6 were on the horizon when the Executive

Committee, convening three days later, agreed that within the Club Crimson Impact would be termed, for now at least, the Community Service Committee. Treasurer Waroff noted that dues payments had increased in December, probably in reaction to new Federal legislation disallowing, as of the first of this year, the deduction of club dues as a business expense. Chairman Arthur I. Hirsch L'63 remarked that while his colleagues on the Admissions Committee were concerned about the loss of dues deductibility, they felt that new members, particularly those to be recruited in Cambridge and Boston, would most likely be much less disturbed than older members by this change in the law.

Chairman Yamin announced that, pursuant to an Athletics Sub-committee recommendation, arrangements were being made to offer the use of the squash courts at off-peak hours to girls of that long-ago neighbor of the Club's, the Brearley School.

The annual meeting on the twentieth produced no change in the leadership, all five officers being reelected. After the dinner that followed, Professor Emeritus John Kenneth Galbraith delighted his good-sized audience with his pithy, witty and wholly original observations. Then the diners rose to their feet, most of them mature men and women, with here a fresh-faced pair of recent graduates and there gallant survivors in their ninth and tenth decades. As hundreds of voices blended together in the opening chords of "Fair Harvard," a few singers must have recalled that the original part of their clubhouse would that year complete a full century as a landmark and a cherished second home.

Outside and in, the old place had never looked better. And the institution it housed, comprising ten thousand and more men and women of Harvard, had never been stronger.

Did the strains of the familiar anthem, quickening memories near for some and far distant for others, touch their hearts, perhaps bringing tears to their eyes? Whether or no, these members looked forward to celebrating, months thereafter, with appropriate "festival rites," the centennial of their clubhouse, another milestone in their Club's continuing progression "from the age that is past, to the age that is waiting before."

## ADMISSIONS COMMITTEE CHAIRMEN (continued)

| | | | |
|---|---|---|---|
| *Charles F. Bound '32 | 1953 | E. Kennedy Langstaff '44 | 1975 |
| Robert G. Stone, Jr. '45 | 1954 | Paul E. Konney '66 | 1976 |
| *Laurence S. Johnson '39 | 1955–1956 | Christopher A. Smith '55 | 1977 |
| Donald E. McNicol '43, L'48 | 1957–1958 | Bengt H. Kjellgren '53, L'56 | 1978 |
| *J. David Lannon '39 | 1959 | Laurence B. Rossbach, Jr. '50, L'53 | 1979 |
| Robert R. Barker '36 | 1960 | William S. Kelly '70 | 1980 |
| John F. Harvey '43, B'47 | 1961 | Cyrus W. Brown II '59 | 1981 |
| John P. Campbell '46 | 1962 | Charles T. Lee '72 | 1982 |
| Robert G. Axtell '48. B '48 | 1963 | John S. Reidy '61, B'63 | 1983 |
| Ralph G. Coburn '33, L'36 | 1964 | Robin L. Farkas '54, B'61, | |
| •Joseph R. Hamlen, Jr. '43, | | Robert C. Bickford '56, L'60 | 1984 |
| Edward S. Davis '54, L'59 | 1965 | Richard E. Gutman '66 | 1985 |
| George W. Gibson '31, B'33 | 1966 | Mark S. Waldman B'76 | 1986 |
| Ian Baldwin '33 | 1967 | Richard M. Broad '75 | 1987 |
| Lawrence S. Munson '42, L'48 | 1968 | John C. Katz '60, L'63 | 1988 |
| *Robert Gilmor, Jr. '57 | 1969 | Roseanne Gaulkin B'55 | 1989 |
| Raymond C. Guth '43, L'48 | 1970 | Joseph J. Handlin '73 | 1990–1991 |
| Carl H. Pforzheimer III '58, B'63 | 1971 | Bahman Mossavar-Rahmani '73, B'79 | 1992 |
| Kelso F. Sutton '61 | 1972 | Katherine L. Harrington G'67, G'77 | 1993 |
| Richard W. Kimball '50 | 1973 | Arthur I. Hirsch L'63 | 1994 |
| Tweed Roosevelt '64 | 1974 | | |

## ADMISSIONS COMMITTEE SECRETARIES

| | | | |
|---|---|---|---|
| *George Blagden, Jr. '90 | 1895–1896 | Volney Righter '26, B'28 | 1944–1946 |
| *S. Vernon Mann, Jr. '95 | 1897–1899 | Barrett W. Stevens '29 | 1947–1948 |
| *G. Herman Kinnicutt '98 | 1900–1902 | Frank S. Streeter '40 | 1949–1951 |
| *Langdon P. Marvin '98, L'01 | 1903–1907 | *Charles S. Brown, Jr. '49 | 1952 |
| *Franklin D. Roosevelt '04 | 1908–1909 | George H. P. Dwight '50 | 1953 |
| *Candler Cobb '08 | 1910–1911 | Philip C. Potter, Jr. '48, L'52 | 1954 |
| *Richard Whitney '11 | 1911–1917 | William M. Evarts, Jr. '49, L'52 | 1955 |
| *DeCoursey Fales '11 | 1919–1921 | *Howard Corning, Jr. '26 | 1956 |
| *F. Higginson Cabot, Jr. '17 | 1922–1924 | *Philip Boyer '33 | 1957 |
| *John K. Olyphant '18 | 1925–1927 | *J. David Lannon '39 | 1958 |
| *John Reynolds '07 | 1928–1929 | Robert R. Barker '36 | 1959 |
| Sheridan Logan '23 | 1930–1933 | John F. Harvey '43, B'47 | 1960 |
| *Nathaniel S. Howe '26 | 1934–1937 | John P. Campbell '46 | 1961 |
| *Morgan D. Wheelock '31 | 1938–1940 | *Robert G. Axtell '43, B'48 | 1962 |
| *Samuel S. Drury, Jr. '35 | 1941–1943 | Ralph G. Coburn '33, L'36 | 1963 |

*Deceased

## ADMISSIONS COMMITTEE SECRETARIES (continued)

*Joseph R. Hamlen, Jr. '43......................................1964
Edward S. Davis '54, L'59,
    George W. Gibson '31, B'33............................1965
William W. Prout '36 ............................................1966
Lawrence S. Munson '42, L'48............................1967
Nicholas Benton '51 ..............................................1968
George H. Waterman III '60 ................................1969
David S. Patterson '57 ..........................................1970
Benjamin R. Richards, Jr. '48, L'53 ....................1971
Wellington A. Newcomb '46, L'53 ......................1972
Kenneth G. Standard '58, L'62 ............................1973
Hrand J. Topjian '57, B'59....................................1974
Harvey L. Thomas III '67, B'70............................1975
Oliver T. Kane '72.................................................1976
Carolyn K. McCandless B'69 ..............................1977
Shelton A. Brooks '49 ..........................................1978

Anthony B. Barton '69 ..........................................1979
*Grant G. Geiger II '74 ..........................................1980
Joseph B. Poindexter '57.......................................1881
James M. O'Neil '50 .............................................1982
Cleveland Jay Harp III Ds'71................................1983
William B. Dunham '52 .........................................1984
Cynthia A. Harris B'74...........................................1985
Joseph J. Handlin '73.............................................1986
Fredi L. Pearlmutter L'71.......................................1987
Susan E. B. Schwartz '78 .......................................1988
*Anthony A. Sirna III '46 .......................................1989
Nancy L. Brenner B'71 ..........................................1990
Richard F. Stern '57, B'61 ......................................1991
William B. Dunham '52 .........................................1992
J. Thomas Westring B'64.........................................1993
Richard S. P. Weissbrod '68 ..................................1994

---

*Deceased

## INDEX OF NAMES

## PHOTOGRAPHIC CREDITS

Jim Strong: 4, 5, 8, 15, 44, 57, 73, 96, 97, 101, 102, 116, 120, 121, 123, 127, 132, 137, 146, 167, 178, 182, 192, 193, 198, 203, 215, 248, 256, 258, 269, 270, 281, 288, 294, 313, 316, 341, 370, 371. Jonathan Wallen: 87, 103, 418. Robert C. Lieberman: 377, 385. Christian Steiner: 365 (left). All others: Harvard Club or Harvard University Archives.